FAULT LINES IN EQUITY

Equity, the body of law developed in the English Court of Chancery, has a long and distinguished history. In the twenty-first century it continues to be an important regulator of both commercial and personal dealings, as well as informing statutory regulation. Although much equitable doctrine is settled, there remain some intractable problems that bedevil lawyers across jurisdictions.

The essays in this collection employ new historical, comparative and theoretical perspectives to cast light on these fault lines in equitable doctrine and methodology. Leading scholars and practitioners from England, Australia and New Zealand examine such contentious topics as personal and proprietary liability for breaches of equitable duties (including fiduciary duties), the creation of non-express trusts, equitable rights in insolvency, the fiduciary 'self dealing' rule, clogs on the equity of redemption, the distribution of assets on family breakdown, and the suitability of unjust enrichment analysis. The authors address specific doctrinal questions as well as the 'meta' issues of organisation and methodology, and their findings will be of value to academics and practitioners alike.

Volume 1 in the series Hart Studies in Private Law

Hart Studies in Private Law

This monograph series brings together in one place two types of book: works which examine in-depth the fundamental doctrines and principles of private law, and works which engage with the theoretical underpinnings of private law. The series thus aims to contribute to ever-evolving debates about the nature of private law such as problems of classification and taxonomy, remedies, the relationship with public law and the boundaries of private law generally. The series includes, but is not confined to, works on contract, tort, unjust enrichment, equity, property and the conflict of laws, welcoming work which intersects with other fields of study to enable a deeper understanding of private law theory and practice.

Fault Lines in Equity

Edited by

Jamie Glister
and
Pauline Ridge

•HART•
PUBLISHING
OXFORD AND PORTLAND, OREGON
2012

Published in the United Kingdom by Hart Publishing Ltd
16C Worcester Place, Oxford, OX1 2JW
Telephone: +44 (0)1865 517530
Fax: +44 (0)1865 510710
E-mail: mail@hartpub.co.uk
Website: http://www.hartpub.co.uk

Published in North America (US and Canada) by
Hart Publishing
c/o International Specialized Book Services
920 NE 58th Avenue, Suite 300
Portland, OR 97213-3786
USA
Tel: +1 503 287 3093 or toll-free: (1) 800 944 6190
Fax: +1 503 280 8832
E-mail: orders@isbs.com
Website: http://www.isbs.com

British Library Cataloguing in Publication Data
Data Available

ISBN: 978-1-84946-219-8

Typeset by Compuscript Ltd, Shannon

PREFACE

Each of the essays in this collection considers an unsettled or unexplored aspect of equitable doctrine or methodology. Equity continues to be an important regulator of commercial and personal dealings as well as informing frameworks for statutory regulation. There is continued sense in considering its doctrines and methodology as a coherent and conceptually distinct whole.

Many of the essays draw upon the jurisprudence of the High Court of Australia. The High Court's continued emphasis upon equity as a distinct and vital source of law, combined with its loyalty to Chancery precedent, means that its judgments, whilst sometimes controversial, provide a useful indicator of fault lines in equity. Joachim Dietrich and Mark Leeming's essays evaluate the merits of the principle of unjust enrichment as an alternative and superior explanation to an historical approach to equitable doctrine and methodology. They compare the jurisprudence of the High Court of Australia and the (then) House of Lords. Dietrich considers the question on the macro level by discussing the two courts' attitudes to unjust enrichment on the one hand and the equitable concepts of unconscionability and remedial discretion on the other hand. He finds that, despite their seemingly dichotomous positions, both courts seek the same objectives of legal certainty and transparency of reasoning and attempt to restrain the unbridled use of general concepts. Further complicating the comparison, neither court is entirely consistent in its methodology. Mark Leeming considers the merits of the principle of unjust enrichment on the micro level in relation to equitable subrogation. He argues that the elegant simplicity of the unjust enrichment framework has difficulty in coping with the complex multi-party scenarios that raise subrogation issues. Pauline Ridge also compares and contrasts the methodologies of the Australian and English courts. She argues that an analysis of the case law on participatory liability in equity as a whole suggests a liability scheme for participation in breach of trust or breach of fiduciary duty that is at odds with both the Privy Council and the High Court.

Two essays draw particularly upon the authors' legal history expertise. Joshua Getzler's essay on assignment of future property and Fiona Burns' essay on the doctrine against clogs on the equity of redemption chart the historical development of those respective areas of law. Getzler demonstrates the complex interaction of statute and equity and suggests that equity undermines the spirit of insolvency law in this area. Burns charts the gradual erosion of the anti-clog doctrine due to legal and economic factors concerning the function of mortgages and the dominance of contract. She shows that English, Australian, Canadian and New Zealand courts have not reacted consistently to these changes and she predicts the imminent demise of the anti-clog doctrine.

By contrast, in his essay Matthew Harding uses legal philosophy to consider the limits of the equitable jurisdiction to allocate family assets on the breakdown of a relationship. He asks why it is that courts exercising equitable jurisdiction do not consider the parties' future needs in allocating family assets, whereas they routinely do so under the statutory schemes. He argues that a distributive norm may apply to the relationship of an unmarried couple that requires the parties to provide material support for each other even after the relationship ends. This would empower courts exercising equitable jurisdiction to consider future needs, although he goes on to explore possible non-doctrinal constraints on the exercise of such a jurisdiction.

Some of the most perplexing problems in equity arise in relation to fiduciaries and trusts. The question of the proper basis of the fiduciary obligation is dealt with by James Edelman who explores the so-called 'self dealing rule' of fiduciary law to determine whether it undermines the argument that fiduciary duties arise only from voluntary undertakings. He argues that the rule is better understood as a collection of distinct rules that are not confined to fiduciary relationships and that apply in a range of different contexts with a range of outcomes. Thus, his 'undertaking' test for imposing the fiduciary obligation remains intact. Jamie Glister unravels the complexities of two problems that beset the remedy of equitable compensation for breach of fiduciary duty, namely, the extent of a custodial fiduciary's duty to restore the trust fund and the application of causation rules to breach of non-custodial fiduciary duties. His essay spans English, Australian, Canadian and New Zealand case law.

Ben McFarlane's essay considers one basis for recognising a non-express trust, as suggested by Lord Browne-Wilkinson's judgment in *Westdeutsche Landesbank Girozentrale v Islington LBC*, and provides an analysis of the circumstances in which such a trust should arise. He argues that the holder of a legal or equitable interest must have acquired the right to that interest by virtue of the same event or transaction that caused the claimant to lose that right (or become subject to a duty in respect of it). The holder of the right must then have knowledge of the matters alleged to affect his or her conscience before a non-express trust over that interest can arise. McFarlane finds support in recent Australian case law for such a trust as well as interesting analogies with the knowledge requirement for recipient liability under the first limb of *Barnes v Addy*. He also finds support in the Australian cases for his thesis that the facts of *Lipkin Gorman v Karpnale* are best explained as an instance of this non-express trust. Michael Bryan also looks at non-express trusts, specifically the remedial constructive trust. He clarifies what is meant by 'remedial' in this context and suggests that proper recognition of remedial constructive trusts has been hindered by a disproportionate fear of the insolvency implications of proprietary interests. He recommends the American Law

Institute's *Restatement (Third) of the Law of Restitution and Unjust Enrichment* as a model for determining when the remedy is appropriate.

Finally, Andrew Butler and Tim Miller's essay considers the ubiquitous rivalry of Australia and New Zealand and argues that, in the context of equity jurisprudence, New Zealand has much to offer.

We hope that this collection highlights the enduring relevance of equity as well as the insights that may be yielded by comparative and inter-disciplinary analysis. All of the essays, apart from Ben McFarlane's, were discussed at a workshop in December 2010 at the University of Sydney. There the authors also benefited from the comments of Simone Degeling, Barbara McDonald, James Penner, John Stumbles and Nicola Bodor. We acknowledge the support of the Ross Parsons Centre of Commercial, Corporate and Taxation Law, and particularly its administrator, Adam Bratt, in facilitating the event. We also thank Richard Hart and all at Hart Publishing.

Jamie Glister
Pauline Ridge
August 2011

CONTENTS

CONTRIBUTORS

Michael Bryan is an Emeritus Professor at the University of Melbourne.

Fiona Burns is an Associate Professor at the University of Sydney.

Andrew Butler is a Partner in the law firm of Russell McVeagh, Wellington.

Joachim Dietrich is an Associate Professor at Bond University.

The Hon Justice James Edelman is a Judge of the Supreme Court of Western Australia.

Joshua Getzler is Professor of Law and Legal History at the University of Oxford, a Fellow and Tutor in Law at St Hugh's College, Oxford, and a Conjoint Professor of Law at the University of New South Wales.

Jamie Glister is a Senior Lecturer at the University of Sydney.

Matthew Harding is an Associate Professor at the University of Melbourne.

Mark Leeming is a Senior Counsel in New South Wales and Challis Lecturer in Equity at the University of Sydney.

Ben McFarlane is a Reader in Property Law at the University of Oxford and a Fellow and Tutor in Law at Trinity College, Oxford.

Tim Miller is a Solicitor with the law firm of Russell McVeagh, Wellington.

Pauline Ridge is an Associate Professor at the Australian National University.

TABLE OF CASES

TABLE OF LEGISLATION

National Legislation

Australia

Canada

New Zealand

United Kingdom

International Legislation

1

Unjust Enrichment versus Equitable Principles in England and Australia

JOACHIM DIETRICH

With every day, and from both sides of my intelligence, the moral and the intellectual, I thus drew steadily nearer to the truth, by whose partial discovery I have been doomed to such a dreadful shipwreck: that man is not truly one, but truly two.

Robert Louis Stevenson, *Dr Jekyll and Mr Hyde*

I. Introduction

In this chapter I contrast the different approaches of the High Court of Australia and of the House of Lords (and Privy Council)[1] in relation to that controversial concept, unjust enrichment. In particular, I will compare the treatment of unjust enrichment with the differing approaches of the courts in relation to equitable concepts, such as unconscionable conduct, and equity's capacity flexibly to shape remedy. In the context of equity, there are discernible though more subtle differences between the views of the High Court and the House of Lords. At first blush, the contrasting judicial positions that I will describe, although not polar opposites, are at least significantly at odds. In part, this is a consequence of highlighting some of the rhetoric contained in judgments in isolation from the decisions themselves. Although the differences of *substance* between the courts are not as stark as some of the rhetoric might suggest, nonetheless, such differences also exist, at least as a result of decisions in the last 15 years or so.[2] I will seek to give some tentative reasons for why the different positions have developed. This interesting exercise may raise more questions than will be answered.

[1] For convenience, general references to the House of Lords include the Privy Council. There are no decisions of the new United Kingdom Supreme Court on point at the time of writing. Given the continuity in the make-up of the Supreme Court from that of the House of Lords, I do not expect the legal positions in the Supreme Court to differ significantly in the near future.

[2] It must be conceded that it is quite artificial to select a limited time period for comparison, in particular since there are obviously discernible differences *within* courts from time to time as a result of the different views of the changing individual members of the courts.

II. Unjust Enrichment and Equity in the High Court

When it comes to the High Court, it is possible to narrate a story of Jekyll and Hyde-like characters. The undesirable characteristics that the High Court ascribes to unjust enrichment are almost as frightening as those of Stevenson's own creation, Mr Hyde. The High Court has asserted, in one case with strong criticism of those who flirt with the opposite views[3] the serious limitations of the unjust enrichment concept. That concept has been variously described by Gummow J as being restrictive in its effect, as a form of 'top-down reasoning' that dictates outcomes,[4] distorts 'well settled' (equitable) principles, and generates fictions, so that dogma restricts 'substance and dynamism' in the law.[5] These sentiments were unanimously endorsed by five members of the Court in *Farah Constructions Pty Ltd v Say-Dee Pty Ltd*.[6] The joint judgment describes unjust enrichment as 'unhistorical'[7] and seemingly considers it to be inimical to common law judicial method and reasoning, particularly when equitable principles are at issue. The joint judgment also rejects, in a reference to Birks' school of unjust enrichment theory,[8] 'a mentality in which considerations of ideal taxonomy prevail over a pragmatic approach to legal development'.[9] More recently, in *Lumbers v W Cook Builders Pty Ltd (In Liq)*,[10] four members of the High Court stated that unjust

[3] See, eg the criticisms by the High Court in *Farah Constructions Pty Ltd v Say-Dee Pty Ltd* [2007] HCA 22, (2007) 230 CLR 89 of the New South Wales Court of Appeal decision overturned in that appeal.

[4] See Gummow J in *Roxborough v Rothmans of Pall Mall Australia Ltd* [2001] HCA 68, (2001) 208 CLR 516 [73]: 'Top-down reasoning' is reasoning 'by which a theory about an area of law is invented or adopted and then applied to existing decisions to make them conform to the theory and to dictate the outcome in new cases'. The term derives from Judge Posner and is also referred to by McHugh J in *McGinty v Western Australia* (1996) 186 CLR 140 (HCA) 232. Gummow J (at [72]) cautions against 'judicial acceptance of any all-embracing theory of restitutionary rights and remedies founded upon a notion of 'unjust enrichment'. To the lawyer whose mind has been moulded by civilian influences, the theory may come first, and the source of the theory may be the writing of jurists not the decisions of judges. However, that is not the way in which a system based on case law develops; over time, general principle is derived from judicial decisions upon particular instances, not the other way around.'

[5] Ibid [74]. The full quote (with footnotes omitted) is:

> Unless, as this Court indicated in *David Securities Pty Ltd v Commonwealth Bank of Australia* [(1992) 175 CLR 353, 378–9], unjust enrichment is seen as a concept rather than a definitive legal principle, substance and dynamism may be restricted by dogma. In turn, the dogma will tend to generate new fictions in order to retain support for its thesis. It may also distort well settled principles in other fields, including those respecting equitable doctrines and remedies, so that they answer the newly mandated order of things. Then various theories will compete, each to deny the others. There is support in Australasian legal scholarship for considerable scepticism respecting any all-embracing theory in this field, with the treatment of the disparate as no more than species of the one newly discovered genus.

[6] *Farah* (n 3) [151]–[156] (Gleeson CJ, Gummow, Callinan, Heydon and Crennan JJ).

[7] Ibid [154].

[8] See especially Peter Birks' final work, setting out his concise account of the law: *Unjust Enrichment*, 2nd edn (Oxford, Oxford University Press, 2005); and P Birks, 'Equity in the Modern Law: An Exercise in Taxonomy' (1996) 26 *University of Western Australia Law Review* 1.

[9] *Farah* (n 3) [154].

[10] *Lumbers v W Cook Builders Pty Ltd (In Liq)* [2008] HCA 27, (2008) 232 CLR 635.

enrichment is not a 'principle which can be taken as a sufficient premise for direct application in particular cases.'[11] They were keen to read down[12] the ambit of the statement of Deane J in 1987, with whom Mason and Wilson JJ generally agreed, in *Pavey & Matthews Pty Ltd v Paul* that unjust enrichment 'constitutes a unifying legal concept which explains why the law recognises, in a variety of distinct categories of case, an obligation on the part of the defendant to make fair and just restitution for a benefit derived at the expense of a plaintiff'.[13]

One can contrast the High Court's reception of unjust enrichment theory with the much more favourable treatment of established equitable concepts such as unconscionability and of 'the cardinal principle of equity that the remedy must be fashioned to fit the nature of the case and the particular facts'.[14] In *Bofinger v Kingsway Group Ltd (formerly Willis & Bowring Mortgage Investments Ltd),*[15] Gummow, Hayne, Heydon, Kiefel and Bell JJ stated in the context of a subrogation claim:

> [A]ll-embracing theories [of unjust enrichment] may conflict in a fundamental way with well-settled equitable doctrines and remedies. Reference was made in the opening paragraph of these reasons to the importance attached by equity to the fashioning of the particular remedy to meet the nature of the case. The administration of the remedies of injunction and specific performance provides perhaps the most obvious examples. So also the remedial constructive trust, as these reasons have sought to demonstrate.
>
> Equity has been said to lack the necessary 'exacting taxonomic mentality' when providing an appropriate remedy for unconscientious activity.[16] The better view is said to be that liability in 'unjust enrichment' is strict, subject to particular defences,[17] while '[t]he unreliability of conscience' offends the precept that like cases must be decided alike and not by 'a private and intuitive evaluation'.[18]
>
> But the experience of the law does not suggest debilitation by absence of a sufficiently rigid taxonomy in the application of equitable doctrines and remedies. And legislatures have taken the same view in Australia, notably by calling upon equitable analogues in framing the remedial provisions laid out in Pt VI of the Trade Practices Act 1974 (Cth).
>
> As these reasons have sought to show, the relevant principles of equity do not operate at large and in an idiosyncratic fashion.[19]

[11] Ibid [85] (Gummow, Hayne, Crennan and Kiefel JJ). See also *Friend v Brooker* [2009] HCA 21, (2009) 239 CLR 129 [7] (French CJ, Gummow, Hayne and Bell JJ). Some of these views echo views expressed by this author prior to these decisions: see J Dietrich, *Restitution A New Perspective* (Sydney, Federation Press, 1998).

[12] Ibid [83]–[86].

[13] *Pavey & Matthews Pty Ltd v Paul* (1987) 162 CLR 221 (HCA) 256–57.

[14] *Warman International Ltd v Dwyer* (1995) 182 CLR 544 (HCA) 559 (Mason CJ, Brennan, Deane, Dawson and Gaudron JJ) quoted with approval in *Bofinger v Kingsway Group Ltd (formerly Willis & Bowring Mortgage Investments Ltd)* [2009] HCA 44, (2009) 239 CLR 269 [1] (Gummow, Hayne, Heydon, Kiefel and Bell JJ); see also [85]–[98].

[15] *Bofinger* (n 14).

[16] Birks, 'Equity in the Modern Law' (n 8) 16–17.

[17] Ibid 67–68.

[18] Ibid 17.

[19] *Bofinger* (n 14) [91]–[94].

Some of the cases in which these views were expressed will be analysed in more depth below. But in summary, the High Court is concerned that the use of unjust enrichment theory will lead to outcomes that are inconsistent with well-established, presumably coherent, equitable principles. There appears to be an undercurrent of distrust of academic developments of unjust enrichment theories and of attempts by academics to shape the law in accordance with their theories.[20] There is strong resistance in particular to manifestations of 'unjust enrichment' theory in which unjust enrichment forms part of a strict taxonomical and conceptual framework which dictates or prescribes particular stages of inquiry for all cases of restitution.[21] Putting it more bluntly, the Court is saying, 'get your hands off equity, we can do without your theoretical meddling'. Well-established concepts such as contribution[22] and subrogation operate coherently and satisfactorily without requiring explanation in terms of unjust enrichment, which adds little or nothing to our understanding of these doctrines. Notably, equity's technique of flexibly tailoring a remedy to suit the circumstances of the case (remedial discretion)[23] is a *virtue* that is consistent with precedent, and when done in accordance with settled principles, does not create dangers of uncertainty. Equity is the High Court's Dr Jekyll when compared to unjust enrichment.

[20] Instructive here is the exchange between Gummow J and Counsel in the transcript of arguments in *Lumbers v W Cook Builders Pty Ltd (In Liq)* [2008] HCATrans 95 (26 February 2008). After Gummow J asked the question 'What is the force of this word "incontrovertible" [benefit]?' he interrupts Counsel's answer with the comments 'Well, why should we buy this package? … It is just slogans.'

[21] See especially Birks, *Unjust Enrichment* (n 8) and earlier formulations of his theories, *An Introduction to the Law of Restitution*, 1989 revised edn (Oxford, Clarendon Press, 1989). Contrast the statement in *Haxton & Ors v Equuscorp Pty Ltd* [2010] VSCA 1 [127] (Dodds-Streeton JA, Ashley and Neaves JJA agreeing) which supports my view that the High Court has rejected Birksian unjust enrichment theory, but suggests a different reason for this rejection: 'The High Court's post-*Pavey* elaboration of unjust enrichment signals a caveat against loose applications of overly general principles and associated "idiosyncratic notions of unfairness". It appears inconsistent with unjust enrichment as the independent category of law advocated by jurists exemplified by Professor Birks.' These two sentences are not easily reconcilable, precisely because Birks' theory is an attempt to move away from unjust enrichment as an "overly general principle"; indeed, much of Birks' writing is critical of the use of general principles, including equitable ones (see n 82). Hence, Birks' theory can be criticised for being technical and dogmatic, not for its reliance on and application of 'overly general principles'. See J Dietrich, 'Giving Content to General Concepts' (2005) 29 *Melbourne University Law Review* 218 and also n 109 below. It should be noted that there is an irony in such an approach to legal reasoning developing around what was historically regarded as too vague and uncertain a notion. Unjust enrichment was, with some justification, seen as an arbitrary appeal to the 'formless void of individual moral opinion': see *Carly v Farrelly* [1975] 1 NZLR 356 (NZSC) 367 (Mahon J); *Avondale Printers & Stationers Ltd v Haggie* [1979] 2 NZLR 124 (NZSC) 144–55 (Mahon J); and hence not a proper basis for the adjudication of legal rights (cf WS Holdsworth, 'Unjustifiable Enrichment' (1939) 55 *LQR* 37, 51).

[22] See *Friend v Brooker* (n 11).

[23] K Mason, 'Opening Address' (1998) 13 *Journal of Contract Law* 1 sums up the progression of legal thought when he states that as a 'rough generalisation … we have progressed from the notion of "where there's a remedy there's a right" past the notion of "where there's a right, there's a remedy", to the notion of "where there's a right, there's an issue of remedies"'.

III. Unjust Enrichment and Equity in the House of Lords

When we turn to the House of Lords, a very different picture emerges: Jekyll and Hyde still exist, but in much less extreme manifestations and their roles have been reversed. From some reading of House of Lords' decisions, one gets a sense that unjust enrichment has the status of the recently-arrived, but more trustworthy, Dr Jekyll, whereas that long-term resident, equity, has some undesirable Mr Hyde-like qualities, for example, legal uncertainty generated by concepts such as unconscionability and remedial discretion.

Unjust enrichment, and specifically, the three-stage steps of analysis advocated by theorists, is now regularly used by the English courts at all levels, and has been endorsed by the House of Lords. The three-stage analysis requires consideration of whether the defendant has been enriched, at the expense of the claimant, and in a way that is unjust. The generally accepted position in relation to the third element is that the claimant must point to some unjust factor, such as mistake, to establish liability; this is consistent with Birks' own earlier views. Prior to his death, however, Birks argued that the preferable approach was an 'absence of basis', that is, if there is *no basis for* a transfer, such as contract or gift, then restitution should follow, and it is that absence of basis that establishes that the enrichment is unjust.[24] Although comments in *Deutsche Morgan Grenfell Group plc v Inland Revenue Commissioners*[25] suggest that Lord Hoffmann sees some merit in the absence of basis analysis when compared to 'mistake' as an unjust factor,[26] the House of Lords continues to apply the unjust factor approach.[27]

So regularly does the House of Lords utilise the three-step process, that it does so at times with little analysis or comment.[28] Importantly, the use of unjust enrichment is prevalent in a range of commercial contexts, such as the ultra vires payments under interest swaps contracts,[29] for recovery of payments

[24] Birks, *Unjust Enrichment* (n 8) particularly chs 5 and 6.

[25] *Deutsche Morgan Grenfell Group plc v Inland Revenue Commissioners* [2006] UKHL 49, [2007] AC 558.

[26] Ibid [20]–[28].

[27] See, eg *Sempra Metals Ltd v Her Majesty's Commissioners of Inland Revenue* [2007] UKHL 34, [2008] 1 AC 561. Leaving aside the absence of basis issue, in *Sempra* there is broad adoption of Birks' theory; see, eg Lord Hope of Craighead's extensive citation of Birks at [27]–[33]. Although Birks argues that the 'interest swaps' cases, such as *Kleinwort Benson Ltd v Lincoln City Council* [1999] 2 AC 349 (HL), support an absence of basis approach as a matter of precedent and logic (*Unjust Enrichment* (n 8) 96–102) this is highly questionable: see S Hedley, 'The Empire Strikes Back? A Restatement of the Law of Unjust Enrichment' (2004) 28 *Melbourne University Law Review* 759, 769–72. It is also clearly not the law in Australia; see, eg *Haxton* (n 21) [127].

[28] See, eg *Yeoman's Row Management Ltd v Cobbe* [2008] UKHL 55, [2009] AC 453 [40] (Lord Scott; Lord Hoffmann, Lord Brown and Lord Mance agreeing).

[29] *Kleinwort* (n 27).

made under a mistake,[30] subrogation,[31] and for work done in precontractual relationships.[32]

The extensive use of unjust enrichment theory in commercial cases contrasts with the reluctance of the House of Lords to allow equitable claims, such as proprietary estoppel, in the same context. For example, in *Yeoman's Row Management Ltd v Cobbe*, the House of Lords was concerned not to allow an estoppel claim despite the defendant unconscionably taking advantage of the plaintiff.[33] In the words of Lord Walker:

> [T]he court should be very slow to introduce uncertainty into commercial transactions by over-ready use of equitable concepts such as fiduciary obligations and equitable estoppel. That applies to commercial negotiations whether or not they are expressly stated to be subject to contract.[34]

Similarly, Lord Scott stated: 'to treat a "proprietary estoppel equity" as requiring ... simply unconscionable behaviour is, in my respectful opinion, a recipe for confusion'.[35] And in the *Actionstrength* case, discussed below, Lord Walker rejected the view that an estoppel could arise on the basis of 'unconscionability on its own'.[36]

Although, as will be seen below, some not dissimilar views have been expressed in the High Court, nonetheless they do reflect a more restrained approach in the use of such equitable concepts. As one commentator has described the English position after *Yeoman's Row Management Ltd v Cobbe*[37] and similar cases: the 'hopes that equity may be able to provide some form of moral compass in the commercial context[38] have been defeated by the judicial imperative for certainty, which accords far more with the law of unjust enrichment'.[39]

In a similar vein is the distrust of a flexible approach to remedy in equity, seen as a threat to 'fixed' property rights and perhaps even the rule of law.[40] Hence the rejection of the remedial constructive trust,[41] contrary to the acceptance of that

[30] *Deutsche Morgan Grenfell Group* (n 25).

[31] *Banque Financière de la Cité v Parc (Battersea) Ltd* [1999] AC 221 (HL).

[32] *Yeoman's Row* (n 28).

[33] Ibid.

[34] Ibid [81] (Lord Brown agreeing), and similarly, Lord Scott at [28]. See also *Thorner v Major* [2009] UKHL 18, [2009] 1 WLR 776; and D Neuberger, 'The Stuffing of Minerva's Owl? Taxonomy and Taxidermy in Equity' (2009) 68 *CLJ* 537.

[35] *Yeoman's Row* (n 28) [16] (Lord Scott; Lord Hoffmann, Lord Brown and Lord Mance agreeing).

[36] *Actionstrength Ltd v International Glass Engineering IN.GL.EN SpA* [2003] UKHL 17, [2003] 2 AC 541 [50].

[37] *Yeoman's Row* (n 28).

[38] A Mason, 'The Place of Equity and Equitable Remedies in the Contemporary Common Law World' (1994) 110 *LQR* 238 and P Millett, 'Equity's Place in the Law of Commerce' (1998) 114 *LQR* 214.

[39] See N Piška, 'Hopes, Expectations and Revocable Promises in Proprietary Estoppel' (2009) 72 *MLR* 998, 1015. It is no coincidence that Piška cites an Australian judge, writing extra-judicially, for the 'hope' of equity's moral compass being used in commercial contexts.

[40] Certainly, Birks had this view about the remedial constructive trust and remedial discretion more generally. See n 82 below.

[41] Eg *Westdeutsche Landesbank Girozentrale v Islington LBC* [1996] AC 669 (HL): Lord Browne-Wilkinson concluding that English law has not recognised such a trust. Similarly, in the Privy Council: *Re Goldcorp Exchange Ltd* [1995] 1 AC 74 (PC) 104 (Lord Mustill).

concept in Australian law.[42] Similarly, in *Foskett v McKeown*,[43] the majority of the Law Lords were adamant that their application of the tracing rules involved nothing more than 'hard-nosed' property law.[44] The tone is set by the statement of Lord Millett: 'Property rights are determined by fixed rules and settled principles. They are not discretionary. They do not depend upon ideas of what is "fair, just and reasonable". Such concepts, which in reality mask decisions of legal policy, have no place in the law of property.'[45] There are echoes of Birks here:

> The business of the lawyer can only be to say with as much precision as possible on what facts proprietary interests arise. 'Do you or do you not have a proprietary interest?' is, and should remain, a technical question, utterly different from 'Do you or do you not deserve to suffer less than these other colleagues in calamity?'[46]

This can be contrasted with the views of the dissenting judges that the majority position involved an unacceptable *extension* of such rules; the minority were willing to adopt a more flexible approach that acknowledges the role of policy.[47]

In short, many members of the House of Lords appear to consider that unjust enrichment and the supposedly sound[48] taxonomy associated with that doctrine, leads to consistency of reasoning; such views can be contrasted with the evident restraint and general scepticism towards 'unconscionability' and discretionary remedies in equity shown by the House, particularly in the context of property.

Two examples are emblematic in illustrating the differences between the jurisprudence of the House of Lords and the High Court. The first concerns the characterisation of common law quantum meruit claims. The House of Lords in *Yeoman's Row Management Ltd v Cobbe*,[49] without real comment, has equated a quantum meruit claim with unjust enrichment, whereas the High Court in *Lumbers*[50] was at pains to deny such a conceptual basis. The joint judgment of Gummow, Heydon, Crennan and Kiefel JJ rejected an unjust enrichment analysis as to whether services are of benefit to a recipient and are obtained at the expense *of* the claimant, as relevant to determining the availability of a claim for *services*.[51]

[42] See, eg *Muschinski v Dodds* (1985) 160 CLR 583 (HCA) and *Bathurst City Council v PWC Properties Pty Ltd* [1998] HCA 59, (1998) 195 CLR 566.

[43] *Foskett v McKeown* [2000] UKHL 29, [2001] 1 AC 102.

[44] Ibid 109 (Lord Browne-Wilkinson).

[45] Ibid 127 (Lord Hoffman and Lord Browne-Wilkinson concurring).

[46] P Birks, 'The Law of Restitution at the End of an Epoch' (1999) 28 *Western Australian Law Review* 13, 56.

[47] See especially *Foskett* (n 43) 112: Lord Steyn accepted that 'wider considerations of policy must be taken into account' in determining whether claimants, whose money had been used to pay insurance premiums, were entitled to a proportionate share of the proceeds of the policy. See also Lord Hope of Craighead, particularly at 120.

[48] For a contrary view, see J Dietrich, 'What is "Lawyering"? The Challenge of Taxonomy' (2006) 65 *CLJ* 549 and J Dietrich, 'The "Other" Obligations Category in the Classification of Obligations', in A Robertson (ed), *The Law of Obligations: Connections and Boundaries* (London, UCL Press, 2004) 111.

[49] *Yeoman's Row* (n 28) [42].

[50] *Lumbers* (n 10).

[51] The joint judgment refers to the 'evident difficulties of definition' of some of the unjust enrichment concepts: ibid [75]. The joint judgment stresses that such concepts were pitched at too high a

Instead, the joint judgment states a very narrow, historically-based rationale for the award of a quantum meruit for services rendered, namely, the need to show the *request* to the plaintiff for the work. The focus of the judgment is on the traditional pleading rules relating to a quantum meruit in order to identify its elements.[52]

The second example, this time in equity, is provided by the High Court's decision in *Farah*.[53] This case concerned third party liability for the knowing receipt of trust or fiduciary property. In this context there is perceived to be a direct conflict between the operation of unjust enrichment theory and equity. *Farah* arose after much debate in England and Australia about the merits of a strict-liability unjust enrichment approach to the receipt of trust property by third parties. In England, at least, there has been strong judicial[54] and extra-judicial[55] endorsement from senior Law Lords of such 'strict' unjust enrichment-based liability, although there is no authoritative decision on point as yet.

level of abstraction in the sense that they were both difficult to define and they did not draw attention to the legal relationships that existed between the parties said to have conferred and received the benefit respectively, and any other third parties involved in the transactions that are said to have resulted in the conferral of benefits. The claim was for building work done by the plaintiff on the defendants' house, done on behalf of a third party with whom the defendants had a contract to build the house; but the views expressed appear to be of more general application.

[52] See, eg *Lumbers* (n 10) [89]–[90] (footnote omitted). See also [79]. (Reference was made to *Bullen and Leake's Precedents of Pleadings*, 1868, 3rd edn, in the appeal transcripts: [2008] HCATrans 95 (26 February 2008)). Such a request can be express or *implied*; and the request must be *by* the defendant *to* the plaintiff.

The response of most commentators reflects the unjust enrichment world view. The approach of the joint judgment has been described as 'unacceptably formalistic' by one case note author: A Goymour, 'Too many cooks: three parties, contracts and unjust enrichment' [2008] *CLJ* 469, 470. She considers (471–72) that 'To find principled answers to complicated questions like the ones raised here is exactly why the law of unjust enrichment needs to be kept alive and nurtured, and not buried beneath rigid forms of action.' And it has been described as a possible attempt to 'resuscitate' the old forms of action and deny 'the existence of unjust enrichment as an independent category of law' by another. See J Edelman, 'Unjust Enrichment and Contract' [2008] *Lloyd's Maritime and Commercial Law Quarterly* 444, 447, 449; and see also M Bryan, '*Lumbers v W Cook Builders Pty Ltd (in liq)*: Restitution for Services and the Allocation of Risk' (2009) *Melbourne University Law Review* 320. Contrast J Dietrich, '*Quantum Meruit* for Services rendered in a Three-party Context: (implied contract, restitution, or unjust enrichment?' [2009] 17 *Restitution Law Review* 98.

[53] *Farah* (n 3).

[54] See, eg *Twinsectra Ltd v Yardley* [2002] UKHL 12, [2002] 2 AC 164, 194 (Lord Millett); *Criterion Properties plc v Stratford UK Properties LLC* [2004] UKHL 28, [2004] 1 WLR 1846 [4] (Lord Nicholls).

[55] See, eg D Nicholls, 'Knowing Receipt: The Need for a New Landmark' in W Cornish, R Nolan, J O'Sullivan & G Virgo (eds) *Restitution—Past, Present & Future: Essays in Honour of Gareth Jones* (Oxford, Hart Publishing, 1998) 231 noting the need for a new landmark case to resolve the difficulties. See also Sir Peter Millett, 'Restitution and Constructive Trusts' in the same work 199, 207; R Walker, 'Dishonesty and Unconscionable Conduct in Commercial Life—Some Reflections on Accessory Liability and Knowing Receipt' (2005) 27 *Sydney Law Review* 187, 202. For extra-judicial endorsement by Australian judges, see K Mason, 'Where Has Australian Restitution Law Got To and Where Is It Going?' (2003) 77 *Australian Law Journal* 358, 368. Against: D Heydon and M Leeming, *Jacobs' Law of Trusts in Australia*, 7th edn (Chatswood, LexisNexis Butterworths, 2006) para [1337].

The High Court categorically rejected the use of unjust enrichment theory to impose strict liability in this context and was highly critical of the New South Wales Court of Appeal's reasoning. The High Court emphasised that long-established authority, including 'seriously considered' *obiter dicta* of the Court in *Consul Development Pty Ltd v DPC Estates Pty Ltd*,[56] precluded an intermediate court from taking such a radical step. The requirement of notice or knowledge as a foundation of recipient liability in equity is too firmly entrenched to be abandoned. Even if the unjust enrichment claim is argued to arise alongside the equitable claim, rather than as a recasting of it,[57] the High Court correctly recognised that this would be to render equity's knowing receipt and its notice requirement, otiose.[58] Hence, the High Court stressed that recipient liability should not be outflanked by the unjust enrichment claim, which should not be used to 'cut down traditional equitable protection'.[59]

All this suggests that the divide between the English and Australian law of restitution is ever widening.[60] It should be noted, however, that in both the examples given, it is almost certain that a court applying unjust enrichment theory to the Australian cases would have reached the same conclusion, a point stressed by a number of commentators.[61] So just how different are the approaches of the courts?

IV. Just How Different Are the Approaches of the High Court and House of Lords?

Although the rhetoric that I have selectively quoted above may suggest otherwise, the differences between the two jurisdictions are not as wide as they appear and there are also similarities in approach, as I will demonstrate below. In this section, I propose to analyse more closely the substance of some of the decisions, focussing on outcomes and substantive reasoning. This analysis demonstrates that the legal positions in the respective jurisdictions and the underlying judicial concerns motivating English and Australian courts are not that dissimilar. Nonetheless, there are still some significant differences of substance between the courts in the two jurisdictions. I will consider both the role and use of equitable concepts and

[56] *Consul Development Pty Ltd v DPC Estates Pty Ltd* (1975) 132 CLR 373. See *Farah* (n 3) [134].

[57] This is consistent with Birks' later writing on the subject, eg P Birks, 'Receipt' in P Birks and A Pretto (eds) *Breach of Trust* (Oxford, Hart Publishing, 2002) 223.

[58] *Farah* (n 3) [134].

[59] Ibid [153]. See also [155]: It was not clear 'how there was any justice in permitting restitution against a defendant who received trust property without notice of that fact'.

[60] Such a view was expressed even before the more recent cases: see Hedley (n 27).

[61] In relation to *Lumbers*, see Goymour (n 52) and Edelman (n 52). For an analysis of how *Farah* might be decided on the basis of unjust enrichment theory, see J Dietrich and P Ridge, '"The Receipt of What?" Questions Concerning Third Party Recipient Liability in Equity and Unjust Enrichment' (2007) 31 *Melbourne University Law Review* 47.

of unjust enrichment, respectively. Then, in the following section, I will tentatively suggest some reasons for those divergences that do in fact exist: are there fundamental differences in judicial method, or ideological differences, at work?

A. Equitable Concepts: Unconscionability and Discretion

Undeniably, despite any views to the contrary that may appear above, both the High Court and House of Lords use broad, general concepts in the equitable jurisdiction and both courts do so in a *restrained* way.

For example, in the context of remedies for breach of fiduciary duty, the Privy Council in *Attorney General (Hong Kong) v Reid*[62] ignored a century of precedent and accepted the use of a proprietary remedy over the proceeds of a bribe given to a fiduciary. Other doctrines have been developed and modernised (sometimes in parallel fashion) so that equitable principles are relevant to the modern world. The protection of innocent guarantors against exploitation is an example.[63] Indeed, in the context of accessorial liability for knowing assistance of a breach of trust or fiduciary duty, the Privy Council has shown a willingness to develop the law on the basis of broad principles, whereas the High Court has been unwilling to go beyond a narrow, precedent-based formulation of doctrine.[64]

In both the High Court and the House of Lords, it has been stressed that general concepts, in equity at least,[65] are developed and used in our law consistently with existing principles and doctrines. Thus, although unconscionability seeks to test the standards of a defendant's conduct against some bench-mark, the question of whether conduct is unconscionable does not roam at large. The notion only comes into play by reference to the specific requirements and operative criteria of individual doctrines informed by that notion. Unconscionability, then, has developed 'in its many guises'.[66]

Thus, in *Tanwar Enterprises Pty Ltd v Cauchi*,[67] the joint judgment, noting that the terms 'unconscientious' and 'unconscionable' are used across a broad range of equity jurisdiction, continued:

> [They] describe in their various applications the formation and instruction of conscience by reference to well developed principles. Thus, it may be said that breaches of

[62] *Attorney General (Hong Kong) v Reid* [1994] 1 NZLR 1 (PC).

[63] See *Garcia v National Australia Bank Ltd* [1998] HCA 48, (1998) 194 CLR 395 and in the House of Lords, *Barclays Bank plc v O'Brien* [1994] 1 AC 180 (HL) and *Royal Bank of Scotland plc v Etridge (No 2)* [2001] UKHL 44, [2002] 2 AC 773, extending that protection further than the High Court's decision; the methodologies of the Australian and English cases differ quite considerably, however.

[64] *Royal Brunei Airlines Sdn Bhd v Tan* [1995] 2 AC 378 (PC); *Barlow Clowes International Ltd (in liq) v Eurotrust International Ltd* [2005] UKPC 37, [2006] 1 All ER 333; in Australia, contrast *Farah* (n 3).

[65] The position may be otherwise in relation to unconscionability under s 21 and s 22 of *The Australian Consumer Law 2010* (Cth).

[66] P Finn, 'Equitable Doctrine and Discretion in Remedies' in Cornish (n 55) 257.

[67] *Tanwar Enterprises Pty Ltd v Cauchi* [2003] HCA 57, (2003) 217 CLR 315 [20] (Gleeson CJ, McHugh, Gummow, Hayne and Heydon JJ).

trust and abuses of fiduciary position manifest unconscientious conduct; but whether a particular case amounts to a breach of trust or abuse of fiduciary duty is determined by reference to well developed principles, both specific and flexible in character. It is to those principles that the court has first regard rather than entering into the case at that higher level of abstraction involved in notions of unconscientious conduct in some loose sense where all principles are at large. … But the phrase 'unconscionable conduct' tends to mislead in several respects. First, it encourages the false notions that (i) there is a distinct cause of action, akin to an equitable tort, wherever a plaintiff points to conduct which merits the epithet 'unconscionable'; and (ii) there is an equitable defence to the assertion of any legal right, whether by action to recover a debt or damages in tort or for breach of contract, where in the circumstances it has become unconscionable for the plaintiff to rely on that legal right. … Thirdly, as a corollary to the first proposition, to speak of 'unconscionable conduct' may, wrongly, suggest that sufficient foundation for the existence of the necessary 'equity' to interfere in relationships established by, for example, the law of contract, is supplied by an element of hardship or unfairness in the terms of the transaction in question, or in the manner of its performance.[68]

In other words, that concept has a limited and *specific* operation according to the particular context within which it is used.[69] Courts in both jurisdictions recognise this and the statements from the English courts quoted above are hence consistent with similar cautions delivered by the High Court. Deane J's classic statement in *Muschinski v Dodds*[70] that 'proprietary rights fall to be governed by principles of law and not by some mix of judicial discretion … and "the formless void of individual moral opinion"', has often been cited, including in the House of Lords.[71] There is agreement that labels such as unconscionability cannot be used to avoid more detailed analysis and resort to established doctrines with their focus on specific elements.

Hence, members of both the House of Lords and of the High Court have expressed concerns about an *unrestrained* (or open-ended) use of 'unconscionability'. It is perhaps ironic that similar concerns also seem to underlie the

[68] Ibid [20], [23]–[26]. See also *ACCC v Berbatis Holdings Pty Ltd* [2000] FCA 2, (2000) 96 FCR 491 [14]–[15], [21] (French J): unconscionability in equity is 'subject to limitations in its factual field of operation by the existence of specific doctrines'. See further Dietrich, *Restitution* (n 11) 48. See also R Bigwood, 'Conscience and the Liberal Conception of Contract: Observing Basic Distinctions' (2000) 6 *New Zealand Business Law Quarterly* 1, 10 (also at (2000) 16 *Journal of Contract Law* 191) noting in relation to the operation of 'conscience' in equity, that the 'inquiry is channelled, and hence disciplined, through specific rules and criteria that express the unconscionability idea and, in turn, serve the desirable purpose of compelling judges to focus the issues and to give precise reasons for their decisions based in conscience.'

[69] Cf *Winterton Constructions v Hambros Aust Ltd* (1991) 101 ALR 363 (FCA) 373 (Gummow J).

[70] *Muschinski v Dodds* (1985) 160 CLR 583 (HCA) 616. Similarly, in the relation to unjust enrichment: *Pavey & Matthews* (n 13) 256 (Deane J) and *David Securities Pty Ltd v Commonwealth Bank of Australia* (1992) 175 CLR 353 (HCA) 379 (Mason CJ, Deane, Toohey, Gaudron and McHugh JJ); and in relation to unconscionability, see K Hayne, 'Address to Commercial Conference' (2002) 23 *Australian Bar Review* 1, 3.

[71] Eg Lord Walker of Gestingthorpe quotes Deane J in the opening paragraph of his judgment in *Yeoman's Row* (n 28) [46].

scepticism of some members of the High Court towards unjust enrichment. As Gummow J has said extra-judicially:

> The reduction of complex bodies of rights and remedies in the law to apparently simple all-embracing terms is productive of definitional disputation which does not assist the resolution of cases as they arise. For that, amongst other reasons, one should be sceptical of the use of 'unjust enrichment' to describe what is 'a result in different relations and in differing forms of litigation'.[72]

Both courts thus are concerned to restrain general concepts (and, similarly, I would suggest, remedial discretion) within the strictures of legal doctrine, precedent and method. However, the courts' focus on which general concepts are more in need of restraint or are more 'unruly', is different. The High Court is more cautious about unjust enrichment, whereas the House of Lords and Privy Council are more cautious about the use of equity, in particular, as already noted, where 'property' rights and/or commercial transactions are at issue. And it is from this difference of emphasis, albeit driven by the same judicial imperatives of legal certainty and transparency of reasoning, that the important differences of substance emerge.

To take property rights first: the concern with certainty and thereby with limiting the reach of proprietary remedies is oft-repeated. Instructive here is the Privy Council's decision in *Re Goldcorp Exchange Ltd*,[73] when contrasted with the New Zealand Court of Appeal decision in *Liggett v Kensington*[74] that it overturned. And I have already mentioned the remedial constructive trust, contrasting its acceptance and use in Australia, with the antipathy towards and rejection of it in England.

In the context of commercial relations, cases such as *Union Eagle Ltd v Golden Achievement Ltd*[75] reflect the focus on respecting properly made commercial contracts (and more broadly, the legal frameworks adopted by commercial parties). In that case, the Privy Council expressly adverted to the need for commercial certainty in refusing relief to a purchaser of land whose contract had been terminated after a 10 minute delay in payment of settlement moneys. The Privy Council was unwilling to resort to equitable concepts to allow relief against forfeiture of property interests or against the termination of contracts. Although many Australian cases have reached similar conclusions on similar facts,[76] and the High Court cases of *Friend v Brooker*,[77] *Tanwar*[78] and *Romanos v Pentagold*

[72] W Gummow, 'Equity; Too Successful?' (2003) 77 *Australian Law Journal* 30, 31 citing *Federal Sugar Refining Co v United States Sugar Equalization Board inc* 268 F 575, 582 (1920).

[73] *Re Goldcorp Exchange* (n 41).

[74] *Liggett v Kensington* [1993] 1 NZLR 257 (NZCA).

[75] *Union Eagle Ltd v Golden Achievement Ltd* [1997] AC 514 (PC).

[76] See N Seddon and M Ellinghaus, *Cheshire and Fifoot's Law of Contract*, 9th Australian edn (Sydney, LexisNexis Butterworths, 2008) para [21.19] and generally paras [21.35]–[21.36].

[77] *Friend* (n 11).

[78] *Tanwar* (n 67).

Investments Pty Ltd[79] can all be seen as examples of the same unwillingness to intervene in the legal frameworks that commercial parties have chosen to adopt,[80] nonetheless it is 'also clear that equitable relief will be available in Australia in circumstances where it would be refused in England' in the same factual context as *Union Eagle*.[81]

In part, the greater caution in England against using equitable principles to unsettle property rights (as exist prior to the application of such principles) and commercial relationships may reflect the influence of Professor Birks, who quite vociferously rejected resort to flexible equitable standards, such as unconscionability and remedial discretion.[82] Yet such views are contrary to the trend of legal development, at least in Australia, that Professor Paul Finn, as he then was, describes as 'an emerging tendency to formulate some range of doctrines, not in terms of distinct, limited and discrete rules of behaviour, but as generalised standards of conduct which in a controlled way are instance-specific in their application'.[83]

I propose to consider one example of the more restrictive approach of the English courts in detail: the law of estoppel. It has rightly been observed that '[t]he English law of estoppel, particularly promissory and equitable estoppel, is narrower than Australian law'.[84] The *Actionstrength* case is instructive.[85]

In that case, the House of Lords rejected liability on the basis of an estoppel, holding that an oral guarantee was unenforceable for lack of writing (as required by Statute of Frauds successor legislation). The creditor argued that it had detrimentally relied on the oral promise of guarantee. The House of Lords rejected this argument: the oral promise of itself could not found an estoppel. Something

[79] *Romanos v Pentagold Investments Pty Ltd* [2003] HCA 58.

[80] A more recent statement supporting this view is provided by *John Alexander's Clubs Pty Limited v White City Tennis Club Limited; Walker Corporation Pty Limited v White City Tennis Club Limited* [2010] HCA 19, (2010) 241 CLR 1 [101] quoting from: *James Baird Co v Gimbel Bros Inc* 64 F 2d 344 at 346 (2nd Circ Ct of Appeals, 1933) (Learned Hand J delivering the judgment of himself, Judge Manton and Judge Swan). See also Kirby J's view in *Tanwar* (n 67) [86] of the need to avoid unpredictability in legal relations; cf the joint judgment at [54]. Compare the willingness of the High Court to intervene in a transaction in a domestic setting in *Bridgewater v Leahy* [1998] HCA 66, (1998) 194 CLR 457 by broadly applying the unconscionable dealing doctrine.

[81] See *Tanwar* (n 67) [6], in which Gleeson CJ, McHugh, Gummow, Hayne and Heydon JJ quote this statement of Handley JA in the New South Wales Court of Appeal decision in *Tanwar*, with approval. See Seddon and Ellinghaus (n 76) paras [21.35]–[21.36] for some examples.

[82] The sources are too numerous to list exhaustively, but see in particular: Birks, 'Equity in The Modern World' (n 8); 'The Law of Restitution at the End of an Epoch' (n 46); 'Annual Miegunyah Lecture: Equity, Conscience, and Unjust Enrichment'(1999) 23 *Melbourne University Law Review* 1; 'Rights, Wrongs, and Remedies' (2000) 20 *OJLS* 1; 'Three Kinds of Objections to Discretionary Remedialism' (2000) 29 *Western Australian Law Review* 1.

[83] P Finn, 'Commerce, The Common Law and Morality' (1989) 17 *Melbourne University Law Review* 87, 90.

[84] *Tipperary Developments Pty Ltd v The State of Western Australia* [2009] WASCA 126 [132] (McLure JA; Newnes JA agreeing).

[85] *Actionstrength* (n 36).

more was necessary[86] such as a representation that the Statute would not be relied on, or that the formalities need not be complied with. The creditor must have been led to assume that the promise would be enforceable. As Lord Bingham concluded:

> There was no representation by St-Gobain [the guarantor] that it would honour the agreement despite the absence of writing, or that it was not a contract of guarantee, or that it would confirm the agreement in writing. Nor did St-Gobain make any payment direct to Actionstrength [the creditor] which could arguably be relied on as affirming the oral agreement or inducing Actionstrength to go on supplying labour. If St-Gobain were held to be estopped in this case it is hard to see why any oral guarantor, where credit was extended to a debtor on the strength of a guarantee, would not be similarly estopped. The result would be to render nugatory a provision which, despite its age, Parliament has deliberately chosen to retain.[87]

This narrow position must be contrasted with the more fluid, but probably broader, position in Australia where, although there is no High Court decision directly on point, *Waltons Stores (Interstate) Ltd v Maher*[88] has been cited in favour of both a broader and narrower position.

The broader view that has been adopted in some Australian cases[89] is that estoppel is made out simply by an oral representation that is relied on. No further representation, such as that the statute will not be relied upon, is required. A majority of the Western Australian Court of Appeal in *Tipperary Developments Pty Ltd v The State of Western Australia*[90] endorsed the broader view and considered *Walton's Stores* to be consistent with that view (alongside cases such as *Riches v Hogben*).[91] Accordingly, establishing the estoppel does away with any argument based on the Statute of Frauds and nothing further is required.[92] Critically, the majority saw Brennan J's judgment in *Walton's Stores* as decisive:

> As s 54A makes an oral agreement to make a written agreement for the disposition of an interest in land ineffective, an equity which gave the assumption the same force as a promise would be ineffective. But, as we have seen, the equity is to be satisfied by

[86] Ibid. See, eg Lord Clyde [35]: 'In order to be estopped from invoking the Statute there must be something more, such as some additional encouragement, inducement or assurance.'

[87] Ibid [9] (Lord Woolf and Lord Walker agreeing). Similarly, Lord Hoffmann at [26] stated that 'To admit an estoppel on these grounds would be to repeal the Statute.' Such statements appear contrary to the widely accepted Australian view that estoppel does not lead to enforcement of the contract but of the equity which is 'created' by the conduct: see, eg *Olsson v Dyson* (1969) 120 CLR 365 (HCA) 379 (Kitto J).

[88] *Waltons Stores (Interstate) Ltd v Maher* (1988) 164 CLR 387 (HCA).

[89] See, eg the early decision of *Riches v Hogben* (1985) 2 Qd R 292 (McPherson J); (1986) 1 Qd R 315 (Full Court).

[90] *Tipperary Developments* (n 84) (McLure JA and Newnes JA, Wheeler JA dissenting).

[91] *Riches v Hogben* (n 89).

[92] *Tipperary Developments* (n 84) [144]–[145]. A statement by Mason CJ and Wilson J in *Waltons Stores* (n 88) 406 for there to be 'something more' was interpreted by the majority in *Tipperary Developments* as a reference to further elements of estoppel needed to be satisfied beyond merely detrimental reliance on a representation or promise. See at [141]–[142].

avoiding a detriment suffered in reliance on an induced assumption, not by the direct enforcement of the assumption.[93]

Wheeler JA in dissent adopted the narrow approach of *Actionstrength*, noting that 'although *Waltons Stores* contains observations which could support a different conclusion' it too supported the narrow view.[94]

Consistent with Wheeler JA's dissent is *Powercell Pty Ltd v Cuzeno Pty Ltd*,[95] in which the New South Wales Court of Appeal adopted the narrower approach and accepted the reasoning in *Actionstrength* as 'conclusive' against a claim on an estoppel.[96] The Court considered the requirement of 'something more', in the nature of a secondary assumption or representation,[97] to be consistent with *Waltons Stores*[98] Further, '[i]t could not without more be inequitable or unconscionable to rely on the law of the land'.[99]

One of the problems with *Actionstrength* and *Powercell* is that these cases rely on the existence of an express, albeit oral, contract as refuting an estoppel without 'something more'. Hence, where A and B agree that A sell land to B, then the oral contract is not enforceable, even where B detrimentally relies on the promise to sell (putting part performance to one side). However, if A merely makes a representation and B is induced to rely on it, such that there is no sufficiently certain, concluded agreement, then B could argue an estoppel: that is, because there is no contract, unenforceable or otherwise, but there *is* a representation that was detrimentally relied on. Hence, Statute of Frauds considerations do not enter. The end result: parties who make clear and precise agreements are worse off than those that do not.[100]

[93] *Waltons Stores* (n 88) 422–23. There is also commentary in support of the broader position. See Andrew Robertson, 'The Statute of Frauds, Equitable Estoppel and the Need for "Something More"' (2003) 19 *Journal of Contract Law* 1, who distinguishes *Actionstrength* from the Australian position as 'based on the notion that promissory estoppel does not operate to provide an independent source of rights, but simply operates to prevent a person from enforcing a strict legal right' (at 10). In Australia, however, '[t]he courts apply a broad doctrine of equitable estoppel that operates as an independent source of rights and provides a cause of action' (at 11). See also at 16–17.

[94] *Tipperary Developments* (n 84) [21]–[24].

[95] *Powercell Pty Ltd v Cuzeno Pty Ltd* [2004] NSWCA 51, (2004) 11 BPR 21,429. Thanks to Sonali Walpola for drawing my attention to this case.

[96] Ibid [71].

[97] Ibid. Although the Court noted at [69]: 'Perhaps the something more did not have to be as explicit as that the respondent would honour the agreement despite the absence of writing.'

[98] *Waltons Stores* (n 88).

[99] *Powercell* (n 95) [73]. The court noted at [80] that the doctrine of part performance ameliorated the harshness of the Statute of Frauds and that if one could rely on estoppel in all cases of detrimental reliance on an oral promise, the Statute would be 'rendered nugatory' and the part performance doctrine 'unnecessary'. In relation to *Riches v Hogben* (n 89) the Court considered that 'it is not apparent that the estoppel was founded only on the making of the agreement rather than on the defendant's subsequent conduct' and the case was not considered to preclude the conclusions reached (see [82]).

[100] Alternatively, the differences in result could turn on the context: *Actionstrength* and *Powercell* were commercial agreements, and *Riches v Hogben* was a domestic situation. N Piška (n 39) suggests in his note on *Yeoman's Row* (n 28) and *Thorner* (n 34) that this is the fundamental divide that exists between cases where estoppel tends to be successfully pleaded and where it is not. Note that, although *Tipperary Developments* (n 84) was a commercial case, the estoppel argument ultimately failed for other reasons.

B. Unjust Enrichment

In England, as we have seen, unjust enrichment provides a mechanism for organising the 'individual instances in which the law does give a right of recovery.'[101] Specifically, this means that the courts apply the stages of analysis that are derived directly from the concept of unjust enrichment itself: there must have been 'enrichment', 'at the expense of' the plaintiff, where some 'unjust factor' justifies restitution. The courts have repeatedly utilised these steps and considered in more detail the content of each stage. There is considerable engagement with academic theory. By way of contrast, in the High Court, unjust enrichment is *at best* utilised as descriptive of conclusions reached by reference to more specific processes of analysis, rather than as part of such analysis and determination of liability itself.

The case of *Sempra Metals Ltd v Her Majesty's Commissioners of Inland Revenue*[102] illustrates the dominance of unjust enrichment in legal discourse in England. In *Sempra*, the House of Lords allowed a claim for pre-judgment *compound* interest on moneys paid under a mistake and recoverable as restitution. Both the majority and minority judgments extensively rely on unjust enrichment analysis to support their conclusions. The majority[103] allowed compound interest as of right, concluding that this reflected the valuation of the actual benefit received. The minority[104] disallowed the compound interest claim, arguing that it should only be available where the claimant proves that such a gain has in fact been received by the recipient. Notable in the judgments is the reliance on academic writing. For example, Lord Hope includes in his judgment extensive citation and endorsement of Professor Birks' writing.[105] It demonstrates the influence of Birks: few other non-judicial lawyers have so significantly shaped the legal landscape, in private law at least, in recent decades.

Yet the decision in *Sempra* also illustrates some of the pitfalls of unjust enrichment theory. The analyses of both minority and majority judgments have been subjected to telling, indeed, I would suggest irrefutable, critique by Pauline Ridge.[106] Ridge points out that, although money is undeniably enriching, what one does with that money need not be. Thus, on the one hand, it cannot be automatically assumed that a defendant has gained the benefit of earning, or saving, interest at compounded rates as a result of the receipt of money. Hence, Birks' subjective devaluation operates: the recipient can deny that the use of the money is subjectively enriching and argue that an objective valuation is not warranted. On the other hand, if the defendant has obtained some *extra* benefit from the use of such money, for example, by investing it in profitable shares, such a gain is not

[101] *Woolwich Building Society v IRC* [1993] AC 70 (HL) 196–97 (Lord Browne-Wilkinson).
[102] *Sempra Metals* (n 27).
[103] Lord Hope of Craighead, Lord Nicholls of Birkenhead and Lord Walker of Gestingthorpe.
[104] Lord Scott of Foscote and Lord Mance.
[105] *Sempra Metals* (n 27) [27]–[31].
[106] See P Ridge, 'Pre-Judgment Compound Interest' (2010) 126 *LQR* 279.

at the expense of the claimant on the basis of subtraction. The claimant would need to show a legal wrong to get at such benefit.[107] Ridge concludes that:

> [A] claim for compound interest on a mistaken payment can only meaningfully be conceptualised in one of two ways, neither of which involve unjust enrichment by subtraction. Either the claim is for C's loss of the use of the mistakenly paid sum or it is for D's gains from the use of the mistakenly paid sum. In either case, the claim cannot be based upon unjust enrichment according to Birks' use of that term but must be based upon a 'wrong' in the sense of breach of a legal duty.[108]

This brief excursus suggests that the complexities of unjust enrichment theory itself and of applying it to problematic facts can lead even senior Law Lords to struggle to apply the theory with consistency.[109] Unfortunately, the unjust enrichment analysis adopted in *Sempra* led the majority to expand the liability of an *innocent* defendant to one that equates with that of a wrongdoer.

As an interesting aside, the House of Lords was also split in *Sempra* as to whether discretion was relevant to the restitutionary remedy. That division did not follow the division as to the outcome of the case. Lord Mance, of the minority on the overall decision, adopted an unjust enrichment analysis, but also reasoned by analogy with equity. He considered that the equitable jurisdiction to award compound interest allowed for such an award in the context of mistaken payment.[110] In doing so, Lord Mance was prepared to import equity's *discretion* into the award of compound interest. Lord Mance stated that 'there is no sustainable reason in modern conditions for continuing to limit [the

[107] Ibid, particularly 287–89. Although the money received by D (say $1000) was obtained by subtraction from C, the extra (say $500) profit was not.

[108] Ibid 288. cf *Sempra Metals* (n 27) [145]: Lord Scott (dissenting) states:

> My Lords I find myself unable to accept the premise on which this proposed development is based, namely that the mere possession of mistakenly paid money—and accordingly the ability to use it if minded to do so—is sufficient to justify not simply a restitutionary remedy for recovery of the money, but a remedy also for recovery of the wholly conceptual benefit of an ability to use the money. Why should a restitutionary remedy be concerned with a benefit that is no more than conceptual? The mistake that had been made and on which the restitutionary claim is based was the mistake of the payer, Sempra in the instant case. The restitutionary claim is not based on any wrongdoing on the part of the recipient.

[109] On the complexities of unjust enrichment see, eg Hedley's conclusion that 'the subject has become more and more technical ...[but] is acknowledged to explain less and less ... There is more and more schematising and theorising, to less and less effect.' S Hedley, 'The taxonomic approach to restitution' in A Hudson (ed), *New Perspectives on Property Law, Obligations and Restitution* (United Kingdom, Routledge-Cavendish, 2004) ch 7, 152 and generally; and also Hedley, 'The Empire Strikes Back' (n 27) 781:

> The high degree of precision that Birks demands ensures that there is a continual battle simply to keep academic theory and judicial pronouncements within hailing distance of one another. The language is becoming denser and more intense. Birks ... acknowledges that his approach is making unjust enrichment abstract and technical.

Practitioners have also expressed concern about the complexity of the theory: see the views noted in the editors' comments by A Burrows and E Peel (eds), *Commercial Remedies: Current Issues and Problems* (Oxford, Oxford University Press, 2003) 'Restitution of Unjust Enrichment: Review of Discussion' 186, in response to the papers by P Birks (ch 13) and R Calnan (ch 14).

[110] Presumably, as a concurrent jurisdiction: see Ridge (n 106) fn 86. Ridge comprehensively rejects any arguments for extending equity's jurisdiction beyond *compensation* for wrongdoing.

availability of compound interest] in a way which may prevent the court from doing equity'.[111]

Some of the majority also expressly accepted a role for discretion and the infusion of equitable principles.[112] Lord Scott, of the minority, however, expressly disavowed a discretionary approach.[113]

A discretionary approach is more in tune with the High Court's views on equitable rights and remedy, but it is an approach that has not generally found favour in English unjust enrichment jurisprudence. For example, in the context of the change of position defence that may defeat a claim for restitution, restitution theorists have widely condemned any attempts by courts to seek to apply a discretionary, equitable approach, such as, for instance, seeking to 'balance the equities' between defendants and plaintiffs.[114]

It is interesting to speculate how the High Court might deal with the issue of compound interest for a restitutionary claim. I would venture that the judgments would closely analyse the existing case law and seek to identify the circumstances in which the authorities have awarded compound interest in equity and the common law. The court would then seek to characterise the claim before it to determine whether it fell within one of the established categories. I doubt that the High Court would start with unjust enrichment theory; indeed, one would strongly suspect that the value of such theory in answering such a tricky question would be decried. The Court would be unlikely to allow compound interest. And almost certainly, the current High Court would not 'fuse' equitable and common law principles. Support for these conclusions is found in the judgment of McHugh and Gummow JJ in *Commonwealth v SCI Operations Pty Limited*,[115] a case concerning statutory provisions that, it was held, determined the extent of any interest claim, but in which the general law was also canvassed.

Despite the widespread use of unjust enrichment theory, however, there are still instances in which the English Courts have not accepted or applied the theory in contexts where, arguably, it could apply. For example, the House of Lords has expressly rejected the applicability and utility of unjust enrichment in the context of proprietary remedies and property law, contrary to the position advocated by Birks. According to Birks, both personal and proprietary responses derive from

[111] *Sempra* (n 27) [239].

[112] Ibid [187]–[188] (Lord Walker), [46] (Lord Hope seemingly in agreement).

[113] Ibid [152]. Lord Nicholls appears to reject any reasoning by analogy with equity and considered the law of restitution was sufficiently flexible in its valuation of benefits (if market value can be shown not to have been received) and in the application of change of position defence ([119]).

[114] This was done in *National Bank of New Zealand v Waitaki International Processing (NI) Ltd* [1999] 2 NZLR 211 (NZCA). For criticisms see, eg Birks, *Unjust Enrichment* (n 8) 214–19; and A Burrows, 'Clouding the Issue on Change of Position' (2004) 63 *CLJ* 276, criticising the English Court of Appeal in *Niru Battery Manufacturing Company v Milestone Trading Ltd* [2003] EWCA Civ 1446, [2004] 1 All ER (Comm) 193 for utilising the language of discretion, such as 'inequitable' and 'unconscionable', in relation to the change of position defence.

[115] *Commonwealth v SCI Operations Pty Limited* [1998] HCA 20, (1998) 192 CLR 285 [72]–[76]. But see Kirby J at [82]–[85] who appears more open to allowing compound interest under the law of restitution.

the same taxonomy of 'causative events'. Thus, proprietary responses derive from unjust enrichment, wrongs and consent. And if a proprietary interest does arise in response to unjust enrichment, it will then continue into the traceable proceeds of any such property initially received.[116]

A number of difficulties arise in relation to this analysis. Birks himself conceded that his views are seemingly contrary to the reasoning of the House of Lords in *Westdeutsche Landesbank Girozentrale v Islington LBC*,[117] though not the result in that case. Further, some commentators have rejected the argument that a proprietary response ever can arise from unjust enrichment, such principle founding only personal liability.[118] Finally, both commentators and the House of Lords in *Foskett v McKeown*,[119] have rejected Birks' taxonomy of causative events giving rise to proprietary responses and see 'property law' as itself a source of legal rights (or as a causative event).[120] In short, there is very little likelihood that Birks' analysis will be accepted. As Lord Millett put it, writing extra-judicially in relation to Birks' claim that a claim to the traceable proceeds of property is based on unjust enrichment:

> This convoluted analysis is not based on anything in any reported case, is not universally accepted by commentators, and is inconsistent with the analysis adopted by the House of Lords in *Foskett v McKeown.*[121] I reject it. I prefer to say with Lord Ellenborough in *Taylor v Plumer* that: '[T]he product of or substitute for the original thing still follows the nature of the thing itself'.[122]

Further, even where the *label* of unjust enrichment is utilised, the courts have not always analysed the problem in terms of such theory. Hence, in *Blue Haven Enterprises Ltd v Tully*,[123] a case in which a landowner had received the benefit of substantial improvements by a mistaken improver, the Privy Council headed part of its judgment as 'unjust enrichment' but then posited the following question: 'The critical question is not whether [the landowner] has been enriched at [the

[116] Birks, *Unjust Enrichment* (n 8) 198–201.

[117] *Westdeutsche* (n 41) discussed by Birks ibid 190–91.

[118] See, eg W Swadling, 'Property and Unjust Enrichment' in J Harris, *Property Problems: From Genes to Pension Funds* (London, Kluwer Law International, 1997) 130, and P Millett, 'Restitution and Constructive Trusts' in Cornish et al (n 55) 199 and 'Proprietary Restitution' in S Degeling and J Edelman (eds), *Equity in Commercial Law* (Sydney, Thomson, 2005) 309.

[119] [2000] UKHL 29, [2001] 1 AC 102. See also Millett, 'Proprietary Restitution' (n 118).

[120] See, eg G Virgo, *The Principles of the Law of Restitution* 2nd edn (Oxford, Oxford University Press, 2006); and in a similar vein, R Calnan, 'Proprietary Remedies for Unjust Enrichment' in A Burrows and E Peel (eds), *Commercial Remedies* (n 109). For Birks' response, see *Unjust Enrichment* (n 8) 32–38, 204.

[121] [2000] UKHL 29, [2001] 1 AC 102, 119.

[122] Millett, 'Proprietary Restitution' (n 118) 313–14, citing *Taylor v Plumer* (1815) 3 M & S 562, 575; 105 ER 721, 726. Despite these contrary views as to the taxonomical basis of proprietary remedies, Millett suggests that there is little difference between Birks' and his own views as to when a proprietary remedy would arise.

[123] *Blue Haven Enterprises Ltd v Tully* [2006] UKPC 17.

claimant's] expense, but whether the circumstances in which that enrichment came about places [the landowner] under an equitable obligation to compensate.'[124]

In answering that question, the Court proceeded to apply principles of proprietary estoppel, and the need to show something in the way of unconscionable behaviour on the part of the recipient of the benefit.[125] The Privy Council thus resorted to traditional established equitable principles. Critically, although the approach is consistent with established precedent, it is contrary to unjust enrichment theory even though the same result may be reached applying such theory. According to unjust enrichment theory, an improver's *mistake* is a sufficient generic unjust factor to justify restitution, provided the mistaken improvement of land amounts to a 'benefit'. A recipient is able to deny the receipt of a benefit on the basis of 'subjective devaluation' unless he or she had freely accepted the benefit or it was incontrovertible. Hence, conduct of the recipient is relevant, but to establishing the existence of a benefit. Instead of adopting this analysis, the Privy Council *assumed* a benefit existed but then focussed on the *conduct* of the landowner and whether it was *unconscionable*, in order to determine liability.

Hence, although the House of Lords has broadly accepted the unjust enrichment principle and adopted the general structure of analysis dictated by the theory, it has been selective in its use of that theory. Judges of the House of Lords are willing to engage with the theory, but not always. The judges appear to be utilising the concepts at their disposal selectively and preferentially, in order to achieve or support the outcomes that they have reached. This may explain why much of the case law in which unjust enrichment theory has been *judicially* developed and applied is met with mixed responses from the theorists: the response is often, 'it is wonderful that the courts have accepted this principle', but the courts have failed to properly apply/analyse/explain or have simply got wrong, significant parts of it.[126]

It remains to consider some reasons as to why there is such a significant divide in rhetoric and less pronounced, but still significant, differences in analytical approaches, between the two courts. The question is all the more interesting because only sometimes do these differences in analysis lead to actual differences in the outcomes of cases. Indeed, as already noted above, the results reached by the High Court in *Lumbers* and *Farah* are consistent with unjust enrichment theory. This means that similar outcomes can be reached by seemingly very different routes. Many of the decisions in one jurisdiction are not necessarily incompatible or inconsistent with the decisions in the other jurisdiction.

[124] Ibid [20].

[125] Ibid [22].

[126] See, eg Birks, *Unjust Enrichment* (n 8) 31–32, 71, 163, 183 and his treatment of *Foskett* (n 43) and *Westdeutsche* (n 41). And such responses are not limited to the United Kingdom. See, eg the recent lament of one unjust enrichment theorist concerning the failure of the Supreme Court of Canada to engage with Birks' theory: M McInnes, 'Taxonomic Lessons for the Supreme Court of Canada' in C Rickett and R Grantham (eds), *Structure and Justification in Private Law* (Oxford, Oxford University Press, 2008) 77. This is ironic, given that unjust enrichment has a firm jurisprudential basis in Canada. Problematically for McInnes, but not for this writer, the Canadian Courts use that concept in a non-technical way.

Why the differences in rhetoric and in approaches? This can only be answered by way of speculation. I offer a few suggestions, in no particular order.

V. Suggested Reasons for the Different Approaches of the Courts

The first possible reason for the differences in approach between the High Court and the House of Lords may be linked to fusion. In part, the High Court's rejection of unjust enrichment could be driven by the almost visceral rejection of the openly pro-fusionist approach of much of unjust enrichment theory.[127] This appears to have riled many of the judges who have an avowed anti-fusionist stance.[128] As both a fusionist[129] and an unjust enrichment theory sceptic, this does leave me feeling rather lonely and torn, at times. The same anti-fusionist agenda is simply not evident in the House of Lords where one sees fusionist reasoning in some judgments.[130]

Interestingly, much of the impetus for fusion among lawyers other than 'unjust enrichment theorists', to generalise somewhat, has come from those advocating a fused, and discretionary, approach to remedy: that all of the remedial armoury of the law should be potentially available to remedy infringements of either equitable or common law 'rights'.[131]

[127] See, eg A Burrows, 'We Do This at Common Law But That in Equity' (2002) 22 *OJLS* 1.

[128] Of the judges in the joint judgment in *Farah*, Heydon J is a co-author of *Meagher, Gummow and Lehane's Equity: Doctrines and Remedy*, 4th edn (Chatswood, LexisNexis Butterworths, 2002) and Gummow J is a co-author of previous editions. See also Heydon JA's judgment in *Harris v Digital Pulse Pty Ltd* [2003] NSWCA 10, (2003) 56 NSWLR 298 (though note the interpretation of this judgment as not strictly anti-fusionist by A Burrows, 'Remedial Coherence and Punitive Damages in Equity' in S Degeling and J Edelman (eds), *Equity in Commercial Law* (Sydney, Lawbook Co, 2005) particularly 391–402, and see also J Edelman, 'A "Fusion Fallacy" Fallacy' (2003) 119 *LQR* 375, 377).

[129] I agree with the views of Deane J in *Waltons* (n 88) 447: 'To ignore the substantive effects of the interaction of doctrines of law and equity within that fused system in which unity, rather than conflict, of principle is now to be assumed is … unduly to preserve the importance of past separation and continuing distinctness as a barrier against the orderly development of a simplified and unified legal system which fusion was intended to advance.' This was cited with approval by Mason P, dissenting, in *Harris v Digital Pulse* (n 130) [154], which judgment is an excellent rebuttal of the anti-fusionist view (see generally [132]–[155]).

[130] I would suggest that some of the judgments in *Sempra* (n 102) are an example.

[131] See, eg P Finn, 'Equitable Doctrine and Discretion in Remedies' (n 55) 251. Other commentators who support such an approach include JD Davies, 'Restitution and Equitable Wrongs' in FD Rose (ed), *Consensus ad Idem: Essays on Contract in Honour of Guenter Treitel* (London, Sweet & Maxwell, 1996) 158; S Evans, 'Property, Proprietary Remedies and Insolvency: Conceptualism or Candour' (2000) 5 *Deakin Law Review* 31; M Tilbury, 'Remedies and the Classification of Obligations' in A Robertson (ed), *The Law of Obligations: Connections and Boundaries* (London, UCL Press, 2004) 11–30; D Wright, *The Remedial Constructive Trust* (Sydney, Butterworths, 1997); Wright, 'The Statutory Trust, The Remedial Constructive Trust and Remedial Flexibility' (1999) 14 *Journal of Contract Law* 221. Ironically, to generalise somewhat again, the *fusionist* unjust enrichment theorists vehemently reject remedial discretion.

A second possible reason for the divergence could be that the High Court has, historically, preferred to focus on parties' conduct rather than on outcomes. Whereas unconscionable *conduct* is the concern of equitable doctrines generally, 'unjust' qualifies the concept of enrichment, which does not refer to conduct but to a particular outcome, namely a defendant's 'enrichment'. Yet many transactions leave a party 'better off' and are thus potentially open to question and subsequent reversal if it can be said that they were 'unjust'. This is one of the difficulties with the unjust enrichment concept. By focussing merely on *outcomes* that ought to be reversed, much of the law could be described as about the reversal of unjust enrichments, without so much as hinting at the reasons for such reversal, other than the epithet 'unjust'. Unconscionability, by way of contrast, draws attention to a defendant's conduct and requires us to consider whether such conduct breaches some legal standard. A similar point has been made by Finn J, writing extra judicially:[132]

> [T]o the extent that it directs attention to outcomes and to the character to be attributed to them, [unjust enrichment] is capable of concealing rather than revealing why the law would want to attribute a responsibility to one party to provide satisfaction to the other. This is particularly so where, as is so often the case, it is conduct in a relationship or dealing—an expectation created and relied upon; a mistake not corrected; etc—which provides the focus of legal attention and which generates the issue of legal policy for which resolution is required. This, I suspect, provides the reason why 'unconscionable conduct' and not 'unjust enrichment' (a possible effect of that conduct) has achieved the currency it has in Australian law.[133]

Related to this issue is Keith Mason's suggestion that the High Court's rejection of unjust enrichment theory is driven in part by a fear of indeterminacy.[134] This could be correct. Certainly, the High Court in *Farah* and *Lumbers* is much more restrictive in its approach than, for example, the earlier Court in *Pavey & Matthews Pty Ltd v Paul*. And even though the High Court continues to espouse the virtues of remedial discretion,[135] much more caution is evident in *application* in this context as well.[136]

So there is evidence of a generally more restrictive approach in the High Court to broad, open-ended concepts. And unjust enrichment *can* be used in an open-ended way that could give rise to greater indeterminacy and unpredictability.

[132] Ibid 252. These views have been adopted by Gummow J in *Roxborough* (n 4) [70]. For further discussion of the dangers of outcome-orientated reasoning, see Dietrich, *Restitution* (n 11) 41–3.

[133] Thus, members of the High Court in *Roxborough* (n 4) made reference, in relation to the money had and received action, to equitable notions of the 'unconscientiousness' of the retention of money, either alongside references to unjust enrichment (Gleeson CJ, Gaudron & Hayne JJ: [24], [23]) and note the references to principles of equitable relief in Kirby J's judgment at [152], or as a preferable alternative to it (Gummow J: [70]–[100]). See also B Kremer, 'Restitution and Unconscientiousness: Another View' (2003) 119 *LQR* 188.

[134] K Mason, 'Values in the Law' (unpublished paper cited with the author's permission) 11.

[135] *Bofinger* (n 14).

[136] I would suggest *Bathurst City Council v PWC Properties Pty Ltd* [1998] HCA 59, (1998) 195 CLR 566 and *Giumelli v Giumelli* [1999] HCA 10, (1999) 196 CLR 101 are examples.

However, interestingly, I would argue that in fact, unjust enrichment has not been used in that way in the United Kingdom,[137] and instead, the theory has been used in a dogmatic and restrictive way that seeks to straitjacket the law within narrow confines.[138] This may explain the views of Gummow J, that at first glance appear contradictory, that unjust enrichment is both too general and all embracing[139] and yet is also dogmatically restricting 'substance and dynamism' in the law.[140] I have described elsewhere the different ways in which the law utilises general concepts and how the potential dangers of unjust enrichment as an open-ended, visceral appeal to justice has been confronted by theorists by adopting the opposite extreme: a highly technical and rule-based theory.[141]

Thirdly, the differences in approach could be a consequence of the fact that statute has dramatically altered the Australian legal landscape in the law of obligations, perhaps much more so than in England. The taxonomy offered by unjust enrichment theorists is essentially one of the common law (including equity) of obligations. Yet this is perhaps the most fundamental of all weaknesses in the taxonomical project.[142] The taxonomy's neglect of statute raises serious doubts about the focus of the taxonomists' energies: what can be gained from such an exercise? In Australia, at least, legislation has *displaced* much of the common law and what is left is (with a few notable, but decreasing number of, exceptions) largely insignificant. And since we are 'stuck with', in many cases, piecemeal legislation, we cannot assume that there is a 'coherent whole' that is merely being obscured by such legislation.[143] For example, in terms of remedy, remedial discretion and taxonomy, much of the writing of Birks et al is rather by the way in Australia, given the impact of legislation such as the Trade Practices Act 1974 (Cth).[144]

Fourthly, the High Court's attitude towards unjust enrichment could be a rejection of the academic tendency constantly to chastise judges for 'getting it wrong', often because they have failed to accept the particular commentator's theory. The consequent judicial reaction may be not to pay too much attention to academic writing at all. Interestingly, this does not seem to have concerned members of the

[137] Compare the use of unjust enrichment in Canada, which is more comparable with the use in Australian courts of 'unconscionability'.

[138] See Dietrich, 'Giving Content to General Concepts' (n 21) particularly 230–33.

[139] See n 72 above.

[140] See nn 4 and 5 above.

[141] Dietrich 'Giving Content to General Concepts' (n 21).

[142] Interestingly, however, when legislation is (rarely) mentioned, it is sometimes seen as an argument in favour of the taxonomical project. Thus, eg Birks, 'Annual Miegunyah Lecture' (n 82) 28 noted that: 'The massively increased output of parliaments, focused now on this problem and now on that, pays scant regard to systematic overview.'

[143] Against: P Birks, 'Definition and Division: A Meditation on *Institutes* 3.13' in P Birks (ed), *The Classification of Obligations* (Oxford, Oxford University Press, 1997) 1. 'Piecemeal legislation has combined with educational practice indifferent to legal taxonomy to return the common law to [a] disorderly heap ...'. This makes classification of obligations all the more important, in Birks' view. And although his taxonomy 'is not the classification of the whole law ... a good map of the law of obligations would make a huge contribution to the coherence of the whole law': 2.

[144] See the quote in the text at n 19 above. The TPA has now been replaced by the Competition and Consumer Act 2010 (Cth).

House of Lords, who are prepared robustly to debate the pros and cons of the theory. The extra-judicial writing of Lord Millett and Lord Nicholls are obvious examples.[145]

Perhaps also the sheer volume of writing on unjust enrichment may be a barrier to some judges engaging with the theory other than in a selective and piecemeal fashion.[146] And there are, of course, dangers in that. Members of the High Court appear unwilling to engage with unjust enrichment theory and there is some justification for this. The theory has become self-referential and the different versions of it have become more intricate and convoluted such that it is difficult for outsiders to follow the debate.[147] This might also explain the preference in the High Court for the use of both more historical and doctrinal sources, rather than of taxonomical and theoretical writing.

VI. Conclusions

What lessons are there for the law from all of this? Perhaps, and I would assume this to be uncontroversial, one might conclude that it is important to avoid the two undesirable extremes of (1) using generic concepts such as unconscionability or unjust enrichment as labels attaching to certain events, and thereby as mechanisms for imposing liability, without adequate and transparent explanation for such liability, or (2) using concepts such as unjust enrichment as part of a dogmatically-asserted, exclusive framework for restitution cases in which theory dictates analysis and solutions. Indications are that the High Court is well aware of the pitfalls of either of these extremes and, in its use of general concepts, the High Court is steering a middle path between them. But so, it seems, is the House of Lords. Unjust enrichment is used selectively, and the role of discretion and flexibility has been acknowledged in some contexts.

Hence, the triumph of unjust enrichment theory in the House of Lords is only partial. Should the views of the High Court on the (lack of) utility of unjust enrichment theory have merit (and they resonate with many of my own views) then perhaps in due course, the United Kingdom Supreme Court may even retreat from its strong commitment to the theory. Dr Jekyll may turn out to have a darker side. It is likely, however, that the Supreme Court will continue to use the skeletal framework of unjust enrichment for analysis. Further, if there is merit in both the use of general concepts and remedial discretion,[148] then Mr Hyde may

[145] See n 55 above.

[146] Certainly, some of the High Court judgments cited above implicitly suggest that complexity is a problem. This complexity, as Hedley has suggested, n 109 above, is a product of attempting to mesh the theory with the actual outcomes of the cases.

[147] See Hedley, 'The Empire Strikes Back' (n 27) and n 109 above.

[148] It is outside the scope of this article to articulate some of those benefits. See articles cited in n 131 above.

yet be redeemed and again accepted more enthusiastically into the English legal community, his virtues evident for all to see. As has already been noted, some members of the House of Lords in *Sempra* appeared willing to infuse their unjust enrichment analysis with a dose of equitable discretion.

What this exercise in identifying contrasts also demonstrates, perhaps even more importantly, is some of the incongruities *within* the courts themselves. I will give two examples. First, the High Court's positive view of the utility of general equitable concepts seems at odds with its focus on precedent-based and historical reasoning in cases such as *Lumbers* and *Farah*. In both cases, the High Court seemed unwilling to articulate general principles or to develop the law beyond the narrow confines of the factual problem at hand and the relevant precedent that disposed of that problem.

Secondly, when one turns to the House of Lords, it has continually asserted the immutability of property concepts and the (in my view) disingenuous approach that the law determines property interests on the basis of supposedly 'hard-nosed' property principles.[149] On this view, there is no need to make policy choices, nor to balance the competing interests of various claimants. For present purposes, the approach seems at odds with the House of Lords' willingness to develop the law of unjust enrichment in new ways, often quite distinctly from precedent and the historical sources of the law of restitution, and to try to look to the underlying reasons for restitution rather than rely on, in some cases, historical fictions. There is not the same commitment to the open articulation of the underlying reasons for decisions when the House of Lords deals with property. As Finn has rightly pointed out, in many situations of supposedly established rules, property interests are 'manufactured … by resort either to maxims, or to estoppels or presumptions',[150] so that there are 'real grounds for questioning the integrity of the requirement that there be an existing (or subsisting) equitable interest in the property the subject of the claim.'[151] Similarly, Evans has convincingly argued that the label or concept of 'property' 'distracts attention from substantive questions and distorts the process of resolving contested claims.'[152] Evans concludes that the 'Courts should be prepared to defend their decisions candidly on the basis of their consequences and should not shelter behind opaque conceptualism.' Were

[149] See *Foskett* (n 43) 109 (Lord Browne-Wilkinson).

[150] Finn, 'Equitable Doctrine and Discretion in Remedies' (n 55) 263. He gives the example of *Reid* (n 62) 4, holding that a fiduciary receiving a bribe holds such bribe on constructive trust for the beneficiary, immediately upon receipt of it, since the fiduciary should have paid it instanter to the principal who is the victim of the breach of duty.

[151] Ibid. See also *LAC Minerals Ltd v International Corona Resources Ltd* (1989) 61 DLR (4th) 14 (SCC) 50 (La Forest J). As Finn stresses, ibid 264, with reference to *Re Goldcorp Exchange* (n 41), in which the issue was whether a secured creditor under a floating charge ought to have priority over unsecured creditors who believed they had interests in specific property held by the insolvent: the issue was determined by the 'ultimately artificial process of discerning or rejecting the existence of an equitable estate in the claimant[s].'

[152] Evans (n 131) 33. And see at 35: Established proprietary concepts such as the resulting trust and institutional constructive trust 'conceal (and do not eliminate) the distributive decisions about which claimants deserve priority.' See generally K Gray, 'Property in Thin Air' (1991) 51 *CLJ* 252.

they to do so, I suggest, there would be considerably less uncertainty in predicting the outcomes of cases once the competing and relevant policies and principles were identified and openly weighed up by the courts. Lord Millett's assertion of 'policy'-free,[153] perhaps even hinting at value-free, determinations of proprietary rights is no more than an illusion.

So it seems that courts that are restrained and conservative in their use of some general concepts are ambitious and liberal in their use of others. Some general concepts are embraced, others are rejected. Courts that are open and transparent in articulating the principles underlying their decisions in some contexts hide behind labels and 'precedent' in others. Some things change, some things stay the same. And perhaps Dr Jekyll and Mr Hyde may turn out not to be so different after all.

[153] *Foskett* (n 43) 127 (Lord Hoffmann and Lord Browne-Wilkinson concurring).

2

Subrogation, Equity and Unjust Enrichment

MARK LEEMING

> [I]t may be said that the underlying purpose of an Income Tax Assessment Act is to raise revenue for government. No one would seriously suggest that s15AA of the Acts Interpretation Act has the result that all federal income tax legislation is to be construed so as to advance that purpose.[1]

> Perhaps the most difficult problems facing rule-makers concern choices as to the level of generality at which to frame the rule, with what degree of precision and with what provision for exceptions: at one extreme is the very precisely worded, very general, purportedly absolute rule which makes few or no concessions to the complexity and particularity of actual events; at the other extreme is the instrument that is so vague and so open-ended as to raise doubts as to whether it can be appropriately referred to as a 'rule' at all. Thus the perfect rule-maker needs … an infallible judgment about what constitutes an appropriate level of generality in a given context.[2]

> There are no categorical rules to direct judges about the selection of appropriate levels of generality.[3]

I. Introduction

Chief Justice Gleeson is writing of the unspoken assumption made in the purposive construction of statutes, while William Twining and David Miers are writing about the formulation of rules, in statute or judge-made law, and yet those very different contexts capture the essence of the divergence that exists between areas of Australian and English law claimed by scholars working in the field of unjust enrichment. This chapter contends that the essence of the divergence is the level of generality attaching to 'unjust enrichment'.[4]

[1] *Carr v Western Australia* [2007] HCA 47, (2007) 232 CLR 138 [6] (Gleeson CJ).

[2] W Twining and D Miers, *How To Do Things With Rules*, 5th edn (Cambridge, Cambridge University Press, 2010) 150.

[3] Ibid 309.

[4] The problem is a recurring one; in a completely different context, it arises in connection with formulating a duty of care: see *Cole v South Tweed Heads Rugby League Football Club Ltd* [2004] HCA

On the one hand, 'unjust enrichment'[5] may be seen as a unifying theme, a helpful aid to analysis and to the development of a coherent body of law, but insufficient standing alone to resolve a justiciable controversy, whose resolution will turn on more particular propositions identified in or extrapolated from the body of existing law. On the other hand, 'unjust enrichment' may be seen as a legal norm in its own right which may directly generate a result in a particular case, through the prism of which the body of existing law is to be interpreted. Naturally, there are intermediate positions. The status afforded to 'unjust enrichment' directly impacts the way legal argument proceeds and is adjudicated, and the precedential force of earlier authorities which may or may not fit well with the conceptual paradigm.

It is unhelpful, not to mention invidious, to ask which approach is *better*. But one can consider which approach is more likely to enhance clarity of reasons, certainty of outcome and coherence.[6] After all, as Andrew Burrows put it:[7]

> The whole point of the restitution movement was to unpack the wording of the old forms of action and their related pleading so that they can be explained in modern transparent terminology that enables us to understand exactly what the judges are doing.

To do that requires a comparative analysis of the law in action, being developed and applied in real cases. That is no small task, and certainly not one fully assayed in this paper, whose purpose principally is to indicate the nature of the inquiry. One high level (and crude) measure is the amount of litigation. For example, the sheer quantity of English litigation following *Barclays Bank v O'Brien*[8] contrasts with *Garcia v National Australia Bank*,[9] although there are other causative factors aside from divergent doctrine.[10] Conversely, one could adopt the low level course chosen by the example considered in this paper, and focus on individual cases. Real cases offer an opportunity to assess how well the conventional (Australian)

29, (2004) 217 CLR 469 [56] (Gummow and Hayne JJ): 'the articulation of a duty of care at too high a level of abstraction provides an inadequate legal mean against which issues of fact may be determined', and [81]: 'as the present case demonstrates, the articulation of a duty of care at a high level of abstraction either presents more questions than it answers, or is apt to mislead'. A related example arises where the availability of an appeal turns on there being a question of law, see *Amaca Pty Ltd v AB & P Constructions Pty Ltd* [2007] NSWCA 220; [2007] Aust Torts Reports ¶81–910 [138]–[139] (Basten JA): 'If the duty of care is defined at a high level of generality, no question of law arose in this case'.

5 The inverted commas are intended to emphasise that the same words are used differently by different authors.

6 For coherence in a body of law see, eg *Sullivan v Moody* [2001] HCA 59, (2001) 207 CLR 562 [55] and the more elaborate analyses by Mason P in *Harris v Digital Pulse* [2003] NSWCA 10, (2003) 56 NSWLR 298 [191]–[213] and Spigelman CJ in *Edwards v Attorney-General* [2004] NSWCA 272, (2004) 60 NSWLR 667 [3]–[10].

7 A Burrows, 'The Australian law of restitution: has the High Court lost its way?' in E Bant and M Harding (eds), *Exploring Private Law* (Cambridge, Cambridge University Press, 2010) 67, 84.

8 *Barclays Bank Plc v O'Brien* [1994] 1 AC 180 (HL), notably *Royal Bank of Scotland Plc v Etridge [No 2]* [2001] UKHL 44, [2002] 2 AC 773.

9 *Garcia v National Australia Bank* [1998] HCA 48, (1998) 194 CLR 395.

10 Plausibly including the size of the legal system, the willingness of courts to entertain summary dismissal applications, and differences in consumer protection statutory regimes.

and the new (English) way of thinking about subrogation perform, in terms of the key measures of clarity, certainty and coherence. Subrogation would seem to be a good area to investigate, for at least three reasons. First, following decisions of the House of Lords and High Court of Australia, the divergence of approach is clear. Secondly, and unlike other more contentious areas,[11] there seems to be no dispute amongst those contending for a unifying law of unjust enrichment that subrogation lies within that area. Thirdly, subrogation problems are necessarily complex, the better to illustrate whether their curial resolution displays clarity, certainty and coherence.

II. Divergent Approaches in Australia and England

Lord Hoffmann wrote in *Banque Financière de la Cité v Parc (Battersea)* that, in addition to contractual subrogation, the term subrogation 'is also used to describe an equitable remedy to reverse or prevent unjust enrichment which is not based upon any agreement or common intention of the party enriched and the party deprived'.[12] That decision seemingly caused Gareth Jones to promote the coverage of subrogation in *The Law of Restitution* from chapter 31 to chapter 3,[13] and certainly caused Charles Mitchell and Stephen Watterson to write, in their introduction to *Subrogation Law and Practice*:[14]

> Twenty years earlier, in *Orakpo v Manson Investments Ltd,* Lord Diplock expressed doubts about the latter proposition, because he considered that 'there is no general doctrine of unjust enrichment in English law.' That is no longer a tenable view, following a series of House of Lords' decisions to the contrary ... including the *Banque Financière* case, where Lord Steyn declared that unjust enrichment is 'an independent source of rights and obligations' which 'ranks next to contract and tort as part of the law of obligations'. Hence Lord Hoffmann's speech in the *Banque Financière* case can now be regarded as a definitive statement of English law.

Those passages highlight the contrast with repeated statements by the High Court of Australia, to the effect that that is precisely what 'unjust enrichment' is *not.*[15] Almost twenty years ago, Mason CJ, Deane, Toohey, Gaudron and McHugh JJ rejected an approach 'that in Australian law unjust enrichment is a definitive legal principle according to its own terms' in *David Securities v Commonwealth Bank*

[11] For example, liability following breach of fiduciary obligation for 'knowing receipt' or 'recipient liability'.

[12] *Banque Financière de la Cité v Parc (Battersea) Ltd* [1999] 1 AC 221 (HL) 231.

[13] See G Jones (ed), *Goff and Jones: The Law of Restitution* 5th edn (London, Sweet & Maxwell, 1998), v; cf ch 31 of the 4th edn (London, Sweet & Maxwell, 1993).

[14] C Mitchell and S Watterson, *Subrogation Law and Practice* (Oxford, Oxford University Press, 2007) 4.

[15] The decisions which follow are also discussed in Joachim Dietrich's chapter (chapter one) in this volume.

of Australia;[16] instead a plaintiff must establish more particular vitiating features such as mistake or total failure of consideration in order to obtain a remedy, although, as *David Securities* itself[17] and *Roxborough*[18] indicate, there is scope for development of the law relating to mistake or total failure of consideration.

Recently, the High Court's criticisms of the English approach have been more frequent, and more pointed. They were repeated in *Farah Constructions v Say-Dee* by Gleeson CJ, Gummow, Callinan, Heydon and Crennan JJ in 2007.[19] In 2008, in *Lumbers v W Cook Builders* Gummow, Hayne, Crennan and Kiefel JJ said, of statements made in *Pavey & Matthews v Paul*,[20] that

> unjust enrichment was identified as a legal *concept* unifying 'a variety of distinct categories of case'. It was *not* identified as a principle which can be taken as a sufficient premise for direct application in particular cases. Rather, as Deane J emphasised in *Pavey & Matthews*, it is necessary to proceed by 'the ordinary processes of legal reasoning' and by reference to existing categories of cases in which an obligation to pay compensation has been imposed. 'To identify the basis of such actions as restitution and not genuine agreement is not to assert a judicial discretion to do whatever idiosyncratic notions of what is fair and just might dictate.' On the contrary, what the recognition of the unifying concept does is to *assist* 'in the determination, by the ordinary processes of legal reasoning, of the question whether the law should, in justice, recognise such an obligation in a *new or developing category of case*'.[21]

In 2009 in *Friend v Brooker*, French CJ, Gummow, Hayne and Bell JJ said:

> [W]hile the concept of unjust enrichment may provide a link between what otherwise appears to be a variety of distinct categories of liability, and it may assist, by the ordinary processes of legal reasoning, in the development of legal principle, the concept of unjust enrichment itself is not a principle which can be taken as a sufficient premise for direct application in a particular case.[22]

Most recently, in an extended passage of the reasons of Gummow, Hayne, Heydon, Kiefel and Bell JJ in *Bofinger v Kingsway Group*,[23] the High Court not merely repeated those views, forcefully, but explained in some detail why the different approach mattered. The passage is *obiter*, because (in striking contrast to *Banque Financière*, where the appeal was run on the basis that there was a restitutionary remedy or nothing)[24] all counsel eschewed any attempt to rely on

[16] *David Securities Pty Ltd v Commonwealth Bank of Australia* (1992) 175 CLR 353 (HCA) 378.

[17] Following the result in *Air Canada v British Columbia* [1989] 1 SCR 1161 (SCC) and anticipating that in *Kleinwort Benson Ltd v Lincoln City Council* [1999] 2 AC 349 (HL).

[18] *Roxborough v Rothmans of Pall Mall Australia Ltd* [2001] HCA 68, (2001) 208 CLR 516 [14]–[21].

[19] *Farah Constructions Pty Ltd v Say-Dee Pty Ltd* [2007] HCA 22, (2007) 230 CLR 89 [151].

[20] *Pavey & Matthews Pty Ltd v Paul* (1987) 162 CLR 221 (HCA).

[21] *Lumbers v W Cook Builders Pty Ltd (in liq)* [2008] HCA 27, (2008) 232 CLR 635 [85] (footnotes omitted, emphasis in original).

[22] *Friend v Brooker* [2009] HCA 21, (2009) 239 CLR 129 [7].

[23] *Bofinger v Kingsway Group Ltd* [2009] HCA 44, (2009) 239 CLR 269 [85]–[98].

[24] *Banque Financière* (n 12) 226 (Lord Steyn): 'On appeal to your Lordships' House counsel for BFC attenuated his submission by making clear that BFC only seeks a restitutionary remedy against OOL.'

the recent English decisions,[25] but it is nonetheless illustrative of the nature of the divergence.

The fact that English law has diverged from its historical roots is clear; Lord Diplock was far from the only English judge to deny the existence of a general doctrine of unjust enrichment—his was the conventional understanding at the time. Of itself, that divergence is not necessarily a bad thing. All law needs to change—or, at least, to contemplate the possibility of change—and a recurring theme of the statements by the High Court is the ongoing vitality of traditional reasoning, notably in the development of equitable principle.[26] As has been noted, the outcome in *Banque Financière* might readily have been achieved by the development of orthodox equitable principles.[27] Likewise, it is possible that the same outcome might have been reached had *Bofinger* been litigated in England.

Mere divergence of *outcome* does not underly the High Court's statements reproduced above. It has been clear for decades that that there are separate bodies of English and Australian law,[28] notwithstanding the much delayed reflection of that fact in the wording of section 80 of the Judiciary Act 1903 (Cth).[29] Moreover, it is easy by focussing on the differences at the level of detail to ignore the similarities in basic structure of the Australian and English legal systems. For example, for all the judicial and academic ink spilt over the nature of the right of an object of a trust to obtain access to trust documents,[30] it remains the case that both legal systems share a common ancestor (the law developed in the English court of chancery), a common institution (the trust) and a common problem (object of trust seeks information about its assets and management). Whatever the English law be as to the liability of third parties assisting in a breach of fiduciary duty

[25] *Bofinger* (n 23) [98]: 'The respondents, led by counsel for the Solicitors, in this Court correctly eschewed any attempt to support the outcome in the Court of Appeal by application of reasoning in the recent English cases.'

[26] For example, the 'vitality to permit further development in an orthodox fashion': *Bofinger* (n 23) [89].

[27] By treating the purely personal 'security' of prioritised payment as being enjoyed by the claimant. See I Jackman, 'Restitution and Subrogation' (1999) 73 *Australian Law Journal* 110, noted in *Bofinger* (n 23) [96].

[28] *Parker v The Queen* (1963) 111 CLR 610 (HCA) 632–33, and see *D'Orta Ekenaike v Victoria Legal Aid* [2005] HCA 12, (2005) 223 CLR 1 [59].

[29] This section referred to the 'common law of England' until those words were replaced by 'common law in Australia' by the Law and Justice Amendment Act 1988 (Cth), s 41.

[30] *Schmidt v Rosewood Trust Ltd* [2003] UKPC 26, [2003] 2 AC 709; *Avanes v Marshall* [2007] NSWSC 191, (2007) 68 NSWLR 595; *McDonald v Ellis* [2007] NSWSC 1068, (2007) 72 NSWLR 605; *Schreuder v Murray [No 2]* [2009] WASCA 145, (2009) 260 ALR 139; L Smith, 'Access to Trust Information: *Schmidt v Rosewood Trust Ltd*' (2004) 23 *Estates Trusts & Pensions Journal* 1; T Cockburn, 'Trustee Duties: Disclosure of Information' [2005] *Murdoch University Electronic Journal of Law* 13; T Graham, 'Disclosure to Discretionary Beneficiaries—the latest on Schmidt' (2008) 14 *Trusts and Trustees* 128; J Campbell, 'Access by Trust Beneficiaries to Trustees' Documents Information and Reasons' (2009) 3 *Journal of Equity* 97; G Dawson, 'A Fork in the Road for Access to Trust Documents' (2009) 3 *Journal of Equity* 39; L Ho, 'Trustees' duties to provide information' in E Bant and M Harding (eds), *Exploring Private Law* (Cambridge, Cambridge University Press, 2010) 343.

(compare *Royal Brunei Airlines v Tan*,[31] *Twinsectra v Yardley*,[32] and *Barlow Clowes v Eurotrust*)[33] and accepting there are divergences with the Australian position confirmed in *Farah Constructions v Say-Dee*,[34] again the common ancestor is the English court of chancery (by its soon to be abolished court of appeal) in *Barnes v Addy*,[35] and both legal systems share the notions of trust, fiduciary, and ancillary liability consequent upon breach. It would be a much harder task to compare the reasoning processes at work in legal systems which do not share the same ancestry; contrast for example the Quebecois law of trusts,[36] or the German law relating to guarantees by spouses.[37]

The statements made by the High Court of Australia reproduced above are directed to a profoundly different methodological approach in resolving hard cases and developing the law. The approach sanctioned and applied by the High Court remains historical, seeking to identify and extrapolate principle from the reasoning contained in the body of case law. The 'unjust enrichment' approach is essentially interpretative; it seeks to focus on the *outcomes* of case law, and to reinterpret the reasons for them so as to fit, as best they may, within a more recently identified conceptual framework or 'taxonomical dogma'.[38] The proposition that grappling in terms with underlying principle may produce a more transparent judicial process than applying and extrapolating from early cases is, certainly, viable. But, with due respect to those who have accepted or assumed as much, it is not self-evident. Nor is it obvious that the result will be increased certainty or coherence. For that approach involves necessarily discarding much of the *reasoning* in the body of existing law; indubitably many of the decisions highlighted in works on restitution were *not* decided for the reasons articulated by their present-day proponents. Lord Mansfield when deciding *Moses v Macferlan* certainly did not share Lord Steyn's view that unjust enrichment is an independent source of rights and obligations which stands next to contract and tort as part of the law of obligations.[39]

This paper takes one decision, *Bofinger v Kingsway Group*,[40] arising on facts that are far from unusual, and identifies (in more detail than has hitherto been

[31] *Royal Brunei Airlines Sdn Bhd v Tan* [1995] 2 AC 378 (PC).

[32] *Twinsectra Ltd v Yardley* [2002] UKHL 12, [2002] 2 AC 164.

[33] *Barlow Clowes International Ltd (in liq) v Eurotrust International Ltd* [2005] UKPC 37, [2006] 1 WLR 1476.

[34] *Farah* (n 19) [151].

[35] *Barnes v Addy* (1874) LR 9 Ch App 244 (CA).

[36] See D Waters, M Gillen and L Smith, *Waters' Law of Trusts in Canada*, 3rd edn (Toronto, Thomson Carswell 2005), ch 28.

[37] See S Kiefel, 'Guarantees by Family Members and Spouses: *Garcia* and a German perspective' (2000) 74 *Australian Law Journal* 692.

[38] See W Gummow, '*Moses v Macferlan* 250 years on' (2010) 84 *Australian Law Journal* 756, 757.

[39] Ibid 757; cf *Banque Financière* (n 12) 227.

[40] *Bofinger* (n 23).

able to be devoted to it)[41] the steps in reasoning which led to the outcome. Unsurprisingly, those steps accord with the High Court's approach referred to above; but it may be asked what mode of reasoning would a court, adhering to an approach founded in unjust enrichment, adopt to resolve the dispute between the five competing parties, how transparent would that reasoning be, and how coherent with the body of the law within which subrogation operates.

III. *Bofinger v Kingsway Group*

A. Facts

The essential facts were these B & B Holdings Pty Ltd carried on the business of property development on land at Enmore. It borrowed, by three separate and independent transactions, $8,278,000 from Kingsway Group Ltd, $1,400,000 from Rekley Pty Ltd, and $350,000 from Mr Skehan, secured by (relevantly) first, second and third registered mortgages over the Enmore land. B & B Holdings' director Mr Bofinger and his wife guaranteed B & B Holdings' obligations under each loan, and granted separate mortgages (six in all) over their home and an investment property (the Willarong Road and Bulwarra Street Properties) to secure those guarantees. The same firm of solicitors acted for each mortgagee, and indeed, Kingsway Group operated from the same address as the solicitors' practice, and one of the partners was a director.

B & B Holdings Pty Ltd defaulted, after which Mr and Mrs Bofinger sold the Willarong Road and Bulwarra Street Properties, and used the proceeds to reduce the indebtedness of B & B Holdings. Importantly, the properties were sold not merely with the consent of Kingsway Group, but also with that of the second and third mortgagees. At around the same time, a liquidator was appointed to B & B Holdings, Kingsway Group went into possession of the Enmore Land, and sold all save two lots, using the proceeds to satisfy the indebtedness to it. In early February 2006, Kingsway Group provided the keys to the unsold lots, and discharges of the mortgages it had obtained over those lots, to Rekley, and the surplus of $701,019 was transferred to the solicitors' trust account on behalf of Rekley.

Mr and Mrs Bofinger sued all three mortgagees and the mortgagees' solicitors, claiming that the surplus was held in trust for them, and that the solicitors had assisted in a breach of trust by causing it to be paid to Rekley.

[41] See M Conaglen and P Turner, 'Subrogation, Accounting and Unjust Enrichment' (2010) 69 *CLJ* 30; P Ridge, 'Equitable Subrogation: Principle and Remedy' (2010) 126 *LQR* 188, both of which were constrained by the limitations of a note.

B. Issues

Pausing there, it may be observed that out of relatively mundane facts (default on borrowings from three non-bank lenders, secured by guarantees by the borrower's principal and his wife) there was ample scope for legal complexity, brought about principally by the overlapping role of the solicitors and the first mortgagee. What is the reconciliation of the rights of the guarantors to the surplus and their obligations under the guarantees to the second and third mortgagees? Are the guarantors' rights qualified by the terms of their guarantees, or some less formal assumed state of affairs? The borrower is being wound up, and the guarantors' solvency cannot be presumed, so what is the nature of their entitlement to the surplus: is it a proprietary interest sufficient to defeat a set-off in the event of their bankruptcy? What is the nature of any fiduciary obligation owed by the first mortgagee to the guarantors, and does it support a claim against the second mortgagee which received the surplus, or the solicitors who caused it to be paid away? Within the defendants' camp, was there a breach of duty (in equity or at common law) when the mortgages over the Willarong Road and Bulwarra Street Properties were discharged, and when the whole of the surplus was transferred to the second mortgagee (bearing in mind that by that stage no security supported either of the guarantees given to the remaining mortgagees)? How do all of those rights fit with the contracts entered into by the parties, and with statute (the local counterpart to section 5 of the Mercantile Law Amendment Act 1856 (Eng),[42] and the Torrens system of title)?

Thus simple facts gave rise to a complex quintipartite dispute. However, not all aspects of that dispute were before the court. The parties chose (and the courts acceded to their choice) to litigate only part of their dispute, and without the benefit of most of the facts. The solicitors had applied for the determination of a separate question whether the surplus was held on trust; if not, then the *Barnes v Addy* claim against them would fall away (being the whole of the claim against them, for, at least at that time, no claim was being made against them by any of their client mortgagees). That meant that the matter proceeded on agreed facts, which were a significantly incomplete account of events, and that the only issue was whether there was an obligation on Kingsway and the solicitors to account to Mr and Mrs Bofinger in respect of the surplus.

C. Steps in the Legal Reasoning

The resolution of the limited dispute involved these steps:

first, noting the effect of the discharge of mortgages on the Willarong Road and Bulwarra Street Properties;

secondly, identifying the principle that a guarantor's equitable right to securities takes priority over a subsequent mortgagee;

[42] Law Reform (Miscellaneous Provisions) Act 1965 (NSW), s 3.

thirdly, determining that that principle applies to land held under Torrens title;
fourthly, determining that the guarantors' agreement did not disentitle them from reliance on the principle;
fifthly, rejecting an extension of the rule in *Otter v Lord Vaux*;[43]
sixthly, rejecting an estoppel by convention on the limited facts before the Court;
seventhly, determining that the relief that was sufficient for the purposes of the limited determination was relief which identified a fiduciary obligation on the part of the first mortgagee, sufficient to engage *Barnes v Addy* liability on the part of the solicitors.

Those steps (which are addressed below) indicate the magnitude of the task assayed by those propounding 'unjust enrichment' as a rule which would resolve the quintipartite dispute. The litigation crystallised a problem which involved the resolution, as between five parties with different interests, all of which were to some extent opposed to each other, of interrelating claims based on contract, equitable subrogation, fiduciary duties, and *Barnes v Addy* liability, in relation to property subject to the Real Property Act 1900 (NSW). A theory of unjust enrichment would have to deal with the interrelating claims; *Farah* shows that that is problematic, not least because different theories of unjust enrichment conceptualise *Barnes v Addy* liability differently.

First step. When Rekley and Mr Skehan agreed to the sale of the Willarong Road and Bulwarra Street Properties, they continued to have the benefit of personal guarantees from Mr and Mrs Bofinger, but those guarantees were no longer secured. It was far from clear at that point that the interests of Rekley and Mr Skehan were aligned to those of Kingsway, or even were aligned as between themselves. In particular, Rekley and Mr Skehan had not obtained agreement with Mr and Mrs Bofinger to deny what would otherwise be their subrogation rights upon Kingsway's debt being discharged. When the solicitors caused the surplus to be held for its benefit, Rekley obtained priority over other unsecured creditors of Mr and Mrs Bofinger (including Mr Skehan); the questions on the alternative analysis rejected by the High Court would include whether that priority in payment amounted to an enrichment which was unjust as those terms are understood.

Second step. The traditional principle is that sureties who discharge the indebtedness of their principal are entitled to the benefit of securities held by the creditor. It has long been established that the same position obtains where there are *puisne* mortgagees. *Rowlatt on Principal and Surety* states as follows:

> The surety's right to the securities of the creditor is prior to that of later encumbrancers, who are subject to the creditor's mortgage. This is on the basis that the surety stands in the place of the creditor he pays off and because the subsequent security is not lessened

[43] *Otter v Lord Vaux* (1856) 2 K & J 650, 69 ER 943; discussed below, text to n 58.

> by the coming in. Thus it does not seem material whether a subsequent encumbrancer had notice of the suretyship.[44]

In *Drew v Lockett,* Sir John Romilly MR said:

> I am of opinion that a surety who pays off the debt for which he became surety must be entitled to all the equities which the creditor, whose debts he paid off, could have enforced, not merely against the principal debtor, but also as against all persons claiming under him. It is to be observed that the second and any subsequent mortgagee is in no respect prejudiced by the enforcement of this equity; when he advances his money he knows perfectly well that there is a prior charge on the property, and if he thinks fit to advance his money on such security, it is his own affair, and he cannot afterwards with justice complain. The amount being limited, it is a matter of indifference to him whether the first mortgagee or the surety is the prior claimant for that amount, and it would be, in my opinion, a violation of all principle if, when the surety pays off the debt, he were not to be entitled, as against the principal debtor and those who claim under him, to be paid the full amount due to him.[45]

That principle was ultimately applied directly, as speaking to the present litigants in its own terms. And while of course a mortgagee owes only limited obligations to the mortgagor when exercising a power of sale, to the extent that the proceeds of sale generate a surplus over and above the mortgagor's indebtedness, the mortgagee has long been regarded as a trustee.[46]

Third step. The facts that the land was held under Torrens title, and the power of sale statutory, did not displace the applicability of those principles, although it is important here (as elsewhere)[47] to reason why that is or is not so, rather than merely to assume it. There are two points: the first is that, although in New South Wales statute does not expressly provide that the surplus is held on trust for the mortgagor,[48] it is well established that the words in section 58(3) of the Real Property Act 1900 (NSW) 'shall be applied' are read in the same way.[49] The second is that the statutory command to apply the proceeds 'in payment of subsequent mortgages, charges or covenant charges (if any) in the order of their priority; and the surplus (if any) shall be paid to the mortgagor, charger or covenant charger, as the case may be' was held not to displace the equitable right of a surety who has discharged the indebtedness to the first mortgagee;[50] that reflects a process of

[44] G Moss and D Marks, *Rowlatt on Principal and Surety,* 5th edn (London, Sweet and Maxwell, 1998) para [7–34].

[45] *Drew v Lockett* (1863) 32 Beav 499, 505–06; 55 ER 196, 198.

[46] *Charles v Jones* (1887) LR 35 Ch D 544, 550 (Kay J): 'although I quite agree that the Court is very reluctant to treat a mortgagee as being a trustee in any sense while any money is due to him, still when he has paid himself, and has money remaining in his hands which is no longer his property, how can he be treated as other than a trustee of such money?'

[47] See *Farah* (n 19) [190]–[198] and H Atkin, 'Knowing Receipt Following *Farah Constructions Pty Ltd v Say-Dee Pty Ltd*' (2007) 29 *Sydney Law Review* 713.

[48] Contrast the Law of Property Act 1936 (SA), s 50; see *Sheahan v Carrier Air Conditioning Pty Ltd* (1997) 189 CLR 407 (HCA) 429–30.

[49] *Adams v Bank of New South Wales* [1984] 1 NSWLR 285 (NSWCA) 299 (Hutley JA).

[50] *Bofinger* (n 23) [79].

statutory construction whereby the general words governing the distribution of a surplus achieved upon exercise of a power of sale are read as subject to the specific rights granted by equity in circumstances where that surplus is attributable to payment by a guarantor.[51]

Fourth step. Equity follows the law. Rights of subrogation can be excluded by agreement,[52] no differently from other equitable rights.[53] Mr and Mrs Bofinger had promised, in their guarantee to Rekley, to waive their 'rights as surety whether legal, equitable, statutory or otherwise which may be inconsistent with this deed or in any way restrict the Lender's rights, remedies or recourse'. But it was held, making allowance for the rule of interpretation that guarantees are construed narrowly in favour of guarantors,[54] that that clause was confined to rights which were inconsistent with the guarantee, which the right of subrogation was not. An alternative argument of construction depending upon a different clause 'Guarantors Not To Claim Benefits or Enforce Rights' was likewise rejected by giving it a narrow construction.[55]

On the footing that the guarantees were not in their terms inconsistent with Mr and Mrs Bofinger's entitlement to subrogation, what of the fact that they had guaranteed B & B's obligations to the second and third mortgagees? The point was that there was no agreement, in substance or otherwise, whereby the second mortgagee would be paid before the guarantors could recover the surplus. Nor was there any agreement which warranted the second mortgagee to be paid from funds contributed by the guarantors ahead of the third mortgagee. Following the discharge of the mortgages over the guarantors' Willarong Road and Bulwarra Street Properties, the second and third mortgagees were merely unsecured and equally ranking creditors of Mr and Mrs Bofinger on their guarantees.

Fifth and sixth steps. Handley JA had decided the case on a basis not raised by any of the parties,[56] namely an extension of the rule in *Otter v Lord Vaux* which prohibits a mortgagor who has paid off a mortgage debt from setting it up in priority to a later mortgage which the mortgagor has granted.[57] That rule turns upon merger of estate, with the result that the land being held under Torrens title was critical: the mortgages were creatures of statute and not subject to destruction by merger.[58] His Honour had also relied on conventional estoppel, but that

[51] 'An intention to eliminate a common law advantage is not lightly to be inferred': R Sullivan, *Sullivan and Driedger on the Construction of Statutes*, 4th edn (Markham, LexisNexis, 2002) 353.

[52] *Equity Trustees Executors & Agency Co Ltd v New Zealand Loan & Mercantile Agency Co Ltd* [1940] VLR 201, 205.

[53] See M Leeming, 'The scope of fiduciary obligations: How contract informs, but does not determine the scope of fiduciary obligations' (2009) 3 *Journal of Equity* 181.

[54] *Andar Transport Pty Ltd v Brambles Ltd* [2004] HCA 28, (2004) 217 CLR 424 [17]–[23].

[55] *Bofinger* (n 23) [60]–[65].

[56] *Bofinger v Kingsway Group Ltd* [2008] NSWCA 332 [28].

[57] *Otter* (n 43).

[58] *Bofinger* (n 23) [76]–[77].

could not be sustained on the (minimal) agreed facts on which the litigation had proceeded.[59]

Seventh step. Finally, the ultimate question was a limited one: what relief was sufficient, consequent upon the limited adjudication that had taken place, to protect the interests of Mr and Mrs Bofinger? The High Court held that the first respondent had been required to account as a trustee of the surplus, in accordance with *Charles v Jones*,[60] and that breach of that obligation would engage *Barnes v Addy*. The Court did not decide (it being unnecessary, and surely inappropriate, on the limited facts presented by the parties, to do so) if Mr and Mrs Bofinger enjoyed a beneficial interest in the amounts in question.[61]

IV. The Role of 'Unjust Enrichment' and 'Unconscionability'

The High Court said that subrogation 'may be seen as preventing the unjust enrichment of the principal debtor who otherwise might escape carriage of ultimate liability'.[62] But that observation *of itself* does not determine any of the steps in the reasoning referred to above; it is addressed at too high a level of generality to do so.[63] In contrast, Giles JA had rejected the Bofingers' claim to subrogation in part by reason of a different construction of the guarantees (the fourth step summarised above),[64] but also in part by relying on the scope afforded by unjust enrichment theory to modify the claimant's right to subrogation. His Honour cited Mitchell and Watterson's work:

> [I]t must be kept in mind that the claimant is not an actual assignee of the creditor's rights, and that the claimant's new rights are awarded for a particular purpose, namely reversing an unjust enrichment at his expense. Hence the claimant does not inevitably acquire new rights which share every characteristic of the rights which were formerly held by the creditor. Sometimes their quality may vary, for a number of different reasons. … For example, the debtor may have changed his position, or may have repaid the sum due. Alternatively, an existing junior incumbrancer may resist the claimant's claim to priority vis-à-vis the junior interest on the basis that it has changed its position; or on the basis that giving the claimant such priority would be contrary to public policy.[65]

[59] Ibid [75].
[60] *Charles* (n 46) 549–50.
[61] *Bofinger* (n 23) [50].
[62] Ibid [88].
[63] Compare (in the different context of the inutility of reliance upon extrinsic material) Gleeson CJ's comments in *Carr* (n 1) [6], reproduced above at n 1, approved in *Alcan (NT) Alumina Pty Ltd v Commissioner of Territory Revenue (NT)* [2009] HCA 41, (2009) 239 CLR 27 [51].
[64] *Bofinger* (CA) (n 56) [12]–[13], [17].
[65] Mitchell and Watterson, *Subrogation* (n 14) 209.

Reliance on that passage suggests an approach which required the existence and extent of the equitable right of subrogation to be preconditioned upon and confined to identifying unjust enrichment at the claimant's expense, which may in turn depend upon considerations of change of position and public policy—that is to say, an approach which gives determinative weight to 'unjust enrichment' in its own right. If so, it is not self-evident that this approach will enhance transparency in reasoning and predictability in outcome.

Likewise, the High Court was critical of the approach adopted by Sackville AJA, which seemed in part to turn upon the plaintiff demonstrating an unconscionable result. His Honour said:

> But in what way is the doctrine of subrogation needed to avoid an unconscionable result? Or, to put the question another way, what would be unjust or inequitable about the net surplus from the sale of the Principal Debtor's assets going to the second mortgagee, as envisaged by s58(3) of the Real Property Act 1900 (NSW) (which deals with the priorities for the application of moneys derived by a mortgagee from the exercise of a power of sale)?[66]

That discloses a similar defect, by seeking to deploy unconscionability at the wrong level. The High Court said:

> But this reasoning does not allow for the circumstance that the surplus was computed only after allowance for the payments which had been made by the appellants to reduce the secured indebtedness of B & B Holdings. These payments had enlivened the doctrine of subrogation, subject to the operation of which, and subject to contrary agreement or inequitable conduct, the parties were to be taken to have conducted their affairs.[67]

In the one appeal, one sees a New South Wales statute, whose relevantly identically worded ancestor is an English Act of 1856, which in turn cannot be fully construed without regard to the legal and equitable rules it was altering. One sees consideration of how the radically different nature of mortgages under Torrens legislation impacted upon on principles formulated under old system title. And one sees the intersection of rights at common law (contract, and estoppel by convention), equity (subrogation, fiduciary obligation and *Barnes v Addy* liability) and statute (Real Property Act 1900 (NSW), and the contemporary local counterpart to the Mercantile Law Amendment Act 1856 (Eng)). There is revealed a continuity with the principles articulated centuries ago. Each step in the reasoning reflects an analysis of the extent to which those principles needed to alter in light of the particular facts and the changed legal environment.

It is asserted that 'in cases of this kind, the claimant's entitlement to subrogation rights can always be explained as a legal response to unjust enrichment'.[68] That may be so; but the question is how certain, how transparent and how coherent would such an explanation be? Parts of that analysis would be straightforward and

[66] *Bofinger* (CA) (n 56) [66].
[67] *Bofinger* (n 23) [82].
[68] Mitchell and Watterson (n 14) 19.

uncontroversial: there is no question but that, as between guarantor and puisne mortgagee, the latter would be unjustly enriched if its rights were not subject to the guarantor's right to a surplus, subject to the guarantors not having bargained away those rights by their contract. But parts would certainly be contentious, for there are multiple, inconsistent unjust enrichment analyses of the same facts (in particular, depending on whether and how the *Barnes v Addy* claims are accommodated within the framework).[69] If (as Mitchell and Watterson would insist) subrogation requires creating a new security when a surety has discharged the liability of his, her or its principal, then the analysis would have to address the mortgages over the two lots, possession of which was given to Rekley, which had ceased to exist following the registration of their discharge; how a new security was to be rationalised against the Real Property Act; and what the effect of the local equivalent of section 5 of the Mercantile Law Amendment Act 1856 was. A theory of unjust enrichment would need to address whether and how the rule in *Otter v Lord Vaux* was to be reconciled with it, and whether and how it intersected with (common law) estoppel by convention. It also seems tolerably clear that the focus on unjust enrichment here, where one is talking of a temporary priority being given to one creditor by the breach of fiduciary obligation of another, coming about (it may well be) because of an earlier breach by the solicitors of both, is unlikely to provide decisive insight into legal analysis. That was the point made by the joint judgment, echoing Goff and Jones: 'there is difficulty in identifying the "unjust" enrichment in subrogation cases, which necessarily involve multilateral, rather than bilateral, relationships'.[70] Every case of subrogation to securities will involve at least four parties: the debtor, the secured creditor, the surety, and those against whom the subrogated surety wishes to enforce the securities. In *Bofinger*, even though the debtor was in liquidation, there were five competing parties.

But let it be assumed that an unjust enrichment analysis were undertaken. *Would the resultant reasoning be less opaque, and would the law be more coherent or more predictable?* It seems likely that the reverse would ordinarily be the case. To reinterpret the expressed reasons for decision in the body of judge-made law gives new leeways of choice to judges, and ultimately is apt to introduce uncertainty in the law. The higher the level of abstraction at which a legal norm is identified, the less likely it is to provide any useful role in determining the outcome of the case.[71] On the other hand, although it may be untidy, it is respectfully submitted that an approach which preserves historical continuity is more apt to provide cogent reasons to the losing litigant, and to give rise to a body of law which is coherent. It is ultimately more apt to enhance certainty and predictability. The point of

[69] See for example the various critical responses by Joachim Dietrich, Steven Hedley, Andrew Robertson and Michael Tilbury to Prof Birks' later taxonomies in A Robertson (ed), *The Law of Obligations: Connections and Boundaries* (London, Cavendish, 2004), reviewed by J Keeler (2005) 26 *Adelaide Law Review* 179.

[70] *Bofinger* (n 23) [97].

[71] *Caltex Refineries (Qld) Pty Ltd v Stavar* [2009] NSWCA 258, (2009) 75 NSWLR 649 [179] (same point in tortious context), and see I Jackman, 'Restitution and Subrogation' (n 27) 111.

setting out in some detail the reasons of the High Court in *Bofinger* is to make it clear that, fairly plainly, they are *not* an example of 'traditional opaque property reasoning without resort to unjust enrichment', asserted to be a vice of judgments adopting a conventional approach.[72] There may be a price to be paid, of complexity, but Coke long ago wrote that *cognitio legis est copulata et complicata.*[73] It is unrealistic to expect a simple legal analysis to resolve a complicated legal dispute. As I have previously written:

> But simplicity comes at a price, and it is important to bear that price in mind. There is an innate attraction to simplicity; it can be difficult to displace a simple understanding with a more complex one. Fullagar J referred to this when he spoke of the 'temptation which is so apt to assail us, to import a meretricious symmetry into the law'.[74]

V. Convergent Unjust Enrichment Rhetoric

After the foregoing focus on Anglo-Australian divergence, the common ground in Anglo-Australian unjust enrichment rhetoric is striking. Three distinguished Australian authors have addressed the points discussed in this paper from the contrary position. They say:

> Restitution's claim to selected parts of traditional equity has also been encouraged by equity's inevitable failure to explain itself according to any rational lines or even, in many cases, to make good its claim that an understanding of jurisdictional roots that were severed in England as long ago as 1875 offers a meaningful springboard for historical enquiries.[75]

That passage discloses, with respect, these problems. First, as formulated, the statement asserts as a premise that there is a single theory 'restitution'. But there are, to say the least, a family of theories, aspects of some of which are inconsistent with each other. Secondly, the strong assertion that equity's explicative failure is 'inevitable' is unsupported by any reasons. Thirdly, the same proposition is counterintuitive; the conventional account of high level themes unifying particular equitable doctrines and remedies can, surely, hardly be said not to be 'rational'. Fourthly, *Bofinger* is itself a good example of continuity with the past: the New South Wales statute was a result of reform to the limitations of subrogation as perceived in the mid nineteenth century, and the reasoning summarised above

[72] Burrows, 'The Australian law of restitution' (n 7) 70.

[73] 'Knowledge of the law is interconnected and complex.' E Coke, *First Part of the Institutes of the Law,* 16th edn (London, F Hargrave and C Butler, 1809), Vol 1, 283.

[74] M Leeming, 'What is a trust?' (2009) 7 *Trusts Quarterly Review* 5, 12–13, citing *Attorney General (NSW) v Perpetual Trustee Co Ltd* (1952) 85 CLR 237 (HCA) 285.

[75] K Mason, J Carter and G Tolhurst, *Mason & Carter's Restitution Law in Australia,* 2nd edn (Sydney, LexisNexis, 2008) 5.

reflects a direct connection with what had been worked out in the nineteenth century.

To similar effect, Burrows has said, in relation to *Farah* and *Lumbers* (and it may safely be assumed that he would place *Friend* and *Bofinger* in the same category) that 'the High Court has lost its way in relation to the Australian law of restitution' and concludes that 'it is essential to the rationality and coherence demanded by the rule of law that unjust enrichment reasoning is restored to its rightful central place'.[76]

Once again, the claim that a central place is 'rightful' assumes the correctness of the author's premise, and is unsupported by reasons. Once again, the proposition is counterintuitive; for most of the history of the English and Australian legal systems, 'unjust enrichment reasoning' has been far from centre stage. And once again, there is an appeal to 'rationality': which, so it is asserted, cannot be achieved but through the new conceptual framework.

Perhaps those authors have something different in mind when referring to 'rationality' from its ordinary meaning. There may be advantages and disadvantages (mostly having to do with the leeways of choice given to courts in developing the law) in an approach which gives greater weight to unifying concepts, and one which focusses on more particular areas of law connected by unifying themes. One could debate whether the conceptual framework of one approach was more or less logically structured than the other, and the advantages and disadvantages that ensued; this seems to be what Peter Birks himself envisaged at one stage.[77] In that sense, it cannot fairly be said that one approach is rational and the other is not. To take an example from a different area, there is (endless) scope for debate as to the merits of a two or three stage approach to determine proximity for the law of negligence or a multifactorial approach.[78] But each of those approaches is *rational*. They are all rational ways of analysing the artifice which is the body of judge-made law.

On other occasions, Birks did appear to propound rationality not so much as a descriptor of a system of law which is logically ordered and free from caprice, but as an ideal which drove taxonomy. For example, he wrote that it is 'a difficult question, and one of great importance to the common law, whether rationality ultimately requires this distinction between enrichment by performance and enrichment in other modes'.[79] That invokes a very different meaning of 'rationality', and seems to presuppose that there is some platonic ideal description of the legal

[76] Burrows (n 7) 85.

[77] P Birks, 'Equity, Conscience and Unjust Enrichment' (1999) 23 *Melbourne University Law Review* 1, 2: 'the recognition of the law of unjust enrichment is a genuine advance in the rationality of the common law. Since rationality and justice go hand in hand, it should not be repudiated.'

[78] Contrast *Anns v Merton London Borough Council* [1978] AC 728 (HL); *Caparo Industries Plc v Dickman* [1990] 2 AC 605 (HL) with the Australian approach, the authorities relating to which are collected in *Caltex Refineries* (n 71) [101].

[79] P Birks, 'At the expense of the Claimant: Direct and Indirect Enrichment in English law' (2000) *Oxford University Comparative Law Forum* 1, text after n 12.

system, or at least the parts of it that fall within the rubric of 'unjust enrichment', which is waiting to be uncovered. It would be a remarkable thing for a single generative principle to resolve cases in the complex congeries of cases said to comprise the law of restitution, something strikingly dissimilar to the position in negligence, which is often merely a bilateral controversy whose essential structure, surely, would be less arduous to identify. To the extent that that body of law extends to areas developed by the chancery court, it would be all the more remarkable, for there is force in the criticism offered by the High Court of the unjust enrichment approach, namely, that:

> Such all-embracing theories may conflict in a fundamental way with well-settled equitable doctrines and remedies. Reference was made in the opening paragraph of these reasons to the importance attached by equity to the fashioning of the particular remedy to meet the nature of the case.[80]

That passage emphasises the historical antipathy of organising the reasoning of the decisions of the chancery court within such a precise structure.

The Victorians—ironically, the same Victorians who enacted the Judicature Acts of 1873 and 1875 and who brought together common law, chancery and civilian superior courts in one building (not to mention filling them with electric light shortly after it became commercially available)[81]—considered that they had achieved a complete understanding of the natural world, and that the twentieth century would amount merely to more careful measurement of natural phenomena. They were quite wrong. 'If scientists today are more modest, it is probably because they recall the absurd spectacle of their nineteenth-century counterparts, whose all-inclusive knowledge of the universe was proved totally inadequate in a few decades.'[82]

There is no necessary reason for the appropriate conceptual framework of a legal system to be as complex as that of the natural world has turned out to be. But there is likewise no reason why modes of thinking that have endured for many decades are necessarily inappropriate. After all, selecting the appropriate level of generality to describe an aspect of our legal system is no easy task. If a case for a new conceptual framework is to be made out, it needs to be justified, not proselytised.

[80] *Bofinger* (n 23) [91]. See also M Leeming, 'Equity, the Judicature Acts and Restitution' (2011) 5 *Journal of Equity* 199 at 222–227.

[81] See D Brownlee, *The Law Courts: The Architecture of George Edmund Street* (Cambridge, MIT Press, 1984) 348–51. I am grateful to Stephen Gageler for the reference to this fascinating account of law and architectural reform.

[82] B Stableford, *The Mysteries of Modern Science* (London, Routledge & Kegan Paul Ltd, 1977) 6.

3

Clogs on the Equity of Redemption: A Story of Changing Equitable Intervention

FIONA BURNS

I. Introduction

Over the last two centuries, there have been some significant changes to the law of mortgages. One important area has been the way that the traditional law against 'clogs on the equity of redemption' has been considered. The long-established view was that the mortgagor and the mortgagee could not agree to terms which would have the effect of clogging or preventing the redemption of the mortgage by the mortgagor, particularly when the full amount owing under the mortgage was paid. Therefore, a number of devices which led (potentially) to the extinguishment of the equity of redemption were considered at one stage to be automatically void.[1] However, this is no longer the case. There has been a dramatic shift away from a literal application of the doctrine against clogs on the equity of redemption (or for the purposes of brevity in this chapter, the 'anti-clog doctrine'). Some courts have modified or relaxed the anti-clog doctrine. Others have suggested that the anti-clog doctrine ought to be jettisoned altogether. Following on from the diverse attitudes of the courts, eminent textbook writers still refer to and discuss the anti-clog doctrine, but the nature of the significant modifications (rather than the broad principle itself) take centre stage.[2]

The focus of this chapter is to consider the anti-clog doctrine as a litmus test for the changing nature of equitable intervention.[3] First, the chapter will briefly

[1] See, eg *Jennings v Ward* (1705) 2 Vern 520, 23 ER 935.

[2] P Butt, *Land Law*, 6th edn (Sydney, Lawbook Co, 2010) paras [1831]–[1847]; *Falconbridge on Mortgages* ch 3 (May 2003); K Gray and S Gray, *Elements of Land Law*, 5th edn (Oxford, Oxford University Press, 2009) paras [6.2.22]–[6.2.46].

[3] Therefore, the chapter will not consider suggestions for reform by law reform bodies such as the Ontario Law Reform Commission, *Report on The Law of Mortgages* (Toronto, Ontario Ministry of the Attorney-General, 1987) 31; Law Commission, *Land Mortgages* (Working Paper No 99, 1987) 68–73, 190–206; Law Commission, *Transfer of Land—Land Mortgages* (Law Com No 204, 1991) paras [6.42]–[6.43].

consider the development of the traditional mortgage and the contribution of the Court of Chancery to its development, noting: the equity of redemption, the equitable right to redeem and the anti-clog doctrine. The Court of Chancery considered the equity of redemption as an important right in property and the anti-clog doctrine was ultimately protective of it. Second, the chapter will identify several changes in the legal environment over the last two centuries which have affected mortgage practice and have had an impact upon the framework of reference in which the equity of redemption, the equitable right to redeem and the anti-clog doctrine are viewed. Third, the chapter will consider how modern courts in England, Australia, Canada and New Zealand have dealt with the anti-clog doctrine. Fourth, it will be concluded that prior to the eighteenth century the broad reach of equity based on 'conscience' was specifically articulated and tailored in the combined operation of the equity of redemption, the equitable right to redeem and the anti-clog doctrine. Since then, other formidable approaches have influenced how mortgages ought to be interpreted and have, in turn influenced equity's jurisdiction.

II. Development of Doctrines Prior to the Twentieth Century

A. The Equity of Redemption and the Equitable Right to Redeem

Mortgages in English law have had a long and complex development which will not be detailed in this chapter.[4] However, in the light of the anti-clog doctrine it is important to note the following.

By the end of the fifteenth century, the basic mechanism by which legal mortgages were created had been settled. Legal mortgages were created by the conveyance of the legal estate[5] subject to a condition that the mortgagor could re-enter the land if the mortgagor repaid the amount which was owed under the mortgage. If the mortgagor failed to repay the amount owed on the due date, then the mortgagee held the land as owner and was no longer bound by the condition. The mortgagor was in a vulnerable position, having no interest in the land and therefore, no right to possession.

By the end of the seventeenth century the legal conveyance of the fee simple was retained, but its effect was modified by a 'proviso for reconveyance' or 'proviso

[4] For a helpful discussion see: AWB Simpson, *A History of the Land Law*, 2nd edn (Oxford, Clarendon Press, 1986) 141–143; C Harpum, S Bridge and M Dixon, *Megarry and Wade: The Law of Real Property*, 7th edn (London, Sweet & Maxwell, 2008) paras [24–007]–[24–018].

[5] Butt (n 2) para [1804].

for redemption'[6] enforceable in the Court of Chancery so that it was subject to a condition subsequent which was the mortgagor's right to make a repayment by the due contractual date.[7] However, the rights of the mortgagor were not merely contractual. The Court of Chancery had become proactive, developing its own unique approach towards the interests and rights of mortgagors. This was enshrined in twin doctrines: the equity of redemption and the equitable right to redeem.[8] At first the Court of Chancery provided relief to mortgagors only in difficult or harsh cases. By the end of the seventeenth century, the Court universally recognised the operation of the equity of redemption and the equitable right to redeem.[9]

It is important to differentiate between the equity of redemption and the equitable right to redeem, although both must be considered in relation to the anti-clog doctrine.[10] The equity of redemption was the mortgagor's equitable estate in the property which in the eyes of equity meant that he remained the owner of the land. It arose immediately when the mortgage was created and had taken effect. The equity of redemption was a proprietary interest which the mortgagor could deal with, subject to the interests of the mortgagee.[11] Since then, courts have held that in reality, despite the existence of the legal mortgage, the mortgagor remained the owner of the land in equity and have even likened the interest of a mortgagor to that of a *cestui que trust*.[12] So innovative was the equity of redemption that modern commentators have observed that it:

> is one of equity's earliest, greatest and most spectacular achievements; it is a classic example of how equity's intervention in particular cases became more universal,

[6] It appears that the proviso for reconveyance had existed well before the seventeenth century, but by the end of the seventeenth century it was an incontestable element of the law of mortgages: see R Turner, *The Equity of Redemption* (Cambridge, Cambridge University Press, 1931) 21.

[7] Butt (n 2) para [1804].

[8] According to Turner (n 6) 56 the phrase 'equity of redemption' first appeared in 1654 in *Duchess of Hamilton v Countess of Dirlton* (1654) 1 Ch R 165, 21 ER 539. An interesting aspect of the equity of redemption is the use of what would be recognised in Christianity as a religious term: see F Alexander, 'Property and Christian theology' in J Witte and F Alexander (eds), *Christianity and Law: An Introduction* (Cambridge, Cambridge University Press, 2008) 205, 206–07.

[9] Simpson (n 4) 245; Butt (n 2) para [1805].

[10] Butt (n 2) para [1805]; P Young, C Croft and M Smith, *On Equity* (Sydney, Lawbook Co, 2009) para [9.240]. See Viscount Haldane LC in *Kreglinger v New Patagonia Meat and Cold Storage Co Ltd* [1914] AC 25 (HL) 35 considering the effect of the Council of Lateran in 1179.

[11] *Casborne v Scarfe* (1738) 1 Atk 603, 605; 26 ER 377, 379. See also *Sparrow v Hardcastle* (1754) 3 Atk 798, 805; 26 ER 1256, 1260; *Tarn v Turner* (1888) 39 Ch D 456, 460–61; Turner (n 6) 69–76; Simpson (n 4) 245. See also the observations of Lord Nottingham in D Yale (ed) *Lord Nottingham: Prolegomena of Chancery and Equity* (Cambridge, Cambridge University Press, 1965) 282 reprinted in D Heydon and P Loughlan, *Equity and Trusts: Cases and Materials*, 7th edn (Sydney, LexisNexis Butterworths, 2007) para [15.2E]; John Brunyate (revised), *FW Maitland, Equity: A Course of Lectures* (Cambridge, Cambridge University Press, 1947) 194. For a modern discussion of the proprietary nature of the equity of redemption see E Cousins and I Clarke, *Cousins on the Law of Mortgages*, 2nd ed (London, Sweet & Maxwell, 2001) paras [17-01]–[17-02].

[12] Turner (n 6) 76–77, 166–75. *Re Sir Thomas Spencer Wells* [1933] Ch 29 (CA). Consider the argument in *Casborne* (n 11) 685; 379.

> persistent and predictable, converting a personal 'right' of action into a proprietary right, an equitable interest which can be bought or devised.[13]

The equitable right to redeem did not arise when the mortgage was initially created but when the contractual date for repayment had passed and the mortgagor had not redeemed the mortgage in accordance with its terms.[14] From a common law perspective, upon the failure to repay on the due date the mortgage was absolute and the mortgagor had no further rights to re-acquire the property. However, from the perspective of equity, a mortgage was primarily regarded as a security. The principal right of a mortgagee was to be repaid the money owed.[15] Once a conveyance had been made for the purpose of security only, it remained redeemable in equity until the equitable right of redemption had been brought to an end by foreclosure or lapse of time.[16]

RW Turner has noted (and disputed) the argument that the establishment of equitable relief was essentially based in contract and the Court of Chancery had determined that the time for repayment was not of the essence of the contract.[17] Turner argued that this would be 'putting into the mind of the Chancellor theories which were not current for at least another half century.'[18] Instead, Turner emphasised that the Chancellors considered that it was 'administering a kind of equitable conscience'[19] and that this can be discerned at two levels. As the mortgage was a security, so long as the mortgagee received what had been bargained for, it did not matter that the payment was late.[20] More broadly speaking however, the Court of Chancery was concerned that the mortgagee did not unduly take advantage of the mortgagor.[21]

Although the equity of redemption and the equitable right to redeem have been clearly differentiated by judges and commentators, they constitute two sides of the one coin. The mortgagor had a right of redemption: expressed as the equity of redemption and the personal right to redeem after the contractual date for redemption had passed.[22] As the mortgagor had a significant equitable estate and as the transaction between the mortgagor and the mortgagee was only a security,

[13] Heydon and Loughlan (n 11) para [15.1]. For a modern discussion of the equity of redemption see *Petranik v Dale* [1977] 2 SCR 959 (SCC) 966–68 (Dickson J).

[14] Cousins and Ross (n 11) 292–294.

[15] *Thornborough v Baker* [1676] 1 Ch Cas 284, 22 ER 364.

[16] Turner (n 6) 61–62. Therefore, the Court of Chancery gave relief to mortgagors who had failed to repay the debt on the contractually stipulated day, so long as the mortgage had not been brought to an end. According to Turner (at 24) this practice began during the reign of Elizabeth 1. Turner points out (at 27) that later, the right to redeem after the date stipulated was presumed by mortgagors. Note the early cases *Emmanuel College v Evans* (1625) 1 Ch Rep 18, 21 ER 494, 495; *Hales v Hales* (1636) 1 Ch Rep 105, 21 ER 520; *Porter v Emery* (1637) 1 Ch Rep 97, 21 ER 518.

[17] Turner (n 6) 41.

[18] Ibid.

[19] Ibid.

[20] Ibid. See also Simpson (n 4) 246.

[21] *Kreglinger* (n 10) 35–36 (Viscount Haldane LC).

[22] E Sykes and S Walker, *The Law of Securities*, 5th edn (Sydney, LawBook Co, 1993) 156.

it would have been against good conscience if the mortgagor had not been able to provide a late repayment before foreclosure.[23]

B. Clogs on the Equity of Redemption or Clogs on the Right of Redemption

A major concern for the Court of Chancery was the ultimate preservation of the mortgagor's interest and entitlement to the land, eventually unencumbered by the mortgage. The Court recognised that the mortgagee may act unconscionably, setting up a mortgage under which the mortgagor lost all hope of re-acquiring the land even upon full payment of the debt. Therefore, the Court of Chancery quickly reacted against any attempts by mortgagees to impose contractual terms which undermined the proprietary nature of the equity of redemption or the equitable right to redeem.[24] By the end of the seventeenth century, there was an automatic right to redeem even when the parties had agreed either before or at the time of entering the deed that there would be no right of redemption.[25] Several phrases were used to communicate this such as: 'once a mortgage, always a mortgage';[26] 'there shall be no clog on the equity of redemption'; and 'the land shall be returned to the mortgagor exactly as he parted with it.'[27] Underlining such justifications was the oft-repeated idea that a mortgage was only security which remains redeemable (even after the original mortgagor's lifetime).[28]

There were three important aspects to the notion of the anti-clog doctrine. First, the Court of Chancery was a court of conscience. The Court wanted to ensure that the mortgagee did not act unconscientiously, abusing its superior practical and bargaining position.[29] Already, there had been a considerable restriction on bargaining through the prohibition of usury.[30]

Second, the effects of any potential clogs on the equity of redemption were interpreted strictly. The Court of Chancery did not countenance any device or provision which either legally or practically prevented the redemption of the mortgage. The Court refused to enforce provisions which: only allowed the right

[23] Under foreclosure, the mortgagor's entire beneficial interest in the property was vested in the mortgagee and the equity of redemption and the equitable right to redeem were extinguished: Butt (n 2) para [18124]. An early case of foreclosure was *How v Vigures* (1628) 1 Ch Rep 32, 21 ER 499.

[24] 'The sense of clog here is of a piece of wood attached to an animal or even a person to restrain movement.' Simpson (n 4) 245.

[25] See, eg *Newcomb v Bonham* (1681) 1 Vern 7, 23 ER 266; *Howard v Harris* (1681) 1 Vern 33, 23 ER 288; (1683) 1 Vern 191, 23 ER 406; *Clench v Witherly* (1678) Rep Finch 376, 23 ER 206.

[26] *Newcomb* (n 25); *Seton v Slade* (1802) 7 Ves 265, 273; 32 ER 108, 111. See also Cousins and Clarke (n 11) paras [18.06]–[18.13].

[27] See generally Turner (n 6) 62, 175.

[28] *Newcomb* (n 25).

[29] *Vernon v Bethell* (1762) 2 Eden 110, 113; 28 ER 838, 839.

[30] P Atiyah, *The Rise and Fall of Freedom of Contract* (Oxford, Clarendon Press, 1979) 65–67. See generally R Tawney, *Religion and the Rise of Capitalism* (Harmondsworth, Penguin Books, 1938).

of redemption to be exercised by the mortgagor personally;[31] extended the date of redemption well into the future so that there could be no early redemption;[32] or provided the mortgagee with collateral advantages such as an option to purchase the land.[33] At one time there were concerns that an express power of sale may have constituted a clog on the equity of redemption.[34] Therefore, 'the result was that the Chancery freely interfered with mortgage transactions with a complete indifference to the terms agreed by the parties; in no branch of the law was the sanctity of agreement less recognised.'[35]

Third, the original phrase which encapsulated the anti-clog doctrine was 'clogs against the equity of redemption', emphasising that the equity of redemption itself could not be fettered, clogged or discharged by the making of the mortgage. Unfortunately, the phrase 'clogs on the equity of redemption' was inaccurate. Equally important and seamlessly juxtaposed to the protection of the equity of redemption,[36] was the protection of the equitable right to redeem.[37] The protection of the personal equitable right to redeem after the contractual date for redemption had passed was articulated by Lord Parker in *Kreglinger v New Patagonia Meat and Cold Storage Company Ltd*:[38] 'The equity which arises on failure to exercise the contractual right cannot be fettered or clogged by any stipulation contained in the mortgage or entered into as part of the mortgage transaction.'[39] Interestingly, Lord Parker highlighted that the anti-clog doctrine protected the equitable right to redeem,[40] indicating a contractual interpretation of mortgages (and the anti-clog doctrine) without necessarily the concern to protect the mortgagor's proprietary interest. This will be discussed further below.[41]

The mortgagor's right to redemption comprised both the personal equitable right to redeem the mortgage (even after the contractual date) and an equitable proprietary interest in the land. Therefore, the anti-clog doctrine may more properly be described as a doctrine which protected the mortgagor from clogs against 'the right of redemption.'[42]

[31] *Newcomb* (n 25).
[32] *Talbot v Braddill* (1683) 1 Vern 183, 23 ER 402; (1686) 1 Vern 394, 23 ER 539.
[33] *Jennings* (n 1).
[34] Turner (n 6) 179.
[35] Simpson (n 4) 246.
[36] An analysis of various texts indicates that most meld the concept of the equity of redemption and the equitable right to redeem: see, eg Gray and Gray (n 2) paras [6.2.7]–[6.2.9]; Butt (n 2) para [1831].
[37] Butt (n 2) para [1831].
[38] *Kreglinger* (n 10).
[39] Ibid 48.
[40] Ibid 48–49.
[41] See Part III (A) (ii).
[42] Sykes and Walker (n 22) 156.

III. Historical Change and the Anti-Clog Doctrine

From the seventeenth century onwards, the anti-clog doctrine became well entrenched in English law. However, there were several important historical changes which led to a fundamental re-evaluation of whether there was any legal or practical necessity for a mortgagor acquiring a specific right of redemption and the associated protection under the anti-clog doctrine.

A. The Mortgage as Bargain

i. The Abolition of Usury

In 1854 laws against usury were abolished.[43] This was an important change in the regulation of the mortgages in the nineteenth century and cannot be ignored. It has been suggested that the abolition of usury had a considerable impact on the anti-clog doctrine. In *Kreglinger* Viscount Haldane LC pointed out that public policy which placed restrictions on the rate of interest also influenced the administration of equity.[44] Equity was ready to interfere with any usurious stipulation in a mortgage or collateral advantage which breached the anti-clog doctrine. Once the law in regard to usury was abolished, the restraint on collateral advantages was loosened, so that courts could relax the rule against collateral advantages so long as they were not unconscionable or did not make the mortgage irredeemable.[45] However, there have been other views. Turner has disputed the connection between the law regarding usury and the doctrine against clogs on the equity of redemption.[46] He argued that there was rarely a reference to usury in the cases examining the anti-clog doctrine, which, in any event, focused on protecting the mortgagor from pressure to contract out of the equity of redemption. On balance, the observations in *Kreglinger* are probably correct in so far as the abolition of one more restriction on the making and content of mortgages would re-enforce the view that mortgagors and mortgagees ought to be able to negotiate the terms of the mortgage, unimpeded by what were regarded as outmoded restrictions.[47]

ii. Will Theory, Contract Law and the New Mortgagor

Whatever the precise influence of the law regarding usury on the anti-clog doctrine, the era in which the usury laws were abolished was dominated by a new

[43] Usury Laws Repeal Act 1854 (UK).
[44] *Kreglinger* (n 10) 35–36.
[45] Ibid. See generally P Devonshire, 'The Modern Application of the Rule Against Clogs on the Equity of Redemption' (1997) 5 *Australian Property Law Journal* 21.
[46] Turner (n 6) 182.
[47] See the comments of Lord Mansfield quoted in Atiyah (n 30) 124.

individualism expressed in the phrases 'freedom of contract' and 'will theory.'[48] Each autonomous individual assumed obligations based on a firm intention articulated by an unambiguous promise in a contractual context. Courts were more reticent to interfere in what may have been regarded as 'bad bargains' and were less likely to prescribe specific contractual terms or standards, particularly when the contracting parties were commercial players who acted on equal terms. From the perspective of mortgages generally, it has been pointed out that the Court of Chancery's proactive attitude towards the fairness of economic exchange declined.[49]

Together with the rise of freedom of contract, the traditional characterisation of the mortgagor, mortgagee and land changed in the light of the new commercial and industrial conditions in the nineteenth century. Formerly, the mortgagor was portrayed as a person (generally of the landed gentry) who had to be protected against the machinations of potential mortgagees who would seek to acquire land which endowed special status on favourable terms.

While land was still regarded as useful, it had become a mere commodity in the nineteenth and twentieth centuries.[50] Moreover, it has been pointed out that mortgagors in modern times were (and are) not necessarily in parlous circumstances, finding it more efficient to borrow against assets rather than seeking further funds from shareholders or partners. Private mortgagors borrowing to purchase a family home will generally be financially secure and wish to become part of the 'property-owning democracy'[51] acquiring social mobility.[52] Significantly, the aim of mortgagees was (and is) to provide finance at a profit, rather than seeking opportunities to acquire land.[53] The predatory nature of some lending practices and the recent global financial crisis may have challenged to some extent this portrayal of the modern mortgagor and mortgagee because mortgagors may not fully understand the complexities of the mortgages they enter into and may be incapable of repaying the mortgage according to its terms. Nevertheless, it underlines the complexity and flexibility of, and necessity for, mortgages today.

Therefore, by the end of the nineteenth century, the very existence of the anti-clog doctrine was seriously challenged in England by the rise of the law of contract or what Atiyah referred to as 'the transition from a law of property to a law of contract relating to property'.[54] Accordingly, the nature and extent of the anti-clog doctrine was scrutinised by some judges through the lens of contract law, rather

[48] See Atiyah (n 30) 212–16.

[49] See, in relation to relief against penalties and forfeiture, C Rossiter, *Penalties and Forfeiture* (Sydney, LawBook Co, 1992) 3–12, 20–23.

[50] A Pottage, 'Evidencing Ownership' in S Bright and J Dewar (eds), *Land Law: Themes and Perspectives* (Oxford, Oxford University Press, 1998) 129, 136–42; A Pottage, 'The Originality of Registration' (1995) 15 *OJLS* 371, 388–93.

[51] See generally Gray and Gray (n 2) para [6.2.14].

[52] Ibid.

[53] Indeed, mortgagees generally take possession of the mortgaged land as a last resort: see Butt (n 2) para [18106].

[54] Atiyah (n 30) 103. See also E Firth, 'Freedom of Contract in Mortgages' (1895) 11 *LQR* 144.

than traditional property norms. The decision of the Court of Appeal in *Santley v Wilde*[55] is a good example. The Court articulated the principle of freedom of contract in the context of an increasingly common provision in mortgages of the time whereby the mortgagor (as lessee) agreed to pay the mortgagee a portion of the net profits from sub-leases or sub-tenancies. It was argued that the collateral provision was a clog on the equity of redemption. The Court held that the mortgage in this case did not prevent the mortgagor from redeeming the mortgage. The mortgage could be redeemed even though it specified that one-third of the net profits derived from the land had to be repaid before redemption could take place. The collateral provision remained enforceable against the mortgagor and was necessary in the light of the commercial risk to the mortgagee and the fact that the security of the lease may not have been sufficient.[56] There was a bargain and as there had been no 'oppression' there was no legal relief available.[57]

Thus, mortgages became bargains and collateral advantages were permissible bargaining tools, rather than automatic evidence of pressure or unconscionable conduct. Significantly also, the remedy for breach of the contract or bargain was damages, not proprietary relief. However, the prevailing right to redeem meant that a mortgagor who did repay what was owed under the mortgage would be entitled to redemption and an unencumbered title.

The decision in *Santley* was not universally endorsed.[58] Nevertheless, the question whether mortgages fell within the broader concept of 'bargain' remained irksome in the debate about the interface between the anti-clog doctrine and freedom of contract. In *Bradley v Carritt*, the House of Lords held by a bare majority that a collateral and personal obligation which continued to operate after the redemption of the mortgage breached the anti-clog doctrine.[59] However, Lord Shand and Lord Lindley (both in dissent) held that the collateral obligation did not fetter the right to redeem.[60] In *Samuel v Jarrah Timber and Wood Paving Corporation Ltd*, the House of Lords held that an option to purchase was a clog on the equity of redemption.[61] However, the Earl of Halsbury LC lamented that: 'A perfectly fair bargain made between two parties to it, each of whom was quite sensible of what they were doing, is not to be performed because at the same time a mortgage arrangement was made between them.'[62] In contrast, three decades

[55] *Santley v Wilde* [1899] 2 Ch 474.

[56] Ibid 476. As Lord Lindley also observed in *Noakes & Co Ltd v Rice* [1902] AC 24 (HL) 36 such a lease was a wasting asset and 'owing to its nature, cannot be given back on redemption in the state in which it was mortgaged'.

[57] *Santley* (n 55). See also Sir FH Jeune at 477.

[58] See, eg *Noakes* (n 56).

[59] *Bradley v Carritt* [1903] AC 253 (HL).

[60] Ibid 279–280 (Lord Lindley), 265 (Lord Shand).

[61] *Samuel v Jarrah Timber and Wood Paving Corporation Ltd* [1904] AC 323 (HL).

[62] Ibid 325. See also Lord Macnaghten (at 327). See also the comments of Lord Parker in *Kreglinger* (n 10) 47. Both the Earl of Halsbury LC and Lord Macnaghten in *Noakes* (n 56) disagreed with the decision in *Santley* (n 55).

later, the Court of Appeal in *Knightsbridge Estate Trust v Byrne*[63] determined that a provision which effectively made a mortgage irredeemable for 40 years was not a clog on the equity of redemption, because to decide otherwise would have interfered with commercial realities.[64] The decision was the apotheosis of freedom of contract.[65]

Nevertheless, the anti-clog doctrine was not swept aside by the rise of will theory and freedom of contract. One reason was that it was already too well entrenched in English law to be directly discarded. Even in *Santley*, Lord Lindley acknowledged a mortgagor's right to redeem.[66] Another reason was that the old law of mortgages was assimilated by the courts into the law of contract. Therefore in *Tarn v Turner*,[67] it was noted that: 'The Court of Equity gives effect to what it sees to be the real contract between the parties though it be not expressed on the face of the instrument.'[68]

Finally, by the time *Santley*, *Bradley*, *Samuel* and even *Knightsbridge* had been decided, the cracks in 'freedom of contract' had already begun to appear. The principle of freedom of bargain could not be applied literally in every case.[69]

iii. Mortgages as Contracts and Equitable Intervention

Although Atiyah described what he termed the 'decline' of equity in the nineteenth century[70] the jurisdiction of equity in relation to mortgages did not decline. First, equity norms were challenged but not jettisoned. The courts still accepted the special nature of mortgages and what has been referred to above as the general right of redemption.[71] Second, from the eighteenth century onwards, equity had created a buoyant jurisdiction to redress equitable fraud.[72] When courts exercising equitable jurisdiction viewed mortgages through a contractual lens, the courts considered them as bargains which could also be subject to equity's jurisdiction to relieve against oppressive or unconscionable conduct.[73]

In *Kreglinger*[74] Lord Parker's famous dictum about collateral advantages in mortgages presented an interesting duality, which was the result of the two separate interpretations and applications of equity's notion of 'conscience.' Lord Parker said that a provision for a collateral advantage would be valid unless it was: '(1) unfair and unconscionable, or (2) in the nature of a penalty clogging the

[63] *Knightsbridge Estate Trust v Byrne* [1939] Ch 441 (CA).
[64] Ibid 454.
[65] See Atiyah (n 30) 675.
[66] *Santley* (n 55) 474–75.
[67] *Tarn* (n 11).
[68] Ibid 459.
[69] Atiyah (n 30) 693–715.
[70] Ibid 392–394, 671–80.
[71] See, eg *Noakes* (n 56).
[72] A significant decision in this regard was Lord Hardwicke in *Earl of Chesterfield v Janssen* (1750) 2 Ves Sen 125, 155–57; 28 ER 82, 99–101. Note also the comments of Lord Haldane LC in *Nocton v Ashburton* [1914] AC 932 (HL) 954.
[73] See, eg *Santley* (n 55) 479 (Romer LJ).
[74] *Kreglinger* (n 10).

equity of redemption, or (3) inconsistent with or repugnant to the contractual and equitable right to redeem.'[75] It has been suggested that *Kreglinger* severed historical restraints in the sense that it changed the law regarding the way that the anti-clog doctrine operated.[76] However, in light of the subsequent case law, it is better to contend that *Kreglinger* united old and new standpoints. On the one hand, consistent with the old perspective in which the mortgage was a security, Lord Parker held that neither a collateral advantage nor a penalty could clog an equity of redemption or hamper the right to redeem. On the other hand, consistent with the collateral advantage viewed as part of a mortgage as a bargain, the collateral advantage (or indeed the mortgage as a whole) could not be unfair and unconscionable. The latter restraint was a very general principle which could be applied to a variety of contractual situations, including the mortgage as a contract. The alleged unfair and unconscionable nature of the mortgage would be determined by reference to the commercial nature of the transaction, the standing of the parties and the level and availability of independent advice. As the outcome would be determined by a variety of factors, a court's determination would not be a foregone conclusion. This duality, namely, the two separate manifestations of equity's conscience, would set the framework for current approaches to the anti-clog doctrine.[77]

B. The New Mortgage

i. The Mortgage as a Charge

It is also important to acknowledge that the fundamental nature of some land mortgages has changed. One change was the shift to a title-by-registration system. The traditional mortgage consisted of a conveyance of the legal estate to the mortgagee subject to the equity of redemption and the equitable right to redeem. However, with the advent of title-by-registration, the mortgage has become and is inherently a pure security interest. The mortgagor retains the legal title to the land and the mortgage takes effect as a statutory charge over the property. While the mortgagee acquires an interest in the land, it is neither a legal estate nor any other estate.[78] The mortgagee acquires a collection of powers and rights which can be exercised in the event that there is a default by the mortgagor in the performance of his or her obligations. Therefore, it is strongly arguable that the legal conditions which wrought the equity of redemption and the anti-clog doctrine no

[75] Ibid 61.

[76] See generally Devonshire (n 45) 28.

[77] The inclusion of mortgages as another species of contract has also had an important effect upon the regulation of mortgages, which have been considered to be contracts for the granting of credit: see, eg the discussion of consumer credit in Gray and Gray (n 2) paras [6.2.49]–[6.2.55].

[78] Butt (n 2) para [1821]. For Australia see, eg Real Property Act 1900 (NSW) s 57; *English Scottish and Australian Bank Ltd v Phillips* (1937) 57 CLR 302 (HCA) 321. For a helpful discussion of the Canadian situation which permits both registration of title and title-by-registration see *Falconbridge on Mortgages* (n 2) §8.20–§8.30 (May 2007).

longer exist—if their main function was recognition of the mortgagor's ongoing ownership of the property and the limited nature of the mortgagee's security.

Nevertheless, the different legal nature of modern mortgages ought not to be overstated as a cogent reason for the demise of a right of redemption or the anti-clog doctrine. Certainly, Turner argued that the Court of Chancery's recognition of the equity of redemption was a nascent portent of the modern mortgage as a statutory charge.[79] Notwithstanding the different legal nature of modern mortgages in title-by-registration systems, judges and commentators have generally stressed that it should not affect the operation of a right of redemption. The conveyancing process may have changed with title-by-registration systems, but basic principles for redemption and the exercise of judicial discretion would remain the same.[80] The registration of a mortgage in a title-by-registration system still diminishes the rights and interests of the mortgagor,[81] so that it is understandable that the mortgagor would wish, upon repayment of the amount owing, to be able to redeem the mortgage, register the discharge of mortgage and regain an unencumbered title. It has also been pointed out that in Australia in the event that the mortgage was created by transfer rather than charge, equity would step in and recognise an equity of redemption protected by caveat or injunction.[82] In the light of what has been considered previously, the recognition of the equity of redemption in this situation means that it would still have a function to play in the regulation of modern mortgages.

ii. Complex Mortgage Transactions

Another factor changing the fundamental nature of mortgages has been the evolution of more complex mortgage transactions or 'products' which have provided the mortgagor with greater flexibility and minimised the commercial risk to the mortgagee.[83] Mortgages have also been part of multi-faceted commercial dealings in which the relationship was not simply that of a mortgagor and mortgagee, but where the mortgage has been the cornerstone securing the liability of a business partner or co-venturer.

IV. Modern Judicial Attitudes to the Anti-Clog Doctrine

The reactions of modern courts to the anti-clog doctrine have been multi-faceted and, in some cases, arguably irreconcilable. For the purposes of this discussion,

[79] Turner (n 6) 128.
[80] *Perry v Rolfe* [1948] VLR 287 (VSC) 302.
[81] Butt (n 2) para [1823].
[82] Ibid para [1824].
[83] Such as mortgages linked to the Consumer Price Index—see ibid [1847]. Such mortgages are neither considered to be against the public interest nor unconscionable: *MultiService Bookbinding Ltd v Marden* [1979] Ch 84 (Ch).

it is necessary to observe that initially the application, consideration or rejection of the anti-clog doctrine falls into two broad subdivisions. The first conforms to the traditional approach of the anti-clog doctrine because it considers contractual terms which potentially clog redemption (often, but not necessarily after the equitable right to redeem has arisen). The second, procedural clogs on redemption, does not appear directly linked to the traditional approach, but has been raised when the mortgagor has queried the conduct of the mortgagee in the actual exercise of mortgage rights.

A. Clogs on Redemption: Contractual Provisions Made at the Time of the Mortgage or as Part of the Mortgage Transaction

Although the anti-clog doctrine has come under serious scrutiny, particularly in recent years, it has not been formally jettisoned by the higher courts in the jurisdictions under consideration. In some cases where the question of the anti-clog doctrine has arisen, courts have decided that although it was not applicable to the particular case, it remained part of the modern law and ought not to be overturned.[84] Five main situations have arisen in modern cases where the courts have endorsed the anti-clog doctrine.

First, courts sometimes refused to recognise provisions that postponed the mortgagor's right to redeem. However, not all provisions which postpone the right to redeem are necessarily void under the anti-clog doctrine. It is possible for a provision to postpone redemption for a reasonable period, so long as that the mortgagor gains the property in its pre-mortgage state on redemption.[85] The question is whether the right to redeem is rendered illusory by the fact that the mortgagor only obtains the unencumbered property for a short time thereafter.[86]

Second, courts have always been wary of the imposition of collateral advantages.[87] However, collateral advantages (such as those operating in the context of tie agreements) are no longer automatically regarded as breaching the anti-clog doctrine, particularly in the light of *Kreglinger*.[88] In that case Lord Parker confirmed the prima facie validity of collateral stipulations unless, inter alia, they were inconsistent with or repugnant to the contractual and equitable right to redeem.[89] However, there have been some singularly important authorities where courts have maintained that the collateral advantage has constituted a breach of

[84] See, eg *Dical Investments v Morrison* (1990) 75 DLR (4th) 497 (ONCA) 503 (Lacoucière JA); *Aribsala v St James Homes (Grosvenor Dock) Ltd* [2007] EWHC 1694 (Ch) [20].

[85] See *Knightsbridge* (n 63); *Hongkong Bank of Canada v Wheeler Holdings Ltd* [1993] 1 SCR 167 (SCC); *Attorney General of Canada v Logan and Farm Credit Corporation* (1997) 155 Sask R 235; Harpum, Bridge and Dixon (n 4) paras [25–089]–[25–090].

[86] *Fairclough v Swan Brewery Co Ltd* [1912] AC 565 (PC) 570.

[87] To the extent that at one time any collateral advantage was deemed to be a clog on the equity of redemption: see *Jennings* (n 1).

[88] *Kreglinger* (n 10).

[89] Ibid 61.

the anti-clog doctrine because the collateral advantage gave the mortgagee the opportunity to force the mortgagor to sell the property[90] or the collateral advantage operated after the mortgage had been repaid.[91]

In *Bradley*,[92] which has been described as the 'high water mark' of the anti-clog doctrine,[93] a shareholder in a tea company mortgaged his shares to a tea broker. However, he also covenanted that he would use his best endeavours as a shareholder to ensure that the broker would be called upon to sell the company's teas. In the event that the company's teas were sold through other brokers, the mortgagor agreed to pay the mortgagee the commission that the mortgagee would have otherwise earned as the tea broker. A majority of the House of Lords held that the collateral advantage breached the anti-clog doctrine, albeit in a rather indirect way. While it was true that the mortgagor was able to redeem the mortgage unrestricted, his dealing with the shares after redemption would remain restrained because of the personal obligation and the financial penalty if he failed to exercise his shareholder powers in favour of the mortgagee. The mortgagor would be compelled to retain the shares in order to be able to exercise some control over the company's decision making process.[94] Sykes and Walker have criticised the decision of the majority of the House of Lords, stating:

> This seems rather circuitous and special reasoning involving too much of a dependence on the possible personal motives of the mortgagor to be entirely convincing. The covenant did not bind the mortgagor qua his ownership of the shares though it might have influenced the position as to whether or not he should sell them. The view of the majority appears almost to involve the proposition that no collateral stipulation can ever survive.[95]

However, the view of the majority was consistent with the traditionally strict approach to collateral advantages.

Third, the anti-clog doctrine has been and remains a significant principle when dealing with options to purchase. Traditionally, options to purchase were considered to be clogs on the equity of redemption because a mortgage cannot be made irredeemable. As options to purchase necessarily enabled the mortgagee to extinguish the equity of redemption and the right to redeem, they offended the proprietary rights of the mortgagor and they were deemed to be void. Lord Macnaghten in *Samuel*[96] commented that the rule 'is founded on sentiment rather

[90] Consider *Browne v Ryan* [1901] 1 IR 653 (CA); cf *British Columbia (Attorney-General) v Malik* [2009] BCCA 202 [37]–[40].

[91] *Noakes* (n 56) 33. Note in contrast the decision in *Biggs v Hoddinott* [1898] 2 Ch 307 where the tie agreement was valid as a collateral advantage because it came to an end when the mortgage was repaid. For a more recent application of the approach, see *Oakdale (Richmond) Limited v National Westminster Bank plc* [1996] EWCA Civ 568, [1997] BCLC 63.

[92] *Bradley* (n 59).

[93] Sykes and Walker (n 22) 74.

[94] *Bradley* (n 59), 260–61 (Lord Macnaghten), 268–69 (Lord Davey), 270 (Lord Robertson).

[95] Sykes and Walker (n 22) 74.

[96] *Samuel* (n 61).

than principle.[97] Nevertheless, there have been several important modern cases in England,[98] Canada[99] and New Zealand[100] where the rule against options to purchase has been applied strictly, notwithstanding early criticism of the rule[101] and attempts to relax the rule in several cases which will be discussed below.[102] Courts have also endorsed the rule against options to purchase where the rule did not strictly apply to the facts of a case.[103]

Fourth, related to the case law in which options to purchase have been treated as clogs on the equity of redemption, is the decision of the English Court of Appeal in *Jones v Morgan*.[104] In this case, the respondents wished to develop land and the buildings on it as a nursing home. One of the respondents borrowed money from the appellant and a charge over the land secured the indebtedness. The necessary repayments under the charge were not made, and the appellant decided to exercise the power of sale. The appellant then entered into a further agreement with the respondents. The appellant agreed to the partial sale of the property on condition that the sale moneys would be used in part to discharge the indebtedness under the charge and that one half of the retained property would be transferred to the appellant. One question was whether the charge as amended by the subsequent agreement breached the anti-clog doctrine. A majority of the Court of Appeal held that it did. Lord Chadwick held first that, notwithstanding the fact that it was the subsequent agreement (rather than the original charge) which enabled the appellant to take a share of the property, both documents were interdependent. It would have been artificial to have considered otherwise, in light of the intention of the parties that the appellant was to have a share in the new development plan.[105] He also held that the later agreement varied the way in which the respondents were entitled to exercise the right of redemption. Originally, they had been entitled to redeem the property upon repayment of all the principal and interest which the charge secured. On redemption they would have acquired the whole of the property unencumbered. The subsequent agreement created two distinct mortgage loans. The respondents were entitled to redeem the part of the

[97] Ibid 326 (Lord Macnaghten).

[98] *Reeve v Lisle* [1902] AC 461 (HL); *Samuel* (n 61); *Lewis v Frank Love Ltd* [1961] 1 WLR 261 (Ch).

[99] *Hoar v Mills (No 2)* [1935] 1 WWR 433 (Sask CA); *Montgomery v Montgomery* (1970) 74 WWR 41 (Alta SC); *Kreick v Wansbrough* [1971] 2 WWR 561 (Sask QB); *Buchko v Truelove* [2003] SKQB 465 [8].

[100] *Harper v Joblin* [1916] NZLR 895 (NZCA); *Bannerman, Brydone, Folster & Co v Murray* [1972] NZLR 411 (NZCA); *Re Supreme Court Registrar to Alexander Dawson Inc* [1976] 1 NZLR 615 (SC).

[101] See *Samuel* (n 61) 326 (Lord Macnaghten).

[102] See Part IV (B).

[103] *Dical Investments* (n 84) 503 (Lacourcière JA, Zuber JA concurring); *Briar Building Holdings Ltd v Bow West Holdings Ltd* (1981) 126 DLR (3d) 566 (ABQB) 568 (MacDonald J). An interesting application of the rule against converting a security into an option to purchase can be found in *Laurin v Iron Ore of Canada* (1977) 82 DLR (3d) 634, 645 (Nfld SCTD).

[104] *Jones v Morgan* [2001] EWCA Civ 995, [2002] EGLR 125. For a discussion of this case see J Devenney, 'A Pack of Unruly Dogs: Unconscionable Bargains, Lawful Act (Economic) Duress and Clogs on the Equity of Redemption' [2002] *Journal of Business Law* 539.

[105] *Jones* (n 104) [69]–[71].

property which was to be sold to a purchaser on payment of the sale funds to the appellant. They were then entitled to redeem the retained property on payment of the principal and interest outstanding. Chadwick LJ (with whom Lord Phillips concurred) held that the second transaction was a re-financing transaction, not an independent collateral contract.[106] Pill LJ dissented and held that there was no clog on the equity of redemption, but a commercial arrangement to facilitate the development of flats.[107]

Finally, the operation of some 'all moneys' clauses has been interpreted as a breach of the anti-clog doctrine. In a seminal decision in the area, *Re Modular Design Group Pty Ltd*,[108] a variety of securities and guarantees were provided by the chargors to a bank. The terms of the securities had the effect of cross-collateralising the obligations of the chargors to the bank and extending the definition of bank to include any assigns of the bank. The bank assigned the securities to the assignees. The chargors owed other moneys to the assignees, but had not consented to the assignment or the cross-collateralisation of the original indebtedness to the assignees. Santow J held that, generally speaking, the 'all moneys' clauses could be considered to be clogs on the equity of redemption, particularly when there was no specific consent by a mortgagor to the accretion of additional indebtedness to the securities.[109]

B. Modifications to the Traditional Anti-Clog Doctrine

In the cases discussed above,[110] the courts have not only accepted the ongoing existence of the anti-clog doctrine but have applied it strictly to the facts because the provisions in question had the effect or potential effect of preventing the redemption of the mortgage. However, a second response to the anti-clog doctrine has been to accept the existence of the doctrine, but create modifications to it which have enabled greater flexibility both in the creation and the interpretation of mortgages. While adhering to the anti-clog doctrine, the courts have been influenced by new commercial conditions which have led to greater reliance on freedom of contract. In some situations, courts have specifically determined that new forms of mortgage, such as index-linked mortgages, have not been

[106] Ibid [93]–[94]. Lord Phillips MR concurred.

[107] Ibid [84].

[108] *Re Modular Design Group Ltd* (1994) 35 NSWLR 96 (NSWSC). Note also *Katsikalis v Deutsch Bank (Asia) AG* [1988] 2 Qd R 641 (QSC); *Estoril Investments Pty Ltd v Westpac Banking Corporation* (1993) 6 BPR 13,146 (NSWSC).

[109] Ibid 104. Note the different situation discussed by Barrett J in *Multi-Span Constructions No 1 Pty Ltd v 14 Portland Street Pty Ltd* [2001] NSWSC 696, (2001) 10 BPR 19,253. In subsequent cases, judges have acknowledged this decision but on an investigation of the documentation before them have declined to find a breach of the anti-clog rule: see, eg *Murphy, Re Bankrupt Estate of; Donnelly v Commonwealth Bank of Australia Ltd* (1996) 140 ALR 46 (FCA); *Windslow Corporation Pty Ltd (in liq) v Olympic Holdings Pty Ltd* [2006] WASC 158; *Olympic Holdings Pty Ltd v Windslow Corporation Pty Ltd (in liq)* [2008] WASC 80, (2008) 36 WAR 342 [70] (Buss JA) and [93]–[95] (EM Heeman JA).

[110] Part IV (A).

against public policy, unconscionable[111] or in breach of the anti-clog doctrine.[112] However, the most marked modification of the anti-clog doctrine has been evident in the treatment of collateral advantages and options to purchase.

As discussed above, in *Kreglinger*[113] the House of Lords held that an independent collateral stipulation could remain in operation after the repayment of the loan,[114] so long as it was not part of the mortgage transaction, although it may be subject to other equitable doctrines. When determining whether a collateral stipulation was independent of the mortgage transaction, the courts would consider the substance (rather than the form) of the transaction,[115] with all the interpretative difficulties that this may entail.[116]

The approach of the House of Lords in *Kreglinger* has been adopted particularly in Australia[117] and Canada.[118] For example, in those jurisdictions a collateral bonus,[119] a participation clause entitling the mortgagee to a percentage of the gross income or profits earned by the mortgagor on the property,[120] an agreement in regard to the transfer of a condominium pre-dating the mortgage[121] and a petrol sale agreement,[122] all of which were considered to be separate transactions from the mortgage, were held not to be clogs on the equity of redemption.[123]

The approach of the courts to options to purchase has also been modified in a variety of ways to take into account the nature and substance of the overall agreement between the parties. Transactions which may have appeared to breach

[111] *Multiservice* (n 83).

[112] *Charmelyn Enterprises Pty Ltd v Klonis* (1981) 2 BPR 9527 (NSWCA).

[113] *Kreglinger* (n 10). For a discussion of English law see A Berg, 'Clogs on the Equity of Redemption or Charming an Unruly Dog' [2002] *Journal of Business Law* 335.

[114] This was notwithstanding such decisions as *Noakes* (n 56). See also *De Beers Consolidated Mines Ltd v British South Africa Co* [1912] AC 52 (HL); Harpum, Bridge and Dixon (n 4) paras [25–094]–[25–095].

[115] *Toohey v Gunther* (1928) 41 CLR 18 (HCA) 194–196.

[116] As Heydon and Loughlan have observed (n 11) 351: 'Issues concerning validity of collateral stipulations are the most confusing in the entire law of mortgages.'

[117] See *Toohey* (n 115) where in particular Issacs J (195–196) and Higgins J (203–205) considered whether or not a collateral bond was an independent transaction. See also *Baker v Biddle* (1923) 33 CLR 188 (HCA).

[118] *London Loan & Savings Co of Canada v Meagher* [1930] SCR 378; *Bainov v Anthem Bambu Lofts Ltd* [2006] BCSC 1227 [16]–[17]. See generally E Belyea, 'Unclogging the Equity of Redemption in Commercial Transactions' (1994) 24 *The Canadian Journal of Business* 161, 177–82.

[119] *London Loan* (n 118).

[120] *North American Life Assurance Company v Beckhuson* [1981] 2 WWR 446 (Alta QB) [12]–[14] (Cawsey J). See also *Standard Trust Company v Panstar Developments Inc* (1993) 30 RPR (2d) 198 (BCSC) 16–17 (Owen-Flood J).

[121] *Bainov* (n 118) [16]–[17].

[122] *Re Petrol Filling Station, Vauxhall Bridge Road, London Rosemex Service Station Ltd v Shell Mex and BP Ltd* (1968) P & C 1 (ChD). Note also the tie agreement in *Esso Petroleum Company Ltd v Harper's Garage (Stourport) Limited* [1968] AC 269 (HL) which was reviewed from the perspective of restraint of trade rather than the anti-clog doctrine.

[123] Unfortunately, the issue whether the option to purchase in *Epic Feast Ltd v Mawson KLM Holdings Pty Ltd (in liq)* [1998] SASC 7106, (1998) 71 SASR 161 was a clog on the equity of redemption was not determined. In that case, there were indications that the option and the mortgage were closely connected.

the anti-clog doctrine have been found not to do so. First, a court may find that the mortgage is in fact a sale agreement, so that the matter stands outside the scope of the anti-clog doctrine.[124] An option to purchase made in favour of a vendor as part of an agreement for the sale of land is valid, because the agreement was never intended to operate as a security.[125]

Second, consistent with the former situation, courts have considered that a mortgage which was collateral to a sale agreement or an option to purchase did not breach the anti-clog doctrine because the mortgage effectively facilitated the purchase.[126]

Third, some courts have differentiated between option agreements which were exercisable when the mortgagor was in default, and options which were exercisable whether or not the mortgagor was in default. In Canada, the validity of an option agreement can turn on whether it was only exercisable on default.[127] When the option operated on default and the court considered that the exercise of the option would be a way of avoiding the traditional foreclosure action, the court would generally determine that the option was a clog on the equity of redemption.[128] However, in contrast, it has been suggested in Australia that an option to purchase which was exercisable on default would be rendered void as a penalty; whereas an option which could be exercisable at any time could breach the anti-clog doctrine.[129] It would appear that in this regard, the Australian application of the anti-clog doctrine is more onerous that the Canadian approach.

Finally, although the main transaction is indisputably a mortgage, an option to purchase will not breach the anti-clog doctrine if it is considered to be a transaction which is separate from and independent of the mortgage.[130] Generally speaking, this is a question of the substance rather than the form of the transaction[131] so that the courts will go beyond whether there are separate documents or only a single transaction.[132] Nevertheless, if the second or subsequent transaction is regarded as entirely separate from and independent of the mortgage, it appears

[124] For an important case as to whether a sale or mortgage existed see *Gurfinkel v Bentley Pty Ltd* (1966) 116 CLR 98 (HCA). Note also *Warnborough Ltd Garmite Ltd* [2006] EWHC 10 (Ch); *Brighton & Hove City Council v Audus* [2009] EWHC 340 (Ch); *BCE Development Corp v Cascade Investments Ltd* (1987) 55 Alta LR (2d) 22 (Alta QB) (Virtue J).

[125] *Ottawa Construction Ltd v Barnhart-Cochrane Construction Ltd* [1953] 4 DLR 571 (ONCA).

[126] *Wily v Endeavour Health Care Services Pty Ltd* [2003] NSWCA 312, (2003) 12 BPR 22,447.

[127] Ibid 645.

[128] *Co-op Credit Centre Union v Greba* (1984) 55 AR 176 (Alta CA); *Osborne Mortgage & Realty v Theroux* (1986) 74 AR 367 (Alta CA) [7]–[8]. In Canada, some courts have been wary of provisions which may sidestep the procedural requirements of foreclosure: *McKay v Herbert & Barnes* [2004] BCSC 1072.

[129] Butt (n 2) para [1832].

[130] Ibid; Gray and Gray (n 2) para [6.2.25]. Note *De Beers* (n 114).

[131] *Westfield Holdings Ltd v Australian Capital Television Pty Ltd* (*Westfield*) (1992) 32 NSWLR 194 (NSWSC) 198 (Young J).

[132] See, eg *Jones* (n 104) where there were two documents several years apart which constituted the one transaction.

that the mortgagor can act contrary to what would otherwise be the requirements of the anti-clog doctrine.[133]

In Canada, some courts have assumed that any agreement subsequent to the original mortgage can legitimately negate the anti-clog doctrine. In *Attorney General of Canada v Logan and Farm Credit Corporation*[134] Hunter J quoted (with approval) the view expressed in academic commentary that

> a mortgagor may, by a separate and independent transaction subsequent to the making of the mortgage, sell or release his equity of redemption to the mortgagee, or give the mortgagee the option of purchasing the mortgaged property and thus in effect deprive himself of his right to redeem.[135]

In *Misley v 420746 BC Ltd and Margolia*[136] McEachern CJ of the Court of Appeal for British Columbia, appeared to go even further when, after reviewing the origins of the equity of redemption and the power imbalance between borrowers and lenders, he opined:

> Once a mortgage has been negotiated, however, the power imbalance disappears, and the courts once again emphasize freedom of contract. Thus where the mortgagor, subsequent to the creation of the security, enters a contract with the mortgagee which makes redemption impossible, or more difficult than it should be, the contract does not constitute a clog on the equity of redemption.[137]

In this case, the Court was not considering options to purchase but whether a demand for additional interest on the mortgagee's judgment in foreclosure proceedings amounted to a clog on the equity of redemption. Nevertheless, the comment starkly demonstrates two important considerations. One is that the anti-clog doctrine and the modifications justified on the basis of separate and independent transactions are sourced in two different legal traditions: the anti-clog doctrine protects a proprietary interest and the enforceability of the separate and independent transaction is based on contract and the free bargaining position of the parties. The other consideration is the potential artificiality of juxtaposing two legal traditions. The traditional equitable approach presumes that the necessitous borrower needs protection; whereas the free bargaining position assumes that parties are able to look after their own interests. It is presupposed that the traditional anti-clog doctrine can be adapted and justified by the right of the parties to freely negotiate contractual rights. The problem is whether the effective reduction or even emasculation of the traditional doctrine can be justified

[133] *Reeve v Lisle* (n 98) 464 (Earl of Halsbury and Lord Brampton), 465 (Lord Lindley). Note also *Dical Investments* (n 84).

[134] *Logan* (n 85) [13]. The quotation was from Falconbridge, *Law of Mortgages*, 4th ed (Toronto, Canada Law Book, 1977) 66.

[135] Ibid 5. In *400091 British Columbia Ltd v Copper Beach Estate Ltd* (1992) 25 RPR (2d) 189 (BCSC) [8] Harvey J held that a right of first refusal was not a clog on the equity of redemption.

[136] *Misley v 420746 BC Ltd and Margolia* (1997) 46 BCLR (3d) 166 [47].

[137] Ibid. See also *Dical Investments* (n 84) 503 (Lacoucière JA); 616 (McKinlay JA); *Brennenstuhl Estate v Trynchy* [2007] Alta QB 703 [93]–101].

by recourse to the free bargain of the parties. Surely it cannot be assumed that a mortgagor is less necessitous when he or she negotiates a separate and independent bargain (which is subsequent to the mortgage and which makes redemption difficult or impossible). Such a position would appear to be an unsatisfactory one as courts ought to follow a consistent doctrinal approach to the making and amendment of mortgages, particularly when the validity of significant provisions is at stake.

C. The Equitable Principle of Unconscionability: The Decline and Abolition of the Anti-Clog Doctrine?

The cases discussed above[138] raise the issue whether and to what extent modern equity operates to protect the proprietary interests of mortgagors and their traditional right of redemption. Over the centuries, the nature and extent of equitable intervention has changed as courts have re-evaluated and modified the anti-clog doctrine. The anti-clog doctrine has been connected to and reflected the equitable concept of conscience, the traditional foundation of the equitable jurisdiction, in four ways. By charting this connection, it is possible to discern the rise of a new articulation of the role of conscience in the mortgage context and the consequent attenuation of the anti-clog doctrine.

First, as previously discussed, the anti-clog doctrine was a manifestation of the conscience of equity because it restated the determination of the Court of Chancery to protect necessitous borrowers from unscrupulous lenders. The intervention of equity was transaction specific, predictable and immutable. All mortgagors acquired an equity of redemption and, assuming the mortgage was not paid out on time, an equitable right to redeem. No mortgage provision could prevent or hamper the right of redemption.

Second, the modification or relaxation of the anti-clog doctrine did not jettison the traditional approach, but it meant that while equitable intervention was still transaction-specific, it was no longer quite as predicable or all-encompassing. For example, the decision in *Kreglinger* and the ongoing modification of the anti-clog doctrine has diminished the capacity of equity to protect uniformly a mortgagor's proprietary interest.

Third, the *Kreglinger* case was a pivotal decision. The House of Lords not only accepted the anti-clog doctrine and modified its operation, but it also endorsed simultaneously, equity's jurisdiction to consider collateral stipulations as part of a bargain. Equity could intervene when the collateral stipulation was unfair and unconscionable.[139] Therefore, for mortgages, equitable intervention could be at two levels: intervention on the basis of the nature of the mortgage as a security; and intervention on the basis of the mortgage as a bargain between

[138] Part IV (A) and (B).

[139] *Kreglinger* (n 10) 61 (Lord Parker). Note Harpum, Bridge and Dixon (n 4) para [25–094].

two parties. Earlier cases such as *Santley*[140] had presaged this duality of equitable intervention referred to above.[141] *Kreglinger* confirmed it and later cases have relied on it. For example in *Modular,*[142] Santow J not only considered that the particular 'all moneys' clause did constitute a breach of the anti-clog, doctrine but that it was also 'unfair and unconscionable' for the assignee to obtain such a collateral advantage.[143] Similarly, in *Jones v Morgan,*[144] the English Court of Appeal considered the applicability of the anti-clog doctrine as well as whether in general the second agreement between the parties was vitiated by unconscionable conduct.[145]

It was possible for matters to have stayed at the point which *Kreglinger* arrived at almost a century ago. However, in two jurisdictions, England[146] and Australia,[147] some judges have been very dissatisfied with the anti-clog doctrine, seeking both the abolition of the anti-clog doctrine and the duality of equitable intervention.

The dissatisfaction in England was evident in those cases where the courts were concerned about the anti-clog doctrine being used to evade a fair bargain between the parties.[148] For example, in *Kreglinger*, Lord Mersey compared the anti-clog doctrine to 'an unruly dog, which, if not securely chained to its own kennel, is prone to wander into places where it ought not to be.'[149] He also said that to apply the anti-clog doctrine 'would give effect to no equity and would defeat justice.'[150] In *Jones v Morgan*[151] Lord Phillips MR observed that 'the doctrine of a clog on the equity of redemption is, so it seems to me, an appendix to our law which no longer serves a useful purpose and would be better excised.'[152]

Nevertheless, the respect for earlier and higher judicial authority has been strong in English case law, so that English judges have been unwilling to abolish the anti-clog doctrine, notwithstanding a broader recognition of oppressive and unconscionable behavior.[153] In *Jones v Morgan*, despite his express misgivings, Lord Phillips MR concurred with Chadwick LJ that a clause in the second agreement created a clog on the equity of redemption and was consequently void.[154]

140 *Santley* (n 55).
141 Discussed in Part III (A) (iii).
142 *Modular* (n 108).
143 Ibid 104. See also *Wily* (n 126).
144 *Jones* (n 104).
145 Ibid [35]–[42], [50]–[73] (Chadwick LJ); [86]–[94] (Lord Phillips MR). The duality is also reflected in English textbooks where the consideration of clogs on the equity of redemption the redemption of oppressive and unconscionable mortgages are separately treated: see, eg Cousins and Ross (n 11) 302–11.
146 Ibid [86] (Lord Phillips MR).
147 *Westfield* (n 131).
148 See Part III (A) (ii).
149 *Kreglinger* (n 10) 46.
150 Ibid.
151 *Jones* (n 104).
152 Ibid [86].
153 As to unconscionable conduct, note also the decision of Goff J in *Cityland and Property (Holdings) Ltd v Dabrah* [1968] 1 Ch 166 (Ch).
154 Jones (n 104) [94].

In *Warnborough Ltd v Garmite Ltd*[155] the Court of Appeal severely criticised the anti-clog doctrine for its inflexibility and failure to accommodate new ways of dealing,[156] but accepted its efficacy in English law.[157] Therefore, the duality of equitable intervention in mortgages identified earlier in the *Kreglinger* case[158] remains in English law.

In Australia, dissatisfaction with the anti-clog doctrine has also been evident. The seminal decision is *Westfield Holdings Ltd v Australian Capital Television Pty Ltd.*[159] In that case, Young J decided that the transaction in question was not a mortgage. However, in obiter dicta, he held (consistent with the bargain cases considered above)[160] that there was no commercial reason why courts ought to invalidate a collateral advantage or an option to purchase in a mortgage.[161] He held that he was not bound by Lord Parker's formulation of equitable intervention in *Kreglinger*, as the earlier Australian authorities did not apply Lord Parker's statement of the law (including the anti-clog doctrine) as the ratio decidendi.[162] Instead, he jettisoned the characterisation of the law by Lord Parker and held that the issue simply was whether there had been unconscionable conduct on the part of the mortgagee.[163]

Since then, there has been acknowledgement[164] and in some cases, endorsement[165] of the approach of Young J in *Westfield*. In the light of this judgment, the anti-clog doctrine was criticised as being too narrow because it did not protect the interests of persons other than borrowers; and too wide because it resulted in highly technical decisions.[166] Notably also, the case law in favour of a single articulation of equity's conscience has continued to evolve almost exclusively in New South Wales. In *Guardian Mortgages v Miller,*[167] Wood CJ at CL

[155] *Warnborough v Garmite Ltd* [2003] EWCA Civ 1544, [2003] All ER (D) 52.

[156] Ibid [42]–[71] (Parker LJ) with whom Judge LJ and Brown LJ concurred.

[157] Ibid [72]–[81] (Parker LJ) with whom Judge LJ and Brown LJ concurred. When the matter was remitted for consideration in the lower court, it was held that there was no clog on the equity of redemption because the transaction was a sale and purchase, rather than a mortgage. In short, the Court was able to take the transaction outside the scope of the anti-clog doctrine: see *Warnborough* (n 124). Note also the opinion of counsel extracted in *Bonham v Fishwick* [2007] EWHC 1859 (Ch) [7].

[158] Part III (A) (iii).

[159] *Westfield* (n 131).

[160] Part III (A) (ii).

[161] *Westfield* (n 131) 202.

[162] Ibid 201.

[163] Ibid 202–203.

[164] *Epic Feast* (n 123) 173. In the decision, the Court declined to make a determination whether the option to purchase was a clog on the equity of redemption because it was not pursued at trial. However, the Court continued to separate considerations of general unconscionability from the anti-clog doctrine.

[165] *Wily v Endeavour Health Care Services Pty Ltd (No 5)* (2003) 11 BPR 21,081; see also W Duncan and W Dixon, *The Law of Real Property Mortgages* (Sydney, The Federation Press, 2007) 105; L Willmott and W Duncan, 'Clogging the Equity of Redemption: An Outmoded Concept?' (2002) 2 *Queensland University of Technology Law & Justice Journal* 359; Devonshire (n 45); Young, Croft and Smith, (n 10) para [9.340].

[166] Willmott and Duncan (n 165) 49–50.

[167] *Guardian Mortgages v Miller* [2004] NSWSC 1236, (2004) 12 BPR 22,833.

commented that the anti-clog doctrine has been 'subsumed by the general test of unconscionability.'[168] In *Sam Management Services (Aust) Pty Ltd v Bank of Western Australia Ltd*[169] Hodgson JA of the NSW Court of Appeal held that as the conduct and requirements of the mortgagee had not been unconscionable, a claim based on an alleged clog on the equity of redemption could not succeed.[170]

The most robust judicial endorsement of Young J has been that of Barrett J in *Lift Capital Partners Pty Ltd v Merrill Lynch International*,[171] who held that there was no Australian authority which compelled the NSW Supreme Court to apply the anti-clog doctrine.[172] He held that the general principle against unconscientious conduct underpinned the doctrine[173] and that the general doctrine of unconscionability 'remains the fulcrum upon which entitlement to equitable relief turns.'[174] When relying on the broad principle of unconscionability current in Australian equity jurisprudence, Barrett J referred to a wide array of authorities which, strictly speaking, had nothing to say about the anti-clog doctrine, but insisted upon their relevance.[175] Moreover, consistent with the emphasis on the mortgage as a bargain, Barrett J held:

> It cannot be said today that a contractual provision freely assented to by a mortgagor is void or unenforceable just because it allows the mortgagee to acquire the mortgaged property or to resist the mortgagor's attempt to redeem. The susceptibility of such a provision to equitable intervention is, however, well established. In a given case, equity will prevent reliance on the provision by the mortgagee if that reliance is unconscientious because of some factor associated with the formation of the contract or something distinct from mere changed circumstances or supervening event operative at the time of reliance.
>
> In determining whether reliance is unconscientious, regard must be had to the nature of the bargain, the circumstances in which it was made and the circumstances in which the mortgagee seeks to assert the mortgagor's promise to defeat the right to redeem.[176]

In the instant case Barrett J held that the mortgagor had acted unconscientiously because the effect of the mortgage was to allow the mortgagor's assets to be subject to lending arrangements under which they passed to a third party free of the mortgagor's interest in them.[177] His Honour also pointed out that the provisions would

[168] Ibid [114]. See also Duncan and Dixon (n 165) 105.

[169] *Sam Management Services (Aust) Pty Ltd v Bank of Western Australia Ltd* [2009] NSWCA 320.

[170] Ibid [59]–[60]. Young JA and Sackville AJA concurred; cf an earlier judgment in regard to the anti-clog doctrine: *Wily* (n 126).

[171] *Lift Capital Partners Pty Ltd v Merrill Lynch International* [2009] NSWSC 7, (2009) 73 NSWLR 404.

[172] Ibid [114]–[120].

[173] Ibid [124].

[174] Ibid [126].

[175] Ibid [126]–[130]. He considered *Muschinksi v Dodds* (1985) 160 CLR 583 (HCA); *Stern v McArthur* (1988) 165 CLR 489 (HCA); *Australian Broadcasting Corporation v Lenah Game Meats Pty Ltd* [2001] HCA 63, (2001) 208 CLR 199; *Commonwealth v Verwayen* [1990] HCA 39, (1990) 170 CLR 394; *Australian Competition and Consumer Commission v C G Berbatis Holdings Pty Ltd (No 2)* (2000) 96 FCR 491 (FCA); *Tanwar Enterprises Pty Ltd v Cauchi* [2003] HCA 57, (2003) 217 CLR 315.

[176] *Lift Capital* (n 171) [136]–[137]. Quoted with approval by Rein J in *Sam Management Services (Aust) Pty Ltd v Bank of Western Australia Ltd* [2009] NSWSC 676, [79].

[177] *Lift Capital* (n 171) [151].

be void as an impermissible fetter on the mortgagor to redeem the mortgaged shares, if, contrary to the opinion expressed, unconscionability was not the essential element of the anti-clog doctrine.[178]

Doctrinally, the decision in *Lift Capital* identified two simultaneous assimilations: the mortgage was incorporated into the broad notion of bargain; and the anti-clog doctrine was subsumed under the concept of unconscionable dealing. The conduct of the mortgagee remained subject to scrutiny, but the frame of reference was different. Therefore, it can no longer be assumed in NSW that the mortgagor's proprietary interest in the land and the right to redeem are automatically protected by equity. The Court may consider special sensitivities to redemption of the mortgage,[179] but the nature of equitable intervention has been transformed by the 'contractualisation' of the mortgage and the 'contractualisation' of equity.

D. Procedural Clogs on Redemption in the Exercise of the Mortgagee's Powers

Finally, there are a miscellaneous category of cases where some litigants have attempted to raise the anti-clog doctrine to deal with a perceived unconscionable exercise of power by the mortgagee, although strictly speaking, the review of the exercise of mortgagee powers did not appear to fall within the traditional anti-clog doctrine. These cases pre-date the decisions in *Westfield* and *Lift Capital* and are not confined to NSW. Whether or not these cases represent the kind of unconscientious conduct referred to by Barrett J in *Lift Capital* remains to be seen. Nevertheless, although some courts may have determined that the particular facts did not raise a question of a clog on the equity of redemption[180] or did not pursue the argument,[181] the courts neither disputed the existence of the anti-clog doctrine nor its application to the exercise of mortgage powers generally.

There have been a number of cases where mortgagors have argued that the actions taken by the mortgagee to exercise powers under the mortgage have had the effect of preventing or making more difficult the redemption of the mortgage. The emphasis in these cases has been on the immediate actions of the mortgagee (in the exercise of statutory powers or powers which exist under the mortgage) which it has been argued breached the anti-clog doctrine.[182]

[178] Ibid.

[179] Ibid [131].

[180] See, eg *Metropolitan Trust Company of Canada and Seaboard Life Insurance Company v Dancorp Developments Ltd* (Supreme Court of British Columbia, Master Patterson, 16 March 1993) 6–8; *Riley v Brown* [2006] NZHC 652 [26]. cf *Devlin v Surfers Paradise Investments Pty Ltd* [1997] QCA 102, [1998] 1 Qd R 404; *Christchurch Foodcourts Ltd v Tony NG Thiam Soon and Betty Goh as Trustees of Global Trust* [2005] NZHC 417 [65].

[181] *Wilson v Pinci* [2005] WASC 114 [6]; *Tyndall Funds Management Australia v CAN 078 545 605 Pty Ltd* [2002] SASC 177 [16]–[18]; *Golden Glory Pty Ltd v Sacco* [2009] VSC 442; *Telecom New Zealand Ltd v Sintel-Com Ltd* [2007] NZCA 499, [2008] 1 NZLR 780 [26]–[27].

[182] The kinds of allegations that have been made include that the mortgagee (or an assignee of the mortgagee): asserted a false and high level of indebtedness which was impossible to pay: *Spalla v*

In *Southwell v Roberts*,[183] for example, the mortgagee was in possession and the mortgagor argued that the mortgagee was not entitled to add to the amount already owed by making permanent and lasting improvements to the land (rather than maintenance and repairs of a recurrent nature). The Court held that the amount expended was unreasonable and disproportionate.[184] Dixon J (as he then was) held that while it was appropriate for a mortgagee to expend funds for the preservation of the property, it was not permissible for the mortgagee to expend funds which significantly altered the identity of the property because that would hamper the redemption of the mortgage.[185] Later cases have confirmed that a mortgagee cannot do anything which would prevent redemption such as leasing the property for a lengthy period[186] or retaining shares in a company associated with the mortgagor during the course of protecting its security.[187] A collusive sale by a mortgagee in breach of its power of sale, does not extinguish the mortgagor's equity of redemption.[188] In the light of the fragmentation of the anti-clog doctrine, it is unclear whether appeals to it in the context of these miscellaneous cases will continue to receive judicial consideration.

V. Conclusion

The equity of redemption, the equitable right to redeem and the anti-clog doctrine have been staple, immutable and predictable features of the law of English

St George Motor Finance Ltd (No 5) [2004] FCA 1262 [34]; calculated interest and additional sums which constituted a clog on the equity of redemption: *Heffernan v Grangewood Securities Ltd* [2001] EWCA Civ 1082 [6]; refused to provide a discharge figure during the course of the litigation proceedings: *Christchurch Foodcourts* (n 180) [19]; failed to provide a discharge of mortgage (although further monies could be outstanding at a later date): *Metropolitan Trust Company* (n 180) 6–8; denied a chargor the right to sue for an accounting and retrieval of property under telecommunications contracts: *Sintel-Com Ltd (in liq) v Telecom New Zealand Ltd* [2006] NZHC 349 [9], [45] (see also *Sintel-Com Ltd v Telecom New Zealand Ltd* [2006] NZHC 1339 [7]; *Telecom New Zealand* (n 181) [26]–[27]); denied the right of a later mortgagee paying out the earlier mortgage the right to sue on that mortgage: *Canadian Imperial Bank of Commerce v McIvor* (QB, Baynton J, 10 July 1998) [45]–[46]; refused to accept an amount calculated by the mortgagor for discharge, instead of the additional amount owing under judgment against the mortgagor: *Misley* (n 136) [7], [31]–[49]; or refused to consent to the assignment of the mortgage: *Instant Funding Ltd v Greenwich Property Holdings Ltd* [2007] NZHC 1527 [42]–[44]. The lodgement of a caveat has been considered to be a means of clogging the proprietary interest of another party: *Sims v Lowe* [1988] 1 NZLR 656 (NZCA). Note also *Riley* (n 180) where the mortgagee, inter alia lodged a caveat to protect her interest under an unregistered mortgage and the court held at [26] that her actions did not amount to a clog on the equity of redemption.

183 *Southwell v Roberts* (*Southwell*) (1940) 63 CLR 581 (HCA).

184 Ibid 598 (Dixon J); 602 (McTiernan J).

185 Ibid 597–598. Note also the argument raised by the mortgagor in *Golden Glory* (n 181) [8].

186 *Tyndall* (n 181) [16]–[18].

187 *Devlin* (n 180).

188 *Swanston Mortgage Pty Ltd v Trepan Investments Pty Ltd* [1994] 1 VR 672 (VICAD) 675 (Brooking J); *Patmore v Upton* [2004] TASSC 77, (2004) 13 Tas R 95 [42]. In Canada, it has also been held that a failure of the mortgagor to defend the foreclosure proceedings did not lead to the extinguishment of the equity of redemption: *Petranik* (n 13) 970 (Dickson J).

mortgages for centuries. They were manifestations of the underlying jurisdiction of equity based on conscience. Specifically, the Court of Chancery was concerned about protecting vulnerable and necessitous borrowers and the recognition and protection of proprietary interests in land.

However, it could not be said today that the anti-clog doctrine or its application in any of the jurisdictions which have been considered is still clear, immutable or predictable. Instead, the law is contradictory and sometimes confused. The reasons for the incongruities and inconsistencies are complex, but they began in the significant legal and social changes in the eighteenth and nineteenth centuries with the creation of the modern capitalist economy; the commoditisation of land; the introduction of title-by-registration; the centrality of contract as bargain; and, following from this, the categorisation of mortgages as a species of contract. This dramatic transformation of the legal and economic environment in which mortgages operate has had an impact upon mortgage practice and the anti-clog doctrine in particular. In the beginning of the twenty-first century, these major changes are still being worked through, as the sometimes confused and contradictory state of the case law on the anti-clog doctrine demonstrates.

Importantly, there has been a fundamental impact on equity. Much has been written about the influence of equity upon the law of contract[189] and there have been some notable decisions in which equitable doctrines, such as undue influence,[190] misrepresentation,[191] estoppel[192] or unconscionable dealing[193] have been applied successfully to prevent egregious reliance on a contract which has been unconscionable in some way.[194] However, leaving aside legal historians such as Atiyah and Simpson, there does not appear to have been a similar recognition of the profound effect that contract law has had on equitable jurisprudence. Perhaps there are two reasons for this. One has been the overwhelming centrality of contract as bargain (even operating in an attenuated fashion) in the modern law, so that lawyers are unaccustomed to thinking about a world where courts simply ignored the terms of the mortgage. Another reason is that references to broad notions of conscience may have blurred or masked ways in which the

[189] See, eg the seminal articles: P Finn, 'Equity and Contract' in P Finn (ed) *Essays on Contract* (Sydney, LawBook Co, 1987) 104; P Finn, 'Unconscionable Conduct' (1994) 8 *Journal of Contract Law* 37.

[190] See, eg *Johnson v Buttress* (1936) 56 CLR 113 (HCA); *Bank of New South Wales v Rogers* (1941) 65 CLR 42 (HCA); *National Westminster Bank plc v Morgan* (1985) AC 686 (HL).

[191] See, eg *Redgrave v Hurd* (1881) 20 Ch D 1; *Hellbut, Symons & Co v Buckleton* [1913] AC 30 (HL); *Munchies Management Pty Ltd v Belperio* (1988) 53 FCR 274 (FCA).

[192] See, eg *Central London Property Trust Ltd v High Trees House Ltd* (1947) 1 KB 130. Note strictly outside the contract context: *Waltons Stores (Interstate) Ltd v Maher* (1988) 164 CLR 387 (HCA); *Verwayen* (n 175).

[193] See, eg *Earl of Aylesford v Morris* (1873) LR 8 Ch App 484; *O'Rorke v Bolingbroke* (1877) 2 App Cas 814; *Commercial Bank of Australia v Amadio* (1983) 151 CLR 447 (HCA); *Garcia v National Australia Bank* [1998] HCA 48, (1998) 194 CLR 395; *Royal Bank of Scotland v Etridge (No 2)* [2001] UKHL 44, [2002] 2 AC 773.

[194] Nevertheless, the impact of equity has not been all encompassing. See, eg *Micarone v Perpetual Trustees Australia Ltd* [1999] 75 SASR 1 (SASC).

Court of Chancery developed equitable jurisprudence before the eighteenth century. Nevertheless, the creation, confusion and potential demise of the anti-clog doctrine is an illustration of notions of contract as bargain influencing settled equity jurisprudence on mortgages. Up to the eighteenth century, mortgagors automatically acquired an equity of redemption and an equitable right to redeem (once the date for contractual payment passed). Their proprietary interest in the land was protected by the anti-clog doctrine. With the advent of will theory and the contract as an almost unassailable bargain between two parties, the frame of reference for examining mortgages changed particularly as far as the anti-clog doctrine was concerned. What was once an acceptable equitable intervention was and remains subject to challenge.

The response to this challenge has differed in the various jurisdictions considered in this chapter. While some courts have applied the former equitable jurisprudence, there have been modifications to the anti-clog doctrine (sometimes leading to its virtual emasculation), inclusion of the anti-clog doctrine in a broad concept of conscience and even suggestions for its abandonment altogether. In England, the challenge of contract has been met mainly by modification of the doctrine. There has been some expressed dissatisfaction with it, but courts have been unwilling to take the step of abandoning it altogether. *Jones v Morgan*[195] represents a new conservatism, a peculiar quandary faced by judges who would have preferred not to have applied the doctrine because the entire mortgage (as amended) was neither oppressive nor unconscionable. In Canada and New Zealand, the challenge to the anti-clog doctrine has been met by the adoption of the kind of modification techniques applied in English case law. In Canada, there has been no direct doctrinal challenge to the existence of the doctrine.[196] Rather, an intensive contractual approach has in some cases severely limited it to a simple and rudimentary fragment in the law. In Australia, a number of approaches have been taken. Despite the view that there is no High Court case in which the anti-clog doctrine has been relied on as the ratio decidendi,[197] the doctrine has not been overruled by that Court. Indeed, on several occasions the High Court accepted its continued existence.[198] There has also been judicial support for the modification techniques applied in English case law.[199] However, in NSW in particular, there has also been a direct challenge to the anti-clog doctrine based on a robust application of a broad equitable doctrine of unconscionability in that State.[200] Whether the High Court will follow the approach of the NSW courts remains to be seen. However, the Court arguably has eschewed broad notions of unconscionability which are unconnected to specific equitable doctrines.[201]

195 *Jones* (n 104).
196 *Falconbridge on Mortgages*, (n 2) §3–10 (May 2003).
197 *Westfield* (n 131) 201; *Lift Capital* (n 171) [114]–[120].
198 *Baker* (n 117); *Toohey* (n 115); *Southwell* (n 183).
199 See, eg *Baker* (n 117); *Toohey* (n 115); *Modular* (n 108); *Wily* (n 126).
200 *Westfield* (n 131); *Lift Capital* (n 171).
201 See, eg *Tanwar* (n 175) [20]–[26] (Gleeson CJ, McHugh, Gummow, Hayne and Heydon JJ).

The contradictory and confused state of the case law in regard to the anti-clog doctrine also indicates that the response and role of equity has markedly changed, both in terms of its reduced predictability and the principles upon which intervention will be based. Today equitable intervention is no longer founded on the strict protection of an equitable proprietary right in a predictable fashion. Instead, courts often apply a modified and sometimes uncertain legal framework which requires the investigation and evaluation of the underlying facts of the case. In NSW, the court may review the mortgage transaction in the light of a broad notion of unconscionable conduct. In any event, a mortgagor can no longer be assured that he or she will automatically regain the property unencumbered by the mortgage or that, having regained the property unencumbered, he or she will not be subject to some other obligation connected indirectly to the original mortgage.

The review of the modern case law on the anti-clog doctrine suggests that it faces an uncertain future. It seems likely that we are witnessing its final demise. There are three reasons for this prognosis. First, taking into account that in each of the jurisdictions considered there would have been hundreds, if not thousands, of contentious mortgages, it is surprising that the anti-clog doctrine has not been raised as much as would have been anticipated.[202] Perhaps this is because today there is a wide array of other legal tools available to mortgagors wishing to challenge a transaction. No doubt other doctrines or statutory provisions were considered by litigants as more helpful than the anti-clog doctrine. Second, in recent times legislatures have become more interventionist in the regulation of mortgages. Not only have mortgagors been able to rely on statute to challenge a mortgage, but the statutory framework may exist without any regard to the anti-clog doctrine. Certainly, the framework for regulation in some jurisdictions has characterised mortgages as consumer or credit contracts, focusing particularly on the contracting process.[203] Moreover, the very right to redeem has been statutorily modified in some jurisdictions.[204] In the case of England, there is the potential for the law of the European Union to permit matters which would have been traditionally against the anti-clog doctrine.[205] Third, it has been assumed in some jurisdictions that a broad notion of unconscionability will best serve the public interest and that it is possible to subsume the anti-clog doctrine under an investigation of unconscionable conduct. Ultimately, while a broad articulation of equity's objectives is superficially attractive and appears to simplify and modernise the law, it ought not to be assumed that the practical result will be any more certain or streamlined.

[202] See Duncan and Dixon (n 165) 105.

[203] See, eg the *Australian National Credit Code*, Part 2 and s 76; and Butt (n 2), paras [18 77]–[18 79]. See also the discussion of specific statutory regulation in England: Gray and Gray (n 2) paras [6.2.47]–[6.2.54].

[204] See, eg Corporations Act 2001 (Cth) s 124(1)(b); Conveyancing Act 1919 (NSW) s 93.

[205] *Cukurova Finance International Ltd v Alfa Telecom Turkey Ltd (British Virgin Islands)* [2009] UKPC 19, [2009] 3 All ER 849 [11], [27]–[28].

4

Assignment of Future Property and Preferences

JOSHUA GETZLER*

I. The Basic Problem: Equitable Protection of Assignees *versus* Protection of Creditors from Assignments

From the time of the Tudors to the present day, the courts of law and equity have sometimes supported and extended the policy of insolvency[1] statutes enforcing parity of creditors, and sometimes cut against. A strong case of the former was Lord Mansfield's extension of the rules of fraudulent preference to encompass not just acts prejudicial to a particular creditor or creditors (such as gifts or transfers at undervalue), but any diminution of the post-insolvency trust pool available to all general creditors, including discharge for value of an obligation owed to a particular creditor, which in effect displaced the statutory scheme of *pari passu* distribution.[2] A strong case of the latter, of judicial undercutting of statutory insolvency principles, is found in the protective trust, which developed as a double discretionary trust in nineteenth-century English law, in turn evolving into the asset protection trust in modern American law. Both these devices, notably the

* I warmly thank Jamie Glister, Magda Raczynska, Peter Turner, and Kristin van Zwieten for comments on draft versions; and John Armour, Simon Douglas, James Edelman, Louise Gullifer, Steven Schwarcz, and Lionel Smith for invaluable discussion. All errors and lacunae are my sole responsibility.

[1] 'Insolvency' will here be used to denote both corporate insolvency and individual bankruptcy, unless the context indicates otherwise.

[2] *Alderson v Temple* (1768) 4 Burr 2235, 98 ER 165; 1 Black W 660, 96 ER 384. See further R Goode, *Principles of Corporate Insolvency Law*, 4th edn (London, Sweet & Maxwell, 2011) 519–25, 569–97. Thus an attempt to assign all of one's assets to a trustee to hold on trust for all of the creditors could be avoided and treated as itself an act of bankruptcy, not because it delayed or hindered a particular creditor but because it attempted a composition of debts outside the regulated process of the bankruptcy laws: see M Lobban, 'Bankruptcy and Insolvency' in W Cornish et al (eds), *The Oxford History of the Laws of England Vol XII, 1820–1914: Private Law* (Oxford, Oxford University Press, 2010) 779, 780–85.

American model, impose powerful restraints on alienability and attachment not always visible to creditors and so distorting risk allocation in credit markets.[3]

My purpose in this chapter is to investigate one important flashpoint in the judicial control of insolvency policies. I examine how the equitable law of future assignments, designed to enforce paid-for promises and uphold the interests of assignees, is in tension with another 'equitable' policy established by statute, namely the jurisdiction to prevent preferential assignments that tend to defraud creditors by blocking recourse against debtors' assets.

The enforcement of assignments of future property has long been one of the most mysterious parts of Chancery jurisdiction. Such assignments are difficult to explain in rational doctrinal terms, and they also bring disturbing consequences. Future assignments can be used to give a wholly non-possessory security to a favoured creditor, who can leapfrog the general creditors to attach receivables, proceeds, after-acquired property or other future assets as they vest. Courts must balance this freedom of assignment against the statutory policies of 'preference recapture', which nullify attempts to transfer assets that serve to reduce the debtor's estate available in insolvency. The basic policy intuition is that to prefer the interests of certain assignees is to defraud the general creditors of their due: 'persons must be just before they are generous'.[4]

The enforcement of future assignments might be reconciled with statutory insolvency policy on the basis that future property assigned under equity never enters the assignor's beneficial estate, and therefore cannot justly be claimed by creditors under the general assignment in bankruptcy.[5] But this answer may not always persuade. For one, we have the counter-example of the floating charge where the after-acquired property certainly does enter the debtor's estate and can be dealt with by that debtor; yet priority can still be accorded to the assignee

[3] Lord Eldon LC early set limits on the use of trusts and charges calculated expressly to avoid credit obligations in English law: compare *Brandon v Robinson* (1811) 18 Ves Jun 429, 34 ER 379 and *Higinbotham v Holme* (1812) 19 Ves Jun 88, 34 ER 451. The policy of constraining rearrangement of priorities conditioned upon insolvency has been continued into modern English law: see, eg *Re Jeavons, ex parte Mackay* (1873) LR 8 Ch App 643 (CA); *British Eagle International Air Lines Ltd v Cie Nationale Air France* [1975] 1 WLR 758 (HL); *Swiss Bank Corp v Lloyds Bank Ltd* [1982] AC 584 (HL); *Perpetual Trustee Company v BNY Corporate Trustee Services Ltd* [2009] EWCA Civ 1160, [2010] Ch 347; *Butters v BBC Worldwide Ltd* [2009] EWHC 1954 (Ch); criticised for applying the *pari passu* principle outside true insolvency contexts in L C Ho, 'The principle against divestiture and the pari passu fallacy' (2010) 25 *Butterworths Journal of International Banking and Financial Law* 3. The *Quistclose* trust arguably cuts across this entire policy, and is accordingly controversial: see R Stevens, 'Insolvency', in W Swadling (ed), *The Quistclose Trust: Critical Essays* (Oxford, Hart Publishing, 2004) 153. American courts by contrast burst constraints on insolvency-triggered trust arrangements from the later nineteenth century: see J Getzler, 'Transplantation and Mutation in Anglo-American Trust Law' (2009) 10 *Theoretical Inquiries in Law* 355. The wider problem of judgment proofing in America is set out in L LoPucki, 'The Death of Liability' (1996) 106 *Yale Law Journal* 1.

[4] *Freeman v Pope* (1870) LR 5 Ch App 538 (CA) 540 (Lord Hatherley LC). See further below, text following note 61, where this quotation is explained.

[5] A rule evolved by the common law courts, taking cognisance of equitable trusts and assignments in interpreting the operation of statutory assignment under the bankruptcy law: *Scott v Surman* (1742) Willes 400, 402; 125 ER 1235, 1236 (Willes CJ).

upon insolvency, attaching to new and circulating assets upon a triggering event.[6] A variant is *post facto* collateralisation of extant debt, where assets that may already have been in the control of the debtor when credit was extended are later subjected to a security in order to guarantee an already-contracted debt, again reducing the assets available to general creditors. But we need not turn to these elaborations of the genus to explore the basic problem, which is the potential of the most simple future assignments to create non-possessory securities disrupting just credit expectations. A survey of English and especially Australian equity, from the days of the early High Court to the present, richly demonstrates the contours of this recurrent problem. The Australian materials turn out to be especially intricate, for overlaying the basic problem of assignment versus preference recapture, we have a spectrum of statutory preference tests emerging from variant federal and state laws governing the related areas of bankruptcy, near-bankruptcy and insolvency. The legislative variances have further impeded the courts in their struggle to find consistent answers to the basic problem.

The insolvency statutes draw deeply from equitable concepts of fraud, and they in turn have been interpreted extensively by judges using equitable ideas.[7] But before we examine how statutory jurisdiction interacts with equitable assignments, we had better establish what those assignments might be.

II. The Operation of Equitable Assignment

A good example of the phenomenon of assignment re-ordering normal priorities is found in *Holroyd v Marshall*,[8] the very decision that established the modern doctrine of assignment of future interests in 1862. In that case a creditor, Holroyd, extended payment to one Taylor, a mill owner, on condition that Taylor should sell his mill inventory to a trustee nominated by Holroyd who would hold it as security and sell it should Taylor be unable to find money to pay off the debt. A further clause of the loan stated that Taylor would assign any further machinery or implements brought into his milling operation so as to add to the security held on trust for sale. Taylor acquired new machinery, and also contracted further unsecured debt, with the new creditors being made aware of Holroyd's security (described in the case sometimes as an 'assignment', sometimes as an 'equitable

[6] See the essays in J Getzler and J Payne (eds), *Company Charges: Spectrum and Beyond* (Oxford, Oxford University Press, 2006).

[7] For a modern survey covering much of preference rules in bankruptcy as well as corporate insolvency, but with a predominantly English focus, see H Bennett and J Armour (eds), *Vulnerable Transactions in Corporate Insolvency* (Oxford, Hart Publishing, 2007). The tangle of Australian statutory instruments before the Corporations Act 2001 (Cth) is dissected in J Edelman, 'The Meaning of Fraud in Insolvency and Bankruptcy: A 400 Year Old Riddle' (2000) 18 *Company and Securities Law Journal* 97.

[8] *Holroyd v Marshall* (1862) 10 HLC 191, 11 ER 999. The best exegesis remains J Keeler, 'Some Reflections on Holroyd v Marshall' (1967–70) 3 *Adelaide Law Review* 360, 468.

charge', most commonly as a 'mortgage', though a modern lawyer would distinguish these concepts).[9] Taylor could not pay his debts; the new creditors then executed judgment, and through Marshall sought to take over the new machinery to recover their judgment debts. Holroyd sued Marshall to assert a prior claim to the after-acquired machinery. Stuart V-C thought that the original assignment was effective to vest Holroyd (through the trustee) with a superior beneficial title, but Lord Campbell LC held that some further assurance was necessary by Taylor to convey an equitable right, and that the judgment creditors should prevail on the common law principle that they had been the first to levy judgment. As counsel for Marshall argued in the further appeal, the general creditors had won the race to the courtroom door, before the assignees had perfected Holroyd's title, so that Holroyd had only a personal equity against Taylor for the assurance of the future property, and this could not bind third parties unless some act of conveyance had occurred on vesting. The fact that the judgment debtors had notice of the prior assignment of future property did not affect the imperfect and merely personal nature of that assignment; on this interpretation the assurance really amounted to a power that had not yet been exercised. The House of Lords reinstated the judgment in Holroyd's favour and, as is well known, Lord Westbury explained the basis of Holroyd's right in terms of the equitable enforcement of a contractual assignment supported by valuable consideration where the contract is 'one of that class of which a Court of Equity would decree the specific performance'.[10] The logic seemed to be that because the contract was capable of specific performance this grounded an instant conveyance of an equitable title once future property had vested in the assignee; no further intervention such as an act of conveyance or assurance was therefore necessary. Lord Chelmsford's judgment did not dwell on the availability of specific performance but rather on the intention of the parties to effect the assurance, and it was this analysis that was expanded and supported in Lord Macnaghten's leading judgment in *Tailby v Official Receiver* in 1888.[11] In that House of Lords case an assignment of existing and future book debts was upheld on the basis that the contract for value had sufficiently identified the subject matter of the assurance and that the parties' intention to effect a transfer immediately on vesting of the future debts was clearly expressed. Lord Macnaghten made clear that the basis of the doctrine was 'the principle that equity considers that done which ought to be done'; the availability of specific performance of the terms of the contract was only a subset or adjunct of that broader principle, and not a

[9] See P Turner, 'Company Charges: Inflexible Interplay of Law and Equity?' (2006) 22 *Journal of Contract Law* 16; for a fuller treatment of securities in land and non-real assets see B McFarlane, *The Structure of Property Law* (Oxford, Hart Publishing, 2008) 582–642, 785–835. In the case of *Associated Alloys v ACN 001 452 106 Pty Ltd* [2000] HCA 25, (2000) 202 CLR 588 it was essential to distinguish a charge over proceeds from a trust assigning proceeds as the former device would be void without registration; the plurality judges (at [6]) made the point that equitable powers over an asset arising under a charge are circumscribed by the essential nature of the institution as a security, whilst an assignment operating as a trust is not so confined.

[10] *Holroyd* (n 8) 209, 1006.

[11] *Tailby v Official Receiver* (1888) LR 13 App Cas 523.

special condition for equitable enforcement of an assurance as Lord Westbury's *Holroyd* judgment might have implied.[12]

This wider approach to equitable enforcement of rights derived from contract has been emphasised by the modern High Court of Australia, for example in *Chan v Cresdon Pty Ltd*,[13] where the majority stated:

> [T]he references in the earlier cases to specific performance should be understood in the sense of Sir Frederick Jordan's explanation adopted by Deane and Dawson JJ in *Stern v McArthur*:[14]
>
> 'Specific performance in this sense means not merely specific performance in the primary sense of the enforcing of an executory contract by compelling the execution of an assurance to complete it, but also the protection by injunction or otherwise *of rights acquired under a contract which defines the rights of the parties*': ... Chapters on Equity in New South Wales, Select Legal Papers, 6th ed (1947), p 52, n(e).[15]

Meagher JA writing both *ex curia*[16] and *in banco*[17] has stringently criticised the High Court's acceptance of 'Sir Frederick Jordan's footnote' on the basis that it is too wide in its understanding of how equitable interests beyond the contract and binding third parties can be generated by a bargain to convey; there may be contingencies or conditions for the hardening of the equitable right, such as third party consents, or formality requirements, or identification and gathering of assets, or complete execution of the consideration, that must be met before a full interest persisting against third parties can vest, and it is impossible to see how the strong equitable protection of agreements to convey suggested by Jordan CJ's note would operate in such contingent transfers. There is also a question whether Jordan CJ was stating at large how equity enforces assurances for value, whether present or future interests, or was confusing the language of future assignments capable of specific performance found in *Holroyd* and applying it too widely. Meagher JA noted[18] that equity may in many instances recognise a personal chose amounting to a power to require steps to be taken to perfect a transfer, without giving a proprietary claim, or even a full right to specific performance, tracking the analysis of interests under an unadministered estate found in *Commissioner of Stamp Duties v Livingston*.[19] Such an interpretation, applied to contractual examples such as estate contracts and assignments of future interests, would allow

[12] Ibid 545–51.

[13] *Chan v Cresdon Pty Ltd* (1989) 168 CLR 242 (HCA).

[14] *Stern v McArthur* (1988) 165 CLR 489 (HCA) 522.

[15] *Chan* (n 13) 253 (Mason CJ, Brennan, Deane and McHugh JJ) (emphasis added). The High Court also adopted the theory of Jordan CJ in two earlier cases: *Hewett v Court* (1983) 149 CLR 639 (HCA) and *Legione v Hately* (1983) 152 CLR 406 (HCA).

[16] R Meagher, 'Sir Frederick Jordan's Footnote' (1999) 15 *Journal of Contract Law* 1. See also R Meagher, D Heydon and M Leeming, *Meagher, Gummow & Lehane's Equity: Doctrine and Remedies*, 4th edn (Chatswood, Butterworths LexisNexis, 2002) paras [7–150]–[7–195].

[17] *Chief Commissioner of Stamp Duties v ISPT Pty Ltd* (1998) 45 NSWLR 639 (NSWCA) 654–55 (Meagher JA).

[18] Meagher, 'Sir Frederick Jordan's Footnote' (n 16).

[19] *Commissioner of Stamp Duties v Livingston* [1965] AC 694 (PC).

a more discriminating approach to the timing and priority of such interests and their defeasibility, should the underlying contract founder; the specific performance base by contrast suggests all-or-nothing enforcement of the contract on its terms. The power concept of an incomplete interest under an executory conveyance also helps explain equitable forfeiture for breach of contractual condition: dealing with such an instance in *Tanwar Enterprises Pty Ltd v Cauchi* the High Court in 2003 ventured a hesitant *obiter dictum* siding with Meagher JA against Jordan CJ's analysis:

> In the New South Wales Court of Appeal, doubt since has been cast upon the support for any such general principle by the authorities cited by Sir Frederick Jordan, beginning with *Tailby v Official Receiver*. It is sufficient for present purposes to observe that, where the issue, as in Tanwar's appeal, concerns alleged unconscientious reliance by vendors upon their contractual right to terminate, it does not assist to found the equity of the purchaser upon the protection of rights to injunctive relief acquired under a contract the termination of which has taken place. Whilst the contracts here were on foot, breach thereof by the vendors would have been restrained. But there was no relevant breach of contract by the vendors, and the contracts were terminated in exercise of a contractual right to do so.[20]

If this negates the Jordan analysis, what can be put in its place? One path to help conceptualise the doctrine (or doctrines) of *Holroyd* and *Tailby* is to contrast assignments of future interests for value with equitable enforcement of gifts. Equity will not perfect an imperfect gift unless steps have been taken tantamount to a positive commitment to make the assurance absent some further negative intervention (so that everything *necessary*—read *sufficient*—to be done by the donor has been done, even if a *locus poenitentiae* remains). Where the assurance of a future or unascertained asset is supported by a valuable consideration that has been fully executed, however, that commitment to convey is embodied in the paid-for bargain *per se*, not in any executed steps to convey the property, which of course is impossible prior to vesting or identification. Because one side has given full value, for example by payment over of loan monies, equity will therefore bestow on that value-giver a power to ensure the other side reciprocates, and does not exploit the futurity of the promised benefit to renege on the promise.[21] Here equity sees a kind of irrevocable floating trust or trust power over the assets of the assignor as they presently stand being constituted via the agreement,[22] with

[20] *Tanwar Enterprises Pty Ltd v Cauchi* [2003] HCA 57, (2003) 217 CLR 315 [57] (footnotes omitted).

[21] S Gardner, *An Introduction to the Law of Trusts*, 3rd edn (Oxford, Oxford University Press, 2011) 325–27.

[22] *Gomez v Graham* (1743) 9 Mod 287, 88 ER 457; *Stuart v Tucker* (1777) 2 Black W 1137, 96 ER 671; discussed in M Leeming, 'What is a Trust?' (2008) 31 *Australian Bar Review* 211, 218–19. This analysis is afforced by the possibility that trusts can effect a transfer of the enjoyment of contractual benefits subject to anti-assignment clauses, underlining the fact that entrustment is not equivalent to assignment: see *Barbados Trust Company Ltd v Bank of Zambia* [2007] EWCA Civ 148, [2007] 1 Lloyd's Rep 495; *Don King Productions Inc v Warren* [2000] Ch 291 (CA); A Trukhtanov, 'Trust of a Non-Assignable Contractual Benefit' (2007) 70 *MLR* 848; P Turner, 'Trusts of Debts of Restricted Assignability' [2008] *CLJ* 23.

the equity waiting to descend on the specified property once it vests in the estate or is identified from within the estate. In a wonderful phrase, Pollock CB labelled such an interest 'a prophetic conveyance'.[23] It is a more powerful equity than that frailer type evoked by a right to insist on specific performance, which is engaged on different grounds and does not depend on executed consideration.[24]

III. Future Assignments and the Problem of Non-Possessory Security

There are many other areas in our law beyond the *Holroyd v Marshall* equity where non-possessory interests may be created by agreement on terms that can disturb third-party credit risk and displace priorities. At common law, reproduced in the sale of goods legislation, documentary sale of chattels allowed title to shift ahead of factual possession;[25] the factual control of the vendor could then mislead rival creditors assessing the vendor's credit risk, amounting to a representation of reputed ownership.[26] In equity the *Lysaght v Edwards*[27] or *Walsh v Lonsdale*[28] doctrine or doctrines shifting a beneficial interest on perfection of an estate contract can have a similar effect; here the specific performance base of the right makes good sense as land interests are each unique.[29] Perhaps the strongest example is floating charge security over corporate assets. These securities were

[23] *Belding v Reed* (1865) 3 H & C 955, 961; 159 ER 812, 814.

[24] *Federal Commissioner of Taxation v Everett* (1980) 143 CLR 440 (HCA) 450–51. For a like argument basing the 'estate contract' trust on fully executed consideration see N Hopkins, 'Acquiring Property Rights from Uncompleted Sales of Land' (1998) 61 *MLR* 486. The case of non-bargain assignments is rather different: see *Norman v Federal Commissioner of Taxation* (1963) 109 CLR 9 (HCA); *Shepherd v Federal Commissioner of Taxation* (1965) 113 CLR 385 (HCA); *Olsson v Dyson* (1969) 120 CLR 365 (HCA).

[25] See, eg *Dennant v Skinner* [1948] 2 KB 164 (KBD); *Sirius Shipping Corporation v The Ship Sunrise* [2006] NSWSC 398; Sale of Goods Act 1979, s 18 r 1 (Eng).

[26] It is no surprise that in the later nineteenth century commercial judges and legislatures aiming to promote a more complex sales law worked together to largely uproot the reputed ownership doctrine: see especially *Re Stockton Iron Furnace Company* (1879) 10 Ch D 335 and *Re Crumlin Viaduct Works Company* (1879) 11 Ch D 755, both decisions of Jessel MR; and *Gorringe v Irwell India Rubber and Gutta Percha Works* (1885) 34 Ch D 128 (CA); see further J Getzler, 'The Role of Security over Future and Circulating Capital: Evidence from the British Economy circa 1850–1920', in Getzler and Payne, *Company Charges* (n 6) 227–51.

[27] *Lysaght v Edwards* (1876) 2 Ch D 499 (ChD).

[28] *Walsh v Lonsdale* (1882) 21 Ch D 9 (CA).

[29] The nature of such interests in land as something less than a full beneficial estate under a trust is discussed in *Chang v Registrar of Titles* (1976) 137 CLR 177 (HCA) 184 (Mason J); *Chan* (n 13) 250–58 (Mason CJ, Brennan, Deane and McHugh JJ); *Tanwar* (n 20); *Jerome v Kelly (Inspector of Taxes)* [2004] UKHL 25, [2004] 1 WLR 1409 [31] (Lord Walker); S Gardner, 'Equity, Estate Contracts and the Judicature Acts: *Walsh v Lonsdale* Revisited' (1987) 7 *OJLS* 60; N Hopkins, 'Acquiring Property Rights' (n 24). Chambers argues that the equity arises from the uniqueness of the property rather than equitable doctrine of consideration. Swadling in contrast has argued that even in a land context specific performance should not have third party implications and constructive trust language should be expelled; and he explicitly rejects the alternative paid consideration theory: see R Chambers, 'The Importance of

recognised in the late nineteenth century, and were promoted with alacrity by Sir George Jessel MR. Such devices swiftly became a dominating presence in corporate finance, attractive because of the strong receivership powers afforded to banks and other lenders. In form they were a hybridisation of future assignments, overlapping charges and powers of the possessor-debtor to deal in the present assets, and it quickly became clear that these devices exacerbated the problem of hidden securities disrupting credit assessment and risk in trade, leading over time to legislative redistribution of assets otherwise subject to security, in order to pay preferred debts and meet some of the unsecured debts and liquidation costs.[30]

Equity's permissiveness in allowing secret conveyances and securities had long troubled the common lawyers,[31] but the exuberant development of hidden securities and assignments by the equity courts of the late nineteenth century provoked outrage in the trading communities, and even opposition amongst some of the senior judges,[32] leading to Parliament introducing a raft of registration requirements, touching *inter alia* assignments of book debts, bills of sale and company charges, and adding to existing formality and notice requirements imposed by Parliament since the original Statute of Frauds.[33] But the legislative overlay did not dispel the sense of policy disquiet in the courts as they were called upon to enforce ever more elaborate non-possessory securities. The dilemma can be modelled as a three-way choice of strategies for the control of secured credit, as John Armour has recently suggested.[34] Should lawmakers restrict the types of instrument that can be deployed, curbing freedom of contract? Or apply a remedial regime of selective enforcement, as where equity courts will allow a bona fide purchaser for value without notice to defeat prior securities? Or should legislatures enforce formal notice and registration requirements, which combine the policies of channelling security interests into a manageable *numerus clausus* and ensuring that contracting parties have knowledge of rival claims when assessing credit risk? The current destabilised world of securitisations and derivatives presents these

Specific Performance', and W Swadling, 'The Vendor-Purchaser Constructive Trust' both in S Degeling and J Edelman (eds), *Equity in Commercial Law* (Sydney, LawBook Co, 2005) 431, 463.

[30] See J Armour, 'Should We Redistribute in Insolvency?' in Getzler and Payne (n 6) 189–225, and other essays in that collection.

[31] See, eg 'Thomas Audley's Reading on Uses (1526)' in JH Baker, *Baker and Milsom's Sources of English Legal History: Private Law to 1750*, 2nd edn (Oxford, Oxford University Press, 2010) 118–19.

[32] Notably Lord Herschell in *Saloman v Saloman & Co Ltd* [1897] AC 22, 41–47 (HL), as to which see P Johnson, *Making the Market: Victorian Origins of Corporate Capitalism* (Cambridge, Cambridge University Press, 2010) 153–59.

[33] For the Statute of Frauds as a surrogate or evasion of a registration system, see P Hamburger, 'The Conveyancing Purposes of the Statute of Frauds' (1983) 27 *American Journal of Legal History* 354. For the politics of land registration see A Offer, *Property and Politics 1870–1914: Landownership, Law, Ideology and Urban Development in England* (Cambridge, Cambridge University Press, 1981); cf S Anderson's critique of Offer's rent-seeking thesis in *Lawyers and the Making of English Land Law, 1832–1940* (Oxford, Oxford University Press, 1992). Offer replies to Anderson in 'Lawyers and Land Law Revisited' (1994) 14 *OJLS* 269.

[34] See J Armour, 'The Law and Economics Debate About Secured Lending: Lessons for European Lawmaking?' (2008) 5 *European Company and Financial Law Review* 3.

dilemmas most sharply, but we can also see the same policy tensions at work in the seedbed English cases of the late nineteenth century.

Just one case, being a *locus classicus* of the post-*Holroyd* law of equitable assignment, will illustrate some of that basic tension between facilitating security transactions and protecting creditor interests. In *Re Lind* a contingent heir executed two mortgages over his expectancy.[35] He then went bankrupt, and in due course received his discharge, ending all extant contractual rights and duties proved in the bankruptcy. The mortgagees had not proved their claims in the bankrupt estate. Post-discharge the heir once more assigned his expectancy for value to a fresh creditor, and when the expectancy was realised executed a further assignment purporting to transfer the present interest to that same later creditor. The prior mortgagees then claimed the estate, and won in the Court of Appeal. Phillimore LJ stated the operative law in terms rejecting the specific performance model of Lord Westbury in *Holroyd v Marshall*, and preferring the trust or equitable charge model of Lord Chelmsford in that case:

> If the assurance rest in contract and if by consequence the only way in which equity fastens upon the property be by the operation of the doctrine of specific performance, then the liability under the contract would be, as it seems to me, discharged by bankruptcy....
>
> In order that the assignment may survive and have its effect it must give to the assignee something more than a mere right in contract, something in the nature of an estate or interest ... notwithstanding ... allusions to the doctrine of specific performance of contracts, it is I think well and long settled that the right of the assignee is a higher right than the right to have specific performance of a contract, that the assignment creates an equitable charge which arises immediately upon the property coming into existence. Either then no further act of assurance from the assignor is required, or if there be something necessary to be done by him to pass the legal estate or complete the title, he has to do it not by reason of a covenant for further assurance the persistence of which through bankruptcy it is unnecessary to discuss, but because it is due from him as trustee for his assignee.[36]

All of this supported the approach of Lord Macnaghten in *Tailby*; equity created a 'higher right' to the security emerging from the contract but not identical to it. But Phillimore LJ also noted that in *Collyer v Isaacs* in 1881 a strong Court of Appeal led by Jessel MR had held that a discharge from bankruptcy gave the debtor a fresh start including discharge of covenants to assign future property;[37] and overall Phillimore LJ seemed to prefer Jessel's logic in *Collyer* but felt bound by the House of Lords

[35] *Re Lind* [1915] 2 Ch 345 (CA).

[36] Ibid 365–66 (Phillimore LJ).

[37] *Collyer v Isaacs* (1881) 19 Ch D 342 (CA). See also *Ex parte Nicholls* (1883) 22 Ch D 782 (CA) 786–87 (Jessel MR), stating that an assignment of future profits as a chose in action has those profits as they accrue vest in the trustee or assignee in bankruptcy, and do not go to the original assignee of the chose; this stream of authority is explored in M Smith, *The Law of Assignment: The Creation and Transfer of Choses in Action* (Oxford, Oxford University Press, 2007) 400–04, but without making reference to the alternative and dominant stream headed by *Tailby* and *Lind*.

decision in *Tailby*. Indeed Phillimore LJ seemed to affirm the *Tailby* doctrine through clenched teeth, concluding his judgment with these reflections:

> I do not understand an assignment which at the time only operates as a contract, but when the property comes into possession operates without more as an actual assurance; and even if this were intelligible I do not understand why in its chrysalis state it is not subject to the laws of a chrysalis, why, being still only a contract, it is not discharged by a discharge of contracts. And I may add that I think it would be better as matter of public policy that all assignments of bare futurities were made impossible. But the law is settled in the other sense by the highest authority...[38]

The rival doctrine of *Collyer v Isaacs* had already been sidestepped in nineteenth century cases where a covenant to assign future property in a family will or settlement had been followed by the bankruptcy of the settlor.[39] *Re Lind* was important because the same doctrine was extended into general credit relations in the commercial economy, and in effect overruled or displaced *Collyer* entirely.[40] It establishes that a future assignment survives and remains operative after the discharge of the founding contract, and so is apt to establish priority over the future property when it vests by attaching an equitable interest independent of the agreement constituting the interest and taking effect outside the promisor's estate. But the nature of the equitable interest that effects this magic still escapes rational explanation, with commentators resorting to opaque metaphors such as 'inchoate interests' and 'empty funds'.[41] It seems to work in practice but not in theory; and Phillimore LJ in *Re Lind* was not the only judge to doubt that it worked well at all.[42]

IV. Preference Recapture and 'Intention to Defraud'

The law of assignments was developed against the backdrop of older laws governing avoidance of fraudulent preferences, or 'preference recapture' in the phrase of

[38] *Lind* (n 35) 368 (Phillimore LJ).

[39] Notably in *Robinson v Ommanney* (1882) 21 Ch D 780 (Kay J), following the older case of *Lyde v Mynn* (1833) 1 Myl & K 683, 39 ER 839 (Lord Brougham LC).

[40] *Lind* (n 35) 375 (Bankes LJ).

[41] See, eg L Gullifer and J Payne, *Corporate Finance Law: Principles and Policy* (Oxford, Hart Publishing, 2011) 237–39. The applicability of the fund concept to assignment of intangibles including future rights is defended in R Goode, 'Are Intangible Assets Fungible?' [2003] *Lloyd's Maritime and Commercial Law Quarterly* 379; R Nolan, 'Property in a Fund' (2004) 120 *LQR* 108. For doubts concerning fund analysis see D Sheehan, 'Property in a Fund, Tracing and Unjust Enrichment' (2010) 4 *Journal of Equity* 225

[42] For example in *Re Wait* [1927] 1 Ch 606 (CA), in the context of a contract to sell goods only partly ascertained, Atkin LJ (at 634) found that criticism of the specific performance theory of equitable assignment set out in *Holroyd* 'seems well founded and weakens its authority'; and further doubted (at 638) the alternative consideration theory: 'Similarly, I fail to see how the payment of the price can convert that which was not an equitable assignment before the payment, into an equitable assignment after the payment'. In *Re Goldcorp Exchange Ltd (in receivership)* [1995] 1 AC 74 (PC) 90 the Privy Council referred to 'the reasoning contained in the judgment of Atkin LJ [in Re *Wait*], which their Lordships venture to find irresistible'.

some modern courts.[43] The jurisdiction to avoid fraudulent preferences forms a key part of the modern system of bankruptcy and insolvency law.[44] It may be seen as a sister doctrine to the basic equitable jurisdiction to avoid contracts for fraud, as where a person dishonestly misrepresents some material fact in order to win an asset which is then sold on to another innocent party.[45] The difference is that the fraudulent preference relates to the pool of assets that would be available to a creditor or creditors on a distribution, not particular assets. Preference recapture has generated a complex and contradictory body of doctrine, which is not surprising when we see how the jurisdiction was constructed over five centuries or more, from a bewildering array of sources. The unwieldy historical rules and procedures are contained in a variety of statutory instruments and a sprawling case law, which is particularly bewildering in federalised Australia;[46] yet America's uniform commercial and bankruptcy laws and the operation of the federal insolvency jurisdiction suggests that cross-federal codification is not a panacea.

The origins of the preference laws lie in some rather simple and elegant texts of classical Roman law. The *actio Pauliana* nullified voluntary transactions or transactions at undervalue to family or friends which defrauded creditors of recourse against the debtor's assets.[47] Later Civilian law developed the reputed ownership doctrine making assets available to creditors where the true owner had represented that a debtor through possession had those assets under his control or within his patrimony and had so helped him to gain extensions or expansions of credit; this was a kind of estoppel preventing the owner from denying the title of the possessor due to the debtor's justified reliance. The two strategies of avoiding preferences and enforcing reputed ownerships could coincide, as where a person sold an asset secretly to a preferred creditor or associate whilst keeping the possession in order to maintain or advance credit relationships with others. Here both doctrines operated in tandem to return or vest the *dominium* of the asset in the debtor's estate so as to be available to the general creditors who could reasonably presume access.

[43] Eg *Ferrier and Knight (As Liquidators of Compass Airlines Pty Limited (In Liq)) v Civil Aviation Authority* (1994) 55 FCR 28 (FCA) 42–63 ('*Compass Airlines*'), reversed on the facts by majority in *Airservices Australia v Ferrier* (1996) 185 CLR 483 (HCA).

[44] See further D Baird, 'Fraudulent Conveyance', in *The New Palgrave Dictionary of Law and Economics* (London, Macmillan, 1998) II, 192; D Baird and T Jackson, 'Fraudulent Conveyance Law and its Proper Domain' (1985) 38 *Vanderbilt Law Review* 829; H Bennett and J Armour (eds), *Vulnerable Transactions in Corporate Insolvency* (n 7) especially chs 3–4, 7–8.

[45] *Small v Attwood* (1831) Younge 407, 159 ER 1051 is an example of how ordinary equitable fraud can resemble fraudulent preference.

[46] See the impressive Australian Law Reform Commission paper: *General insolvency inquiry* (ALRC 45, 1988), available at http://www.austlii.edu.au/au/other/alrc/publications/reports/45/ accessed 17 June 2011.

[47] D.42.8.1.–25, D.22.1.38.4; the surrounding sources are summarised in M Radin, 'Fraudulent Conveyances at Roman Law' (1931) 18 *Virginia Law Review* 109. The name '*actio Pauliana*' is post-classical, possibly a glossatorian interpolation; for an outline of the content of the *actio* see W Buckland, *A Textbook of Roman Law from Augustus to Justinian*, 3rd edn, revised P Stein (Cambridge, Cambridge University Press, 1966) 596.

The twin doctrines of voidable preferences and reputed ownerships circulated in the early court of Chancery and the commissions of bankruptcy as species of fraud and estoppel, with Scottish law as a possible bridge moving ideas between the Continental and English law. The reputed ownership doctrine was set out by the statute 21 Jac 1, c 19 (1623–24), probably codifying existing curial practice. A version of the preference doctrine was legislated as early as 1376 and 1379,[48] but its modern incarnation is found in the 1571 Statute of Elizabeth, the famous 13 Eliz 1, c 5, extended by 27 Eliz 1, c 4 in 1585, then reiterated in James's first bankruptcy statute of 1601, 1 Jac 1, c 15, and repeated and adapted in many statutes to follow over the next four centuries.[49] Each statute used slightly different language to define the triggering conduct for preference avoidance, as many judges have noted to their dismay in the reams of litigation that followed. The 1585 statute seemed to go well beyond its 1571 predecessor, stating that any attempt to reduce an estate in order to hide assets from creditors could be avoided, even for example where the assignment preceded the contracting of the debt. This left a question of measuring the requisite level of intention necessary to characterise a preference as fraudulent. The original 1571 Statute of Elizabeth allows any conveyance of property made for 'the purpose of delaying, hindering or defrauding creditors' to be avoided by any person thereby prejudiced, subject to a defence of bona fide purchase for value that could be raised by the assignee. As Parliaments have reiterated the words 'for the purpose of' with variants such as 'with intent', 'with a view to', 'with real intent', 'the main purpose', or, with maximal baroque expansiveness, 'to the intent or whereby his creditors shall or may be defeated or delayed', courts have struggled through numerous cases to define the necessary mental element on the debtor's part in making such an undue preference, drawing on parallel equitable doctrines of fraud in a search for principle. A jurisprudence developed exempting involuntary payments on the part of the debtor from the sweep of preference controls, together with a defence of bona fide purchase on the part of the favoured creditor. As a corollary, payments in the 'ordinary course of business' or in the ordinary maintenance of family were not 'voluntary' preferences and did not compromise the good faith of the assignee; and in reverse extraordinary transactions by a near-insolvent trader or company would fix the transferee with notice and impugn the transaction. Legislation in jurisdictions including the USA and Australia later hardened the uncodified position and made it a stipulation that a transaction for value in the run up to insolvency must be in the 'ordinary

[48] 50 Edw 3, c 6; 2 Ric 2, st 2 c 3.

[49] For exhaustive history of the older law see W Roberts, *A Treatise on the Construction of the Statutes 13 Eliz c.5. and 27 Eliz. c.4. relating to Voluntary and Fraudulent Conveyances, and on the nature and force of different considerations to support deeds and other legal instruments, on the Courts of Law and Equity* (London, Butterworth, 1800); S Worthington, *May on Fraudulent Conveyances*, 2nd edn (London, Stevens and Haynes, 1887). A fresh view of eighteenth century developments is found in E Kadens, 'The Last Bankrupt Hanged: Balancing Incentives in the Development of Bankruptcy Law' (2010) 59 *Duke Law Journal* 1229, and of nineteenth century developments in Lobban, 'Bankruptcy and Insolvency', (n 2).

course of business', thus converting a form of evidence tending to negate intention to voluntarily prefer into a substitute test.[50]

The judges in interpreting and applying these statutes seemed to regard them as re-enactments of a much older inherent curial jurisdiction to regulate insolvencies; but the statutes could in turn provoke new departures. In the 1749 case of *Ryall v Rolle* it was held that the reputed ownership doctrine could apply beyond corporeal choses in possession and embraced fractional and incorporeal interests left in a debtor's control,[51] and moreover that the bona fides of a purchaser who had left a vendor in possession after the sale did not bar the claim. Another important curial augmentation, mentioned earlier, came with Lord Mansfield from the late 1760s, who developed the doctrine that conveyances that had the purpose of disturbing the ordained statutory scheme of *pari passu* distribution could be avoided as an undue preference, even if the transaction was supported by consideration and even if made precedent to an act of bankruptcy. Whether this extension of preference recapture used the same concepts of *mens rea* as in a direct statutory fraudulent preference was contested; some judges used a presumptive fraud analysis, others a strict liability approach based on the effect of the transaction. Lord Mansfield's concept of presumptive fraud based on the equity of the statute was then reflexively codified in legislation separate from the original Elizabethan legislative root-stock.[52] The requisite mind state triggering avoidance under this statutory jurisdiction was especially contested; for many judges the *actus reus* was enough to presume a *mens rea*, but the search for a *mens rea* element seemed to intensify and converge with the older dishonesty requirements, when the making of such a voidable preference came to be classified itself as an independent act of bankruptcy triggering statutory assignment to an official trustee in bankruptcy.[53]

[50] *Taylor v White* (1964) 110 CLR 129 (HCA); *Harkness v Partnership Pacific Ltd* (1997) 41 NSWLR 204 (NSWCA). For comparison of the statutory 'ordinary course' tests see G McCormack, 'Swelling Corporate Assets: Changing what is on the menu' (2006) 6 *Journal of Corporate Law Studies* 39; A Keay, 'The Avoidance of Pre-Liquidation Transactions: An Anglo-Australian Comparison' [1998] *Journal of Business Law* 515.

[51] *Ryall v Rolle (Rowles)* (1749) 1 Atk 165, 26 ER 107; Ves Sen 165, 28 ER 490 (Lord Hardwicke LC); see J Getzler and M Macnair, 'The Firm as an Entity before the Companies Acts', in P Brand, K Costello and WN Osborough (eds), *Adventures of the Law* (Dublin, Four Courts Press, 2005) 267, 275–76; also available at http://ssrn.com/abstract=941231 accessed 17 June 2011.

[52] The passage of the English bankruptcy laws was tortuous, as Lobban (n 2), has shown. For our purposes the key legislation begins with the English Bankruptcy Act 1824 ss 3, 8, 108, 122, and culminates in the Bankruptcy Act 1861 s 70 and the Bankruptcy Act 1883 ss 4(1), 29, 47–49 (reproduced and enlarged in New South Wales by the Bankruptcy Act 1861 (NSW) ss 1–2 and the Bankruptcy Act 1887 (NSW) ss 4, 51, 54–56).

[53] The history of distributions and preferences counting as acts of bankruptcy under nineteenth century statutes was traced in *Williams v Official Assignee of the Estate of William Dunn* (1908) 6 CLR 425 (HCA) 432–42 by Griffith CJ; and the history of judicial interpretation from the time of Lord Mansfield was laid out by Kitto J in *Taylor v White* (1964) 110 CLR 129 (HCA) 142–46. Twentieth century developments were analysed in *Robert Reid Pty Ltd v Cassidy* (1966) 114 CLR 558 (HCA), with Taylor J and Windeyer J taking an expansive view embracing all transfers of value, but Kitto J leading the majority to exclude payments of debt or liquidated sums, counting only deliberate conveyances

V. Curial Extensions of the Statutory Preference Scheme

The long history of interaction between statute, law and equity in the field of insolvency has often been noted by the courts, and stands as a rebuttal of the once-fashionable view that statute law and judge-made law inhabit separate spheres and cannot influence each other. This intense interaction was demonstrated in two cases in the Federal Court of Australia in the early 1990s, reviewing English, Australian and American principles relating to 'preference recapture'. The *Garuda* case dealt with avoidance of transfers made with intent to defraud creditors,[54] for example where a preferential payment harms the recovery chances of a present or anticipated creditor, and fixed on a broad test of *mens rea* including natural inferences from conduct. The *Compass Airlines* case focussed on near-bankruptcy dispositions that have the effect of disrupting the statutory scheme of *pari passu* distribution,[55] independent of party intentions. The Federal Court in *Compass Airlines* relied on a scholarly 1936 judgment of Jordan CJ to drive home the symbiotic relationship between statutory and judicial rules in this area, with the legislature and the courts extending and innovating in the law in a complex to-and-fro relationship:

> In *Page v Commonwealth Life Assurance Society Ltd*,[56] Jordan CJ said that the policy of the bankruptcy law has always been regarded as a useful guide in determining the operation and limitations of the letter of the law. His Honour gave two instances, (i) proceedings which, although within the letter of the law, had been regarded as obnoxious to the policy of the bankruptcy law, and therefore, avoided by it,[57] and (ii) limitations upon the application of the letter of the law which have been extracted from its 'general policy'. Although Jordan CJ did not advert to them, the decisions of Lord Mansfield from which the law of preferences developed illustrate proposition (i). The 'running account' doctrine may perhaps be seen as an illustration of proposition (ii).[58]

In the case of *Page v Commonwealth Life Assurance*, Jordan CJ investigated the insolvency statutes and decisions since the Statute of Elizabeth, and concluded that by analogy with the survival of contractual claims to be proved in an estate, it was possible for a plaintiff to proceed with a tort claim against the assignee in insolvency of a company alleged to have committed the tort of malicious prosecution prior to the insolvency. The fact that the tort claim was unliquidated and

and charges of property. See also *Re Gunsbourg* (1920) 2 KB 426 (CA) on how relation back of the trusteeship on bankruptcy affects a preference which is itself the act of bankruptcy.

54 *Re PT Garuda Indonesia Limited v Richard John Grellman* (1992) 107 ALR 199 (FCA).

55 *Compass Airlines* (n 43).

56 *Page v Commonwealth Life Assurance Society Ltd* (1935–36) 36 SR (NSW) 85 (NSWSC) 89.

57 Citing *Higinbotham* (n 3); *Re Johns* [1928] 1 Ch 737 (ChD).

58 *Compass Airlines* (n 43) [73]. The imbrication of statute and equity is also strongly evidenced in *Nelson v Nelson* (1995) 184 CLR 538 (HCA).

judgment was uncertain at the time of insolvency did not mean that the right in action was discharged by the insolvency, and the plaintiff could attempt to prove the claim against the insolvent pool of assets, notwithstanding contrary nineteenth century decisions. Jordan CJ thus demonstrated how the statutory insolvency principles giving discharge were subject to curial extension.

The work of the courts in extending insolvency principles in the common law system also calls into question the orthodoxy that English insolvency law (and by descent that of Australian law) is party-designed, with the agencies of the law used simply to guide and police the ex ante and ex post negotiations. This position is contrasted with the Continental (and perhaps American) approach to insolvency which supposedly is more inclined to use the power of the state coercively to reorder property and contract rights outside party wills.[59] The over-riding of party wills through preference recapture in the common law systems would seem to blur this distinction; the question resolves to *which* party-designed rights will the law allow to stand in an insolvency?

VI. 'Intent to Defraud' and Equitable Fraud—The *Mens Rea* Problem

We must next look more closely at a central question in application of the insolvency doctrines derived from the Statute of Elizabeth; that is, the requisite mind state for finding a preference. One way to conceive this is by comparison with breach of trust. A trustee makes an undertaking to hold an asset for a beneficiary and is subject to an equitable liability that enforces this undertaking by requiring a substitutive payment if an *ultra vires* payment away occurs. A debtor makes an undertaking to repay a loan, and is likewise subject to a liability enforcing that duty, but is free to treat the loan value as his own and need only find a replacement value; unlike a trustee he is *expected* to use the loan value for his own benefit, and will generally not be hemmed in by certain stipulated types of usage. However if the debtor takes action, paying away assets expressly so to prevent a particular creditor having normal recourse against his estate, then this is seen as a species of fraud. In breach of trust cases it has been stated by high authority that no dishonest intent need be found on the part of the trustee to find breach of trust;[60] but this may be a modernising departure from an older equitable approach which

[59] J Sgard, 'Bankruptcy Law, Majority Rule, and Private Ordering in England and France (16th–19th centuries)' (working version at International Society for New Institutional Economics, June 2009, available at http://extranet.isnie.org/uploads/isnie2009/jerome.pdf accessed 17 June 2011); J Sgard, 'Do Legal Origins Matter? The Case of Bankruptcy Laws in Europe 1808–1914' (2006) 10 *European Review of Economic History* 389. The variance between parties' ex ante desire for controlled distribution and ex post desire to grab and run at the expense of overall value is set out in T Jackson, *The Logic and Limits of Bankruptcy Law* (Cambridge, Massachusetts, Harvard University Press, 1986) 7–67.

[60] See, eg *Royal Brunei Airlines v Tan* [1995] 2 AC 378 (PC) 384–85 (Lord Nicholls).

saw wrongful handling of assets or incorrect exercise of powers as themselves a species of fraud; an entrusted person did the wrong thing when he or she *ought* to have known better. It is in a like tradition that a 'fraudulent' intent on the part of the debtor is the gist of the preferences jurisdiction; there may be no malicious intent to do the creditors out of their rights, but debtors ought to know it is wrong voluntarily to transfer away assets when they have an inkling that they cannot pay their debts. The analogy with the breach of trust doctrines of dishonest assistance and knowing receipt grows stronger when one regards the position of the third party assignee of a preference; here bona fide receipt for value will protect the transaction from impeachment, but knowledge of the debtor's fraudulent transaction will lead to the preference being voided. As in trust law, so in preference law presumptions are used to find a culpable mind state of the transacting parties, whether debtor or assignee, and the relevant tests hover between subjective and objective poles, or real versus presumptive fraud.

At the objective end of the spectrum in presuming a fraudulent preferential intent lies the decision of Lord Hatherley LC in *Freeman v Pope* in 1870, a case concerning a voluntary settlement of a clergyman's life policy on a third party when the settlor was already in financial distress. Lord Hatherley began with the famous statement: 'The principle on which the statute of 13 Eliz 1, c 5 proceeds is this, that persons must be just before they are generous, and that debts must be paid before gifts can be made'.[61] He continued:

> [I]n the absence of … direct proof of intention, if a person owing debts makes a settlement which subtracts from the property which is the proper fund for the payment of those debts, an amount without which the debts cannot be paid, then, since it is the necessary consequence of the settlement (supposing it effectual) that some creditors must remain unpaid, it would be the duty of the Judge to direct the jury that they must infer the intent of the settlor to have been to defeat or delay his creditors, and that the case is within the statute.[62]

At the other subjectivist end we have the approach of Lord Esher MR in *Re Wise* in 1886:

> It must be recollected that the statute of Elizabeth applies, and may make a deed void, even though the grantor never becomes a bankrupt. But this case was at first argued not upon that footing, but upon the assumption that, if the natural or necessary effect of what the settlor did was to defeat or delay his creditors, the court must find that he actually had that intent. That proposition or doctrine I entirely abjure.[63]

Australian courts have tended to the first view, with the High Court and Federal Court recently approving the inferential approach of *Freeman v Pope*;[64] but in

[61] *Freeman* (n 4) 540.

[62] Ibid 541.

[63] *Re Wise* (1886) LR 17 QBD 290 (CA) 299. See further G Moffat, *Trusts Law*, 4th edn (Cambridge, Cambridge University Press, 2005) 278–87.

[64] *Marcolongo v Chen* [2011] HCA 3, (2011) 85 ALJR 380; *G and M Aldridge Pty Ltd v Walsh* [2001] HCA 27, (2001) 203 CLR 662 [29]–[30]; *Cannane v J Cannane Pty Ltd (in liq)* [1998] HCA 26, (1998)

earlier cases the High Court could tilt to the second, stricter view. In a 1934 case concerning a fraudulent preference aiming to defeat creditors, Starke J held that '[f]raud ... is not to be presumed: the burden of proof is upon those who impeach the disposition',[65] and Dixon J held that:

> [a] real intent to defeat or delay creditors must exist, and the question always is whether, upon all the circumstances of the transaction, the transfer or other disposition was in fact made with that intent. The burden of proof is upon those alleging that it was so made.[66]

The debate has turned on the classical equitable question of the degree to which a *mens rea* may be inferred from circumstances, and whether 'fraud' connotes a falling below a due prudential standard of common honesty or connotes something worse involving personal viciousness. When bankruptcy earlier had connotations of criminal dishonesty (with incarceration for unpaid debts being supplemented by more extreme sanctions including mutilation and even execution in the seventeenth and eighteenth centuries)[67] it was natural that a stronger proof of subjective intent to a criminal justice standard should be sought. Like requirements pertain today in areas such as corporate directors' personal liability for continuing to trade when insolvent, where super-added criminal liability is on the menu of sanctions: here 'the intent to defraud creditors must be express or actual and real: nothing constructive imputed or implied will do'.[68] But where the core sanction is simply avoidance of a bad transaction, which after all is a core remedy of civil equity jurisdiction, the *mens rea* may not be so demanding.

After lengthy debates weighing the rival formulations, the Federal Court and the High Court have now decided that the modern test for inferring a fraudulent preference was the contextual approach set out by Lord Hatherley in *Freeman v Pope*.[69] But the courts have also acknowledged that there cannot be one uniform test for all preferences across the gamut of bankruptcy and insolvency. It is worth noting here some of the complex effects of federalism on Australian law in this area.[70] The Constitution s 51 (xvii), together with s 109, allows the Commonwealth to legislate in the field of bankruptcy and insolvency so as to occupy the field. The Commonwealth's bankruptcy legislation until 1996 reproduced the old English formula of 'intent to defraud' etc,[71] but after 1996 was amended to revolve around a debtor's 'main purpose' being to defeat creditors' rights under a statutory distribution. In any case the legislation could only operate if there was an actual

192 CLR 557 [12] (Brennan CJ and McHugh J); *Compass Airlines* (n 43); *Garuda* (n 54); *Noakes v Harvy Holmes* (1979) 26 ALR 297 (FCA) 303 (Brennan J).

[65] *Williams v Lloyd* (1934) 50 CLR 341 (HCA) 361.

[66] Ibid 372.

[67] E Kadens, 'The Last Bankrupt Hanged: Balancing Incentives in the Development of Bankruptcy Law' (2010) 59 *Duke Law Journal* 1229.

[68] *Hardie v Hanson* (1960) 105 CLR 451 (HCA) 458 (Dixon CJ).

[69] See cases cited in n 64.

[70] See, eg *Gould v Brown* (1998) 193 CLR 346 (HCA).

[71] Bankruptcy Act 1966, s 121.

bankruptcy, so bringing Commonwealth powers into play. It appears that once bankruptcy occurs, State laws must give way to the Commonwealth bankruptcy scheme; but State laws can govern near-bankruptcy situations where a conveyance prejudices a creditor's interests prior to a bankruptcy.[72] To further complicate matters, States also provided rules for corporate insolvency by reference to the Commonwealth bankruptcy rules for natural persons; but these State insolvency jurisdictions have now been replaced by the Corporations Act 2001 (Cth), passed by the Commonwealth after a referral of power by the States.

In the recent case of *Marcolongo v Chen*,[73] the older statutory concept of 'intent to defraud' was interpreted differently by the New South Wales Court of Appeal and the High Court. The facts of the case were that during a litigation over damage to land the plaintiff gave notice of a property preservation order over other lands owned by the alleged tortfeasor, so as to ensure there were assets available to satisfy any judgment. The owner nonetheless sold the land for value to a third party. On winning the tort action the plaintiff could not satisfy the judgment debt against the owner's remaining assets, and so sought to reverse the land transfer to the third party under section 37A of the Conveyancing Act 1919 (NSW), which states that 'every alienation of property, made … with intent to defraud creditors, shall be voidable at the instance of any person thereby prejudiced', unless the purchaser acquired in good faith and without notice of such intent to defraud. The plaintiff succeeded at trial on the basis that the owner's motives in transferring the land ahead of the judgment satisfied the legislative test. In the Court of Appeal Allsop P and Young JA each investigated the various formulae for preferential intent arising from the tangled State and Commonwealth statutes, and found that the judicial interpretations of the necessary intention in one legislative context might not map onto another legislative context. In particular, the Commonwealth jurisdiction to police assignments subverting the post-bankruptcy distribution (ie that jurisdiction descended from Lord Mansfield's extension of Elizabethan preference law) might allow an easier inference of intention than the state law's concern with pre-bankruptcy subversion of creditor rights, derived directly from the Statute of Elizabeth, where a stronger intention amounting to dishonesty might have to be proved to a standard beyond inference from the natural effect of conduct. By this move the Court of Appeal revived and adopted the tougher Dixonian test for state bankruptcy laws based on the Statute of Elizabeth, though there are interesting questions of *stare decisis* at work here. *Noakes* in the Federal Court,[74] which formed the basis for the doctrine of inferred intentionality in *Garuda*[75] and *Cannane*,[76] at least dealt with a law of similar provenance to the New South Wales preference law, being the Norfolk Island version of the good old

[72] See further W Lee, 'Trusts and Bankruptcy' (1973) 47 *Australian Law Journal* 365, 365–67.
[73] *Marcolongo* (n 64), reversing *Chen v Marcolongo* [2009] NSWCA 326.
[74] *Noakes* (n 64).
[75] *Garuda* (n 54).
[76] *Cannane* (n 64).

1571 Act. But the later Federal Court and High Court decisions in *Garuda* and *Cannane* did concern the operation of preferences in defiance of the statutory bankruptcy scheme, not those prejudicial to particular creditors. The 'Mansfield' form of preference recapture has connotations of a public law or police action, the 'Statute of Elizabeth' form a breach of a duty to private persons.[77] The Court of Appeal in *Marcolongo* allowed the appeal, finding no preference in the absence of a directly proven subjective motive to defraud creditors; but this decision was vulnerable for relying on the wrong stream of preference authority in stating the subjective *mens rea* test.

On further appeal the High Court restored the trial result in *Marcolongo*, and swung the test of intentionality back to one of objective inference from conduct. The plurality accepted that fraud in common law and equity had multiple shades of meaning, betokening any falling down in prescribed standards of conduct including wrongful exercise of powers; much depended on the context of the inquiry. In the context of the anti-preference jurisdiction the basic notion of an 'intention to defraud' had also attracted multiple meanings, depending in many cases on the precise statutory wording. Nonetheless the majority found that according to the main trend of judicial interpretation of the legislation, 'the term "defraud" was designed to reproduce the meaning of the expression "delay, hinder or defraud" in the Elizabethan Statute',[78] and moreover that as a question of policy the modern legislative provisions 'should receive a liberal construction in effecting their purpose of suppressing fraud'.[79] Authority for this liberal approach came from a Privy Council appeal[80] from a New South Wales case that in turn had adopted Kindersley V-C's statement in *Thompson v Webster* that in testing for intent to defraud, 'the Court is to decide in each particular case whether, on all the circumstances, it can come to the conclusion that the *intention* of the settlor, in making the settlement, was to defeat, hinder or delay his creditors'.[81] The High Court plurality also favoured Kindersley V-C's view that something more than a voluntary conveyance was necessary, but also that the necessary intent could be found from the circumstances of a pre-insolvency transaction. The onus of proof lay on the party seeking to avoid that transaction, but they did not, as the Court of Appeal supposed, have to show an active dishonesty or deceit, in the sense of an 'actual and real intention' to defraud or cause harm or loss to the creditor. It was enough if, by an ordinary process of civil proof, the court could find an intention on the part of the transferor to hinder, delay or defeat creditors, even if no active thought of harming the creditor was present; this was the very type of objective dishonesty that equity characteristically suppressed in its fraud jurisdiction, and

[77] See the comments on fraudulent preference as a 'breach of duty' engaging limitation statutes in *Giles v Rhind* [2008] EWCA Civ 118, [2008] 3 WLR 1233 [36]–[55] (Arden LJ).

[78] *Marcolongo* (n 64) [19].

[79] Ibid [20].

[80] *Godfrey v Poole* (1888) 13 App Cas 497 (PC) 503.

[81] *Thompson v Webster* (1859) 4 Drewry 628, 632; 62 ER 241, 242 (emphasis in original).

was familiar enough from areas such as dishonest assistance. The Court's prior decision in *Farah Constructions Pty Ltd v Say-Dee Pty Ltd* made this very point:

> As a matter of ordinary understanding, and as reflected in the criminal law in Australia…, a person may have acted dishonestly, judged by the standards of ordinary, decent people, without appreciating that the act in question was dishonest by those standards.[82]

The earlier authority of *Cannane* then had to be quarantined, where Brennan CJ and McHugh J had spoken of 'the onus of proving an actual intent'. The *Marcolongo* plurality seemed to think that the application of this test involved a distinction between implied intent in fact and constructive intent as a legal implication, commenting that in *Cannane* 'their Honours were adding the word "actual" as a periphrasis to emphasise that, while the existence of the intent might be inferred from the evidence, it was to be found as a fact'.[83]

Moreover the intent only had to be operative, not dominant: the statute 'does not require for its operation that the proscribed intent to defraud be the sole intent'.[84] The *Marcolongo* plurality's approach therefore leads to these conclusions: the intent to delay, hinder etc through a transfer is to be found, circumstantially if necessary, as a question of fact; it must be an operative but not necessarily a sole or predominant intention; it is to be proved by the claimant seeking to void the transaction; but the characterisation of the transferor's intent as fraud triggering the statutory jurisdiction is determined via an objective test. This shifted the law away from the Court of Appeal's subjectivist test and ensured a favourable result for the plaintiff. On the facts of the case, both transferor and transferee obviously knew of the pending tort claim and expedited the land transfer to defeat it, and so the statutory tests were amply met. This also meant that the proviso defence of bona fide purchase was inapplicable since there was notice. Heydon J in a separate judgment agreed that the appeal should be allowed, but did not need to refine the statutory test since on the facts it 'was as "actual" and "dishonest" an intent as it is possible to have'.[85] At any rate, the plurality result in *Marcolongo* gives a clear enough restatement of the relevant test, which is to pull the statutory pre-insolvency preference scheme into alignment with equity's mixed objective-subjective understandings of fraud, and there for now the law of Australia rests.

We cannot be entirely sure that the mixed objective-subjective preference test will always apply, however, since legislative variations will continue to bedevil the system. An added complexity in the Australian federal context arises from a third raft of legislation dealing with a special case, namely where a debtor contemplates bankruptcy or is within a short time period of bankruptcy. Here a different legislative test has been applied, namely whether the *effect* of the conveyance would be to give one creditor a preference over other creditors. A colonial version of this provision from New South Wales was interpreted by the Privy Council in 1861

[82] *Farah Constructions Pty Ltd v Say-Dee Pty Ltd* [2007] HCA 22, (2007) 230 CLR 89 [173].
[83] *Marcolongo* (n 64) [34].
[84] Ibid [57].
[85] Ibid [87].

to require nonetheless a fraudulent intention to prefer,[86] drawing on subjectivist streams of past preference case law; but the High Court of Australia, interpreting a similar provision of the Federal Bankruptcy Act in 1933, produced a strict liability interpretation. After referring to the subjectivist views of the Privy Council and other courts, Starke J stated:

> Whatever assistance, however, we may derive from these decisions upon other Acts, the decision of this Court in the present case depends upon the true construction of the *Federal Bankruptcy Act 1924–1930*. Now that Act says nothing about the view or intention of the debtor nor about any choice or selection by him. It simply declares that a conveyance, transfer or assignment, made within a certain time before bankruptcy, having the effect of giving the creditor a preference, shall be void. It looks to the effect of the transaction and not to the intent, or state of mind, of the debtor.[87]

Rich and Dixon JJ ruled that despite the similarity of the old New South Wales legislative language decided by the Privy Council in 1861, the very different context of the federal legislation meant that its view of the words' meaning was irrelevant.[88]

VII. *Actus Reus*, Voluntarism and Mixed Motives in Assessing Preferences

A further key idea in the courts' exegesis of preference law is that a conveyance can only amount to a fraudulent preference if entirely voluntary on the part of the debtor, on the basis that to 'prefer' another person must involve an elective intention directly to favour or advance the interests of that person by some freely chosen path. Hence a debtor cannot be said to prefer a creditor in a fraudulent manner, to choose to advance the one creditor at the expense of other creditors, if the debtor's mind was driven by an entirely different motive when making the disposition. So for example any trace of coercion including threat of litigation by a creditor, or even a request for payment implying disturbances to supplies if not met, might exclude the operation of the preference doctrine. This proviso is notably vague, and so has given great discretion to the courts in protecting creditor–debtor transactions which divorced from intentions nonetheless do have the effect of advantaging one creditor at others' expense. It adds yet another complication to the search for an intention triggering preference recapture.

Where there is an assignment of future property it would seem that the correct moment to assess the intentionality and voluntarism of the debtor would be at the time of the entering into the contract, as that would be the moment when the

[86] *Bank of Australasia v Harris* (1861) 15 Moo PCC 97, 15 ER 429 (PC) (Knight Bruce LJ).
[87] *S Richards & Co Ltd v Lloyd* (1933) 49 CLR 49 (HCA) 62.
[88] Ibid 59–60.

assignee is vested with the 'higher right' automatically to receive the assets when acquired. No further assurance of the property is later required once that property falls in; the property automatically 'feeds the equity', and the voluntary state of the assignor is irrelevant.[89] If there is still a lingering question whether the consideration moving from the assignee has to be executed fully before that higher right is perfected, then it may be that intention has to be tested up to the moment of perfection by payment of the entire consideration. Formalities rules for the shifting of equitable interests through assignments for value do not give a clear answer to the question when the constructive trust vehicle effecting a disposition of the beneficial interest is constituted, and so do no more than suggest some useful analogies.[90]

A detailed discussion of the correct test for voluntarism of preference arose in the 1909 High Court case of *Muntz v Smail.*[91] The case is interesting at a number of levels: Griffith CJ, Barton and O'Connor JJ each gave judgments looking at direct intention rather than motive as the key test for voluntary preference, whilst Isaacs J vehemently argued for a motive test admitting a much greater range of pressures as factors that might protect a conveyance from avoidance for fraud. The policy choices expressed in these judgments are subtle; Isaacs J on the one hand uses subjective tests and embraces extrinsic materials such as the bargaining power of the parties in order to deny the autonomy of their choices, but does so in order to protect their constrained choices from triggering redistribution through preference recapture, and hence in a sense is protecting party autonomy from control by the state. By contrast, in the 1920 case of *Commissioner of Stamp Duties (Qld) v Jolliffe*,[92] Isaacs J in a powerful dissent pushed hard for a strictly objective test of trust constitution, refusing to admit evidence of subjective motive, and so exposing the trust holder of an illegal bank account to extensive fiscal imposts. Perhaps the facts of *Muntz* explain why Isaacs J inconsistently chose a subjective approach on the preference front. A cattle dealer, Eyles, relied on external credit to finance his buying and selling of stock, and fell into payment difficulties. He owed Smail money he could not repay on a promissory note shortly due; Muntz was another creditor. Eyles was preparing to declare bankruptcy when a buyer presented by Smail offered him a price on his stock sufficient to retire the debt to Smail. Eyles was worried that to accept the sale would be unfair to the other creditors, but Smail indicated that he would pay a good price to ease Eyles' indebtedness and at the moment of decision told Eyles 'that I expected him to carry out his contract

[89] *Crofts v Middleton* (1855) 2 Kay & J 194, 203; 69 ER 749, 753; *Eyre v Burmester* (1862) 10 HLC 90, 11 ER 959 (HL).

[90] See the discussion of *Oughtred v IRC* [1960] AC 206 (HL) and *Neville v Wilson* [1997] Ch 144 (CA) in Meagher, Heydon and Leeming, *Meagher, Gummow and Lehane* (n 16) paras [7–155]–[7–195].

[91] *Muntz v Smail* (1909) 8 CLR 262 (HCA).

[92] *Commissioner of Stamp Duties (Qld) v Jolliffe* (1920) 28 CLR 178 (HCA). The majority decision favouring a subjectivist view of intention to constitute a trust was possibly confined in *Kauter v Hilton* (1953) 90 CLR 86 (HCA) 97; *Associated Alloys* (n 9) [27]–[42]; and probably overruled in *Byrnes v Kendle* [2011] HCA 26, especially at [65] (Gummow and Hayne JJ) and [116] (Heydon and Crennan JJ).

with me'. Eyles acceded, instructing his agent to sell and make the proceeds over to Smail. Muntz later sued to avoid the sale as a preference. The court acknowledged that on the evidence Eyles was striving to do the right thing for his creditors, but the majority found that he had acted 'with a view of' creating a preference of one creditor over other creditors, no matter his bona fides, and so triggered a statutory avoidance and recapture. Griffith CJ cited Jessel MR's statement in *Ex parte Griffith; In re Wilcoxon that* 'that the mind of the debtor was influenced not by the demand of the creditor for a preference, but by his desire to accede to the demand and to give him a preference'.[93] He then gave a careful distinction between intention and motive, drawing on the leading nineteenth century English authorities.[94] He concluded:

> These cases establish that the question to be determined, so far as it depends on the state of mind of the debtor, is: What was the substantial object which he desired to achieve by the act alleged to be a preference? The words 'intention,' 'view,' 'object,' 'motive,' 'purpose,' have all been used by learned Judges in different cases, sometimes as if they were synonymous, and confusion has arisen from not distinguishing between an intention and the motive which induces that intention. But I think that the phrase 'substantial object which he desired to achieve' expresses what was meant by all of them.
>
> In the case of *Sharp v Jackson*[95] the disposition attacked was the conveyance of an estate to make good a breach of trust which had been committed by the debtor, and the Court held, on the evidence, that the question of preferring the beneficiaries was not substantially present to his mind at all. It is a matter of daily experience that men often do acts desiring to achieve a particular object, and incidentally achieve a result quite different from that which was contemplated. It is quite possible for a man to be impelled to do an act that results in a preference to a creditor by a desire to achieve a quite different result. The fact may be difficult of proof, but if it is established he cannot be said to have acted with the view to prefer. In my opinion it is essential to bear in mind the distinction between the motive or reason which induces a man to desire to achieve a particular object and the desire itself. The object desired is alone relevant for the present purpose.[96]

Griffith CJ then addressed a clever argument of Hayden Starke, counsel acting for Smail, to the effect that Eyles had not sold his stock to Smail but had made an assignment of the content of any future fund that might accrue from a sale, and that following Parke J's judgment in *Hunt v Mortimer*,[97] such an assignment of a futurity fell out of the definition of a fraudulent preference. Griffith CJ held that what Eyles had agreed to was a sale with a collateral agreement to pay the proceeds through an intermediary, and there was no evidence that 'the idea of assigning the future purchase money itself was present to the mind of either party'; hence *Hunt v Mortimer* could not apply. In any case any such putative assignment of a

93 *Ex parte Griffith; In re Wilcoxon* (1883) 23 Ch D 69 (CA) 72.
94 *Muntz* (n 91) 271–76.
95 *Sharp v Jackson* [1899] AC 419 (HL).
96 *Muntz* (n 91) 273–74.
97 *Hunt v Mortimer* (1829) 10 Barn & Cress 44, 109 ER 367.

book debt would have failed for want of registration (an objection explored more thoroughly in Barton J's judgment). However, Griffith CJ did not reject outright Starke's theory that an assignment of a future interest inherently could not be a preference.

Perhaps Griffith CJ in *Muntz* did not quite explain the full significance of Parke J's decision on assignment in *Hunt v Mortimer*. The decision was issued in 1829, 33 years before *Holroyd v Marshall*. Note also that this was one of Parke's early judgments as a new justice of King's Bench, before he went on to the Exchequer and then the House of Lords as Wensleydale. In *Hunt v Mortimer* an insolvent trader had borrowed in order to fill a large order from the East India Company, taking the money from a creditor who knew him to be insolvent or nearly so, and agreeing that he would transfer back to the creditor the proceeds of the future sales to the Company in order to acquit the debt. Parke J stated that the assignment of future profit was safe from preference recapture because the credit injection, being given in return for an assignment of the profits from its use in trade, had never joined the debtor's general assets:

> There is no pretence for calling this a fraudulent preference. The money was not lent by the defendants on the general credit of the bankrupts, but on the faith of the monies which were to be received from the East India Company; and the arrangement between the bankrupt and the defendant had the effect of an equitable assignment of that particular fund, to which the plaintiffs (who as assignees are entitled only to such effects as the bankrupt had both legally and equitably) have no claim. In this case, it is true, there was no notice of the arrangement to the East India Company; but notice is not necessary in such cases to give an effect to an equitable assignment between the parties, though it is so for the purpose of preventing the title of assignees attaching, on the ground of the bankrupt being the apparent owner of that fund at the time of the act of bankruptcy, within the meaning of that clause of the late Bankrupt Act, founded on the repealed Statute of the 21 Jac. 1. Here no notice was required, because the monies received from the East India Company were paid over to the defendants long before the act of bankruptcy of both bankrupts. I think therefore that the direction and the verdict were right.[98]

In effect Parke J was here identifying something resembling a *Quistclose* trust, being a secret injection of credit into a distressed debtor with an equity to recover with super-priority against the proceeds should the rescue fail. The reputed ownership doctrine then extant[99] prevented him from a full partitioning of the initial credit fund itself, but he could use the equitable assignment to partition the profit stream from the insolvent estate.

We turn now from the magisterial Griffith CJ in *Muntz* to the mercurial Isaacs J. Now Isaacs J is always interesting whether in dissent or leading the court, most

[98] Ibid 46–47, 368–69.

[99] See, eg *Dearle v Hall* (1823) 3 Russ 1, 20–24; 38 ER 475, 482–84 (Sir Thomas Plumer MR), building on *Ryall* (n 51), in turn building on Elizabethan and Jacobean insolvency statutes: see J Getzler and M Macnair, 'The Firm as an Entity before the Companies Acts' (n 51) 272–76.

particularly, as in *Muntz*, when he is in dissent and writing at the top of his voice. He began his judgment abruptly by kicking away Starke's assignment theory:

> Whether the agreement made between Eyles and Smail constituted an equitable charge which, after insolvency and apart from the order and disposition clause, would have given Smail a right to specific performance, or whether it was merely a personal undertaking to resell through Smail, leaving Smail to collect the purchase money, and alternatively an undertaking to re-sell through another agent approved by Smail, the proceeds being handed to Smail, is, I think, perfectly immaterial on the point of fraudulent preference.[100]

He then assailed the whole tenor of Griffith CJ's analysis, emphasising positive law rather than abstractions concerning mind states:

> The whole matter depends on the construction of a few words in sec. 73 of the *Insolvency Act 1890*, namely, 'with a view of giving such creditor a preference over the other creditors.'
>
> A good deal of argument was addressed to us with respect to the expression 'with a view,' as to whether 'view' meant 'intention' or 'motive,' or some similar word. In my opinion not very much turns on the difference between these words. There is probably a subtle distinction between all of them which may have its value in the field of metaphysics, but for the purpose of fraudulent preference is really immaterial. The phrase 'with a view' was not newly coined for the occasion of the *English Bankruptcy Act 1869*; it was employed by Lord *Mansfield* in the very first of the series of cases in which he laid the foundations of this branch of the law—*Alderson v Temple*[101] (in 1768), and in *Rust v Cooper*[102](1777).[103]

After reviewing the authorities back to Mansfield, Isaacs J concluded:

> It is the will or wish—the *voluntas*—of the debtor to select for preferential treatment one creditor in order to favour him at the expense of the rest—the state of mind of the debtor which causes him to 'prefer' one creditor to another—which is the 'view to give a preference' struck at by the Statute. If the appellant be right—that the mere deliberate payment in full is enough to stamp it as a fraudulent preference—then all the cases as to pressure and mixed motive have been wrongly decided. There is really no escape from this dilemma.[104]

Isaacs J then listed authorities showing that a sense of legal obligation to pay a debt could of itself exclude any finding of a fraudulent preference: 'where the debtor's dominant motive was to fulfil a previous obligation contracted while solvent, or an obligation which he *bona fide* believed to exist, it negatived the supposition of his acting with a view of giving a "preference".'[105] This shows that Isaacs J regarded

[100] *Muntz* (n 91) 291.
[101] *Alderson* (n 2).
[102] *Rust v Cooper* (1777) 2 Cowp 629, 98 ER 1277.
[103] *Muntz* (n 91) 292.
[104] *Muntz* (n 91) 297.
[105] Ibid 302–03.

this particular branch of preference recapture as entirely separate from the cases of near-bankruptcy or evasion of the statutory scheme.

The final element of Isaacs J's dissent concerned the Starke theory of equitable assignment, and here too he was receptive to the debtor's viewpoint:

> If it be necessary to determine whether the agreement amounted to an equitable charge upon the proceeds, I am of opinion it did. The basis of the transaction of Eyles' purchase was that the proceeds of the cattle should be applied in payment of the notes. That necessitated, according to the natural course of things, that the notes should not be dishonoured, and therefore that some time before their due dates the cattle should be resold either through Smail or some other agent approved by him, and the proceeds appropriated in the first instance to discharge the notes. Eyles says 'The proceeds were to go to him.' Without this term of the agreement, the bargain would never have been made, the cattle never bought, and they or their proceeds would not have come into the estate. The sale was not made upon Eyles' general credit (see *Hunt v Mortimer*). It was, in my opinion, an equitable assignment to secure Smail. Being verbal it is not struck by Part VI. of the *Instruments Act 1890*. Applying not to any 'debt' owing by a possible purchaser, but to the proceeds when either in the hands of Eyles or his agent, it was not concerning a 'book debt' within the meaning of the *Book Debts Act 1896*. Consequently it was an assignment which, on the principle of *Alexander v Steinhardt, Walker & Co*,[106] and *Palmer v Culverwell, Brooks & Co*,[107] and other cases of that class gave, as between Smail and Eyles, an equitable security to Smail.[108]

This passage is very hard to credit. In *Hunt* the assignment of sale profits was given in return for new money injected to fund new trading activity, and this was why the assigned proceeds were held to be separate from the general estate. No such analysis could pertain in *Muntz*. And Isaacs J does not bother to explain what magic makes an assignment of future profits fall outside the statutory preference prohibition. The two commercial cases he cited simply affirm that the equity of a forward assignment for value arises at the time of contractual assurance and hence can give priority in a later insolvency; preferences were never at issue in those authorities.

VIII. New Money and Running Accounts in Pre-Insolvency

Later Australian courts clarified the tools to be used where transacting involving new money occurs in the run up to a bankruptcy. The basic idea is that new money, or credit that cycles through the business, of its nature leaves the level of assets at a neutral or even higher level, and so does not extract preferential payments from

[106] *Alexander v Steinhardt, Walker & Co* [1903] 2 KB 208 (KBD).
[107] *Palmer v Culverwell, Brooks & Co* (1902) 85 LT 758.
[108] *Muntz* (n 91) 304–05.

the general estate of the trader.[109] The High Court has exempted from preference recapture one-off transactions that are made not with the intent to reduce overall assets but which maintain or enlarge the asset pool, as demonstrated in the 1959 decision in *Burns v Stapleton*.[110] This case concerned securities over an equity of redemption that were issued by a trader in a near-bankruptcy context. The Court found that the effect of an equitable mortgage given in order to bring fresh stock into the debtor's business for immediate resale had not adversely affected the pool of assets available post-bankruptcy and hence could stand outside preference recapture; but the court did avoid certain other charges issued at the same time by the debtor in an attempt to secure extant unsecured debts; these were clearly preferences reducing the estate in a context where the creditors knew of the debtor's distress and hence could not claim a defence of bona fide receipt. In a twist on this analysis, the High Court has more latterly found that a secured creditor with a right to take the assets of a defaulting company that chooses through a receiver to keep the company as a going concern and continue to pay traders from the insolvent company's capital resources commits no preference, as that secured capital was never available for distribution to the unsecured pool.[111] By a 3:2 decision the High Court has also held that an equitable lien arising on tender of consideration relating to some identified property is immunised from preference recapture; the equity arises outside the will of the parties by operation of law in order to protect the consideration, and by so taking value out of the general estate trumps the preference recapture regime.[112]

The second category of exemption involves the distinctive Australian doctrine of the 'running account', which allows repayments of debt made to level a fluctuating credit account, so as to maintain the mutual exchange of goods and credit within an established and continuous commercial relationship. Again the basis for this exception is that such mutual transfers do not purport to create a preference, and do not in effect diminish the final pool of assets available to the assignee but might instead enlarge that pool or leave it in a neutral state.[113]

Isaacs J had another and better opportunity to explore the workings of future assignments on insolvency some fifteen years after *Muntz*, in the 1924 case of *Carey v Palmer*.[114] This time he had Smail's counsel, now Starke J, alongside him on the bench to help him make the majority. The facts were that Carey provided credit to Johnstone, an importer, for the express purpose of purchasing goods to trade, with the contract providing that Johnstone should sell the goods on without

[109] English authorities supporting this approach are adduced in L Smith, 'Security' in A Burrows (ed), *English Private Law*, 2nd edn (Oxford, Oxford University Press, 2007) paras [5.159]–[5.160]. A theoretical and empirical case for allowing new money credit to attach to collateral ahead of prior creditors is given in S Schwarcz, 'The Easy Case for the Priority of Secured Claims in Bankruptcy' (1997) 47 *Duke Law Journal* 425.

[110] *Burns v Stapleton* (1959) 102 CLR 97 (HCA).

[111] *Sheahan v Carrier Air Conditioning Pty Ltd* (1997) 189 CLR 407 (HCA).

[112] *Hewett* (n 15).

[113] *Compass Airlines* (n 43).

[114] *Carey v Palmer* (1924) 34 CLR 380 (HCA).

delay and pay the sale proceeds directly to Carey's bank account, who would then pay over a profit share and issue fresh credit to the borrower. The importer was facing bankruptcy and made a private composition with Carey transferring to him all his stock in trade and fixtures; the trustee in bankruptcy avoided this transfer as a preference. Carey counterclaimed that the original credit agreement made him assignee of all future stock bought with the loan money, hence he could keep the present stock in trade as outside the preference, because never part of the importer's estate. Knox CJ affirmed his own majority doctrine in *Jolliffe's* case[115] requiring that there be a 'real intention' of the parties to make a charge or trust, which was not evinced in the credit-purchase arrangement, and hence found no equitable assignment. Moreover the fraudulent attempt to transfer the stock pre-bankruptcy strongly suggested that the original agreement was not taken to have created any proprietary rights.[116] Hence according to Knox CJ the transfer was to be avoided as a preference; but in this case his was the minority opinion. Isaacs J in the majority did not refer to his own dissenting judgment in *Jolliffe* but in effect applied his objective test for trust intentions from that case to find an equitable assignment based on the content and context of the credit agreement:

> The dominant purpose of the instrument as evident from its tenor was that Carey should not have to rely on the personal undertaking of Johnstone to repay the money lent as a mere unsecured debt. He was to be entrusted with the money only upon the terms that it should be applied exclusively to purchasing goods for the business, that it should be transformed into goods, and that the goods, once purchased, were to be retransformed 'as soon as possible' by business operations into money and that money should be handed *in specie*, that is, the full actual proceeds, to the appellant, and these should be in the sole control of the appellant for distribution according to agreement.... the official assignee became entitled to the goods, but subject to the trust or interest in favour of Carey.[117]

Starke J agreed with this, adding that according to *Tailby* 'the mode or form of the agreement is absolutely immaterial, provided the intention of the parties is clear'.[118] He added that Bills of Sale legislation did not apply to control of a fund or transfers of money.[119] Both judges agreed that neither the bankruptcy nor the avoided later transfer of stock could undermine the equity created years before by the original agreement. On appeal in the case of *Palmer v Carey*, the Privy Council allowed the appeal, and followed Knox CJ's minority judgment in the High Court.[120] Lord Wrenbury held that a duty to pay sale proceeds from a separate fund had to be imposed unequivocally and in such a manner as to be

115 *Jolliffe* (n 92).

116 *Carey* (n 114) 388–89. In *Williams* (n 65) 368–72, Dixon J similarly used the technique of refusing to find a valid transfer of beneficial interest by perfected declaration of trust in order to stop a purported preference in its tracks.

117 Ibid 389–91.

118 Ibid 392.

119 Ibid 392–93.

120 *Palmer v Carey* [1926] AC 703 (PC).

capable of specific performance; only then would an equitable assignment be found. No discussion of the controversy over *Holroyd* was broached. There was, in fact, a midway point between debt as a personal claim and assignment of value as a chose:

> An agreement for valuable consideration that a fund shall be applied in a particular way may found an injunction to restrain its application in another way. But if there be nothing more, such a stipulation will not amount to an equitable assignment.[121]

On the facts Lord Wrenbury found that under the agreement Johnstone was to take as owner the loan monies, the goods and the sale proceeds, and then be subject to a contractual duty to pay over to the account. The key finding of fact seems to be that no separate fund of the proceeds was intentionally charged; the court looks for something more definite than colloquial language of benefit in order to constitute new equitable rights.[122]

IX. Restraining the Preference Jurisdiction: The 1930s

The law of preferences and assignment in Australia took a sharp turn in direction in the 1930s, perhaps reflecting some of the distress of the time in the credit economy. In *Robertson v Grigg*,[123] a case of 1932, a High Court panel of six, now including Dixon J, were able to push the law in the opposite direction to that outlined in *Palmer v Carey*, one far more favourable to creditor freedom. The facts were that Miles, a road builder, took a £1000 loan in early 1929 from a financier Grigg who agreed to back Miles' attempt to win a major set of contracts by tender from the West Australian Main Roads Board. The loan agreement stipulated that the money was to be used only to fund the road contract performances, with 10 per cent interest to be levied and capital to be paid back 'from repayments to be made from progress payments as the work proceeds and the same are due from Main Roads Board'. A few months later a further £1000 was advanced on similar terms, with an oral agreement to continue with fresh cycles of loans and repayments from the forward contract earnings. Miles then wrote to the Board asking them to send all his contract payments automatically to Grigg and with receipt by Grigg counting as full discharge. When Miles was bankrupted in 1930 the trustee in

[121] Ibid 706, citing Lord Truro in *Rodick v Gandell* (1852) 1 DeG M & G 763, 777; 42 ER 749, 754.

[122] *Palmer v Carey* despite its bare reasoning has proved a useful precedent when judges wish to deny that an equitable interest binding third parties has arisen in relation to a specific fund imprinted with a contractual purpose: see, eg *Swiss Bank Corp* (n 3) 596 (Lord Wilberforce), cf Browne-Wilkinson J at first instance: [1979] Ch 548 (ChD) 566–68. *Re Schebsman (dec'd)* [1944] Ch 83 (CA) 100–07 (du Parcq LJ) is the *locus classicus* of the basal doctrine that benefit does not automatically equate with beneficial interest.

[123] *Robertson v Grigg* (1932) 47 CLR 257 (HCA).

bankruptcy sought to recover the payments to Grigg as passing under an unregistered and therefore void assignments of book debts colliding with the bills of sale acts, or else as void preferences. The Court protected the payments on the basis that, even according to a stringent test for a clear and potent intention to charge future receivables as set out in *Palmer v Carey*, the parties' agreements, written and verbal, showed a sufficient substantive intention to make an assignment of Miles' future contract earnings from their first dealings in early 1929. This was a curious finding in that a later course of conduct was used to help characterise the legal nature of an earlier transaction.[124] The Court then asserted that as a matter of statutory interpretation contract earnings were not to be classified as book debts of a business and so escaped registration requirements. No intentional preference was found as Miles and Grigg were really working together to inject regular finance into Miles' ordinary course of business. Finally there could be no application of the statutory rule catching all estate-reducing payments made within six months of the act of bankruptcy independently of intention, because equitable title to the future road profits had been set up in 1929, the year before the insolvency, and the date of the assignment of future earnings, not accrual of those earnings, was the relevant date of the transfer of value to Grigg. This was a patent case of equitable assignment of future rights creating a non-possessory security that other creditors could not easily discover, and then protecting it from all preference recapture. The precise date of Miles' bankruptcy (9 August 1930) may be significant, arousing the sympathy of the Court for unfortunates caught in the downturn. Whatever the merits, later cases have ratified like financial agreements applying assignments of future rights to shift the benefit of credit flows, and to insulate them from the bankruptcy laws.[125]

These issues were rehearsed again in the 1937 case of *Palette Shoes Pty Ltd (in liq) v Krohn*,[126] which provides the last major case of this study. This was another instance of a credit arrangement, this time for manufacture and sale of shoes. The arrangement was a little more complex than that in *Carey v Palmer* or *Robertson v Grigg*, though the basic form was similar. The credit scheme may be represented on a time line as follows:

1. P makes shoes and sells them, to retailers and other customers (R), on credit for £x.
2. P presents a debit note to K, a financier, for £x less sales tax and a 5.5 per cent credit charge. Call this sum £x – (£t + £c) = £n (where t = tax, c = credit charges, and n = net turnover).
3. K immediately pays £n over to P, who uses the money to cover costs and make some operating profit.
4. R eventually pays P the sum of £x, discharging the P – R credit sale at stage 1.

[124] Cf *Paul v Constance* [1977] 1 WLR 527 (CA).

[125] *Re Ferdinando Antonio Puntoriero and Tonetta Puntorier Ex Parte: Nickpack Pty Limited v Richard Andrew Gagie* [1992] FCA 257.

[126] *Palette Shoes Pty Ltd (in liq) v Krohn* (1937) 58 CLR 1 (HCA).

5. P immediately pays £x over to K.
6. K divides £x up according to the agreed distribution, to pay £t to the state and to retire the debt £n paid over earlier to P; K retains £c as the credit charge or profit on the loan. The credit cycle then starts again to generate £n' and £c' etc.
7. P becomes insolvent owing large debts to other creditors, and with K having invested £n' in P's business. After the insolvency R stands ready to pay £x'. K claims £x' as committed to K under the credit agreement, such that the receivables are made subject to an equitable claim on accrual and so come out of the insolvent estate, P's liquidator claims that £x' should go into the trust for insolvency to be made available to the general creditors.

Latham CJ thought it crucial that P had a duty to pay the whole proceeds of the credit sale (ie £x sums) over to K:

> There was not to be any subsequent adjustment as in *Palmer v Carey*. It is evident that the moneys were to be kept separate from the moneys of the company….in such circumstances, the beneficial interest in the moneys, when received by the company, belonged to the plaintiffs and never to the company and that the company held the moneys in trust for the plaintiffs.[127]

It is not clear why the splitting of profits by Carey and transfer back to Johnstone in the case of *Palmer v Carey* was inconsistent with a trust. But Latham CJ had a second string:

> If, contrary to what I have said, the moneys did become the property of the company upon receipt from the customers, the agreement, being made for consideration, constituted a good equitable assignment of the fund. No particular form is required to constitute an assignment of future personal property. A promise for consideration to assign future property, such property being capable of ascertainment or identification, operates to bind the conscience of the assignor and to bind the property itself from the moment when the contract becomes capable of being performed. The principle that is applied is not a principle depending upon the possibility of a court of equity decreeing specific performance, as had been stated by Lord *Westbury* LC in *Holroyd v Marshall*. The relevant principle is that equity considers as done that which ought to be done. See *Tailby v Official Receiver*, per Lord *Macnaghten*, and the discussion of the question in *In re Lind* … There is no reason why this principle should not be applied to money where it is clear that the money is to be kept separate by the assignee from his own moneys and where it can be identified…. [Whether a trust or an assignment of future value], [i]n neither case is there any assignment of a book debt and Part IX of the Instruments Act is not applicable.[128]

Dixon J analysed rather more carefully the statutory history as to why companies should have to register assignments of book debts in the same manner as traders,

[127] Ibid 14–15 (footnote omitted).
[128] Ibid 16–17 (footnotes omitted).

without corporate exemption. This was important because if K's right to the proceeds of P's sales amounted to an assignment of book debts then K would fail to assert his interest due to want of registration. Dixon J then adopted the *Re Lind* gloss on *Tailby* to describe how assignment of future interests worked, putting the matter in terms of an equity arising because full value has passed from the creditor to bind over the debtor to convey property once vested:

> As the subject to be made over does not exist, the matter primarily rests in contract. Because value has been given on the one side, the conscience of the other party is bound when the subject comes into existence, that is, when, as is generally the case, the legal property vests in him. Because his conscience is bound in respect of a subject of property, equity fastens upon the property itself and makes him a trustee of the legal rights or ownership for the assignee. But, although the matter rests primarily in contract, the prospective right in property which the assignee obtains 'is a higher right than the right to have specific performance of a contract,' and it may survive the assignor's bankruptcy because it attaches without more *eo instanti* when the property arises and gives the assignee an equitable interest therein.[129]

The next question was how to characterise the P-K credit relationship. Agency and trust could be excluded since K never had any right to the shoes nor to the immediate proceeds of their sale. This was why legislative registration requirements pertaining to bills of sale and assignment of book debts did not apply. However elements of these relationships pertained in that P had to keep £x, the sale proceeds, in a separate fund, as if P had an agent or trustee's duty to account. P then had a duty to pay the proceeds in the fund to K who had given valuable consideration for them. By introducing the idea of future proceeds segregated in a fund, with the equitable assignment acting upon the future contents of the fund, Dixon J could justify enforcing their transfer by the agreement as assets outside the company's beneficial estate, and hence outside the insolvency. The question of preference did not overtly arise in this case, but the policy implications of the decision were troubling, as instead of having to defend a preferential effect of payment, the creditor had instead succeeded in winning priority for an unregistered and thus well-nigh undiscoverable assignment of the *value* of book debts. With such a powerful hidden security over future value available to tilt priorities in one's direction, the rival creditors were placed in an inferior position, in breach of the spirit if not the letter of the insolvency laws. *Palette Shoes v Krohn* remains a *locus classicus* of Australian equity, and the case demonstrates how equity can not only enlarge the policy of a statute, or prevent the wrongful use of a statute, but can also undermine a considered statutory policy. Whether this last type of operation of equity can be justified is both a doctrinal and a political question.

[129] Ibid 26–27.

X. Conclusion: New Statute, Old Story?

A new chapter is set to open in the relationship between equity and statute in Australia when the Personal Property Securities Act 2009 (Cth) comes into operation in early 2012. The new legislation promotes the free assignability of debt and is likely to encourage post facto collateralisation and securitisation of future interests. At the core of the new securities regime will be an integrated national system of registration and notice, and a key question will be how assignments of present and future debts will be fitted into that system. If the past is any guide, we can confidently expect that trusts and equitable assignment will add new layers of complexity to the already intricate legislative scheme, just as equity penetrated the Torrens system of land registration almost from its inception. The cycle of interaction between equity and statute in the credit economy, familiar since the time of the Tudors, is set to continue.

5

The Fiduciary 'Self Dealing' Rule

JAMES EDELMAN*

I. Introduction: Fiduciary Duties and Disabilities

The concept of fiduciary duty is surrounded in mystique. The very word 'fiduciary' misleads in this context. Fiduciary bears the meaning of trust and confidence, from the Latin *fiducia*.[1] But trust and confidence are not necessary conditions for the presence of a fiduciary relationship.[2] I have argued elsewhere that we must take the step of recognising that fiduciary duties are simply duties which are expressed or implied into voluntary undertakings.[3] The Supreme Court of Canada has recently taken this step.[4] Without such a rationalisation it is impossible to understand many fiduciary puzzles such as why a contract can 'modify' and 'mould' fiduciary duties;[5] why fiduciary duties can be excluded by agreement (express or implied);[6] why a fiduciary duty which arises in the context of a contractual undertaking, will not usually survive the termination of a

* My thanks to Steven Elliott and Joshua Getzler for lengthy discussion and debate on this issue, and to the participants and organisers of the workshop at which this paper was presented for stimulating suggestions and for a very engaging conference.

[1] J Morwood (ed), *Pocket Oxford Latin Dictionary* (Oxford, Oxford University Press, 2001) 56; *Oxford English Dictionary*, 2nd edn (Oxford, Oxford University Press, 1989) definition 3: 'Of the nature of, proceeding from, or implying trust or reliance'.

[2] R Meagher, D Heydon and M Leeming, *Meagher, Gummow & Lehane's Equity: Doctrine and Remedies*, 4th edn (Chatswood, Butterworths LexisNexis, 2002); *Hospital Products Ltd v United States Surgical Corporation* (1984) 156 CLR 41 (HCA) 69 (Gibbs CJ), 141–42 (Dawson J); *White v Jones* [1995] 2 AC 207 (HL) 271–73 (Lord Browne-Wilkinson); *Breen v Williams* (1996) 186 CLR 71 (HCA) 93 (Dawson and Toohey JJ); F Maitland, *Equity: A Course of Lectures*, rev edn (Cambridge, Cambridge University Press, 1936) 42–43.

[3] J Edelman, 'When do fiduciary duties arise?' (2010) 126 *LQR* 302.

[4] *Galambos v Perez* [2009] SCC 48, [2009] 3 SCR 247.

[5] *Hospital Products* (n 2) 102 (Mason J); *Boardman v Phipps* [1967] 2 AC 46 (HL) 123–25 (Lord Upjohn); *New Zealand Netherlands Society 'Oranje' Inc v Kuys* [1973] 1 WLR 1126 (PC) 1129–30; *Hilton v Barker Booth & Eastwood (a firm)* [2005] UKHL 8, [2005] 1 WLR 567 [30] (Lord Scott).

[6] *Kelly v Cooper* [1993] AC 205 (PC) (implied exclusion); *Citibank NA v QVT Financial LP* [2007] EWCA Civ 11 (express exclusion); cf the doubts expressed in *Premium Real Estate Ltd v Stevens* [2009] NZSC 15, [2009] 2 NZLR 384.

contract.[7] These puzzles can only be explained once fiduciary duties are understood as terms of voluntary undertakings.[8]

One possible criticism of this deconstructionalist thesis of fiduciary duties is that it does not address fiduciary disabilities, and co-relative principal immunities. The two most common disabilities are said to be prohibitions against fiduciary 'self dealing' and the requirement of fiduciary 'fair dealing'. This chapter focuses on the first of these doctrines, self dealing. The thesis is that there is no single self dealing rule and certainly no rule which is peculiar to any fiduciary law.

II. The so-called Self Dealing Rule

The most famous expression of the self dealing and fair dealing rules is that of Megarry V-C in *Tito v Waddell (No 2)*:

> The self-dealing rule is ... that if a trustee sells the trust property to himself, the sale is voidable by any beneficiary ex debito justitiae, however fair the transaction. The fair-dealing rule is ... that if a trustee purchases the beneficial interest of any of his beneficiaries, the transaction is not voidable ex debito justitiae, but can be set aside by the beneficiary unless the trustee can show that he has taken no advantage of his position and has made full disclosure to the beneficiary, and that the transaction is fair and honest.[9]

The same approach is taken in Australia. In *Clay v Clay*, in a joint judgment of the High Court of Australia, the Court said the following:

> The 'fair-dealing rule' provides that a transaction whereby the beneficial interest of a beneficiary is purchased by the trustee is not voidable *ex debito justitiae*, but may be set aside, unless the trustee can show that no advantage has been taken. ... [T]he 'self-dealing rule' is that the sale by the trustee of the trust property to himself is voidable by any beneficiary *ex debito justitiae* ...[10]

These statements represent the orthodoxy in England and Australia in relation to self dealing and fair dealing. But, closely examined, a single doctrine of self dealing is, in fact, an illusion. There are several entirely different situations which are described in the cases as 'self dealing'. They are as follows:

(a) where a trustee, having legal title over an asset, purports to convey title to himself;

(b) where a trustee purports to enter a transaction to sell a trust asset to a nominee of the trustee;

[7] *Attorney General v Blake* [1998] Ch 439 (CA) 453–55; *Bolkiah (Prince Jefri) v KPMG (a firm)* [1999] 2 AC 222 (HL) 235. But survival may occur where this was objectively intended.

[8] J Edelman, 'Four fiduciary puzzles' in E Bant and M Harding (eds), *Exploring Private Law* (Cambridge, Cambridge University Press, 2010) 298.

[9] *Tito v Waddell (No 2)* [1977] Ch 106 (ChD) 241.

[10] *Clay v Clay* [2001] HCA 9, (2002) 202 CLR 410 [51]–[52].

(c) where a trustee purports to enter a transaction which will extinguish or overreach the rights of the beneficiary of the trust;
(d) where a company director purports to sell company assets to himself; and,
(e) where a company director purports to sell company assets to a nominee.

In all of these cases the outcome of the case can be resolved by reference to well established doctrines without resort to a description such as 'self dealing' and without resort to verbal formulae such as whether the transfer is voidable *ex debito justitiae.*

A. Trustee Purports to Convey Title to Himself

This self dealing scenario has deep roots. The orthodoxy quoted above from *Tito v Waddell* and *Clay v Clay* can be traced back as far as Lord King.[11] However, the immediate difficulty in this scenario of a beneficiary having a power to set aside the transaction is that it is a nonsense. There is no *trans*action to set aside. A purchase of property requires two parties. A sale of an asset by a legal owner to himself has no effect on legal relations. Millett LJ succinctly described this as the 'two party rule'.[12]

There are no real exceptions to the two party rule. However, one apparent exception is subsection 72(3) of the Law of Property Act 1925 (UK), which provides that 'After the commencement of this Act a person may convey land to or vest land in himself.'[13] In *Rye v Rye* the question before the House of Lords was whether that subsection permitted two tenants in common of land to grant a lease by parol so that one freeholder could evict the other.[14] At common law *nemo potest esse tenens et dominus*—no-one can be tenant and landlord of the same property. Could subsection 72(3) have altered this principle? If so, it would mean that a smaller estate in land would not merge into a larger estate held by the same person.[15] That person would accept something which is already his own and would owe duties to himself in relation to it.[16] Although Lord MacDermott found the question to be difficult, in the leading speech Viscount Simonds said that his mind recoiled against so 'fanciful and whimsical' a construction of the statute and

[11] See M Conaglen, *Fiduciary Loyalty* (Oxford, Hart Publishing, 2010) 126, citing *Whitackre v Whitackre* (1725) Sel Cas t King 13, 25 ER 195.

[12] *Ingram v Inland Revenue Commissioners* [1997] 4 All ER 395 (CA) 423. See also *The People's Prudential Assurance Co Ltd v The Australian Federal Life and General Assurance Co Ltd* (1935) 35 SR (NSW) 253 (NSWSC) 265; *Clay* (n 10) [51]–[52].

[13] See also the Property Law Act 1969 (WA), s 44; Conveyancing Act 1919 (NSW), s 24; Property Law Act 1952 (NZ), s 49.

[14] *Rye v Rye* [1962] AC 496 (HL).

[15] Cf W Blackstone, *Commentaries on the Laws of England*, 9th edn (London, Strahan and Cadell, 1783) vol II, 177.

[16] As Lord Denning expressed the point in *Rye* (n 14) 514: 'If A grants a tenancy to himself A, can he mutter a notice to quit to himself and expect the law to take any notice of it?'

held that there had been no suggestion in any of the textbooks that the subsection had given birth to such a 'monstrous child'.[17]

There are two possible explanations for section 72(3), neither of which alters the effect of the two party rule. The first explanation is that the purpose of the statutory provision was to liberalise the barring of entails, not to alter the common law two party rule. A sale to oneself could rid the title of an entail and permit sale outside the family. A second possible explanation,[18] also concerned with conveyance rather than contract, is that it was possible at common law to convey to a grantee for uses for the benefit of the grantor, so that when the Statute of Uses 1535 executed the use the grantor would have conveyed to himself. The argument might be that when the 1925 statute repealed the Statute of Uses, the 1925 statute was concerned not to abolish the possibility of the creation of a trust upon an executed use. In either case, the effect of section 72(3) could hardly be to permit a person to make a conveyance of his own title (whether held absolutely or on trust) to himself alone.

A potentially anomalous exception to the two party rule was acknowledged by Lord Denning in *Rye v Rye* when he suggested that a man who is sole executor can convey to himself as devisee.[19] This principle was applied (without citation of Lord Denning's obiter dictum) in *Holder v Holder*.[20] In that case the defendant was an executor of an estate who had ineffectively renounced his executorship. Later he succeeded at auction in purchasing a farm from the estate. The other executors (and potential legatees) brought an action against him to set aside the sale. The Court of Appeal held that the sale was good and that the rule against self dealing did not apply. The reasons given are unconvincing. Harman LJ was the only judge to address the problem. His Lordship argued that even though the defendant was still the executor, the defendant was not in the position of both seller and buyer because he did not take part in instructing the valuer; he did not assume the duties of an executor; and he had acquired no special knowledge as an executor.

All of this may be true but it is beside the point. The will of the deceased had created the office of executor, which the defendant had accepted and had not properly renounced. Title to the property passed to the defendant at the time he accepted the office as executor even though he was not a proving executor in the probate. The sale at auction was to himself. Presumably if he had failed to complete he would have had a duty to bring an action against himself. One can only imagine the amusement for the lawyers he would instruct on each side of such a farcical action.

[17] Ibid 505–06.

[18] Speculated in B McPherson, 'Self-dealing Trustees' in A Oakley (ed), *Trends in Contemporary Trust Law* (Oxford, Oxford University Press, 1996) 135, 142, and suggested by the High Court of Australia in *Clay* (n 10) [51]–[52].

[19] *Rye* (n 14) 514.

[20] *Holder v Holder* [1968] Ch 353 (CA).

Executors with legal title to assets should not be treated any differently from trustees or any other legal owner. The principle is well established that the two party rule prevents a trustee, like any other person holding legal title, from purchasing from himself. In relation to trustees, Romilly MR once described such a purchase as a 'mere piece of waste paper'.[21] In any event, this exception for executors aside, there is nothing unique about the two party rule, nor any reason why it is confined to fiduciaries.

Following the lead of Sir Richard Arden in *Campbell v Walker*,[22] another attempt to defend an independent self dealing rule was made by Lord Eldon in *Ex parte Lacey*.[23] In the context of a trustee in bankruptcy who purchased part of the bankrupt estate at auction, the Lord Chancellor said:

> The rule I take to be this; not, that a trustee cannot buy from his Cestuy que trust, but, that he shall not buy from himself. … A trustee, who is entrusted to sell and manage for others, undertakes in the same moment, in which he becomes a trustee, not to manage for the benefit and advantage, of himself. It does not preclude a new contract with those, who have entrusted him. It does not preclude him from bargaining, that he will no longer act as a trustee. The Cestuys que trust may by a new contract dismiss him from that character: but even then that transaction, by which they dismiss him, must according to the rules of this Court be watched with infinite and the most guarded jealousy; and for this reason; that the Law supposes him to have acquired all the knowledge a trustee may acquire; which may be very useful to him; but the communication of which to the Cestuy que trust the Court can never be sure he has made, when entering into the new contract, by which he is discharged. I disavow…that the trustee must make advantage. I say, whether he makes advantage, or not, if the connection does not satisfactorily appear to have been dissolved, it is in the choice of the Cestuy que trusts, whether they will take back the property, or not if the trustee has made no advantage. It is founded upon this; that though you may see in a particular case, that he has not made advantage, it is utterly impossible to examine upon satisfactory evidence in the power of the Court, by which I mean, in the power of the parties, in ninety-nine cases out of an hundred, whether he has made advantage, or not. Suppose, a trustee buys any estate; and by the knowledge acquired in that character discovers a valuable coal-mine under it; and locking that up in his own breast enters into a contract with the Cestuy que trust: if he chooses to deny it, how can the Court try that against that denial? The probability is, that a trustee, who has once conceived such a purpose, will never disclose it; and the Cestuy que trust will be effectually defrauded.[24]

The obvious problem with this reasoning is that the knowledge of the trustee is irrelevant if the two party rule applies. If there is no transaction there is nothing to set aside. If there were any doubt about this clear proposition, it is dispelled

[21] *Denton v Donner* (1856) 23 Beav 285, 53 ER 112. See also *Lewis v Hillman* (1852) 23 Beav 285, 290; 53 ER 112, 114; *Franks v Bollans* (1868) LR 3 Ch App 717 (CA); *Farrar v Farrar's Ltd* (1888) LR 40 ChD 395 (CA) 404; *Hodson v Deans* [1903] 2 Ch 647 (ChD) 653. These cases are discussed in McPherson, 'Self-dealing Trustees' (n 18) 138–41.

[22] *Campbell v Walker* (1800) 5 Ves Jun 678, 31 ER 801.

[23] *Ex parte Lacey* (1802) 6 Ves Jun 625, 31 ER 1228.

[24] Ibid 626–27, 1228–29.

by the decision of the Privy Council, on appeal from the New South Wales Court of Appeal, in *Williams v Scott*.[25] In that case a co-executor holding legal title under a will trust purported to purchase trust property and then mortgage it to Scott. Scott later purported to foreclose and sell to Williams. Williams refused to complete and an action for specific performance was refused by the Privy Council. Yet, if the contract by which the executor had purported to purchase the property had been merely voidable then Scott ought to have obtained good title and the contract with Williams should have been specifically enforceable.[26]

Although the two party rule is a general common law principle which means that self dealing by a trustee is simply void, and not voidable, it might be said that there is room for operation of the self dealing doctrine and the peculiar notion of voidability *ex debito justitiae* in the context of a sale by a trustee to a nominee. We turn now to that situation.

B. Trustee Purports to Sell a Trust Asset to a Nominee of the Trustee

A second possible scenario arising from the dicta in *Tito v Waddell* and *Clay v Clay* is that it might involve a situation in which a trustee sells a trust asset to a nominee. Is it meaningful in this situation to speak of the transaction being voidable *ex debito justitiae*?

The first difficulty here is that 'nominee' is not a term of art, nor a recognised legal category. Sometimes the term is used to describe an agent of the nominator. On other occasions it is used to describe a person who holds as trustee for the nominator. In cases where a trustee purports to sell a trust asset to an agent nominee then the two party rule applies. The agent is acting for the trustee so the sale is from the trustee to himself. The transaction is simply void.[27] As Lord President Hope said in the Inner House of the Court of Session:

> I know of no case, and none was cited to us, where it has been held that a nominee may contract with his principal so as to create new rights and obligations involving no third party whatever which are to be held only on his principal's behalf. That seems to me to conflict with the principle that a man cannot contract with himself.[28]

A second use of 'nominee' is to describe a situation in which a trustee sells an asset to a person nominated to hold the asset on trust for the trustee. So, for instance, a trustee sells a trust asset to his wife, to hold for him on trust.[29] It might be thought that there is a need for this transaction to be voidable *ex debitae justitiae* to avoid

[25] *Williams v Scott* [1900] AC 499 (PC).

[26] McPherson (n 18) 140–41.

[27] *Re Bloye's Will Trust* (1849) 1 Mac & G 488, 494–95; 41 ER 1354, 1357; *Campbell* (n 22); *Randall v Errington* (1805) 10 Ves Jun 423, 32 ER 909; *Ex parte Bennett* (1805) 10 Ves Jun 381, 32 ER 893; *Watson v Toone* (1820) 6 Madd 153, 56 ER 150. See McPherson (n 18) 140.

[28] *Kildrummy (Jersey) Ltd v IRC* [1990] STC 657 (C Sess, IH) 662.

[29] *Robertson v Robertson* [1924] NZLR 552 (NZSC).

the third party obtaining any benefit. Lord Eldon's reasoning quoted above might be called in aid of this reasoning on his reasoning that the voidability of such a transaction arises because of the non-justiciability of issues of knowledge.

However, there is no need for such voidability. First, the notion that such a transaction is voidable ignores the difference between authorised and unauthorised transactions. If the trustee is authorised to sell the legal title to the third party then, provided that the third party is bona fide, the third party will obtain an unimpeachable title.

Alternatively, if the transaction is unauthorised and the nominee purchases the asset with knowledge of the trustee's lack of authority then the nominee will not be a bona fide purchaser and the nominee will hold his rights on trust for the original beneficiary. The beneficiary does not need to rely upon any voidability of the nominee's rights. The beneficiary can simply demand conveyance of the rights.[30] The same outcome occurs, although more indirectly, even if the nominee purchases *without* knowledge of the beneficiary's equitable rights. The nominee undertakes to hold the legal title on trust for the trustee who, in turn, holds his equitable rights on sub-trust for the beneficiary. It was once thought that in such a situation the sub-trustee would drop out.[31] The better analysis is that the sub-trust remains,[32] but there is still no need for a voidability analysis because the beneficiary can demand that the trustee obtain a reconveyance of the legal rights from the nominee and the beneficiary can then demand conveyance of those rights. Describing the transfer to the nominee as voidable *ex debito justitiae* adds nothing to this conventional analysis.

A further problem with Lord Eldon's reasoning was explained in *Holder v Holder*. Danckwerts LJ rejected the argument of Lord Eldon that it is impossible to ascertain the state of knowledge of a trustee, referring to the well known statement of Bowen LJ that 'the state of a man's mind is as much a fact as the state of his digestion', and also to the 'almost daily experience of any judge engaged in ascertaining the knowledge and intentions of a party to proceedings'.[33]

In summary, in circumstances in which the trustee purports to sell the trust asset to a nominee, nothing is added to conventional understanding of trust law, and the law is only confused, by describing the situation as involving a transfer which is voidable *ex debito justitiae.*

C. Trustee Purports to Enter a Transaction Which Will Extinguish or Overreach the Rights of the Beneficiary of the Trust

A third possible meaning of self dealing is where the beneficiary of a trust is a party to a transaction with the trustee. Although this might, very loosely, be

30 *Saunders v Vautier* (1841) 4 Beav 115; 49 ER 282.
31 *Grainge v Wilberforce* (1889) 5 TLR 436.
32 *Nelson v Greening & Sykes (Builders) Ltd* [2007] EWCA Civ 1358 [54]–[57].
33 *Holder* (n 20) 398.

described as a sale by the trustee to himself, the two party rule is not infringed if the contract can be construed as an agreement by the beneficiary to relinquish his equitable rights against the trustee so that the trustee will hold the legal title outright.

Although a contract between a trustee and a third party which purports to overreach the interest of the beneficiary cannot have such effect unless the trustee is acting within authority,[34] the interest of the beneficiary can always be overreached in cases where the beneficiary is a party to the transaction or when the beneficiary ratifies the unauthorised transfer. In relation to an attempt by the trustee to overreach the interests of the beneficiary in an unauthorised sale to a third party, that attempt is ineffective unless ratified. As O'Sullivan, Elliott and Zakrzewski have explained, 'this is in fact the converse of rescission. The right is to elect to divest an existing beneficial interest, whereas rescission involves regaining a title lost or obtaining a new beneficial interest in traceable substitutes.'[35]

In relation to an attempt by the trustee to overreach the beneficiary's interest in a transaction with the beneficiary, this is capable of being a valid contract. Prior to 1873, the effect of such a contract was that the beneficiary who tried to enforce the trust in the Court of Chancery would be in breach of contract and could be sued at law. After the Judicature Acts the beneficiary could not bring an action on the trust, because to do so would involve circuity of action.[36] This instance of self dealing plainly does not cause a contract to be voidable *ex debito justitiae*; just the opposite, as Millett LJ explained, it is a perfectly valid and enforceable contract.[37] It may be that some of the authorities discussed above involving purported sales by a trustee to himself or to his agent might be re-explained as situations in which the trustee is entering a transaction to extinguish the beneficial interest. Although the transaction would not be voidable simply because of the nature of the transaction as 'self dealing', it is possible that the transaction might nevertheless be voidable for other reasons. This would depend upon application of well established principles concerning whether the trustee obtained fully informed consent to, or waiver of, a conflict of interest. On one view such a transaction would also attract the attention of the equitable doctrine of fair dealing. This chapter does not consider the detail of the doctrine of fair dealing, but it suffices to note that Conaglen has made a powerful argument that the fair dealing doctrine is not independent of the traditional and well known rules relating to conflict of interest and profiting from a fiduciary position. The doctrine of fair dealing, on this argument, is a misnomer: it is not concerned with substantive fairness at all.[38]

[34] *Ingram* (n 12) 423; *Clay* (n 10) [51].

[35] D O'Sullivan, S Elliott and R Zakrzewski, *The Law of Rescission* (Oxford, Oxford University Press, 2007) para [1.58].

[36] *Hirachand Punamchand v Temple* [1911] 2 KB 330 (CA) 337 (Vaughan Williams LJ).

[37] *Ingram* (n 12) 424.

[38] M Conaglen, 'A Re-Appraisal of the Fiduciary Self-Dealing and Fair-Dealing Rules' (2006) 65 *CLJ* 366.

D. Company Director Purports to Sell Company Assets to Himself

In *JJ Harrison (Properties) Ltd v Harrison*[39] a director of a property company, Peter Harrison, acquired a property from the company at an undervalue. Harrison failed to disclose to the other voting directors that a planning application had been made and that the architects were confident that it would be granted. Harrison later made vast profits from developing and selling the land. When, many years later, the non-disclosure was discovered the company brought an action against Harrison for breach of fiduciary duty seeking an account of profits, a constructive trust over the profits and equitable compensation. The Court of Appeal held that Harrison held the land on constructive trust for the company.

The first point to note about this result is that the doctrine applies whether or not the director is the person to whom the company assets are conveyed. It does not matter whether the company assets are conveyed as a result of 'self dealing' by the director or whether they are sold as a result of dealing by a director with a third party who has knowledge of the director's lack of authority. In both cases there is a great deal of authority in support of the proposition that the person who receives an asset of the company, with knowledge that it is transferred without authority, holds that asset on constructive trust for the company.[40] The best known decision for this general proposition is *Rolled Steel Products (Holdings) Ltd v British Steel Corporation*.[41] In that case, Rolled Steel Products (Holdings) Ltd owed £400,000 to another company, S Ltd, owned by one of the Rolled Steel directors. S Ltd itself owed twice that sum to the British Steel Corporation.[42] The Rolled Steel director was a personal guarantor of S Ltd's debt to Rolled Steel. Rolled Steel and British Steel devised a proposal for British Steel to lend money to Rolled Steel which would be used to repay Rolled Steel's debt to S Ltd. S Ltd would then use those funds to repay (in part) the debt it owed to British Steel. Rolled Steel would also give British Steel security for the debt owed to it.

The effect of the proposed arrangements was that Rolled Steel would discharge its debt to S Ltd and S Ltd would discharge part of its debt to British Steel, reducing the contingent liability of the Rolled Steel director. This arrangement was made possible by the security given by Rolled Steel to British Steel and by a loan to Rolled Steel from British Steel. Although the director of Rolled Steel was personally interested in this proposal he did not declare an interest and voted in favour of the proposal. Subsequently the Rolled Steel security was called upon by British Steel. When Rolled Steel was placed into receivership, the receiver sought

[39] *JJ Harrison (Properties) Ltd v Harrison* [2001] EWCA Civ 1467, [2002] BCC 729.

[40] *Russell v Wakefield Waterworks Co* (1875) LR 20 Eq 474 (ChD) 479; *Belmont Finance Corp v Williams Furniture Ltd (No 2)* [1980] 1 All ER 393 (CA) 405; *Paragon Finance plc v D B Thakerar & Co* [1999] 1 All ER 400 (CA) 408; *Re Sharpe; Masonic and General Life Assurance Co v Sharpe* [1892] 1 Ch 154 (CA) 172; *Soar v Ashwell* [1893] 2 QB 390 (CA) 398.

[41] *Rolled Steel Products (Holdings) Ltd v British Steel Corporation* [1986] Ch 246 (CA).

[42] For simplicity, the British Steel group companies are treated interchangeably here.

recovery of the payments made pursuant to the security. This claim failed because Rolled Steel was still under an obligation to repay money borrowed from the British Steel Corporation's subsidiary. However, the Court of Appeal held that the payments under the guarantee were held on constructive trust because the British Steel subsidiary had received them with knowledge of the lack of authority.

One puzzle is why a trust arises in these cases. If a third party knows[43] that a company director has no authority to sell company assets then the company is not bound by any contract which the agent makes with the third party[44] unless the company chooses retrospectively to ratify it.[45] In relation to any conveyance of company assets, the company can bring a personal claim against the third party recipient for unjust enrichment at the company's expense.[46] Given the existence of a personal claim, why is there a need for a constructive trust?

The answer suggested by the Court of Appeal in *JJ Harrison* is that the trust arises by manifestation of consent, in the same way as a trustee who makes an express declaration of trust by conduct. Although, as a director, Harrison was not a trustee, he assumed the same duties as those of a trustee in relation to company property.[47] When the company asset was transferred to Harrison he became a trustee because these duties were then related to a particular asset.[48] This analysis might explain some cases but it is questionable whether the mere knowledge of an unauthorised transfer is sufficient in all cases to manifest an (objective) declaration of trust.[49]

Another possible answer is that the trust arises as a response to the same event as the personal claim.[50] It is the unjust enrichment of the third party at the expense of the company which gives rise to the company's personal claim for restitution. The claim that the rights are held on trust might even be thought to be a more perfect means of obtaining restitution since the claimant has a power to obtain the very enrichment held by the defendant which the claimant transferred. In this light, the trust which arises might be better described as a resulting trust, responding to unjust

[43] It is possible that the doctrine also extends to situations in which the third party only has notice of the director's lack of authority: see *Nelson v Larholt* [1948] 1 KB 339 (KBD), and also *Eddis v Chichester Constable* [1969] 2 Ch 345 (CA) 358. These cases are difficult to reconcile with the principle that carelessness does not preclude a contract from arising by ostensible authority and only dishonesty or irrationality will suffice: see *Thanakharn Kasikorn Thai Chamkat (Mahachon) v Akai Holdings Ltd (in liq)* [2010] HKCFA 63 (Lord Neuberger of Abbotsbury NPJ).

[44] *Heinl v Jyske Bank (Gibraltar) Ltd* [1999] Lloyd's Rep Bank 511 (CA) 521 (Nourse LJ citing dicta of Slade and Browne-Wilkinson LJJ in *Rolled Steel Products* (n 41) 295, 297, 304). Contrast the situation of ostensible authority when a third party has no knowledge of the lack of authority but relies upon the agent's position as director: *Auxil Pty Ltd v Terranova* [2009] WASCA 163, (2009) 260 ALR 164 [176]; *Akai Holdings* (n 43).

[45] *Heinl* (n 44) 533.

[46] *Criterion Properties plc v Stratford Properties LLC* [2004] UKHL 28, [2004] 1 WLR 1846 [4] (Lord Nicholls); *Primlake Ltd (in liq) v Matthews Associates* [2006] EWHC 1227 (Ch) [335].

[47] *JJ Harrison* (n 39) [25]. See also *Re Lands Allotment Co* [1894] 1 Ch 616 (CA) 631, 638; *Cook v Deeks* [1916] AC 555 (PC) 564; *Belmont Finance* (n 40) 405; *Paragon Finance* (n 40).

[48] See also *Sharpe* (n 40) 172; *Soar* (n 40) 398.

[49] The subjective views of the trustee being irrelevant: *Twinsectra Ltd v Yardley* [2002] UKHL 12, [2002] 2 AC 164 [71]; *Re Kayford Ltd (in liq)* [1975] 1 WLR 279 (ChD); *Re Multi Guarantee Co Ltd (No 3)* [1987] BCLC 257 (CA); *Mills v Sportsdirect.com Retail Ltd* [2010] EWHC 1072 (Ch) [53]–[54].

[50] *Nelson v Larholt* (n 43) 342–43.

enrichment.[51] Comments to similar effect were made in *Nelson v Nelson*.[52] In that case, Mrs Nelson transferred land into the name of her children in order to obtain a subsidised government loan. Just as a director can transfer company assets in circumstances in which the company has no intention to benefit the recipient, so too Mrs Nelson had no intention to benefit her children by conferring the use and enjoyment of the property upon them. Her intention was to make a paper transfer but to reserve the use and enjoyment of the land to herself. After the property was sold, her daughter denied that Mrs Nelson had any interest in the proceeds of sale. Deane and Gummow JJ quoted from Professors Scott and Fratcher and explained that such a result would unjustly enrich the daughter.[53] The award made by the High Court of Australia was that the proceeds were held on resulting trust (subject to conditions).

Whichever answer is given to the question of why a trust arises in the case of an unauthorised disposition of a claimant's asset, it is clear that the answer is not confined to circumstances in which the defendant is engaged in 'self dealing' nor is it confined to situations in which the defendant is a fiduciary.

E. Company Director Purports to Sell Company Assets to a Nominee

As we have seen in the scenario of a trustee who sells trust assets to a nominee, the word 'nominee' is not a term of art. This is equally true when a company director purports to sell company assets to a 'nominee'. There are two possibilities in this case of an unauthorised sale by a company director of company assets. First, the nominee of the company director could be an agent for the company director. In that case, the situation is identical to the case of a company director conveying company assets to himself. The unauthorised sale would not have any effect unless ratified, and any conveyance of title would be held on trust for the company.

Secondly, the nominee of the company director could be a person who agrees to purchase the company asset and undertakes to hold it on trust for the company director. If the nominee knows that the asset has been transferred without authority then, as explained above, the contract between the nominee and the company can be avoided and the asset would then be held by the nominee on trust for the company. Alternatively, if the nominee does not know that the transfer is unauthorised, then the nominee would hold on trust for the company director who would, in turn, hold his equitable interest on trust for the company (for the reasons explained above).

III. Conclusion

The purpose of this chapter has been to shine a torch on the so-called principle against fiduciary self dealing. Examined closely, there is no such doctrine, nor is

51 R Chambers, *Resulting Trusts* (Oxford, Oxford University Press, 1997).
52 *Nelson v Nelson* (1995) 184 CLR 538 (HCA).
53 Ibid 564. See also 597 (Toohey J).

there a single consequence that the sale is voidable *ex debito justitiae*. Instead, the situations considered as 'self dealing' are a disparate group of cases involving of a number of different but well established rules, none of which is capable of being generalised to relationships commonly regarded as fiduciary.

A better approach to this area of the law would be to consider each instance of purported self dealing in its own context. The different contexts apply different principles and conflation of all the principles into a 'rule' against self dealing is not helpful. In summary, the principles are:

1. If the case is one involving an attempted sale, or conveyance, by any person to himself or his agent then, fiduciary or not, it is void.
2. If the sale is an authorised transaction between a trustee and a nominee who undertakes to hold on trust for the trustee, then the interest of the beneficiary will be overreached by the transaction.
3. If the 'sale' is between the trustee and the beneficiary and it can be construed as an agreement by the beneficiary to relinquish his equitable rights then the agreement will be valid and the trustee will hold the rights absolutely, subject to well know rules of avoidance which are unconcerned with substantial fairness but which are sometimes compendiously, and confusingly, described as 'fair dealing'.
4. If the sale is an unauthorised transaction between a trustee and a nominee who undertakes to hold on trust for the trustee, then:
   a. if the nominee was not a bona fide purchaser for good faith the nominee will hold on trust directly for the beneficiary; or
   b. if the nominee was a bona fide purchaser for good faith of the legal title then the nominee will hold the title on trust for the trustee (as agreed), who will then hold his equitable rights on sub-trust for the beneficiary. The beneficiary can compel conveyance of the legal rights to himself by demanding that the trustee obtain conveyance from the nominee and then by executing the trust.
5. If the purported sale and conveyance is of company assets by a director from the company to himself, without authority, then the contract of sale will be ineffective (unless ratified by the company) and the director will hold those assets on trust for the company.
6. If the sale and conveyance is of company assets by a director, without authority, to a nominee to hold on trust for the director, then:
   a. if the nominee had knowledge of the lack of authority of the company director then there will not be an effective contract (unless the company chooses to ratify) and the nominee will hold any asset conveyed on trust directly for the company; or
   b. if the nominee director had no knowledge of the lack of authority of the company director (and possibly also no notice) then the contract will be valid and the nominee will hold the assets on trust for the director, who will hold them on sub-trust for the company (as explained in 4b above).

6

Participatory Liability for Breach of Trust or Fiduciary Duty

PAULINE RIDGE

I. Introduction

Confusion surrounds the equitable liability of a third party to a trust or fiduciary relationship who participates in a breach of the trust or fiduciary duty, but without necessarily receiving trust property.[1] Compounding this confusion is the absence of consensus in courts that share a common Chancery law heritage. Notably, the English courts, including the Privy Council within that term, and the High Court of Australia take quite different approaches to the liability, although drawing upon the same nineteenth century trust law precedents. The Canadian common law is different again, although reliant upon the same cases.[2] Until recently, the jurisdictional differences were excused on the basis that the Australian and Canadian courts had not yet had the opportunity to consider the Privy Council's rationalisation of this form of equitable participatory liability in *Royal Brunei Airlines Sdn Bhd v Tan* (*Royal Brunei*) in 1995.[3] This still may be so with respect to the Canadian law, which will not be considered further in this chapter, but it seems clear now that the Australian law is set on a different path.[4]

The English approach is one of broad principle. In *Royal Brunei*, Lord Nicholls gathered together the nineteenth century trust law precedents and reformulated them as a loss based 'accessory' liability that attaches to a third party, D, who procures or assists in any breach of trust by the fiduciary, F.[5] From the twentieth century trust law precedents he identified a requirement of 'dishonesty' on the

[1] This chapter does not deal directly with recipient liability, that is, liability based upon D's receipt of trust property in breach of the trust.

[2] *Air Canada v M & L Travel Ltd* [1993] 3 SCR 787 (SCC). See generally D Waters, M Gillen and L Smith, *Waters' Law of Trusts in Canada*, 3rd edn (Toronto, Thomson Carswell, 2005).

[3] *Royal Brunei Airlines Sdn Bhd v Tan* [1995] 2 AC 378 (PC).

[4] New Zealand law is not considered in this chapter. *Royal Brunei*'s dishonesty test has been adopted in that country: *US International Marketing Ltd v National Bank of New Zealand* [2003] NZCA 295, [2004] 1 NZLR 589.

[5] The liability was formulated in terms of trusts; its application to fiduciaries generally is discussed below.

part of D. The High Court of Australia in 2007 in *Farah Constructions Pty Limited v Say-Dee Pty Limited (Farah)* did not endorse *Royal Brunei*, although widely tipped to do so.[6] Instead, the Court adhered more closely to the nineteenth century precedents, as well as to its own 1975 decision in *Consul Development Pty Ltd v DPC Estates Pty Ltd* (*Consul*),[7] by continuing to differentiate between acts of procurement[8] by D and assistance by D on the one hand, and between honest breaches of duty by F, and dishonest and fraudulent breaches of duty by F, on the other hand. In Australia, D's liability to the claimant beneficiary or principal, C, continues to turn on D's knowledge of F's breach of duty, rather than on D's dishonesty as under the reformulated English model.

Neither the English approach nor the Australian approach is universally endorsed. The optimism generated by *Royal Brunei* dissipated following the interpretation and reinterpretation of its dishonesty test by the House of Lords[9] and the Privy Council[10] respectively. The Australian law remains uncertain as the High Court in *Farah* did not completely rule out the possibility of following *Royal Brunei* in the future.

How is it that two quite different liability schemes have emerged from reliance upon essentially the same equitable precedents? And is either approach defensible? In this chapter I critically evaluate the use of the equity case law by the Privy Council in *Royal Brunei* and the High Court in *Farah* and propose an alternative scheme that more accurately reflects the equitable cases. Of course, the principled use of precedent[11] is not the only consideration in formulating a participatory liability scheme for breach of trust or fiduciary duty. Other relevant matters include policy concerns, the statutory and common law regulatory context for third parties who interact with trustees and fiduciaries, and whether there are jurisdictional idiosyncrasies that might warrant different approaches being taken. Nonetheless, a fundamental step in formulating a defensible participatory liability

[6] *Farah Constructions Pty Ltd v Say-Dee Pty Ltd* [2007] HCA 22, (2007) 230 CLR 89. For approval of *Royal Brunei* by Australian lower courts see, eg *Beach Petroleum NL v Abbott Tout Russell Kennedy* [1999] NSWCA 408; (1999) 48 NSWLR 1, 87 (Spigelman CJ, Sheller and Stein JJA); *The Hancock Family Memorial Foundation Ltd v Porteous* [1999] WASC 55, (1999) 32 ACSR 124 [77] (Anderson J); *Aequitas v AEFC* [2001] NSWSC 14, (2001) 19 ACLC 1006 [392] (Austin J). But see *NCR Australia v Credit Connection Pty Ltd (in liq)* [2004] NSWSC 1 [164] (Austin J) and *Cadwallader v Bajco Pty Ltd* [2002] NSWCA 328 [199] (Heydon J).

[7] *Consul Development Pty Ltd v DPC Estates Pty Ltd* (1975) 132 CLR 373 (HCA).

[8] The High Court used the phrase 'knowingly induced or immediately procured': ibid [161]. It is difficult to discern any difference in meaning between these terms. Hence, 'procurement' will be used to include inducement in this paper. But see P Finn, 'The Liability of Third Parties for Knowing Receipt or Assistance' in D Waters (ed), *Equity, Fiduciaries and Trusts* (Toronto, Carswell, 1993) 195, 212 where separate scenarios of inducing a breach of fiduciary duty and procuring a breach of fiduciary duty are described.

[9] *Twinsectra Ltd v Yardley* [2002] UKHL 12, [2002] 2 AC 164.

[10] *Barlow Clowes International Ltd (in liq) v Eurotrust International Ltd* [2005] UKPC 37, [2006] 1 WLR 1476. One judge has referred to the precedential 'nightmare' caused by these decisions: *Attorney General of Zambia v Meer Care & Desai* [2007] EWHC 952 (Ch) [351], [358] (Peter Smith J).

[11] I use the term 'precedent' to mean cases relevant to the legal issue in question, whether or not binding upon the court.

scheme for breach of trust or fiduciary duty must be to ensure that it is firmly and appropriately founded upon the equitable precedents.

Part II of the chapter outlines the points of doctrinal difference between the English and Australian schemes. Part III describes and evaluates the Privy Council and the High Court's use of the equity case law in *Royal Brunei* and *Farah*. I argue that there are flaws in both the High Court's literalist, narrow reading of a selected few cases and the Privy Council's broad-brush treatment of the case law. Although Lord Nicholls' methodology is preferable, he did not draw upon a sufficiently wide sample of the relevant precedents and, consequently, his proposed accessory liability scheme in *Royal Brunei* is flawed. Part IV demonstrates how a broader consideration of the equity cases concerning participatory liability suggests an alternative way of organising the case law and formulating a principle. In light of these findings, Part V makes some suggestions as to how the doctrinal differences outlined in Part II might be resolved.

II. Doctrinal Differences

Broadly speaking, there are three clear points of doctrinal difference between the English and Australian schemes as presently formulated and one potential point of contention.[12]

A. How Many Categories of Liability?

The first point of difference concerns whether there is one, all-encompassing, 'accessory liability' or two categories of liability, namely,

(i) knowing assistance by D in a dishonest and fraudulent design by F; and,
(ii) knowing procurement by D in any breach of trust by F.

According to *Royal Brunei*, accessory liability, based upon D's dishonesty, applies to all breaches of trust by F and to all types of involvement by D apart from receipt of trust property by D. Conversely, the High Court in *Farah* adhered to the two distinct forms of liability present in the nineteenth century case law in relation to a D involved in a breach of trust or fiduciary duty without receiving trust property: namely, assisting in a dishonest and fraudulent breach of trust or fiduciary duty by F,[13] and procuring any breach of trust by F.[14]

[12] There are doctrinal questions that cannot be jurisdictionally apportioned. See generally C Mitchell, 'Assistance' in P Birks and A Pretto (eds), *Breach of Trust* (Oxford, Hart Publishing, 2002) 139.

[13] *Barnes v Addy* (1874) LR 9 Ch App 244 (CA).

[14] *Fyler v Fyler* (1841) 3 Beav 550, 49 ER 216; *Alleyne v Darcy* (1854) 4 I Ch R 199; *Eaves v Hickson* (1861) 30 Beav 136, 54 ER 840.

B. Does Liability Turn on D's Knowledge or D's Dishonesty?

Traditionally, D's liability has depended upon whether D 'knew' of a dishonest and fraudulent breach of duty by F. This formulation was derived from the so-called 'second limb' of Lord Selborne LC's *ex tempore* judgment in *Barnes v Addy* concerning the equitable liability of agents of trustees:

> [S]trangers are not to be made constructive trustees merely because they act as the agents of trustees in transactions within their legal power, transactions perhaps of which a court of Equity may disapprove, unless … they assist with knowledge in a dishonest and fraudulent design on the part of the trustees …[15]

Attention focussed upon whether D could be liable for something less than actual knowledge of F's wrongdoing. The *Baden* scale of knowledge, comprising five levels of possible cognition ranging from actual knowledge to constructive knowledge became ubiquitous in this context.[16] Confusing the issue was that the requirement of knowledge arose both in relation to the first limb of *Barnes v Addy*, that is, where D received trust property in breach of a trust, and in relation to the second limb, where D participated in a breach of trust without necessarily receiving trust property. Minds differed over whether a lower threshold for liability, and hence a lower level of knowledge, might apply under the first limb where D's liability might be justified in property law terms.[17] That is, in relation to recipient liability, it could be argued that the protection of C's property rights should override concern with the state of D's conscience (as indicated by D's knowledge) and, if this is so, it is easier to say that D should be liable for something less than actual knowledge where D received trust property in breach of the trust.[18]

In *Royal Brunei* Lord Nicholls rejected knowledge as the sole determinant of D's liability in relation to the second limb of *Barnes v Addy*. Instead, according to Lord Nicholls, the question is whether D acted as an honest and reasonable person in all the circumstances would have acted. D's knowledge is one (important)[19] factor in a wider factual matrix from which the court decides whether D acted dishonestly. The *Baden* scale was said to be unhelpful in this inquiry because '"knowingly" is inapt as a criterion when applied to the gradually darkening spectrum where the differences are of degree and not of kind.'[20] After some confusion generated by the House of Lords in *Twinsectra v Yardley*, the Privy Council confirmed in *Barlow*

[15] *Barnes* (n 13) 251–52.

[16] *Baden v Société Générale pour Favoriser le Developpement de l'Industrie en France SA* [1993] 1 WLR 509 (ChD). True constructive notice is not included in the *Baden* scale: Simon Gardner, 'Knowing Assistance and Knowing Receipt: Taking Stock' (1996) 112 *LQR* 56, 57–58.

[17] J Dietrich and P Ridge, '"The Receipt of What?": Questions Concerning Third Party Recipient Liability in Equity and Unjust Enrichment' (2007) 31 *Melbourne University Law Review* 47, 58–60.

[18] *Consul* (n 7) 410–11 (Stephen J).

[19] See generally Gardner, 'Knowing Assistance and Knowing Receipt' (n 16) 66–68.

[20] *Royal Brunei* (n 3) 391 (Lord Nicholls).

Clowes International Ltd (in liq) v Eurotrust International Ltd (Barlow Clowes) that dishonesty was to be determined according to an objective standard.[21]

Conversely, in *Farah* the High Court held that in relation to a D who assists F in a dishonest and fraudulent breach of duty, D's liability turns upon D's knowledge, rather than upon a higher-level conclusion of dishonesty. That is, the second limb of the *Barnes v Addy* formulation was retained. According to the High Court, the *Baden* scale is a helpful tool in describing degrees of knowledge and should be used in interpreting the Court's 1975 decision in *Consul* which continues to bind Australian courts.[22] Accordingly, and applying the *Baden* scale to the judgments in *Consul*, level (iv) of that scale, 'knowledge of circumstances which would indicate the facts to an honest and reasonable man' suffices for D's knowing assistance liability in Australia. This will capture the 'morally obtuse' D who does not recognise an impropriety that would have been recognised by an 'ordinary person'.[23] It is not stated explicitly in *Farah* whether the same standard of knowledge is required for a D who procures, rather than assists, F's breach of duty.[24]

Thus, the most explicit point of contention between Australia and England at present is whether a single criterion of knowledge suffices for D's liability or whether instead, the court should determine whether D acted dishonestly by considering a matrix of facts including, but not limited to, the state of D's knowledge.[25]

C. The Ambit of Liability

It is not clear whether the English formulation of accessory liability extends to breaches of fiduciary duty not involving either a trust or property under F's control.[26] Lord Nicholls' reasoning in *Royal Brunei* focuses upon liability for breach of an express trust and, specifically, the liability of agents acting for trustees, although in his concluding remarks he refers to 'a breach of trust or fiduciary obligation'.[27] Much of his reasoning makes sense only in the context of express trusts. The ambit of liability is considerably widened by the fact that breaches of fiduciary duty by company directors also are treated as instances of breach of trust on the basis that the company property is treated as trust property.[28] But it has not

[21] *Barlow Clowes* (n 10).

[22] *Farah* (n 6) [175].

[23] Ibid [177].

[24] In *Consul* (n 7) 414 Stephen J rejected the respondent's argument that D had actively induced F to breach his fiduciary duty and commented, 'Even were this so I doubt whether, in the absence of knowledge by [D], [C] would be entitled to equitable relief'.

[25] The equally important question of the content of D's knowledge (eg, must D recognise that a breach of *trust* has occurred?) has not received as much attention. See, eg *Barlow Clowes* (n 10) [28]; cf *United States Surgical Corporation v Hospital Products International Pty Ltd* [1983] 2 NSWLR 157 (NSWCA) 253. See generally Mitchell, 'Assistance' (n 12) 195–200.

[26] See, eg Mitchell (n 12) 160.

[27] *Royal Brunei* (n 3) 392.

[28] *Soar v Ashwell* [1893] 2 QB 390 (CA). For a recent example, see *Statek Corporation v McNeill Alford* [2008] EWHC 32 (Ch).

been authoritatively spelt out in England whether liability extends to breaches of fiduciary duty not involving property. Conversely, in Australia the two High Court cases in which accessory liability has been considered, *Consul* and *Farah*, involved 'pure' alleged breaches of fiduciary duty in which no property, trust or otherwise, was misapplied.[29]

D. Remedies

A possible jurisdictional difference between the Australian and English schemes concerns the remedies available for equitable participatory liability. Until very recently, the English courts did not need to consider anything other than loss-based remedies and it seems to have been assumed that the remedy is loss-based only.[30] On the other hand, in Australia gain-based remedies seem uncontroversial. So far, the difference can be attributed to the different factual scenarios that have come before the senior courts in each jurisdiction. Thus, for example, the Australian courts have dealt with 'pure' fiduciary breaches involving alleged exploitation of business opportunities by D that should have been offered to C,[31] or where D appropriated C's product and product market for his own profit-making purposes.[32] The most natural remedy in these scenarios, if the claim were established, is gain-based and certainly none of the courts involved showed any concern with that. On the other hand, the availability of gain-based remedies for accessory liability has been raised less frequently in the United Kingdom and, perhaps as a consequence, it tends to be assumed that the remedy is loss-based.[33]

III. Different Approaches to Precedent

The most striking difference between *Royal Brunei* and *Farah* concerns the style of judicial reasoning in each case and, particularly, their different treatment of the

[29] *Consul* (n 7) 396–97 (Gibbs J).

[30] Cf *Fyffes Group Ltd v Templeman* [2000] 2 Lloyd's Rep 643 (Comm); *Ultraframe (UK) Ltd v Fielding* [2005] EWHC 1638(4) (Ch), [2006] FSR 17; *Sinclair Investment Holdings SA v Versailles Trade Finance Ltd* [2007] EWHC 915 (Ch), [2007] 2 All ER (Comm) 993; *Aerostar Maintenance International Ltd v Wilson* [2010] EWHC 2032 (Ch).

[31] Eg *Consul* (n 7); *Farah* (n 6).

[32] *United States Surgical Corporation* (n 25).

[33] Underlying the uncertainty is a conceptual question regarding the nature of D's liability. The question that is raised, although mostly by commentators and mostly in regard to civil participatory liability generally, is whether D's liability should be conceptualised as an independent 'primary' liability or as a duplicative 'secondary' liability. See generally P Ridge, 'Justifying the Remedies for Dishonest Assistance' (2008) 124 *LQR* 445. See also P Sales, 'The Tort of Conspiracy and Secondary Liability' [1990] *CLJ* 491; S Elliott and C Mitchell, 'Remedies for Dishonest Assistance' (2004) 67 *MLR* 16, 46; M Clapton, 'Gain-Based Remedies for Knowing Assistance: Ensuring Assistants Do Not Profit From Their Wrongs' (2007–08) *Alberta Law Review* 989.

same, or similar, precedents. The difference in judicial method is one significant reason why the outcome of *Royal Brunei* has been preferred to that in *Farah*.

The facts of *Royal Brunei* concerned the principal director and shareholder of a travel agency company that held payments received for airline tickets on trust for the airline. The director, through his negligent mismanagement of the company, caused the company to breach this trust. The *only* question of law before the Privy Council was whether the director could be liable under the second limb of *Barnes v Addy* despite the breach of trust not being part of a 'dishonest and fraudulent design', as per Lord Selborne's dicta in that case. Yet the litigation was viewed as an opportunity to resolve wider uncertainties besetting the doctrine:

> A conclusion cannot be reached on the nature of the breach of trust which may trigger accessory liability without at the same time considering the other ingredients including, in particular, the state of mind of the third party.[34]

The way was then open to consider all elements of the liability.

In *Farah* before the High Court, equitable participatory liability was not raised by the facts and had not been the primary focus of the parties' detailed submissions in a very lengthy case. The question in *Farah* was whether the wife and daughters of the director of a joint venture company could be liable for participation in the company's alleged breach of fiduciary duty. The focus in the New South Wales Court of Appeal and the High Court was upon whether they were recipients of trust property (the first limb of *Barnes v Addy*); however, in the alternative it was argued that they were liable under the second limb of *Barnes v Addy*. The High Court reinstated the primary judge's decision that there was no breach of fiduciary duty, yet went on to consider both limbs of *Barnes v Addy* in light of its strong disagreement with the approach of the Court of Appeal. But the Court declined to consider whether Lord Nicholls' formulation of accessory liability should be adopted in Australia because this question was not in issue before it.[35] 'For now', Australian courts should continue to observe the distinction between the second limb in *Barnes v Addy*, as it was applied in *Consul*, and the earlier nineteenth century procurement cases.

Thus, the potential of the *Royal Brunei* litigation to reform equitable participatory liability for breach of trust was fully exploited by Lord Nicholls, whereas the High Court in *Farah* chose to decline such a task. With respect, it is unfortunate that the High Court did not take up the opportunity presented by *Farah*. The respondents' suggested reformulation of the second limb of *Barnes v Addy* clearly resonated with the momentous changes made in *Royal Brunei* and, without any stretch of the imagination, raised the question of whether *Royal Brunei*'s principle of 'accessory liability' should be adopted in Australia. Occasions for the High Court to provide guidance on such an important question of commercial law do not come up every day in Australia. The smaller volume of commercial litigation

[34] *Royal Brunei* (n 3).
[35] *Farah* (n 6) [160].

and the diluting effect of Australia's federal system in which there are multiple appellate courts of equal standing impedes the building of a solid and consistent jurisprudence on these matters at the Court of Appeal level which might then warrant a High Court challenge. Thus, opportunities for doctrinal clarification, however slim, should be grasped.

Bearing in mind then, that the law in Australia may yet be changed by the High Court in a more suitable case, how did the courts in *Royal Brunei* and *Farah* use the equitable precedents in formulating their versions of the liability?

A. The Use of Equitable Precedent in Royal Brunei and Farah

In *Royal Brunei* Lord Nicholls explicitly moved away from a close reading of the case law because, in his view, this approach was responsible for many of the problems besetting this area of law. Specifically, he jettisoned the traditional precedent of *Barnes v Addy*, on the ground that it had been applied as though it were a 'statute', and '[t]his approach has been inimical to analysis of the underlying concept'.[36] He then considered the matter as one of principle, taking into account all case law on third parties and breach of trust, whether binding or not.

The case law was used at two steps in his reasoning. First, the nineteenth century cases involving third parties and breach of trust were referred to in order to highlight an apparently illogical element in the reasoning of Lord Selborne in *Barnes v Addy* that directed attention to the trustee F's state of mind in order to determine whether D should be liable. Why should a dishonest D assisting a dishonest F be liable, but not a dishonest D assisting an honest F? Lord Nicholls pointed to the handful of trust cases contemporaneous with *Barnes v Addy* in which a dishonest and fraudulent breach was not required where D had procured, rather than assisted, the breach of trust by F. This apparent inconsistency in the precedents presented an opportunity to reconsider the underlying concept of participatory liability in relation to breach of trust. The highlighting of these cases by Lord Nicholls was a significant innovation for they had been overlooked by many judges and scholars.[37]

Secondly, the twentieth century *Barnes v Addy* case law was discussed in relation to the touchstone for D's liability. In considering the relevant law, Lord Nicholls drew on the decisions of judges in other jurisdictions (regardless of their level of seniority) as well as academic commentary. He used the twentieth century cases to extract a requirement of 'dishonesty' on the part of D, although most of those cases did not use that terminology. Under Lord Nicholls' approach, the detail of individual cases was given much less prominence in the reasoning process; instead, the precedents were balanced with a normative inquiry as to when

[36] *Royal Brunei* (n 3).

[37] But see *Elders Trustee & Executor Co Ltd v EG Reeves Pty Ltd* (1987) 78 ALR 193 (FCA) 238–39 (Gummow J) citing C Harpum, 'The Stranger as Constructive Trustee' (1986) 102 *LQR* 114.

third parties dealing with trustees should be subjected to equitable liability.[38] In this context, he considered scenarios that were particularly problematic in the twentieth century *Barnes v Addy* case law such as where D's conduct had been either careless or reckless.

The judicial methodology in *Royal Brunei* is the antithesis of that employed by the High Court in *Farah*. In *Farah* the High Court rejected the respondents' suggested reformulation of the second limb of *Barnes v Addy*.[39] Instead, the Court adhered to the literal reading of Lord Selborne's judgment as it was applied in *Consul* and to a literal reading of the same nineteenth century cases relied upon by Lord Nicholls in *Royal Brunei* concerning procuring and inducing breaches of trust. Consistently with this style of 'reasoning based on decisional precedent',[40] the judgment in *Farah* does not expressly indicate whether the Court approved or disapproved of the judgments in *Consul*, nor why it was considered unnecessary to consider the many Australian lower court decisions since then, let alone the international case law and commentary. This may have been due to the Court's decision to postpone full consideration of *Royal Brunei* for another day or it could be because only *Consul* was a binding precedent for Australian courts. There is also a paucity of normative reasoning in the judgment.

B. Which Approach Should Be Preferred?

What should be made of the differences in the use of the equitable precedents in these two leading cases? I will begin by considering *Farah*. The judicial method in *Farah* matches what Finn J has extrajudicially described as a 'theology of doctrine' approach to legal reasoning.[41] Under this approach, attention is paid primarily to the detail and presentation of doctrine in earlier cases at the expense of consideration of their context or of the underlying principle contained in those cases. To pursue Justice Finn's religious metaphor, it is a fundamentalist, literal approach to exegesis. The texts chosen for exegesis in *Farah* were the 1874 decision of *Barnes v Addy* and the 1975 decision of *Consul*.

Focussing on the detail of previous cases, without explaining why that detail is significant, has the potential to mislead lower courts as to why the law is as it is. It also assumes that the earlier courts got it right, which they may well have done, but not necessarily, and not necessarily for reasons that are enduring and which a

[38] Lord Nicholls rejected the options of no liability or strict liability.

[39] *Farah* (n 6) [183]. The respondents' reformulation replaced the dishonest and fraudulent breach requirement with 'a significant breach' and replaced 'assistance' with 'participated in a significant way'.

[40] M Kirby, 'Overcoming equity's Australian isolationism' (2009) 3 *Journal of Equity* 1, 19.

[41] P Finn, 'Knowing Receipt and Knowing Assistance: Balkanising Equity' (25th Annual Banking & Financial Services Law & Practice Conference, New Zealand, July 2008) 5. See also Finn, 'The Liability of Third Parties' (n 8); P Finn, 'Internationalization or isolation: the Australian cul de sac? The case of contract law' in E Bant and M Harding (eds), *Exploring Private Law* (Cambridge, Cambridge University Press, 2010) 41, 47.

contextual, principled analysis would elicit. With respect, the lack of explanation in *Farah* as to why the Court was adhering to the formulations in earlier case law, rather than adopting the Privy Council's changes to that law, is unhelpful to the lower courts, practitioners and legal scholars.

Even if we accept that *Farah* was not an appropriate factual vehicle in which to confront the challenge of *Royal Brunei*, the deference given by the High Court to *Consul* still seems misplaced given that *Consul* is not a strong precedent. The case concerned whether D, the corporate vehicle of a solicitor's young articled clerk, had knowingly participated in a breach of fiduciary duty by F, a property manager employed by the solicitor. D exploited property development opportunities which should have been offered by F to C, the solicitor's property development company, but which were instead offered by F to D. The appeal largely turned on how Hope J's findings of fact at first instance should be construed.[42] These concerned the young clerk's motivations, his knowledge of F's conduct and his knowledge of the solicitor's financial position.

A majority of the NSW Court of Appeal, Jacobs P dissenting, held that D was liable as a third party to F's breach of fiduciary duty.[43] D appealed to the High Court on the basis that actual knowledge of F's breach of duty was required and had not been shown. D relied upon the English Court of Appeal's 1969 decision in *Carl Zeiss Siftung v Herbert Smith & Co [No 2] (Carl Zeiss Siftung)*.[44] C responded that constructive knowledge[45] sufficed and relied upon two recent English Chancery Division cases that appeared to conflict with *Carl Zeiss* on this point.[46] The majority in the High Court in *Consul* consisted of Gibbs J and Stephen J, who both gave considered judgments, and Barwick CJ who agreed with Stephen J. It has been customary to read Stephen J's judgment in the High Court in conjunction with Jacobs P's judgment in the Court of Appeal as Stephen J drew upon Jacobs P's statement of the law. The dissenting judge in the High Court, McTiernan J, gave a reasoned judgment which turned primarily upon Hope J's findings of fact.

[42] Hope J found that although D and F deliberately hid their property dealings from the solicitor (which suggested D knew of F's wrongdoing), this was because the clerk believed that it was inappropriate for himself as articled clerk and F as an employee of the solicitor to be engaging in dealings similar to C's own property dealings. Moreover, the clerk wished to forestall awkward questions by the solicitor as to why D did not invest in the solicitor's own companies. Hope J also found that D believed reasonably that C was not interested in or financially able to pursue the property development opportunities. *Consul* (n 7) 405–07 (Stephen J).

[43] *DPC Estates Pty Ltd v Grey and Consul Pty Ltd* [1974] 1 NSWLR 443 (NSWCA). Hardie JA held that the clerk breached a fiduciary duty owed directly to the solicitor's companies, but he also agreed with Hutley JA who held that the clerk was liable under *Barnes v Addy* because he must have known that he was encouraging F to breach a fiduciary duty.

[44] *Carl Zeiss Stiftung v Herbert Smith & Co [No 2]* [1969] 2 Ch 276 (CA).

[45] ie, 'the sort of knowledge a reasonable and honest man would have had in the circumstances after making due inquiry': *Consul* (n 7) 400 (Gibbs J).

[46] *Karak Rubber Co Ltd v Burden* [1972] 1 WLR 602 (ChD); *Selangor United Rubber Estates Ltd v Cradock [No 3]* [1968] 1 WLR 1555 (ChD).

The High Court in *Farah* applied *Consul* in relation to two questions of law. First, what degree of knowledge sufficed for D's liability under the second limb of *Barnes v Addy*? This question was directly in issue in *Consul*, although only Stephen J gave a considered judgment on the question of whether recourse could be had 'to the doctrine of constructive notice'.[47] Gibbs J did not consider it necessary to reach a final view on the correctness of the English cases and assumed, without deciding the point, that they were consistent.[48] According to the Court in *Farah*, because Stephen J rejected level (v) knowledge on the *Baden* scale,[49] and Gibbs J left the point open, therefore level (iv)[50] is the limit for D to be liable. With respect, this is highly mechanistic reasoning on a question which has occupied countless pages of the law reports well beyond 1975 and the decision in *Consul*. Nor is the reasoning particularly persuasive given that one equally could argue that, of the four judges in *Consul*, McTiernan J clearly favoured level (v)[51] and Gibbs J found it unnecessary to express a concluded view.[52] This is not to say at all that Stephen J's reasoning and that of Jacobs P in the Court of Appeal is not persuasive, but the High Court did not refer expressly to that reasoning, instead relying on what it considered to be the ratio of the case.

The second question of law in *Farah* for which the High Court relied upon *Consul* was whether a dishonest and fraudulent breach of duty by F was required for the knowing assistance liability of D (the very question at issue in *Royal Brunei*). This question was not addressed in *Consul*. The respondents in *Farah* referred to passages in Gibbs J's judgment in which he describes the dishonest and fraudulent requirement 'by reference to equitable principles'.[53] The High Court dismissed the respondents' argument that Gibbs J thereby was referring to *any* breach of trust or fiduciary duty.[54] Neither the respondents' argument nor the High Court's rejection of it is self-evident from Gibbs J's judgment in *Consul*. The

[47] Resolution of this question was necessary in his view because it had not been shown that D either had actual knowledge of F's breach or had calculatedly abstained from enquiry. *Consul* (n 7) 408 (Stephen J).

[48] Gibbs J considered that, on the facts as the clerk believed them to be, the fiduciary would not have had a conflict of interest. Therefore D had not knowingly participated in any breach of fiduciary duty and it was unnecessary to decide whether constructive notice sufficed. *Consul* (n 7) 400 (Gibbs J).

[49] ie, 'knowledge of circumstances which would put an honest and reasonable man on inquiry': *Baden* (n 16).

[50] ie, 'knowledge of circumstances which would indicate the facts to an honest and reasonable man': ibid.

[51] McTiernan J agreed with the Court of Appeal's overturning of Hope J's findings. In his view, the clerk had undermined the loyalty of F and therefore D should be liable. *Barnes v Addy* supported this outcome, but if it were necessary he would accept 'whatever extension of doctrine' might be involved in the *Selangor* and *Karak* decisions. *Consul* (n 7) 385–86.

[52] Ibid 398.

[53] Ibid. Gibbs J cited the judgment of Ungoed-Thomas J in *Selangor United Rubber Estate* (n 46) in which Ungoed-Thomas J stressed that 'dishonest and fraudulent design' was to be understood by reference to equitable principles rather than criminal law or tort or contract. It is not clear from Ungoed-Thomas J's judgment whether this meant that the natural meaning of 'dishonest and fraudulent' was to be read down, eg, by reference to the concept of equitable fraud.

[54] *Farah* (n 6) [181].

focus of Gibbs J's reasoning in the passages relied upon was on whether *Barnes v Addy* liability (under both limbs) extended to situations where there is no misapplication of trust property. Gibbs J argued that breaches of *fiduciary* duty sufficed, as opposed to merely breaches of trust, but it is not clear that he envisaged that any such breach would suffice, whether dishonest and fraudulent or not, first because he was not drawing a distinct line between knowing receipt and knowing assistance and secondly, because he was not considering that question.[55] Thus, *Consul* is not a strong precedent in relation to either of the two grounds upon which it was relied by the High Court in *Farah*.

There are two final reasons why the High Court's reliance in *Farah* upon its earlier decision in *Consul* might be misplaced. *Consul* was decided at a time when English cases, although not binding upon the High Court,[56] were accorded deference and respect that they would not receive automatically now.[57] In 1975 it was still possible to appeal from State courts of appeal directly to the Privy Council. Appeals from the High Court to the Privy Council were abolished in July of 1975, only four months after judgment was given in *Consul*.[58] It was unlikely that the High Court would have embarked upon a radical reshaping of the English law or that it would have considered itself free to depart from the English law in order to meet local conditions.[59] Secondly, the English cases under consideration in *Consul* were very early examples of the twentieth century's resurgence of interest in *Barnes v Addy* and dealt with an unsettled question of law.[60] At that stage, the two limbs of *Barnes v Addy* were not so clearly differentiated, nor had the possibly distinct rationales for liability been thought through. For all these reasons, it seems unwise to place too much weight on the sparse ratio decidendi and obiter dicta of *Consul*. This leaves us with the High Court's reliance in *Farah* upon *Barnes v Addy* as correctly stating the law concerning equitable liability for assistance in a breach of trust and fiduciary duty and the Court's acknowledgement of a distinction between this form of participatory liability and D's liability for procuring a breach of trust by F.

Given these criticisms of the use of precedent in *Farah*, the principled approach taken by Lord Nicholls on behalf of the Privy Council in *Royal Brunei* must be preferable, whether or not we agree with his conclusion as to the law. Consideration of both precedent and principle is essential in courts of final appeal. This is all the more so when it is universally agreed that the cases are in disarray. But was Lord

55 *Consul* (n 7) 396–97 (Gibbs J).

56 *Public Transport Commission (NSW) v Murray-More (NSW) Pty Ltd* (1975) 132 CLR 336 (HCA).

57 Ibid 341 (Barwick CJ). See generally A Mason, 'The Break with the Privy Council and the Internationalisation of the Common Law' in P Cane (ed), *Centenary Essays for the High Court of Australia* (Sydney, Lexisnexis Butterworths, 2004) 69.

58 Privy Council (Appeals from the High Court) Act 1975 (Cth). The Act commenced on 8 July 1975: Commonwealth, *Gazette: Special*, No. S129, 1 July 1975. *Consul Development v DPC Estates* was decided on 26 February 1975.

59 Finn, 'Internationalization or isolation' (n 41) 44.

60 *Carl Zeiss Stiftung* (n 44); *Selangor United Rubber Estates* (n 46); *Karak Rubber Co* (n 46).

Nicholls' principled approach to the precedents correct? He took a helpful step in drawing attention to other nineteenth century case law on third party liability for breach of trust, but did these cases justify collapsing the distinction between assisting and procuring a breach of trust? In the next part of this chapter it will be argued that Lord Nicholls' collection of the relevant equitable precedents was incomplete and, hence, his formulation of equitable accessory liability is flawed.

IV. Extracting a Defensible Principle

A. Identifying the Relevant Precedents

Royal Brunei and *Farah* focussed upon five nineteenth century cases concerning participation in breaches of express private trusts. *Barnes v Addy* and two or three additional cases in which it was held that a third party who procured or induced a breach of trust could be liable were cited.[61] These precedents are clearly relevant as they involve participation in breach of trust.[62] But it is possible to go much further in identifying relevant equity cases from which a participatory liability principle might be drawn. A flaw in Lord Nicholls' reasoning is that he *only* considered cases concerning participation in breach of trust.

Obvious candidates for comparison with participatory liability for breach of trust and fiduciary duty are those equitable doctrines on the fringes of fiduciary law[63] where third parties are involved, such as undue influence and breach of confidence. One example is the liability of a third party financial institution that knowingly accepts a guarantee tainted by the debtor's undue influence over the guarantor.[64] Similarly, a third party who receives confidential information in circumstances where he or she knows or ought to know that it is confidential will be subject to equitable liability.[65]

[61] *Barnes* (n 13); *Fyler* (n 14); *Eaves* (n 14). The Privy Council also cited *Attorney-General v Corporation of Leicester* (1844) 7 Beav 176, 49 ER 1031. The High Court also cited *Alleyne* (n 14). The two latter cases applied *Fyler*. See generally Harpum, 'The Stranger as Constructive Trustee' (n 37) 141–44.

[62] For reasons of space and clarity I will not attempt to comprehensively consider their twentieth or twenty-first century counterparts.

[63] Opinion is divided on whether these doctrines form part of fiduciary law. P Finn, *Fiduciary Obligations* (Sydney, Law Book Co, 1977); M Conaglen, *Fiduciary Loyalty* (Oxford, Hart Publishing, 2010) 236–44. My arguments do not depend upon which view is correct.

[64] Eg, *Bank of New South Wales v Rogers* (1941) 65 CLR 42 (HCA). See generally R Meagher, D Heydon and M Leeming, *Meagher, Gummow & Lehane's Equity: Doctrine and Remedies*, 4th edn (Chatswood, Butterworths LexisNexis, 2002) para [15.150].

[65] *Prince Albert v Strange* (1849) 1 Mac & G 25, 41 ER 1171. See generally Meagher, Heydon and Leeming, *Equity* (n 64) para [41–110]. Even a D who acquires notice of the confidentiality of information after its receipt will be bound by the confidentiality obligation, although there are unresolved questions concerning whether D's change of position should be accommodated. *Wheatley v Bell* [1982] 2 NSWLR 544 (NSWSC); *Johns v Australian Securities Commission* (1993) 178 CLR 408 (HCA) 459–60 (Gaudron J).

It is possible to go beyond these fiduciary-related doctrines to areas of equity where D's third party liability has evolved into an independent cause of action. There are two overlapping doctrines that meet the description of an independent cause of action that could equally be conceptualised as third party liability of the same form as that encountered in participatory liability for breach of trust or fiduciary duty:

(i) The liability in England of financial institutions who accept a security in circumstances where the surety is subjected to undue influence or misrepresentation by the debtor and where prescriptive duties of information disclosure have not been met by the financial institution;[66]

(ii) The liability in Australia of financial institutions who accept a security in circumstances where there is a risk of misunderstanding by the surety arising from a relationship of trust and confidence between the surety and debtor and where the institution has not ensured that the surety is fully informed.[67] This liability does not depend upon an equitable wrong having been committed by the debtor; hence, it will not always be possible to conceptualise this as a third party liability.[68]

If we accept that each of these independent causes of action may be conceptualised alternatively as third party liability, then there is a range of equitable participatory liability which can usefully be considered alongside third party liability for breach of trust or fiduciary duty.[69]

A seemingly obvious group of participatory liability cases to include when collecting instances of equitable participatory liability concerns D's personal liability for receipt of trust property (the first limb of *Barnes v Addy*). But these will be excluded for now. Despite their historical twinning with knowing assistance cases, they raise slightly different considerations due to their proximity to tracing and priorities claims. Rightly or wrongly, the liability sometimes turns on the protection of C's property interests, rather than on the state of D's conscience.[70] A similar ambivalence between the protection of property interests and a concern with D's conscience can be seen where a third party without notice receives the benefit of a gift or transaction tainted by an equitable wrong other than breach of trust, although less attention has been paid to these equally problematic instances

[66] *Royal Bank of Scotland Plc v Etridge [No 2]* [2001] UKHL 44, [2002] 2 AC 773. See also C Rickett, 'The financier's duty of care to a surety' (1998) 114 *LQR* 17. Rickett argues that the lender's liability in such cases can be conceptualised as either secondary liability dependent on notice of the primary wrong or primary liability based upon the lender's own wrongdoing.

[67] *Garcia v National Australia Bank Ltd* [1998] HCA 48, (1998) 194 CLR 395.

[68] The Australian doctrine of unconscionable dealings could be included as a category (iii) to the extent that the weaker party's special disadvantage is the product of another's equitable wrongdoing, eg, where a financial institution takes a security with notice that the surety is under the undue influence of the debtor. See, eg *Commercial Bank of Australia Ltd v Amadio* (1983) 151 CLR 447 (HCA) 464 (Mason J).

[69] This is not a novel approach: see R Austin, 'Constructive Trusts' in P Finn (ed), *Essays in Equity* (Sydney, LawBook Co, 1985) 196, 200; Finn (n 8) 212–13.

[70] Dietrich and Ridge, '"The Receipt of What?"' (n 17) 58–60. See also Harpum (n 37) 126.

of liability.[71] It is possible, and desirable in my view, to reconcile these cases with non property-related instances of equitable participatory liability, but for now it is safest to exclude from consideration cases where a property law analysis might be relevant so that there is no distortion of the analysis.[72]

What becomes clear from considering a broad range of equitable participatory liability cases including, but not limited to, participation in breach of trust and fiduciary duty is that the cases fall into two distinct groups of third party participation, as will now be discussed.

i. Group 1: Participation in an Equitable Wrong for Personal Gain Beyond Remuneration for Services

The first group of equitable participatory liability cases covers a range of types of participation, but whatever the level of involvement in the primary equitable wrong the participants all derive some benefit from the wrong other than simply professional remuneration. This group takes in almost all instances of equitable participatory liability.

At one end of the spectrum of cases in Group 1 are third parties who actively procure the primary wrong.[73] Thus, a solicitor who knowingly induces an unsuspecting trustee client to breach the trust by investing the trust fund with another client of the solicitor who owes money to the solicitor, will be liable to restore the trust fund.[74] Similarly, a company director who procures a breach of trust by a corporate trustee[75] and a creditor who persuades a debtor wrongfully (through undue influence or misrepresentation, for example) to extract security from a relative will be liable.[76] In all these cases the bona fides of the party committing the primary wrong is irrelevant to D's liability.[77]

Closer to the middle of the spectrum of cases in Group 1 are those third parties who have actively facilitated the primary breach, without necessarily procuring it.[78] An example is the articled clerk and his corporate vehicle in *Consul* who allegedly

[71] Eg a volunteer who receives property tainted by undue influence must rescind the gift regardless of whether he or she had notice of the undue influence: *Bridgeman v Green* (1757) Wilm 58, 97 ER 22; *Tottenham v Green* (1863) 32 LJ Ch 201, 206; *Addie v Campbell* (1841) 4 Beav 401, 49 ER 394. See also Meagher, Heydon and Leeming (n 64) para [15.150]; A Burrows, 'The Australian law of restitution: has the High Court lost its way?' in Bant and Harding (eds), *Exploring Private Law* (n 41) 67, 81.

[72] Cases concerning receipt of trust property would be relevant in an extended study: eg *Harries v Rees* [1867] 37 LJ Ch 102.

[73] Eg *Syrimi v Hinds* (1996) 6 NTLR 1 (NTCA).

[74] *Fyler* (n 14). The principle in *Fyler* was applied in *Alleyne* (n 14) and *Attorney-General v Corporation of Leicester* (n 61).

[75] *Elders Trustee & Executor Co Ltd* (n 37) (procurement not found on the facts). See generally *Australian Securities Commission v AS Nominees Ltd* (1995) 62 FCR 504 (FCA) 523 (Finn J).

[76] *John Owen & JM Gutch v Sarah Homan* (1853) 4 HL Cas 997, 1034; 10 ER 752, 767 (Lord Cranworth LC). The House of Lords held strong suspicions as to the lack of probity of the creditor in this case, although no positive finding was made that the creditor procured the debtor's misrepresentation.

[77] Eg *Eaves* (n 14).

[78] Eg *Mayor of Salford v Lever* [1891] 1 QB 168 (CA). At F's suggestion, D agreed to pay a bribe to F so that F would ensure that C entered a contract for the supply of coal by D.

participated in breaches of fiduciary duty by F, a senior employee of the solicitor to whom the clerk was articled.[79] The clerk did not procure or induce F's equitable wrong, but he actively facilitated it by jointly financing the tainted property dealings. Similarly, financial institutions that benefit from securities tainted by an equitable wrong, such as undue influence or misrepresentation, may have facilitated that wrong through not complying with the requisite standard of advice[80] or by taking the benefit with notice of the breach of primary duty.[81] And a publisher who knowingly publishes confidential information may be treated as actively facilitating the primary wrong, rather than simply taking the benefits subsequently.[82]

At the other end of the spectrum in Group 1 are those third parties who passively facilitate the primary equitable wrong. An example comes from the Privy Council's decision in *Cook v Deeks*.[83] D, a company controlled by F, took a business opportunity that F, in breach of fiduciary duty, diverted from the principal company, C. Similarly, in relation to the equitable wrong of breach of confidence, a publisher who attempts to publish material knowing that it only could have been obtained in breach of confidence by another, F, will be injuncted from publishing regardless of whether the publisher actively induced F's breach of confidence.[84]

One case that sits in Group 1, albeit a little uncomfortably, is *Eaves v Hickson*[85] which was cited in both *Royal Brunei* and *Farah*. A father, D, forged a marriage certificate in order to ensure that his illegitimate children would qualify for distributions under a trust. The trustees, in innocent reliance on the forgery, committed a breach of the trust by distributing to the children. Sir John Romilly MR held that D must pay into court whatever could not be recovered from the children and the trustees must then make up any shortfall to the trust. The problem with fitting this case into Group 1 is that the father did not derive a direct personal benefit; nonetheless, he did receive an indirect financial advantage from his children's welfare being provided for through the trust. Perhaps this is a case where it is clearer to conceptualise D's liability as an independent cause of action (fraud) which may also be seen as a third party liability for another equitable wrong (breach of trust). Nowadays, if the trustees acted reasonably, they would be excused from liability and D would be pursued for fraud.

Thus, Group 1 of equity's participatory liability cases encompasses those Ds who procure an equitable wrong, those who facilitate an equitable wrong, and those who participate in an equitable wrong simply through receiving the benefit of a transaction tainted by the wrong. What unites the third parties in Group 1 is

[79] *Consul* (n 7).

[80] *Royal Bank of Scotland Plc v Etridge [No 2]* (n 66); *Garcia* (n 67).

[81] *John Owen & JM Gutch* (n 76); *Bank of New South Wales v Rogers* (n 64).

[82] Eg *Attorney General v Guardian Newspapers (No 2)* [1990] 1 AC 109 (HL). Toulson J in *Fyffes* (n 30) 670 describes the facts thus: 'The *Sunday Times* knowingly assisted Mr Peter Wright to breach his duty of confidentiality to the British Government by publishing extracts from his memoirs as an MI5 agent.'

[83] *Cook v Deeks* [1916] AC 554 (PC).

[84] *Abernethy v Hutchinson* (1824) 3 LJ Ch 209; *Prince Albert* (n 65).

[85] *Eaves* (n 14).

that they derive some advantage, other than professional remuneration, from the relevant transaction or conduct which constitutes the primary equitable wrong. Group 1 cases can be found in relation to many primary equitable wrongs.

ii. Group 2: The Provision of Services by Pure Agents that Facilitate an Equitable Wrong

The second, and remaining, group of third parties who attract equitable participatory liability, but who do not fit the pattern in Group 1, I will call 'pure agents'. Pure agents are third parties providing agency services to the primary wrongdoer that facilitate the occurrence of an equitable wrong. Unlike Group 1 participants, they receive no direct benefit from the tainted dealings other than, possibly generous, remuneration for their services. Generally, they are related to the primary wrongdoer only by the agency relationship. Solicitors[86] and accountants[87] predominate in this group.

Significantly, Group 2 cases are found only in relation to breach of trust and breach of fiduciary duty. That is, there appears to be no other equitable wrong in relation to which equity imposes participatory liability upon agents involved in the primary wrong through the provision of professional agency services alone. This is the group described by Lord Selborne in *Barnes v Addy* where he was at pains to restrict their liability.[88] This is also the group focussed upon by Lord Nicholls in *Royal Brunei*, when discussing whether a negligent participant in a breach of trust should be liable to C.[89]

Ironically, the concerns expressed by both Lord Selborne in *Barnes v Addy* and Lord Nicholls in *Royal Brunei* in relation to imposing liability on professional agents who facilitate a breach of trust through careless performance of their duties do not reflect the factual scenario in *Royal Brunei* which did *not* concern a 'pure agent'. Mr Tan, the company director of the corporate trustee in *Royal Brunei*, belongs in Group 1: he carelessly facilitated a breach of trust by the trustee company, which he controlled, for his own financial ends. Lord Nicholls implied that Tan made no personal gain from his mismanagement of the trustee company because the trust money was used for the company's 'ordinary business purposes'.[90] But given that Tan controlled the company and was its principal shareholder, any gain received by the company (through meeting its cash shortfalls by recourse to the trust fund) was Tan's gain. He was more than a pure agent who received only remuneration for services. He was the company's alter ego and thus benefitted directly from the breach of trust. The facts of *Royal Brunei* therefore fall into Group 1 even though Lord Nicholls' reasoning was pertinent only to Group 2 instances of participatory liability.

[86] Eg *Barnes* (n 13); *Carl Zeiss Stiftung* (n 44); *Twinsectra* (n 9).
[87] Eg *Barlow Clowes* (n 10).
[88] *Barnes* (n 13) 251–52.
[89] *Royal Brunei* (n 3) 391.
[90] Ibid 383.

An odd case which is difficult to categorise, but which probably falls into Group 2, is *Midgley v Midgley*.[91] There, an over-zealous solicitor, who actively encouraged and procured a breach of fiduciary duty by the executor of a deceased estate, was held liable to the estate along with the defaulting executor and the solicitor's clients who received payment of a statute-barred debt from the estate in breach of trust. The solicitor was said to be 'the instigator and schemer of the whole thing'.[92] On the one hand, the facts seem suited to Group 1, as D actively procured the breach of trust. On the other hand, D received no benefit, other than his professional remuneration, and was retained as an agent providing professional services. It seems likely that D's liability actually depended upon tracing, for most of the misapplied funds remained in D's trust account.[93] Leaving the possibility of tracing aside, however, the facts seem to be an extreme and unusual example of Group 2 participatory liability.

B. The Rationales for Liability in Group 1 and Group 2

In Group 1 participatory liability cases there is an acknowledged consensus as to the rationale for liability whatever the nature of the primary equitable wrong, namely: the prevention of D's exploitation for gain of C's vulnerability arising from the primary wrong. The New South Wales Supreme Court decision in *Khan v Khan* contains a helpful statement of the rationale.[94] In that case, the purchasers' application for specific performance of a contract for the sale of land was refused on the ground that the purchasers had notice of undue influence exercised upon the vendor by her religious leader. Barrett J noted that the liability of a third party to undue influence

> involves the kind of secondary liability based on knowing participation discussed in *Royal Brunei Airlines Sdn Bhd v Tan*. The third party recipient of benefit [D], who knowingly takes with notice of the undue influence exerted upon the disponer [C] by the person having ascendancy [F], takes unfair or unconscientious advantage of a situation in which a force against which equity will grant relief is known by him or her to be at work.[95]

The same rationale is given in cases of breach of confidence,[96] unconscionable dealings and related doctrines.[97] It is not uncommon for the courts and commentators discussing the rationale for equitable participatory liability in relation

[91] *Midgley v Midgley* [1893] 3 Ch 282 (CA). See Harpum (n 37) 142–43.
[92] Ibid 301 (Lindley LJ).
[93] But see Sales, 'The Tort of Conspiracy and Secondary Liability' (n 33) 504, n 38.
[94] *Khan v Khan* [2004] NSWSC 1189, (2004) 62 NSWLR 229.
[95] Ibid 235. Barrett J based his analysis on Meagher, Heydon and Leeming (n 64) para [15.150].
[96] In the leading case of *Prince Albert* (n 65) 44–45; 1178–9 it was said that a third party who knowingly took advantage of 'a breach of trust, confidence or contract by another' would be liable in equity. See generally Mitchell (n 12) 164–65; R Toulson and C Phipps, *Confidentiality* (London, Sweet & Maxwell, 1996) 92; Meagher, Heydon and Leeming (n 64) para [41–035].
[97] *Amadio* (n 68) 462 (Mason J).

to wrongs other than breach of trust or fiduciary duty to refer to that form of liability. There is also some cross-referencing in the case law on participatory liability for breach of trust and fiduciary duty back to other forms of equitable participatory liability.[98] Overwhelmingly then, it appears that the rationale for Group 1 cases is the same whatever the nature of the primary equitable wrong.

The rationale for liability in Group 2, the provision of services by pure agents that facilitate a breach of trust or fiduciary duty, is not as clear-cut. The substantive rationale appears to be that D is so implicated in F's fraud that he or she should be treated as also committing an equitable wrong even though D received no gain other than remuneration for services.[99] But the substantive rationale does not appear to be the sole, or even primary, rationale for liability in Group 2 cases. It is bolstered by far more pragmatic, policy-driven concerns. The liability in Group 2 is grounded in the ability of pure agents to act as 'whistle-blowers' on trustee or fiduciary misconduct. Plus, there is a deterrent function: the threat of such liability may deter pure agents from providing their services in situations of breach of trust or fiduciary duty and thus lessen the opportunities for such breaches. In other words, given that Group 2 consists only of breach of trust and fiduciary duty cases, it would seem that the liability here is bound up with the historically strong prophylactic and protective function of equity's trust jurisdiction.[100]

V. Implications of a Broader Consideration of the Equitable Precedents

Having identified two distinct groups of participatory liability in the case law, does this cast any light upon whether the English or Australian participatory liability schemes outlined in Part II should be preferred? It will be recalled that the doctrinal differences between the two schemes for breach of trust and fiduciary duty concern:

(i) whether there is one category of liability for breach of trust or fiduciary duty, namely, accessory liability (*Royal Brunei*) or two categories of liability, namely, knowing assistance by D in a dishonest and fraudulent design by F and knowing procurement by D of any breach of trust (*Farah*).
(ii) whether D's liability turns on D's knowledge (*Farah*) or D's dishonesty (*Royal Brunei*).
(iii) whether accessory liability as expounded in *Royal Brunei* extends to fiduciary breaches not involving property under F's control.
(iv) whether the remedies are loss-based only.

98 Eg *Fyffes* (n 30) 670.
99 *Harries v Rees* [1867] 37 LJ Ch 102, 106–07 (Rolt J); Harpum (n 37) 116.
100 Finn (n 8) 197; Ridge, 'Justifying the Remedies for Dishonest Assistance' (n 33) 446–47.

My intention here is simply to make some suggestions as to how these differences may be resolved and to suggest a way forward in developing the law on participatory liability for breach of trust and fiduciary duty.

A. How Many Categories of Liability?

A consideration of equitable participatory liability as a whole demonstrates that both the Privy Council and the High Court's categorisations are flawed. Lord Nicholls' collapsing of knowing assistance cases and procurement of breach of trust cases into a uniform accessory liability for breach of trust incorrectly conflates two forms of liability that have different rationales and involve factually different scenarios. On the other hand, the High Court's signalling in *Farah*, albeit cryptic, of the need to distinguish procurement cases from assistance cases in relation to breach of trust or fiduciary duty better accords with my suggested categorisation of Group 1 and Group 2, although, again, the failure to consider the full range of equitable participatory liability precedents meant that the need to confine the second limb of *Barnes v Addy* to pure agents who receive only remuneration for their services (Group 2) was overlooked.

Furthermore, both the substantive and pragmatic rationales for Group 2 liability strongly support retention of the dishonest and fraudulent breach requirement in the second limb of *Barnes v Addy*. If D is liable because of his or her implication in F's fraud and failure to prevent F's fraud through disclosure or refusal of the agency services, then both F's wrongdoing and D's knowledge of that wrongdoing must be of a high order. This suggests that the dishonest and fraudulent breach element of liability under the second limb of *Barnes v Addy* is an essential element in justifying D's liability and furthermore, that D's state of knowledge of F's dishonest and fraudulent breach should closely equate to actual knowledge. Agents should only be liable for participation in egregious breaches by F that could be detected and, possibly, prevented.[101] This accords with Lord Selborne's reservations in *Barnes v Addy* itself against too readily imposing liability on the agents of trustees.[102]

Thus, what is missing from both the English and Australian participatory liability schemes is explicit recognition that liability under the second limb of *Barnes v Addy* is a narrow and exceptional liability that is confined to agents receiving only remuneration for services.[103] Once this is appreciated, the obvious question is whether Group 2 liability should wither away altogether on the basis that there is

[101] See also Gardner (n 16) 77.

[102] *Barnes* (n 13) 251–52. See also *Harries* (n 99) 106–07 (Rolt J): '[I]t is well settled that, as a general rule, the solicitor or agent of a personal representative or trustee is accountable only to his principal; that as a general rule the *cestui que trustent* cannot call on the agent to account as trustee, unless fraud can be made out against him personally, or unless he, knowing of the fraud of the trustee, has derived personal benefit therefrom, or unless some other special equity is established against him.' Rolt LJ cites *Lockwood v Abdy* (1845) 14 Sim 437, 60 ER 428 and *Fyler* (n 14).

[103] Harpum (n 37) 148.

adequate common law and statutory regulation of agents providing professional services to trustees that facilitate a breach of trust.[104]

B. Does Liability Turn on D's Knowledge or D's Dishonesty?

Although most attention has focussed upon whether the touchstone for liability should turn on D's knowledge or D's dishonesty, analysis of a broader range of equitable participatory liability cases suggests that this is a second-order question that is much more easily resolved once the cases are correctly classified and their rationales properly understood. In relation to Group 1, participation in an equitable wrong for personal gain, D's knowledge or notice of the primary wrong is universally acknowledged to be the appropriate touchstone for liability. This is so even in relation to areas of third party liability which, as yet, are not fully explored.[105] The emphasis on D's knowledge has not been contentious except where Group 1 cases have been wrongly considered as Group 2 cases, that is, as *Barnes v Addy* knowing assistance liability.[106] Outside participatory liability for breach of trust or fiduciary duty, the courts seem far more relaxed about a 'jury question' approach to knowledge or notice and there is a rich jurisprudence concerning what is necessary for liability.[107] In other words, there is more confidence that the knowledge question can be answered.

Of course, this apparently insouciant attitude towards the requisite knowledge may be because D's potential liability often is limited to transaction reversal or an account of gains made.[108] Thus, it may be helpful to consider an approach to Group 2 liability that balances the degree of wrongdoing with the extent of knowledge of the primary equitable wrong and the potential remedy. If so, a 'sliding scale' of knowledge determined by the degree of F's wrongdoing and the remedy sought, may be appropriate.

On the other hand, in relation to Group 2, pure agents, knowledge as the touchstone of liability has been far more problematic, particularly in relation to whether something less than actual knowledge or actual notice is sufficient. This makes sense when one considers that this is an exceptional liability under which D must bear the potentially onerous and unbounded losses of C, rather than the reversal of a transaction or return of a gain received. As discussed above, both the substantive and pragmatic rationales for Group 2 liability suggest that a very high touchstone of liability should apply, namely, actual knowledge or the equivalent standard of equitable notice.

[104] See, eg Finn (n 8) 195.

[105] Eg participatory liability for breach of confidence: *Johns* (n 65) 459–60 (Gaudron J).

[106] Eg *Royal Brunei* (n 3) 386.

[107] Eg *Amadio* (n 68) 467–68 (Mason J), 477 (Deane J). This adds weight to calls for knowledge (or dishonesty) questions to be decided as 'jury questions': R Walker, 'Dishonesty and Unconscionable Conduct in Commercial Life—Some Reflections on Accessory Liability and Knowing Receipt' (2002) 27 *Sydney Law Review* 187, 195, 197. See also *Twinsectra* (n 9) [134] (Lord Millett); Mitchell (n 12) 212.

[108] Finn (n 8) 207, n 71.

C. The Ambit of Liability

Recognising that the same principles apply to Group 1 cases regardless of whether a trust or fiduciary relationship is involved means that this form of participatory liability does not depend upon the misapplication of property under the control of the trustee or fiduciary. Group 1 encompasses participation in all types of equitable wrong including breaches of fiduciary duty not involving any misapplication of property. Equally, as suggested above, Group 1 can encompass receipt of property cases. Conversely, the strong historical link between the second limb of *Barnes v Addy* and the protection of *trust* beneficiaries suggests that Group 2 liability should be reined in accordingly.

D. Remedies

Finally, once Group 2 is confined within appropriate limits, it becomes clear that the liability is loss-based for, by definition, Group 2 agents have made no gain. Agents of a trustee or fiduciary who profit through assistance in a breach of trust or fiduciary duty belong in Group 1 where gain-based remedies are available. The rationale for Group 1 cases, namely, preventing exploitation by D of C's vulnerability, lends itself most naturally to gain-based or transaction-reversal remedies, however a range of equitable remedies tailored to the particular facts is available. This may explain why there has been little concern about the availability of gain-based remedies even where the cases involved trustees or fiduciaries.[109] Only a loss-based remedy is suited to Group 2 cases and, as noted already, the potentially onerous effect of such remedies helps explain the reluctance to impose liability expressed by Lord Selborne in *Barnes v Addy.*

VI. Conclusion

My objective in this chapter has been to evaluate the use of case law in the formulation of the English and Australian participatory liability schemes for breach of trust and fiduciary duty as epitomised by the judgments in *Royal Brunei* and *Farah*. The methodological differences in the two decisions raise questions about how the law can develop in a way that respects the accumulated wisdom of precedent without becoming stultified by it. So far as judicial method is concerned, Lord Nicholls' judgment in *Royal Brunei* is a model of senior appellate court reasoning. The strength of the judgment is that it seeks to explain, as well as expound, the relevant law. But the accessory liability principle arrived at by Lord Nicholls in *Royal Brunei* is flawed because his choice of relevant equitable precedents was

[109] Eg *Consul* (n 7); *United States Surgical* (n 25).

too narrow in that he confined himself to considering cases in which there was a breach of trust.

Looking at equitable participatory liability as a whole, rather than at breach of trust cases only, makes it clearer that there are two distinct forms of liability. The first, and larger, Group 1 is much easier to find a rationale for. Here one principle can be used to encapsulate the liability whether D's participation is in the form of procurement, assistance, or passive receipt of a benefit. The liability arises because D exploits for gain C's vulnerability arising from the primary equitable wrong. The second form of liability, that of Group 2 pure agents who facilitate the breach of primary duty through rendering professional services, does not appear in relation to any equitable wrong other than that of breach of trust or fiduciary duty and rests on an historical over-protection of trust beneficiaries that might not be warranted today in light of contemporary common law and statutory regulation of professional agents. This suggests that Lord Nicholls in *Royal Brunei* incorrectly conflated two distinct forms of liability into 'accessory liability' and that his policy discussion, whilst directed to 'pure agents', was given in a case that did not involve that scenario. A proper understanding of the relevant equitable precedents opens the way for a more soundly based legal principle to be formulated.

The High Court in *Farah* offered little by way of explanation for why Australian courts should continue to apply the law as stated in *Barnes v Addy* and applied in *Consul*. The judgment founds itself almost exclusively upon precedent, but in this instance the precedent of *Consul* is not helpful. The 'theology of doctrine' approach to legal reasoning taken in *Farah* is not symptomatic of all contemporary High Court equity decisions,[110] however, and given that the High Court in *Farah* did not rule out a full consideration of *Royal Brunei* when the matter is properly before it, there remains an opportunity for the equitable case law to be revisited in Australia.

[110] Finn, 'Knowing Receipt and Knowing Assistance' (n 41) 5. See *Friend v Brooker* [2009] HCA 21, (2009) 239 CLR 129 for a recent illustration of the effectiveness of combining contextual analysis of the older precedents with an appreciation for principle and policy matters in relation to the doctrine of equitable contribution.

7

Equitable Compensation

JAMIE GLISTER*

I. Introduction

This chapter examines, from a comparative perspective, the principles of equitable compensation in two specific areas: where trust property has been misapplied by a trustee, and where a fiduciary has committed a breach of the no conflict rule by failing to disclose material facts to his or her principal. The first involves discussing the famous decisions of *Re Dawson*,[1] *Target Holdings v Redferns*,[2] and *Youyang v Minter Ellison Morris Fletcher*.[3] The second concerns *Brickenden v London Loan & Savings Co*,[4] and how Australia, Canada, England and New Zealand have each retreated from the strict causation rule laid down by Lord Thankerton in that case.

It was, perhaps, not surprising to discover that Australia and *Youyang* are outliers in respect of the first issue. Although the *Youyang* decision seems to fit neatly with theories of substitutive performance, the enforcement of primary duties and the taking of accounts, nonetheless it would probably have been decided differently in Canada, England or New Zealand. By contrast, in respect of the second discussion it was interesting to find that New Zealand equity jurisprudence might be characterised as more traditional than that of the other jurisdictions. As Andrew Butler and Tim Miller explain in their chapter in this book, and despite the views of some in New South Wales, New Zealand equity is not always heretical!

I use the labels 'substitutive' and 'reparative' regularly in this chapter, and those terms should be explained at the outset.[5] They are closely linked to 'primary' and

* Thanks to Nicola Bodor for excellent research assistance.

[1] *Re Dawson (dec'd); Union Fidelity Trustee Co Ltd v Perpetual Trustee Co Ltd* [1966] 2 NSWR 211 (NSWSC).

[2] *Target Holdings v Redferns* [1996] 1 AC 421 (HL).

[3] *Youyang Pty Ltd v Minter Ellison Morris Fletcher* [2003] HCA 15, (2003) 212 CLR 484.

[4] *Brickenden v London Loan & Savings Co of Canada* [1934] 3 DLR 465 (PC).

[5] The terms were used by Dr Elliott in his doctoral thesis and published work: see S Elliott, *Compensation Claims Against Trustees* (DPhil thesis, University of Oxford, 2002); S Elliott, 'Remoteness Criteria in Equity' (2002) 65 *MLR* 588; S Elliott and J Edelman, '*Target Holdings* considered in Australia' (2003) 119 *LQR* 545; S Elliott and C Mitchell, 'Remedies for Dishonest Assistance' (2004) 67 *MLR* 16; J Edelman and S Elliott, 'Money remedies against trustees' (2004) 18 *Trust Law International* 116. They have since been adopted by other commentators: see, eg C Rickett, 'Equitable Compensation: Towards

'secondary',[6] in that a plaintiff who seeks substitutive compensation is trying to enforce a primary duty and one who seeks reparative compensation is trying to enforce a secondary duty. With primary duties the enforcement vehicle is an order for account, and if that account reveals an unauthorised disbursement then the beneficiary can simply falsify that entry. The trustee must then either restore the property or compensate with ('substitute') his own money. The availability of an accounting order against non-trustee custodial fiduciaries means that no distinction is required between 'true trust' situations and other situations involving custodial fiduciaries, but for a primary enforcement analysis to make sense in this context there must be an initial custodial fiduciary relationship.[7] In contrast, reparative compensation involves a money payment to compensate for the harm caused to the principal or beneficiary by the breach of duty. The size of the award is measured by reference to the amount lost, although, as will be discussed below, the governing rules may not always be the same as those that regulate the quantification of damages at common law. But whether the analogy with common law damages is close or not, the plaintiff will still be enforcing a secondary obligation to pay compensation for loss.

II. Misapplication of Trust Property

Re Dawson is normally cited in any discussion of equitable compensation for breach of trust. Street J's judgment appears to be quoted whenever a breach of trust case is heard in the Commonwealth,[8] but it is interpreted to mean different things. It is argued in this paper that the reach of *Re Dawson* is narrower than sometimes appreciated, in that it can only ever apply to breaches of trust or other custodial fiduciary relations that involve the misapplication of trust property (and

a Blueprint?' (2003) 25 *Sydney Law Review* 31; J Edelman, 'Money awards of the cost of performance' (2010) 4 *Journal of Equity* 122.

[6] For particularly clear explanations of the primary/secondary distinction in this context see: R Chambers, 'Liability' in P Birks and A Pretto (eds), *Breach of Trust* (Oxford, Hart Publishing, 2002) 1; L Smith, 'The measurement of compensation claims against trustees and fiduciaries' in E Bant and M Harding (eds), *Exploring Private Law* (Cambridge, Cambridge University Press, 2010) 363.

[7] Of course a trust beneficiary is not limited to a substitutive claim. If the complaint is that not enough assets were obtained then the beneficiary can 'surcharge' the account (which would then be taken on the footing of wilful default). Surcharging involves taking the account as if the trustee had indeed acquired those assets, with the effect that the trustee is made liable for the assets' value. But in such cases the response is reparative and the secondary duty is in play, even if the principles that apply to such a claim are still plaintiff-friendly. A good recent example is *Whitefish Lake Band of Indians v Canada (A-G)* [2007] ONCA 744, where the Crown sold an Indian band's timber rights for less than market value. The sale (and therefore the breach) took place in 1886 and the assessment of equitable compensation occurred in 2007. The assessment could take account of what would have happened if the correct amount had been received, held on trust and invested for the intervening years. See also *Guerin v R* [1984] 2 SCR 335 (SCC).

[8] It is accurately described as an 'ubiquitous decision' in G McLay, 'Equitable Damages' in A Butler (ed), *Equity and Trusts in New Zealand*, 2nd edn (Wellington, Thomson Reuters, 2009) 911, 927.

perhaps not to all of them). In the case itself, after discussing a number of older authorities,[9] Street J said:

> The principles embodied in this approach do not appear to involve any enquiry into whether the loss was caused by or flowed from the breach. Rather the enquiry in each instance would appear to be whether the loss would have happened if there had been no breach.[10]

So, according to Street J, the question is not whether the breach caused the loss but is whether the loss would have happened if there had been no such breach. This is a rather wordy formulation and one might assume that (i) a loss of property from a trust and (ii) a breach of a duty to keep property safe and disburse it within the terms of the trust[11] are two ways of saying the same thing. As the authors of *On Equity* say, apart from the court's inherent and statutory powers to relieve the trustee, liability is strict.[12] In fact this is not quite right because there will be times when trust property is lost through theft or destruction and where a reasonable trustee would not have insured against that risk. Here there is loss to the trust estate, and there is a factual failure to keep the property safe, but there is no breach of duty. This means that we have to be careful to distinguish between factual loss and breach-related loss,[13] and it is suggested that this is what Street J meant in the *Re Dawson* quote. However, the point is that once a breach has been found then no causal enquiry is required. The only question is whether the trustee's duty to keep trust property safe was breached and, apart from those rare cases of uninsured theft and destruction indicated above, in most cases where trust property is lost the answer will be yes.

[9] *Caffrey v Darby* (1801) 6 Ves Jun 488, 31 ER 1159; *Clough v Bond* (1838) 3 My & Cr 490, 40 ER 1016. Street J quoted a long passage from the judgment of Lord Cottenham LC in the latter case, where the Lord Chancellor cited *Phillips v Phillips* (1676) 2 Freem Ch 11, 22 ER 1024; *Powell v Evans* (1801) 5 Ves Jun 839, 31 ER 886; *Tebbs v Carpenter* (1816) 1 Madd 290, 56 ER 107; *Hancom v Allen* (1774) 2 Dick 498, 21 ER 363; *Howe v Earl of Dartmouth* (1802) 7 Ves Jun 137, 32 ER 56. Just after the quoted part of his judgment, Street J discussed *Salway v Salway* (1831) 2 Russ & My 215, 39 ER 376.

[10] *Re Dawson* (n 1) 215. At this point in his judgment Street J was simply distinguishing the trustee obligation to repay a trust fund and a normal personal debt. This was in the context of whether there was 'sufficient peculiarity in the obligation' to justify departing from the common law rule in relation to damages payable in foreign currency (the words of Lord Radcliffe in the earlier case of *Re United Railways of Havana & Regla Ware-Houses Ltd* [1961] AC 1007 (HL) 1060, applied in *Re Dawson* (n 1) 214). Having found that there was sufficient peculiarity, Street J considered the content of the trustee's obligation at 216: '[The obligation of a defaulting trustee] has always been regarded as tantamount to an obligation to effect restitution *in specie*. … Authority for the form of relief being such as to require an actual restoration to the estate or to place it monetarily in the same position as if there had been an actual restoration is not lacking.'

[11] See *Low v Bouverie* [1891] 3 Ch 82 (CA) 99 (Lindley LJ): 'The duty of a trustee is properly to preserve the trust fund, to pay the income and the corpus to those who are entitled to them respectively, and to give all his *cestuis que trust*, on demand, information with respect to the mode in which the trust fund has been dealt with, and where it is.' See further D Hayton, 'Unique Rules for the Unique Institution, the Trust' in S Degeling and J Edelman (eds), *Equity in Commercial Law* (Sydney, LawBook Co, 2005) 279, 286–90.

[12] P Young, C Croft and M Smith, *On Equity* (Sydney, Thomson Reuters, 2009) para [2.490].

[13] Strictly, a breach is a breach whether there is factual loss or not; but we normally only know about the breach because loss has been suffered: see discussion in text to n 17 below.

Unfortunately the *Re Dawson* approach has been called 'a stringent concept of causation'.[14] It is said to require 'some causal connection between the breach of trust and the loss to the trust estate for which compensation is recoverable, viz the fact that the loss would not have occurred but for the breach'.[15] However, these references to causation and but for tests are needlessly confusing. It is much easier to strip out the second sentence from the *Re Dawson* quote and simply put the issue like this: in relation to the safety of trust property, the question is solely whether there has been a breach of trust. There is really no causation point at all, yet many judges still feel compelled to ask what would have happened if there had not been a breach.[16] Later events are relevant, of course, but they should only be used to establish the current value of the property that was held on trust before the breach. The clock is not stopped in respect of the subsequent valuation of this *prior* property; however, it is stopped in respect of the subsequent valuation of *wrongly disbursed* property. Once that disbursement has been ignored, and the account falsified, the current value of the disbursed property is irrelevant.

The confusion happens because we normally only know about the initial breach because of the occasioning of the later loss. If the breach is spotted before the property is actually lost then the breach is remedied by taking the property out of harm's way. But that should not obscure the point that the relevant breach occurs when the property is put in harm's way, not when that harm actually occurs. *Salway v Salway*, where a receiver was liable for property lost when a bank failed, is a good example of this.[17] The receiver, Mr White, deposited the funds on terms that meant he parted with absolute control. This parting of control was the relevant breach of duty, even though it was completely extraneous to the failure of the bank. Of course, if the breach had been recognised before the bank failed it could have been remedied without any money payment at all. This shows exactly what is meant by substitutive performance and substitutive compensation.

Imagine a case where a trustee wrongly sold 100 shares in BP plc in late March 2010.[18] At that point one BP share in London was worth around 630p. If the beneficiary sued the trustee at the end of June, when a BP share was worth around 300p, then *Re Dawson* would require the trustee to restore 100 BP shares, or to pay equivalent equitable compensation—around £300. If the beneficiary waited to sue

[14] *Bank of New Zealand v New Zealand Guardian Trust Co Ltd* [1999] 1 NZLR 664 (NZCA) 687, 681. See also *O'Halloran v RT Thomas & Family Pty Ltd* (1998) 45 NSWLR 262 (NSWCA) 277.

[15] *Target Holdings* (n 2) 434.

[16] Moreover, *Re Dawson* is often used as authority for a general 'equity is harsh on defaulting fiduciaries and trustees' point: a recent example is Pembroke J in *Thomas v SMP (International) Pty Ltd (No 4)* [2010] NSWSC 984 [73]. *On Equity* (n 12) paras [2.480]–[2.530] also refers to 'equity's strict approach to causation' and seems to cite *Re Dawson* and *Brickenden* (n 4) as authority for that general statement.

[17] *Salway* (n 9). In fact the unlucky receiver paid money into two failing banks, one after another. The case is further discussed in Elliott, *Compensation Claims* (n 5) 159ff, along with *Cocker v Quayle* (1830) 1 Russ & My 535, 39 ER 206. Elliott regrets that neither case was pressed before the House of Lords in *Target Holdings*.

[18] I realise that a trust whose terms prohibited the selling of any shares would be very rare indeed.

until late October then the equitable compensation payable would be £430, since BP shares were then trading at 430p. Of course, in such a situation the beneficiary would often be better advised to adopt the initial breach. However, the example is given to illustrate that *Re Dawson* is about putting the trust back in the position that it held before the breach, and to show that later events will naturally have an effect on how much money is required to do this. Indeed, this is exactly what happened in *Re Dawson* itself, except that the case involved currency movements rather than share prices.

To turn the example around: imagine that a trustee wrongly *bought* 100 shares in BP plc in late March 2010.[19] By late October 2010 those shares would be worth much less, with the main cause being the fall in BP's share price after the Gulf of Mexico oil leak. Under *Re Dawson* the beneficiary could simply falsify the account and claim compensation in respect of the £630 price. The beneficiary might additionally surcharge the account, given that the shares were bought for £630 and one might expect a competent trustee to increase the value of trust assets by a certain percentage in seven months. In any event, the point is that the substitutive and reparative claims are not the same thing: *Re Dawson* is often used as authority for the latter, when it is really only directed to the former.

A. The Problem of Intermediate Income

Re Dawson stands for putting a trust back into the position it was before the breach. That is, restoring—*in specie* or by monetary equivalent—the corpus of the trust as it stood before the breach. That sounds like a simple idea, but there are difficult questions: should dividends that would have been paid, or interest that would have been earned, be included? Some of these items might be seen as part of the trust corpus: eg dividends not yet paid but where the shares were already trading ex-dividend at the date of wrongful disbursement, or interest earned daily but not capitalised until the end of the month. But they quickly shade into the reparative realm of compensation for loss rather than failure to keep property safe. Only some forms of income can properly be seen as being part of the trust corpus at any given date.

Another issue is whether, in the cases of monetary compensation assessed according to *Re Dawson* principles, the award should include interest from the date of breach. Such an award would look very much like compensation for interest that the trustee failed to earn, which according to this analysis would be for a reparative claim. Yet it is clear that interest can be awarded on top of the sum necessary to put the trust back where it was before the breach (and indeed was

[19] Gummow J gives the example of wrongful purchase of shares in W Gummow, 'Compensation for Breach of Fiduciary Duty' in T Youdan (ed), *Equity, Fiduciaries and Trusts* (Toronto, Carswell, 1989) 57, 89. That example was cited in *O'Halloran* (n 14) 276.

awarded in *Re Dawson* itself).[20] The answer to this apparent problem is that the interest award is not compensation for what the trust ought to have earned, but is instead disgorgement of a notional profit made by the trustee. As Buckley LJ said in *Wallersteiner v Moir (No 2)*:

> It is well established in equity that a trustee who in breach of trust misapplies trust funds will be liable not only to replace the misapplied principal fund but to do so with interest from the date of the misapplication. This is on the notional ground that the money so applied was in fact the trustee's own money and that he has retained the misapplied trust money in his own hands and used it for his own purposes. Where a trustee has retained trust money in his own hands, he will be accountable for the profit which he has made or which he is assumed to have made from the use of the money.[21]

Having outlined what I argue to be the true reach of *Re Dawson* and substitutive compensation, we can now turn to the leading recent cases: *Target Holdings v Redferns*,[22] a 1995 decision of the House of Lords, and *Youyang v Minter Ellison Morris Fletcher*,[23] a 2003 decision of the High Court of Australia. These decisions, on quite similar material facts, demonstrate very different approaches to the question of equitable compensation for misapplied trust property. While *Youyang*, at least in the High Court, adopts a substitutive model, *Target Holdings* indicates that all breach of trust cases should treated as reparation claims, including those that involve loss to the trust estate.

B. *Target Holdings v Redferns*

In *Target Holdings v Redferns*, a finance company, Target, agreed to lend money to Crowngate Developments to enable Crowngate to purchase two plots of land for £2m.[24] In fact Crowngate was participating in a fraud whereby it would only pay £775,000 for the land. In reliance on a surveyor's report prepared by another defendant, Target agreed to provide £1.7m towards the supposed £2m purchase

[20] Interest was also awarded in *Youyang* (n 3). That award was made pursuant to section 94 of the Supreme Court Act 1970 (NSW) (now see the Civil Procedure Act 2005 (NSW) s 100), but interest was also included under case law: see D Browne (ed), *Ashburner's Principles of Equity*, 2nd edn (London, Butterworth & Co, 1933, repr 1983) 147–149.

[21] *Wallersteiner v Moir (No 2)* [1975] QB 373 (CA) 397.

[22] *Target Holdings* (n 2).

[23] *Youyang* (n 3).

[24] It is easy to forget that *Target Holdings* only concerned an application for leave to defend a breach of trust claim. It was not a substantive case in that respect. The trial judge had nearly entered summary judgment for Target, the Court of Appeal allowed an appeal from Target on that point and entered judgment for them, and Redferns appealed to the House of Lords. In fact, although Redferns won the appeal and were granted leave to defend the breach of trust claim subject to paying £1m into court, it seems clear that they were going to lose the substantive case. Although the House of Lords proceeded on the basis that all parties had acted honestly, in the penultimate paragraph of his judgment Lord Browne-Wilkinson commented that it was likely that Redferns' breach actually *would* have caused the loss, since otherwise the fraudulent transaction would never have been able to go through at all: *Target Holdings* (n 2) 441.

price. That advance was to be secured by a first mortgage on the property. Redferns, a firm of solicitors, were instructed to act for both Crowngate and Target.

Only £1.525m of the £1.7m loan was to be used for the purchase of the two plots of land. The balance was to be used to pay insurance premiums. £1.525m was duly transferred to Redferns to hold on bare trust in their client account for Target. Once the properties had been conveyed to Crowngate, and the relevant charges had been executed in favour of Target, then Redferns would have had the implied authority to pay the funds to the order of Crowngate. However, in the event nearly all of the money, £1.49m, was paid away by Redferns in breach of trust without Crowngate acquiring the property and without the proper charges being granted to Target. Such charges were eventually executed almost a month later. Crowngate defaulted on the mortgage repayments and was eventually wound up. Target sold the properties for £500,000 and claimed equitable compensation from Redferns in the amount of £990,000, being £1.49m less the £500,000 obtained by the sale.

In the Court of Appeal, Target was awarded the claimed £990,000. Peter Gibson LJ (with Hirst LJ agreeing) held that where a trustee wrongfully pays money away to a stranger then the trust immediately suffers loss and the trustee comes under an immediate duty to restore the money lost. This, it is argued, is the proper *Re Dawson* position. It is not necessary to ask what loss flowed from the breach; only breach must be shown. The current value of the lost property must also be established, but in cases involving wrongful disbursements of money this will be easy. To this extent the Court of Appeal was correct, but the problem was that the majority appeared to ignore the eventual execution of the charge.[25]

Although Target did not obtain a charge over the properties until nearly a month after the transfer in breach of trust, it did eventually obtain a valid security and was able to realise £500,000 on the sale of the property. Owing to a slump in the property market, this sum would have been all that Target could have recouped even if the charges had been obtained properly in the first place. That fact clearly carried weight with Lord Browne-Wilkinson, who began his speech by asking whether trustees are 'liable to compensate the beneficiary not only for losses caused by the breach but also for losses which the beneficiary would, in any event, have suffered even if there had been no such breach?'[26] His Lordship accordingly saw the important point as being the causation of loss, not the initial paying-away in breach of trust. Although he agreed that a trustee who wrongly transfers property in breach of trust comes under an immediate duty to restore the fund, Lord Browne-Wilkinson continued:

> But the fact that there is an accrued cause of action as soon as the breach is committed does not in my judgment mean that the quantum of the compensation payable is ultimately fixed as at the date when the breach occurred. The quantum is fixed at the date of judgment at which date, according to the circumstances then pertaining, the compensation

[25] *Target Holdings Ltd v Redferns* [1994] 1 WLR 1089 (CA) 1103–04 (Peter Gibson LJ, with Hirst LJ agreeing). Ralph Gibson LJ dissented at 1098–1100.

[26] *Target Holdings* (n 2) 428.

> is assessed at the figure then necessary to put the trust estate or the beneficiary back into the position it would have been in *had there been no breach*.[27]

The last five words are of vital importance. Under a reparative approach we ask what would have happened if no breach had occurred, whereas under a substitutive approach we ask what the position was before the breach occurred. 'Had there been no breach' can be interpreted both ways. In *Target Holdings* the House of Lords interpreted it in a reparative sense, since their Lordships found that the loss to Target had been wholly caused by the fraud of the third parties, rather than by Redferns' breach.[28] Of course that is vital in examining the causation of loss, but it is beside the point if one takes the substitutive approach. To apply plaintiff-friendly rules to determining questions about the causation of loss is still to apply an analysis that focuses on loss rather than breach. In short, talking about the dodgy surveyor begs the question of Redferns' duty to preserve the trust fund.

Whereas the Court of Appeal's judgment in *Target Holdings* had been variously described as harsh, chancy, and startling,[29] the decision of the House of Lords was generally well received.[30] Professor Rickett welcomed Lord Browne-Wilkinson's clear articulation of the 'loss-focused nature of equitable compensation',[31] and Professor Burrows argued that, since equitable compensation has exactly the same aim as compensatory damages, the House of Lords decision was correct.[32] However, a different view was taken by a dissentient camp including Lord Millett, Professor Birks and Dr Elliott.[33] They agreed with the outcome in *Target Holdings* but argued that the award of equitable compensation should not depend on causation beyond the fact of breach of trust. To hold otherwise would be to ignore the significance of the accounting relationship and the possibility of enforcing a primary duty.[34] The result was correct because the eventual execution of the charge could be seen as the belated performance of the trustee's primary duty; but the case was right for the wrong reasons.

[27] Ibid 437 (emphasis added).

[28] Ibid 431. It must be stressed that Lord Browne-Wilkinson concluded this while approaching the case on the assumed footing that all parties were honest. As mentioned above, n 24, in reality it was suspected that the fraud meant that funds could not have been obtained from elsewhere, and so Target's loss in fact *was* caused by the breach of trust.

[29] D Heydon, 'Causal Relationships Between a Fiduciary's Default and the Principal's Loss' (1994) 110 *LQR* 328, 329 ('harsh and chancy'); R Ham, 'Trustees' Liability' (1995) 9 *Trust Law International* 21, 23 ('startling').

[30] J Ulph, 'Harmony in the law: hitting the target' (1995) 9 *Trust Law International* 86; R Nolan, 'A targeted degree of liability' [1996] *Lloyd's Maritime and Commercial Law Quarterly* 161; C Rickett, 'Where are We Going with Equitable Compensation?' in A Oakley (ed), *Trends in Contemporary Trust Law* (Oxford, Oxford University Press, 1996); D Capper, 'Compensation for Breach of Trust' [1997] *Conv* 14; A Burrows, 'We Do This At Common Law But That in Equity' (2002) 22 *OJLS* 1.

[31] Rickett, 'Where are We Going?'(n 30) 29; cf Rickett, 'Towards a Blueprint?' (n 5).

[32] Burrows, 'We Do This At Common Law' (n 30) 10–11.

[33] P Millett, 'Equity's Place in the Law of Commerce' (1998) 114 *LQR* 214, 226; P Birks, 'Equity in the Modern Law: An Exercise in Taxonomy' (1996) 26 *University of Western Australia Law Review* 1, 45–48; Elliott, 'Remoteness Criteria' (n 5) 590. These are called the 'dissentient English camp' in S Elliott and J Edelman, '*Target Holdings* considered in Australia' (n 5) 550.

[34] See further, Birks, 'Equity in the Modern Law' (n 33) 47.

On a point of history, it would have been interesting if the Court of Appeal had seen the later execution of the charge as amounting to restoration of the trust estate. It is highly possible that the judgment would then have been upheld on appeal. Indeed, leave to appeal to the House of Lords would probably not have been granted in the first place. Lord Browne-Wilkinson was troubled by the thought that, on the Court of Appeal's reasoning, an honest and otherwise non-negligent trustee could be liable for a fall in the housing market after he had released his client's money one day before he acquired the mortgage security.[35] His Lordship expressly approached the relevant equitable rules with 'a strong predisposition against such a conclusion'.[36] He did not consider the point that getting the security a day late might amount to restoration.

C. *Youyang v Minter Ellison Morris Fletcher*

A classic *Re Dawson* approach was taken in the Australian case of *Youyang*, where a firm of solicitors, Minters, paid money away in breach of trust. Youyang agreed to invest $500,000 in E C Consolidated Capital Ltd (ECCCL), a client of Minters, and entered into an agreement with ECCCL in September 1993. Under the agreement $260,000 would be used to obtain a bearer deposit certificate from a third-party bank, Dresdner; $20,000 would be used for expenses incurred by ECCCL; and the remaining $220,000 would be invested in ECCCL's activities on the international money and securities markets. The bearer deposit certificate would guarantee the return of $500,000 on maturity in September 2003, whatever happened to the rest of the initial investment. The plan was that at worst Youyang would get back their $500,000 at the end of the ten year term and at best they would share in the profits made by ECCCL.

Youyang transferred $500,000 to Minters to hold on bare trust and then disburse according to the agreement. On 24 September 1993 Minters duly transferred $260,000 to Dresdner, but only obtained a certificate of indebtedness in return. This was not within the agreement and it could not operate to give Youyang any security in the event of the insolvency of ECCCL. Minters then paid $20,000 to themselves as payment for ECCCL's expenses, and $220,000 to ECCCL directly. A year after the agreement, ECCCL asked Youyang to execute a deed poll which would authorise the withdrawal of the $260,000 fund from Dresdner and its deposit in another bank on the same terms. Youyang agreed and the deed poll was executed by a director, Mr Hayward. Youyang was not told of the original failure to obtain a proper bearer deposit certificate, and neither was a proper certificate obtained from the second bank. In effect Youyang was nothing more than an unsecured creditor of ECCCL, and ECCCL failed in 1997 with no assets to pay unsecured creditors.

[35] *Target Holdings* (n 2) 432.
[36] Ibid 433.

Minters conceded that the $260,000 had been paid away in breach of trust, and it followed that since the proper security was not obtained they were not authorised to release the $220,000 directly to ECCCL either. However, the solicitors contended that no loss to Youyang had been caused by the breach. At trial Brownie AJ awarded equitable compensation to Youyang based on the misapplication of the $260,000, but refused to award compensation regarding the second payment. The judge reasoned that even if there had been no breach of trust by the failure to obtain the proper bearer deposit certificate Youyang would have had the capital returned in 2003 but would have lost the rest of the investment.[37]

On appeal, the New South Wales Court of Appeal found by a majority that no compensation should be payable in respect of either amount. All three judges found that the loss of the $260,000 was not caused by Minters obtaining the wrong deposit certificate but was instead caused by Mr Hayward's subsequent voluntary execution of the deed poll on behalf of Youyang.[38] It was therefore common ground that the award of Brownie AJ should be reversed. However, whereas Hodgson JA would have awarded compensation in respect of the second payment of $220,000,[39] Handley JA and Young CJ in Eq found that this second payment was consequential upon the first breach, that no further loss had been suffered, and that accordingly no compensation should be payable.[40] Youyang appealed to the High Court of Australia.

In a unanimous judgment, Gleeson CJ, McHugh, Gummow, Kirby and Hayne JJ held that Minters were liable to compensate Youyang for the total initial amount of $500,000. The court held that several breaches of trust had occurred on 24 September 1993, that liability had been incurred by Minters on that date, and that later events involving the execution of the deed poll had no relevance:

> The execution of the deed poll … could be of significance on questions of causation if what had been brought about was the release of an existing bearer certificate of deposit and its replacement by a 'non-bearer' instrument. But that was not the order of events that transpired. Youyang was not provided at any stage with the security for which it had bargained.[41]

[37] *Youyang v Alexander* [2000] NSWSC 698 [2], [27], where the judge notes that the investment was intended to be 'speculative'. This can be compared to the House of Lords decision in *Target Holdings*, where the loss of money was—on the assumed facts at least—caused by the fraudulent activities of third parties.

[38] *Youyang v Minter Ellison* [2001] NSWCA 198 [17]–[18] (Handley JA), [29]–[30] (Hodgson JA), [75]–[82] (Young CJ in Eq).

[39] Ibid [34]–[38]. Unlike Handley JA and Young CJ in Eq, Hodgson JA at [35]–[36] considered the second breach to be independent of the first, and therefore to have its own consequences. Hodgson JA also disagreed with the view of Handley JA that Youyang would in any case have continued with the second payment of $220,000 even if they had known that the deposit certificate was not consistent with the agreement. For the view of the High Court on this point see *Youyang* (n 3) [60].

[40] *Youyang* (NSWCA) (n 38) [17]–[18] (Handley JA), [88] (Young CJ in Eq).

[41] *Youyang* (n 3) [63]. At [32] the Court found that all three payments by Minters were breaches of trust: the $260,000 to Dresdner, the $20,000 to Minters themselves as payment for services to ECCCL, and the $220,000 to ECCCL.

Compensation was payable in respect of the whole $500,000 even though the $220,000 that was to be Youyang's contribution to ECCCL's investment activities would have been lost if the initial deposit certificate had been properly obtained. In contrast, the House of Lords had refused to award £990,000 compensation to Target on the basis that this loss would have been suffered even without a breach by Redferns. In distinguishing the *Target Holdings* case, the High Court referred with approval to the extra-judicial writing of Lord Millett where he had argued that the eventual execution of the charge in *Target Holdings* should be seen as notional restoration of the trust estate.[42]

Clear differences in approach are apparent in the decisions of, on the one hand, the New South Wales Supreme Court and Court of Appeal, and, on the other hand, the High Court of Australia. Although Brownie AJ differed from the Court of Appeal as to the result, this difference was based on an essentially factual question of what event should properly be seen as the cause of the loss to Youyang. The Court of Appeal unanimously held that Mr Hayward's voluntary execution of the deed poll was the cause, whereas Brownie AJ had found that Minters had caused Youyang to lose the opportunity of having $500,000 returned in September 2003. Neither Brownie AJ nor a majority of the Court of Appeal would allow compensation in respect of the $220,000 paid to ECCCL because they found that Minters' actions did not cause this loss. Both decisions therefore show a reparative approach that, similarly to the analysis adopted by Lord Browne-Wilkinson in *Target Holdings*, focuses on the causation of loss to the claimant rather than the breach of trust by the trustee.[43] In contrast, the High Court of Australia focused on the breaches of trust. Regarding the $220,000, which might be compared with the £990,000 in *Target Holdings*, the High Court found 'no ground to dismiss from consideration the breach respecting the balance of the $500,000. Each component of the $500,000 was paid away in breach of trust and not one cent of the moneys was recouped by Youyang from the "investment" with ECCCL.'[44]

D. *Comparing Target Holdings* and *Youyang*

As we have seen, the High Court of Australia distinguished the two cases on the basis that, unlike in *Target Holdings*, the relevant security in *Youyang* was never obtained. From the point of view of a substitutive response, this solution is very attractive: the argument is simply that Redferns eventually performed their primary duty whereas Minters did not. However, this view does not seem to accord with the causation discussion and reparative approach apparent in Lord Browne-Wilkinson's speech.

[42] Millett, 'Equity's Place' (n 33) 227; referred to with approval in *Youyang* (n 3) [45].

[43] Brownie AJ found the claimants to be 20% contributorily negligent on the same facts in a parallel negligence action, but considered contributory negligence to be inapplicable to awards of equitable compensation: see *Youyang* (NSWSC) (n 37) [36]–[38].

[44] *Youyang* (n 3) [65].

If the correct view of *Target Holdings* is that Redferns' liability was extinguished by executing the charge, then the question becomes: if the charge had not been executed, would Redferns have been liable for all of the misapplied property, not just £500,000?[45] The substitutive analysis would suggest that Redferns would be liable for the full amount since the basis of liability is the failure to perform the duty to keep the property safe and deliver it *in specie*. The remedy is simply the amount of money it costs to reimburse the amount that was wrongly paid away. Yet Lord Browne-Wilkinson suggested that the important factor was that of causation of loss, not trustee performance. His Lordship adopted the comments of McLachlin J in the case of *Canson Enterprises v Boughton*, and held that 'losses are to be assessed as at the time of trial, using the full benefit of hindsight … it is essential that the losses made good are only those which, on a common sense view of causation, were caused by the breach.'[46] Lord Browne-Wilkinson had already noted that the loss in the *Target Holdings* case was wholly caused by the fraud of third parties, so it would seem to follow that whether or not the charge was executed would only be relevant to loss caused by the failure to execute the charge. That is, if the charge had not been executed then, according to Lord Browne-Wilkinson's analysis, Redferns would be liable for the breach, but with hindsight that liability should extend only so far as the amount that Target Holdings would have received on realisation of a properly-executed security. Of course, a different result would be found if the substitutive analysis favoured by the High Court of Australia was applied: in that instance the liability to reinstate all property paid away in breach would remain.

Compare *Youyang*, where the High Court ordered Minters to pay compensation of $500,000 plus interest dating from September 1993. Compensation was awarded in respect of the entire sum, despite the fact that the second payment would have gone outright to ECCCL even if the proper security had been obtained for the first payment. Even if Minters had originally obtained the proper security document it was known with hindsight that the second payment would have been lost on ECCCL's insolvency, but this knowledge did not affect the compensatory award. Simply put, the courts below asked whether Minters' actions had harmed the plaintiff, whereas in accordance with the classic *Re Dawson* approach the High Court only needed to know that the money had been paid away in breach.

The award of compensation in respect of the second payment in *Youyang* therefore shows the High Court of Australia adopting an analysis different to that of the House of Lords. Although *Target Holdings* was distinguished on the ground that in that case the proper security had eventually been obtained, in fact the two

[45] £500,000 being the amount realised on the sale of the property. Of course, Target could only realise this amount because of the charge executed in its favour.

[46] *Canson Enterprises Ltd v Boughton & Co* [1991] 3 SCR 534 (SCC) 555–56; adopted *Target Holdings* (n 2) 439. It is argued that such adoption was mistaken because *Canson Enterprises* was not a case involving loss to a trust estate.

cases betray differing views as to the basis of equitable compensation in cases where property is lost from the trust estate.[47] In this context the facts of *Youyang* would be materially identical to those of *Target Holdings*, if in the latter case Redferns had never obtained the proper charge.

E. Restoration

Millett and Birks argue, apparently with the support of the High Court of Australia, that the eventual execution of the charge in *Target Holdings* meant that the trust was notionally restored. However, as Edelman J has pointed out in a recent article,[48] this analysis begs the question of what would have happened if Target had refused to accept the mortgage that Redferns eventually acquired for them. If Target was entitled to refuse the mortgage then presumably Redferns could only perform their duty by reimbursing the amount of misapplied money to the trust fund.

If a solicitor pays out money one day early, and obtains the mortgage for her client the next day, can the client refuse the mortgage and require restoration of the trust fund? Edelman says the answer is yes, and that the important point in *Target Holdings* was that Target could properly be seen to have elected not to pursue this course. Another view is that the solicitors may act as their client's agents in accepting the new mortgage.[49] It may also be possible to conceptualise the problem slightly differently: that is, to see the breach of trust as the failure to get in the security rather than the paying out of the money. If the breach is analysed this way then the breach can be unilaterally remedied simply by getting in the security. Millett[50] and Hayton[51] have argued that the breach could be viewed like this, rather than an as 'unauthorised application of funds', although this is certainly not the prevailing view and the analysis of the High Court of Australia in *Youyang* goes the other way. Nonetheless, there may be some attraction to a model that does not require a principal to ratify or acquiesce in his fiduciary's attempt to fix their mistake, and which does not depend on the fiduciary having his principal's authority to do so.

[47] I therefore disagree with the authors of *On Equity*, who say that *Target Holdings* and *Youyang* are consistent with each other: (n 12) para [2.520].

[48] Edelman, 'Money awards' (n 5).

[49] This is the argument made in Conaglen's reply to Edelman: M Conaglen, 'Explaining *Target Holdings v Redferns*' (2010) 4 *Journal of Equity* 288. Of course this model depends on the agency including the relevant authorisation, which may vary with particular cases.

[50] P Millett, 'Equity—The Road Ahead' (1995) 6 *King's College Law Journal* 1, 7: '[the breach] did not consist of a payment to the wrong person or of the wrong amount. The solicitor was authorised to pay the amount which he paid to the person to whom he paid it. The breach of trust consisted in his failure to obtain an executed mortgage deed.' And, to the same effect: Millett (n 33) 224.

[51] D Hayton, 'Fiduciaries in Context: An Overview' in P Birks (ed), *Privacy and Loyalty* (Oxford, Oxford University Press, 1997) 287. Hayton cites Millett ibid.

F. Accounting

Falsifying an account will have the effect of enforcing a primary duty, and this will result in a classic *Re Dawson* model where analysis is directed solely towards questions of breach. However, this means that the model is only available where there is an accounting relationship. Any references to *Re Dawson* being general authority for a plaintiff-friendly response to all equitable relationships are therefore beside the point, and, more importantly, even 'bare trust' situations must be analysed to see if there is an accounting relationship present.[52] Although the accounting model will be apt for ongoing custodial fiduciary relationships, it might not be appropriate for short-term examples like those in *Target Holdings* and *Youyang*. Indeed, both seem very similar to two cases cited by Dr Getzler.[53] In *Dooby v Watson*,[54] Kekewich J found that no relevant relationship of trustee and beneficiary existed when a client gave funds to her solicitor to perform a single investment. That case might be better viewed as concerning a trust that had actually been fully performed, but the Irish case of *Mare v Lewis*,[55] which also held that a trust relationship did not exist, is not so easily explained. Chatterton V-C held that there was no accounting relationship absent a general agency,[56] and said:

> I have not found, nor have I been referred to any case, to show that the mere giving of a sum of money to a person to invest in a certain class of securities makes that person subject to the equitable obligations of a trustee. If, for instance, a person goes to his stockbroker and directs him to invest money for him in railway shares, without specifying in what company, does the mere receipt of the money by the broker, for such purpose, constitute him a trustee for his employer, and make him subject to all the responsibilities attaching to a trustee in the investment of trustee?[57]

The last sentence can be parsed. Not all trusts involve duties to invest. If the Vice-Chancellor was saying that a broker who holds client money does not have a duty to invest it *qua* trustee, but does have a duty to choose a suitable investment *qua* broker, then this is unproblematic. But it would be more controversial if his Lordship was saying that there was no trust at all. If this is the correct view then the analysis is inconsistent with *Youyang*.

In *Target Holdings v Redferns*, Lord Browne-Wilkinson famously drew a distinction between traditional and commercial trusts:

> In the modern world the trust has become a valuable device in commercial and financial dealings. The fundamental principles of equity apply as much to such trusts as they do

[52] See Birks, 'Equity in the Modern Law' (n 33) 19.

[53] J Getzler, 'Equitable Compensation and the Regulation of Fiduciary Relationships' in P Birks and F Rose (eds), *Restitution & Equity Volume 1: Resulting Trusts and Equitable Compensation* (London, Mansfield Press, 2000) n 89.

[54] *Dooby v Watson* (1886) LR 39 ChD 178.

[55] *Mare v Lewis* (1869) 4 IR (Eq) 219.

[56] Ibid 239: '[I]t is clear that a single instance of handing money to a person, to be by him laid out on a single security, would not be held a sufficient ground for directing an account. This is not an item in an unsettled account; it is a single detached transaction.'

[57] Ibid 238.

> to the traditional trusts in relation to which those principles were originally formulated. But in my judgment it is important ... to distinguish between the basic principles of trust law and those specialist rules developed in relation to traditional trusts which are applicable only to such trusts and the rationale of which has no application to trusts of quite a different kind.[58]

This categorisation met with a mixed response.[59] However, perhaps a similar distinction is justified, at least where *Re Dawson*-style substitutive accounting liability is concerned. Getzler argues that there is a duty to 'get the history right' and concludes that the account basis may only be applicable to continuous and custodial trusteeship.[60] So it would in fact be correct to distinguish between different types of trusts: not by classifying them as commercial or otherwise, but by asking the (undoubtedly similar) question whether there is an ongoing relationship that would allow one party to call on the other for an account. If this is correct then although the High Court's decision in *Youyang* looks like a restatement of orthodox equitable principle against those who would seek to deny equity a role in commerce, it might be that the Court actually extended equity's reach by eliding an existing distinction between ongoing relationships and short-term, one-off events.[61]

III. Non-custodial Fiduciary Duties

A substitutive response that focuses on enforcement of a primary duty will only be applicable to situations that involve custodial fiduciary relations with a correlative

[58] *Target Holdings* (n 2) 435.

[59] The passage was cited with approval in *Guardian Trust Co* (n 14) 684. It is viewed more warily in A Butler, 'Introduction to Equity in Context' in Butler, *Equity and Trusts* (n 8) 1105. The High Court of Australia did not endorse the comments in *Youyang*, and in R Meagher, D Heydon and M Leeming, *Meagher, Gummow & Lehane's Equity: Doctrine and Remedies*, 4th edn (Chatswood, Butterworths LexisNexis, 2002) para [23–015] ('*Meagher, Gummow & Lehane*') the distinction is called 'hitherto unnoticed and not easily explicable'. On the other hand, extrajudicially Mason CJ has called it a 'commendable development': A Mason, 'Equity's Role in the Twentieth Century' (1997) 8 *King's College Law Journal* 1, 14. The authors of *On Equity* give it a generally favourable response (n 12) paras [4.940], [6.80], [18.290], and Young CJ in Eq has commented judicially that the courts 'must not be too technical' when applying equitable principles to commercial relationships: *Youyang* (NSWCA) (n 38) [97]. (The distinction also gets very favourable treatment in *On Equity* at para [18.210], but that section was written by Lord Browne-Wilkinson himself!) In *Bairstow v Queens Moat Houses* [2001] EWCA Civ 712 [53] Robert Walker LJ questioned whether a better dividing line might be between custodial and non-custodial fiduciary duties. The commercial/traditional distinction was relied upon at trial in *Re Paycheck Services; HMRC v Holland* [2008] EWHC 2200 (Ch) [215]–[217], although on appeal the relevant distinction appeared to be that *Target Holdings* was not an unlawful dividend case: [2009] EWCA Civ 625 [95]–[98]. Although Canadian courts have struggled with accommodating pension funds with the law of trusts, a more general traditional/commercial distinction does not appear to have gained a footing in that jurisdiction.

[60] Getzler, 'Equitable Compensation' (n 53) 249–50.

[61] As a practical matter, professional conduct rules will mean that money given to solicitors will be held in a client trust account, and *Youyang* could be supported on this basis. That said, the High Court noted that Youyang was not a client of Minters (unlike Target and Redferns): *Youyang* (n 3) [48]. Moreover, the same conduct rules do not apply to other investment professionals. (Thanks to Matthew Conaglen for this point.)

duty to account. Still, a remedy of 'reparative' equitable compensation remains available in cases involving breaches of non-custodial fiduciary duties:[62] although it is not available for a breach of the no profits rule,[63] it is available for breach of the no conflicts rule.[64] The following discussion focuses on the case of *Brickenden v London Loan & Savings Co*,[65] and its treatment in the various jurisdictions. That case concerned the issue of causation of loss following a breach of the no conflict rule. However, before discussing the comparative differences in respect of causation, it will be helpful to comment on the 'duty to disclose'.

A. *Duty to Disclose*

It is obvious that fiduciaries must disclose any personal interest or any competing professional interest to their principals. It is equally obvious that fiduciaries must disclose lots of other things not related to conflicts of interest. The potential confusion lies in conflating the two points into a single duty to disclose, and a good illustration of this is *Canson Enterprises v Boughton*,[66] where a solicitor failed to

[62] This point is certainly not free of controversy. Many think compensatory remedies to be inapplicable to breaches of fiduciary duty and instead argue that the appropriate response is an account of profits or rescission of the transaction. Although such responses might sometimes look compensatory, eg in the case of a money payment made where rescission is impossible, in fact the true goal is the stripping of a wrongful profit or the reversal of a wrongful transaction: see, eg S Worthington, 'Corporate governance: remedying and ratifying directors' breaches' (2000) 116 *LQR* 638, 664ff; P Millett, 'Proprietary Restitution' in Degeling and Edelman, *Equity in Commercial Law* (n 11) 309. There is certainly force in these arguments. However, if it is now right to see fiduciary duties as proper duties, and not disabilities, then I do not see the problem in saying: 'In breaching the no conflict rule you caused us to sell our house too cheaply. You must pay us the difference between the current value of the house and the amount we received on sale. We have moved in to our new $800,000 house now, and the money will help pay off some of the mortgage, *but you also cost us the opportunity to buy a $1m house and enjoy the greater uplift in value*'. I do not see any 'scope of duty' or remoteness problems here in linking that loss directly to the breach of *fiduciary* duty (rather than to an allied *non*-fiduciary duty; cf Worthington, 665). I think the real question is whether we really see fiduciary duties as duties or not. Of course, if the better view is that they are disabilities then one can still note that, whatever the principle, there is now just too much positive law to deny that equitable compensation exists, is available for breach of fiduciary duty, and is more than just a hidden profit-stripping or rescinding remedy: see M Conaglen, *Fiduciary Loyalty* (Oxford, Hart Publishing 2010) 87; cf C Mitchell, 'Book Review—*Fiduciary Loyalty*' (2010) 4 *Journal of Equity* 165.

[63] This seems obvious, but apparently it is not. The point is very clearly explained in V Vann, 'Causation and breach of fiduciary duty' [2006] *Singapore Journal of Legal Studies* 86, 91–92, citing A Phang and P Lee, 'Restitutionary and Exemplary Damages Revisited' (2003) 19 *Journal of Contract Law* 1, 10. Even if the no profit rule is just an example of the no conflict rule (see *Commonwealth Bank of Australia v Smith* (1991) 42 FCR 390 (FCA) 392; cf *Chan v Zacharia* (1984) 154 CLR 178 (HCA) 198–99) it is clear that the proper response is gain-based. If the making of the unauthorised profit caused loss to the principal then *ipso facto* there is a breach of the no conflicts rule. See, eg *Fyffes Group Ltd v Templeman* [2000] 2 Lloyd's Rep 643 (Comm).

[64] It is less clear that equitable compensation, as opposed to rescission and money awards given when rescission is impossible, is available for breach of the fiduciary dealing rules; on which see M Conaglen, 'Equitable compensation for breach of fiduciary dealing rules' (2003) 119 *LQR* 246, and Conaglen, *Fiduciary Loyalty* (n 62) 85–96, 125–39; cf R Nolan, 'A fiduciary duty to disclose?' (1997) 113 *LQR* 220, and Edelman J's chapter in this volume.

[65] *Brickenden* (n 4).

[66] *Canson Enterprises* (n 46).

tell his client that the land the clients were buying was being 'flipped' by being bought and resold at an inflated price by an intermediate purchaser. The clients bought the property but suffered heavy losses when the subsequent development of the land ran into difficulties because of the negligence of unconnected building contractors. An agreed set of facts assumed that the solicitor had not stood to gain personally from the scam, but it was also assumed that the clients would not have bought the land if they had been aware of the flipping. The case actually involved a duty/duty conflict because the solicitor was also working for the intermediate purchasers, but the judgments of McLachlin J and LaForest J rather disregard this point and both refer to the other principal as a 'third party'.[67] In short, the Court did not appear to distinguish between non-disclosure as a breach of a normal duty and non-disclosure as a breach of the fiduciary duty to avoid conflicts.[68]

Such a distinction is important because the remedial response will be different. Where a solicitor breaches a non-fiduciary duty by failing to disclose something then a court will naturally look to what harm that non-disclosure actually caused to the principal. In contrast, when the failure to disclose goes to the loyalty of the fiduciary then, as is discussed in the section on *Brickenden* below, special rules as to causation and quantification of loss can apply.

All of the judges in *Canson Enterprises* referred to the solicitor breaching a 'fiduciary' duty to disclose,[69] yet a majority of the Supreme Court found the solicitor not to be liable for the development losses on the grounds of causation, foreseeability and intervening cause.[70] This appears paradoxical, and the issue is even more clouded when we remember that there *was* in fact a breach of fiduciary duty. The answer must be: first, that the judges disregarded the existence of the second principal, meaning that there was no relevant conflict; secondly, that they then spoke of a *prescriptive* fiduciary duty to disclose. Such a prescriptive fiduciary

[67] Ibid 542 (McLachlin J), 558 (LaForest J).

[68] I deliberately use the undecided 'normal'. Whether these obligations are best viewed as common law duties or as equitable duties of skill and care probably does not matter if the remedial response is the same, but it is at least possible that the remedial response will not be exactly the same. The minority judges in *Canson Enterprises* thought it necessary to take a different, equitable path to what in that case was the same destination: ibid 546–47 (McLachlin J). Even Millett LJ's famous judgment in *Bristol & West Building Society v Mothew* [1998] Ch 1 (CA) 16–17 only refers to common law rules being used 'by analogy' (although extra-judicially Millett has put the point more strongly (n 33) 226). Quite apart from this point, it may be questioned whether it is right to draw sharp distinctions between the classic, proscriptive fiduciary duties and other duties: see Getzler (n 53); J Getzler, 'Am I My Beneficiary's Keeper? Fusion and Loss-Based Fiduciary Remedies' and D Heydon, 'Are the Duties of Company Directors to Exercise Care and Skill Fiduciary?', both in Degeling and Edelman (n 11) 239, 185. Also, in *Youyang* (n 3) [38]–[40], the High Court referred to the *Mothew* statement and questioned 'whether the unique foundation and goals of equity, which has the institution of the trust at its heart, warrant any assimilation even in this limited way with the measure of compensatory damages in tort and contract'. The authors of *Meagher, Gummow & Lehane* (n 59) para [23–020] certainly disagree with the notion, lamenting in respect of the *Mothew* judgment that 'such a statement should emerge from such a source'.

[69] Including those in the Supreme Court of British Columbia and the Court of Appeal of British Columbia: (1989) 61 DLR (4th) 732 (BCCA); (1988) 52 DLR (4th) 323 (BCSC).

[70] *Canson Enterprises* (n 46) 580–86.

duty might be better described as an incident of the general (non-fiduciary) obligations that fiduciaries owe to their principals.[71]

Outside Canada, even the necessity of disclosing a conflict is not always seen as a fiduciary duty. The classic position is simply that disclosure will normally make a defence of informed consent available to an action for breach of the no conflict rule.[72] There are some relatively recent comments to the effect that conflict disclosure is a fiduciary duty,[73] and as a practical description this is true because a lack of such disclosure will automatically mean that the no conflict rule has been breached due to a lack of informed consent. That said, framing the issue in positive terms does not really add anything and for the sake of hard cases it might be clearer always to say 'duty not to' rather than 'duty to' or 'duty of'. Semantics aside, and while accepting that even a *substantive* prescriptive/proscriptive distinction is not invariably upheld,[74] it is certainly true that the other jurisdictions have not followed Canada in holding that there is a general, positive, fiduciary duty to disclose.

B. The Strict *Brickenden* Rule

In *Brickenden v London Loan & Savings Co*, a solicitor, Brickenden, failed to inform one of his clients, the London Loan & Savings Company, that he was personally interested in the financial affairs of Mr and Mrs Biggs. The Biggs intended to borrow money from the loan company and use it to restructure debts. Part of this restructuring would involve repaying debts owed to Brickenden, so the solicitor had a clear personal interest in the matter. Brickenden did not disclose the interest,[75] the transaction went ahead, and eventually the loan company sued him. The case has many interesting features—for example there is a strong suspicion that Brickenden and the vice-president of the loan company were in cahoots[76]—but

[71] See P Finn, 'The Fiduciary Principle' in Youdan, *Equity, Fiduciaries and Trusts* (n 19) 25–26, citing *Jacks v Davis* (1982) 141 DLR (3d) 355 (BCCA) and *Laskin v Bache* [1972] 1 OR 465 (Ont CA), and noting the growing practice of Canadian jurisdictions to regard general disclosure as being a 'fiduciary' duty. See also Nolan, 'A fiduciary duty to disclose?' (n 64).

[72] *National Mutual Property Services Pty Ltd v Citibank Savings Ltd* [1998] FCA 564; *P & V Industries Pty Ltd v Porto* [2006] VSC 131[23]–[25]; *On Equity* (n 12) para [7.300].

[73] Young JA has said, in the conflict context, that a fiduciary duty encompasses 'the obligation to make full disclosure of all material facts': *Glandon Pty Ltd v Strata Consolidated Pty Ltd (No 3)* (4 June 1990, unreported), repeated *Crawley v Short* [2009] NSWCA 410 [108], with the agreement of Allsop P and Macfarlan JA on this point.

[74] See, eg *Item Software (UK) Ltd v Fassihi* [2004] EWCA Civ 1244, [2004] BCC 994 [38]–[44], concerning a positive fiduciary duty to disclose misconduct; disapproved in *P & V Industries* (n 72) [26]–[32]; doubted but followed in *Brandeaux Advisers (UK) Ltd v Chadwick* [2010] EWHC 3241 (QB) [47].

[75] In fact Brickenden had made three advances to Biggs and the first was disclosed to the loan company but the second and third were not.

[76] Both Brickenden and the company's vice-president, Mr McCormick, were charged with fraud and conspiracy in respect of the advances made to Biggs. The loan funds mysteriously appeared before the company's Board had made the final decision to approve the loan, and it does not seem that Brickenden attempted to defend himself on the breach of duty point.

it has become famous for its rule to the effect that a defaulting fiduciary may not argue in his defence that his principal would have gone ahead with the transaction regardless of the fiduciary's breach. Lord Thankerton said, in a paragraph which was reproduced as the headnote in the Dominion Law Reports:

> Where a party, holding a fiduciary relationship, commits a breach of his duty by non-disclosure of material facts, which his constituent is entitled to know in connection with the transaction, he cannot be heard to maintain that disclosure would not have altered the decision to proceed with the transaction, because the constituent's action would be solely determined by some other factor. Once the Court has determined that the non-disclosed facts were material, speculation as to what course the constituent, on disclosure, would have taken is not relevant.[77]

In many cases, especially those involving duty/interest conflicts, it is abundantly clear that the principal would not have proceeded if full disclosure had been made. In such cases the causal link between breach of duty and loss will be obvious, and may not even be discussed. However, *Brickenden* had to be decided on a different ground because Mr Brickenden's non-disclosure was not the only thing that caused the loan company to go ahead. At trial Raney J had found that there was 'no equity in the mortgaged properties above the prior mortgages, not including Brickenden's $5,000 mortgages'. This is a difficult finding to interpret, but given that Brickenden had actually declared his initial $5,000 mortgage it can only mean that the new loan company securities would have been worthless regardless of whether Brickenden declared his second and third mortgages (and regardless of whether all of his mortgages were postponed to the loan company's). If there was no equity in the Biggs' property then the new loan company mortgages were worthless, *and should have been known to be worthless*, regardless of Brickenden's personal interest. On this point Crockett J in the Supreme Court commented:

> While it may for this reason well be said that Brickenden was not wholly responsible for the unfortunate transaction, he cannot invoke the connivance or dereliction of others as an excuse for his own breach of duty. ... He assuredly ought not to be allowed in such circumstances to excuse himself on the ground that [an officer] of the company with whom he negotiated ought not in any event to have accepted his proposal.[78]

While Lord Thankerton's dictum provides for a complete ban on counterfactual evidence, perhaps Crockett J's more limited prohibition on the calling of evidence might have been a more satisfactory ground on which to rest *Brickenden*. Another possibility was suggested by Heydon: that a fiduciary in a duty/interest conflict must account for any profits made, independently of any inquiry whether the profits would still have been made had he carried out his duty.[79] In any case, the rule is certainly stated in terms wider than necessary to decide the case, and all jurisdictions have now withdrawn from its strict application to some degree.

77 *Brickenden* (n 4) 469.
78 *Biggs v London Loan & Savings Co* [1933] 3 DLR 161 (SCC) 168–69.
79 Heydon, 'Causal Relationships' (n 29) 332.

Nevertheless, even if Lord Thankerton's rule is not applied any more, discussion of the relevant principles of causation often takes place within a discussion of *Brickenden*. This is particularly the case in those common law countries where *Brickenden* was binding authority, and less so in England. The jurisdictions appear to have now arrived at similar points with respect to causation of loss in the context of breach of fiduciary duty, but some important differences still remain.

C. *Brickenden* Today

In New Zealand it has been said that the 'absoluteness' of the *Brickenden* rule is now gone,[80] although for a time the rule had been applied.[81] In the *Guardian Trust Co* case, Tipping J said in the context of 'true' fiduciary duties that there is still a very plaintiff-friendly response, but that there is a small causal get-out:

> Questions of foreseeability and remoteness do not arise in this kind of case either. Policy dictates that fiduciaries be allowed only a narrow escape route from liability based on proof that the loss or damage would have occurred even if there had been no breach.[82]

The defendant in *Gilbert v Shanahan* made use of the escape route,[83] but the defendant in *Taylor v Schofield Peterson* was not so lucky. In the latter case Hammond J seemed to emphasise the narrowness of the escape route with the double use of the word 'precisely':

> [I]t was for the respondent to lay an evidentiary foundation for the proposition that the appellant would nevertheless have acted in precisely the same manner. That was not done, nor can it fairly and appropriately be inferred that he would have acted in precisely the same way.[84]

This high standard of proof/narrow escape route was confirmed in the recent Supreme Court case of *Premium Real Estate Ltd v Stevens*.[85] In that case an estate agent failed to inform her clients that a prospective purchaser was someone who frequently bought residential property and quickly resold it at a profit. The agent had worked for the purchaser in the past and hoped to be instructed on the resale.

[80] *Everist v McEvedy* [1996] 3 NZLR 348 (NZHC) 356 (Tipping J). Tipping J has said similar things extrajudicially: A Tipping, 'Causation at Law and in Equity—Do we have fusion?' (2000) 7 *Canterbury Law Review* 443.

[81] *Farrington v Rowe McBride & Partners* [1985] 1 NZLR 83 (NZCA) 93; *Sims v Craig Bell & Bond* [1991] 3 NZLR 535 (NZCA) 545–46.

[82] *Guardian Trust Co* (n 14) 687. This passage was in Tipping J's separate reasons, but it was approved by the Supreme Court in *Amaltal Corporation Ltd v Maruha Corporation* [2007] 3 NZLR 192 (NZSC) [30].

[83] *Gilbert v Shanahan* [1998] 3 NZLR 528 (NZCA).

[84] *Taylor v Schofield Peterson* [1999] 3 NZLR 434 (NZHC).

[85] *Premium Real Estate v Stevens* [2009] NZSC 15, [2009] 2 NZLR 384; discussed at greater length in J Glister, 'Breach of fiduciary duty: *Brickenden* lives on (*Premium Real Estate v Stevens*)' (2011) 5 *Journal of Equity* 1. The case is also examined, and a different view taken, in Andrew Butler and Tim Miller's chapter in this volume. (Note: the report has *Premium Real Estate Ltd v Stevens*, but the neutral citation has *Stevens v Premium Real Estate Ltd*.)

The Court was unanimous in finding a breach of 'the fiduciary duty of loyalty', and all agreed that the agent could not keep the commission earned on the sale, but the judges differed as to the amount of compensation that should be awarded. Those differences concerned the issue of causation: was it enough for the agent to show that the clients would, on the balance of probabilities, have sold their house for less than its true value?

Mr and Mrs Stevens sold their house to Mr Larsen for $2.575m. Larsen made some minor improvements, pitched it at a different market, and sold it a few months later for $3.555m. The trial judge found that the house was actually worth $3.25m at the time of the initial sale, but the point of difference emerged because there was evidence that the Stevens would have sold for $2.8m. The Stevens had counter-offered with $2.8m to an earlier prospective buyer, and they had wanted to counter-offer with $2.8m to Mr Larsen.[86] Because of this evidence, Elias CJ would only award the plaintiffs equitable compensation in the amount of $2.8m less $2.575m, whereas Blanchard, McGrath and Gault JJ, with Tipping J agreeing, awarded $3.25m less $2.575m.[87] The majority held that the defendant had not adequately shown that the plaintiffs would have sold at $2.8m: 'to say as the Court of Appeal did that the Stevens were likely to have sold it at $2.8m, too easily permits the errant fiduciary to find the "narrow escape route".'[88] This result is important because it arguably shows that, more than a simple disagreement over whether a fact had been proved on the balance of probabilities,[89] the majority thought that the defendant had a higher standard of proof to satisfy.

Brickenden has been applied,[90] and more recently distinguished,[91] several times in Australia, but the High Court has not decided the issue. The majority in *Maguire v Makaronis* found that an entitlement to rescission in that case

[86] Part of the reason that Mr and Mrs Stevens had been prepared to accept $2.8m is that the agent only valued the house in the mid-high $2m range. This was substantially below what the trial judge later found to be the true value, but Courtney J found that the agent had not been negligent or dishonest: the house was close to a cliff and was only on a unit title, so there was a legitimate disagreement over how it should be appraised.

[87] In fact the Supreme Court agreed that compensation should be determined on the basis that commission would have been paid, even though that commission was actually forfeited. The eventual compensation was therefore: ($3.25m less commission) minus ($2.575m less commission).

[88] *Premium Real Estate* (n 85) [86].

[89] I think it is possible to explain the case as involving a disagreement over facts, but I prefer the view that the judges actually disagreed about the relevant standard of proof: Glister, 'Breach of fiduciary duty' (n 85) 12–13.

[90] *Smith* (n 63) 394; *Wan v McDonald* [1992] FCA 4, (1992) 105 ALR 473, 501–02; *Gemstone Corporation v Grasso* (1994) 62 SASR 239 (SASC in banco) 243, 252. For extra-judicial and academic support of *Brickenden*, in varying degrees, see K Handley, 'Reduction of Damages Awards', in P Finn (ed), *Essays on Damages* (Sydney, Lawbook Co, 1992) 127 (although cf Handley AJA in *Rigg v Sheridan* [2008] NSWCA 79 [56]); *On Equity* (n 12) para [2.530]; *Meagher, Gummow & Lehane* (n 59) para [23–020] (although cf Heydon (n 29)).

[91] *Beach Petroleum NL v Abbott Tout Russell Kennedy* [1999] NSWCA 408, (1999) 48 NSWLR 1; *ASIC v Citigroup Global Markets Australia Pty Ltd (No 4)* [2007] FCA 963, (2007) 160 FCR 35 [366]; *Mantonella Pty Ltd v Thompson* [2009] QCA 80, (2009) 2 Qd R 524 [89]–[111]. Pembroke J has recently said of the rule in *Brickenden* that 'taken literally, [it] does not represent the law of New South Wales': *Thomas* (n 16) [75].

arose immediately on the breach of fiduciary duty, and so there was no reason to consider any further causal issue.[92] Kirby J in the minority appeared to support the rule, subject to a certain textual interpretation:

> It contains within its formulation words which adequately meet the need for there to be some connection to the breach so as to exclude events which are too remote. Thus it must be shown that any facts not disclosed by the fiduciary were 'material'. What is forbidden is 'speculation'. … Facts will not be 'material' if the relevant loss would have happened if there had been no breach.[93]

In 1998, Priestley JA said that he thought *Brickenden* should be followed in Australia unless and until the High Court said otherwise.[94] However, a year later in *Beach Petroleum v Kennedy* the New South Wales Court of Appeal concluded that *Brickenden* was not authority for the general proposition that a court was precluded from considering what would have happened if the duty had been performed.[95] In 2002 the same court found that *Brickenden* was not applicable at all in cases involving a fiduciary duty/duty conflict, although this position is doubtful.[96] Moreover, the Court thought that it would be for the *principal* to prove that, but for the non-disclosure, he or she would not have entered into the transaction. By contrast, in a recent duty/duty case in the Victorian Supreme Court it was said that once the plaintiff had shown loss they were entitled to recover, unless the *fiduciary* could show that the loss would have occurred in any event.[97] In contrast to New Zealand's narrow escape route, there are no suggestions that an Australian defendant will have to prove that fact on anything other than the balance of probabilities.[98]

Even without a High Court decision, it seems that *Brickenden* has been abandoned in Australia. This has generally been done through a process of interpretation and distinguishing (one case even refers to the 'general approach suggested by *Brickenden*'),[99] but the nettle was truly grasped by White J in *Short v*

[92] *Maguire & Tansey v Makaronis* (1997) 188 CLR 449 (HCA). Compare the comments at 468 and 474.

[93] Ibid 493. As Conaglen points out, this circular approach to materiality renders the *Brickenden* rule meaningless: M Conaglen, 'Remedial ramifications of conflicts between a fiduciary's duties' (2010) 126 *LQR* 72, n 77.

[94] *O'Halloran* (n 14) 280–81.

[95] *Beach Petroleum* (n 91) [444].

[96] *White v Illawarra Mutual Building Society Limited* [2002] NSWCA 164 [138], [145]. In *Nationwide Building Society v Various Solicitors (No 3)* [1999] PNLR 606 (ChD) 663 Blackburne J rejected a submission that *Brickenden* should be confined to duty/interest conflicts. In *Smith* (n 63) 394 the Full Federal Court applied *Brickenden* to a duty/duty conflict.

[97] *Watson v Ebsworth & Ebsworth (a firm)* [2008] VSC 510 [136] (Beach J, citing Tipping J in *Guardian Trust Co* (n 14) 687). The comment was obiter because the judge found for the defendants on the initial liability point, but the point was closely examined.

[98] In *Cassis v Kalfus (No 2)* [2004] NSWCA 315 [98] Hodgson JA (with whom Handley JA agreed) concluded 'on the balance of probabilities' that the plaintiff would not have gone ahead with the transaction.

[99] Ibid.

Crawley (No 30).[100] After discussing the Australian treatment of *Brickenden*, White J concluded:

> In my view, there is a conflict between the reasoning in *Brickenden* and the requirement that there be a causal relationship in a claim for equitable compensation between the breach of fiduciary duty and the loss for which compensation is sought. Mr J D Heydon QC (as his Honour then was) pointed out that if the principle exists as it is expressed in *Brickenden*, 'its operation without reference to issues of causation supports by analogy the recoverability of damages against trustees independently of a causal link between breach and loss.' Authority which binds me establishes that the plaintiffs must establish that, but for the breach of fiduciary duty, the losses would not have been incurred.[101]

Brickenden was a Canadian appeal, but the case no longer represents the law there either.[102] In Canada it is open to a fiduciary to show, although the onus is upon him to do so, that his principal would have suffered the loss in any event.[103] In *Hodgkinson v Simms*, LaForest J called this a long-standing equitable principle and further said that such evidence must be 'concrete'.[104] However, although the use of 'concrete' in Canadian cases might be compared to the New Zealand 'narrow escape route', this is not borne out by the cases that follow. I can only find two cases that refer to the evidence being 'concrete', and in neither of those was the point of any relevance.[105] A few years before *Hodgkinson v Simms*, McKinlay JA had said in *Berk* that proof would be 'difficult' and 'speculation' would not suffice,[106] but then two paragraphs later the judge referred to the defendant establishing proof on the balance of probabilities.

It is also clear that English courts will examine the question of whether a plaintiff would still have carried on with the transaction notwithstanding the defendant's non-disclosure. *Brickenden* was never binding in England in the first place, and it does not seem to have been relied on by any English court until

[100] *Short v Crawley (No 30)* [2007] NSWSC 1322 [407]–[428]. The Court of Appeal allowed an appeal from this judgment in part, but made no comment on the *Brickenden* issue: *Crawley* (n 73).

[101] Ibid [427]–[428], citing Heydon (n 29) 331.

[102] See J Berryman, 'Equitable Compensation for Breach by Fact-Based Fiduciaries: Tentative Thoughts on Clarifying Remedial Goals' (1999) 37 *Alberta Law Review* 95. There is a recent decision of the Alberta Court of Appeal which states that 'where a fiduciary is in breach of duty, he or she may not avoid liability by demonstrating that the loss would have occurred in any event...Inevitability of loss is irrelevant in determining liability for a breach of fiduciary duty': *Finch v Ross, Todd & Company* [2006] ABCA 98 [23] (Conrad, Picard and Martin JJA). However, the only authorities cited are a 1985 case from the British Columbia Supreme Court (*Island Realty Investments Ltd v Douglas* (1985) 19 ETR 56) and a 1914 decision of the Manitoba Court of King's Bench (*British America Elevator Co v Bank of British North America* (1914) 20 DLR 944), and this case must be regarded as an anomaly. An earlier decision of the Ontario Court of Appeal, *Raso v Dionigi* (1993) 12 OR (3d) 580 [23], restated the strict *Brickenden* approach, but that case must now be viewed as having been overtaken on this point by *Hodgkinson v Simms* [1994] 3 SCR 377 (SCC).

[103] See *Commerce Capital Trust Co v Berk* (1989) 57 DLR (4th) 759 (Ont CA) [13].

[104] *Hodgkinson* (n 102) [76].

[105] *Prenor Trust Co of Canada v Nunn* [1998] CanLII 18150 (Alta QB) [17]; *Reid v Graybriar Industries Ltd* [2006] ABQB 519 [143].

[106] *Berk* (n 103) [13]–[15].

Bristol and West Building Society v May May & Merrimans (No 1) in 1996.[107] In 1997 *Brickenden* was considered by the Court of Appeal in *Swindle v Harrison*, but although the three judges agreed on the result of the case they did so for completely different reasons.[108] The best that can probably be taken from the case is a recognition that each judge emphasised that the plaintiff would have gone ahead regardless of the breach, and obviously this would only be worth emphasising if the plaintiff's counterfactual conduct was relevant—so *Swindle v Harrison* is inconsistent with *Brickenden*. Two years after *Swindle v Harrison*, Blackburne J concluded in another case that 'nothing in the authorities compels me to disregard any inference which, on the evidence, can properly be drawn as to what would have happened if the fiduciary had performed his duty'.[109] The same view was taken by the Court of Appeal in *Gwembe Valley Development Company Ltd v Koshy*, where *Brickenden* was cited but it was found that 'the court is not precluded by authority or by principle from considering what would have happened if the material facts had been disclosed'.[110] There are no hints in England to the effect that counterfactuals will be especially difficult for the defendant to establish, and it is also worth noting that the cases do not prescribe where the onus lies. Instead English courts are content to say that it is open to them to consider the question.

It therefore seems that New Zealand cases are the outliers. Australian and English cases do not qualify the standard of proof with words like narrow or heavy;[111] and the 'concrete' requirement in Canada does not actually appear

[107] *Bristol and West Building Society v May May & Merrimans (No 1)* [1996] 2 All ER 801 (Ch D).

[108] *Swindle v Harrison* [1997] 4 All ER 705 (CA). Evans LJ drew a distinction between fraudulent and non-fraudulent breaches; Hobhouse LJ thought that *Brickenden* was not relevant to a claim for compensation; Mummery LJ held that *Brickenden* was relevant to the question of breach of duty (ie, a fiduciary cannot excuse non-disclosure on the grounds that the principal would have acted in the same way), but his Lordship did not consider it relevant to the question of causation. See further Conaglen, 'Remedial ramifications' (n 93) 82.

[109] *Nationwide* (n 96) 671–72.

[110] *Gwembe Valley Development Company Ltd v Koshy* [2003] EWCA Civ 1048, [2004] WTLR 97 [143]–[147]. Since *Gwembe Valley* the water has been slightly muddied by Jonathan Parker LJ's comments in *Murad v Al-Saraj* [2005] EWCA Civ 959, [2005] WTLR 1573 [103]–[108], where his Lordship perhaps muddled the distinction between the no profit rule and the duty/conflict part of the no conflict rule. Jonathan Parker LJ cited Lord Thankerton's dictum in between Lord Russell's speech in *Regal (Hastings) v Gulliver* [1967] 2 AC 134 (HL) and a part of Mummery LJ's judgment in *Gwembe Valley* where reference was made to directors' unauthorised profits. His Lordship concluded by saying that 'the "no conflict" rule is neither compensatory nor restitutionary: rather, it is designed to strip the fiduciary of the unauthorised profits he has made whilst he is in a position of conflict'. Yet *Brickenden* is a case about equitable compensation awarded in response to loss suffered after a breach of fiduciary duty. Plaintiff loss is beside the point in cases that involve breach of the no profit rule (unless there is also a breach of the no conflict rule), so *Brickenden* simply has no application to no-profit cases. See Vann, 'Causation and breach of fiduciary duty' (n 63) 92: 'If the quantification of an account of profits and the quantification of equitable compensation are the same in a given case, that is merely fortuitous.'

[111] This is not surprising given that in those jurisdictions the burden is not always viewed as being on the defendant. English cases simply provide that the court may consider the issue (which presumably means that the burden is on whichever party seeks to establish the point), whereas Australian cases vary in their comments on this point (again, presumably meaning that the position can change depending on the way particular cases are argued).

to change the normal standard either. However, in New Zealand the evidential requirement is harder to satisfy. In *Premium Real Estate v Stevens* the Chief Justice of New Zealand dissented on exactly this point: in refusing to award compensation referable to the market value of the house, as opposed to the price that the plaintiffs would have been willing to accept, Elias CJ disagreed that a fiduciary should be entitled only to a narrow escape route. Instead her Honour found that 'like any civil onus, it is discharged by the defendant on the balance of probabilities if the fact asserted is found to be more likely than not.'[112] This, indeed, is the position in Australia, Canada and England.

IV. Conclusion

There are clear jurisdictional differences apparent in the treatment of equitable compensation. In respect of property misapplied from a custodial fiduciary relationship, Australia takes a substitutive approach and asks simply whether the disbursement was authorised or not. If not, the trustee cannot take credit for it when the account is taken—regardless of whether a similar disbursement (eg, to the same person, on the same terms, one day later) would have been authorised. This is undoubtedly attractive from a position of pure theory, although it would seem to place a lot of honest trustees at the mercy of a court's jurisdiction to relieve. We might also wonder whether cases involving breaches of trustee investment duties could instead be litigated as 'no authorisation to disburse' cases.[113] Perhaps because of these concerns, the other jurisdictions take a reparative approach to equitable compensation.[114] Indeed, searching for 'Youyang' returns no hits at all

[112] *Premium Real Estate* (n 85) [38].

[113] Similarly, the misapplication of company assets is more commonly treated as the improper exercise of a director's power rather than as a shortfall in the taking of an account: see, eg *O'Halloran* (n 14) and *Bishopsgate Investment Management Ltd (in liq) v Maxwell (No 2)* [1994] 1 All ER 261 (CA). But this might not always be the case.

[114] Even though *Canson Enterprises* (n 46) was not a breach of trust case, the comments on causation are applied to equitable claims in Canada generally. The fullest discussion is found in *Blanco v Canada Trust Co* [2003] 9 WWR 79 (Man CA) [46]–[60], a case with very similar material facts to *Youyang* and *Target Holdings*. The limitation regime prevented a breach of trust claim but would allow a breach of fiduciary duty claim, so strictly the discussion is in the context of fiduciary duty rather than trust; however, it is clearly directed to the same point. Significantly, the Court spoke of the defendant's actions as being at the low end of a 'continuum of conduct', where the loss would be seen 'from a common sense perspective, to have nothing to do with [the breach]'. This is clearly the language of reparative compensation. The position in New Zealand is slightly trickier to interpret, but courts there have generally followed *Target Holdings*: see *Sojourner v Robb* [2006] 3 NZLR 808 (NZHC) [153] and *Guardian Trust Co* (n 14) (although cf *Guardian Trust Co* in the High Court: [1999] 1 NZLR 213 (NZHC)). See further A Butler, 'Civil Liability' in Butler (n 8) 263; McLay, 'Equitable Damages' (n 8) 931.

on www.nzlii.org, www.canlii.org or www.bailii.org. It returns only Australian hits on www.commonlii.org.[115]

The picture in respect of *Brickenden* is more surprising. As Butler and Miller discuss in their chapter, New Zealand equity jurisprudence is not generally received well in New South Wales. One wonders if this has now become an automatic reaction rather than a considered one. For example, the authors of *On Equity* say that the New Zealand cases of *Everist v McEvedy* and *Gilbert v Shanahan* go too far and should be 'viewed with great caution'.[116] Putting aside the fact that, since *On Equity* was published *Premium Real Estate* has arguably shown that New Zealand law has actually gone 'less far' than Australian law, those two earlier decisions certainly went no further than two New South Wales Court of Appeal cases: *Beach Petroleum v Kennedy* and *Cassis v Kalfus (No 2)*. None of this is to defend *Brickenden* or the majority's view in *Premium Real Estate*, but it is interesting to note that—in this context at least—New Zealand equity jurisprudence is more traditional than that of the other jurisdictions.

[115] Searches conducted on 26 April 2011.

[116] *On Equity* (n 12) para [2.530].

8

Trusts and Knowledge: Lessons from Australia

BEN McFARLANE*

I. Introduction

In *Westdeutsche Landesbank Girozentrale v Islington LBC*,[1] Lord Browne-Wilkinson set out four propositions which he regarded as 'fundamental to the law of trusts'.[2] The second of these—to be referred to in this chapter as the 'second proposition'—was as follows:

> Since the equitable jurisdiction to enforce trusts depends upon the conscience of the holder of the legal interest being affected, he cannot be a trustee of the property if and so long as he is ignorant of the facts alleged to affect his conscience, i.e. until he is aware that he is intended to hold the property for the benefit of others in the case of an express or implied trust, or, in the case of a constructive trust, of the factors which are alleged to affect his conscience.[3]

Whilst admitting that this formulation 'may call for some expansion', Lord Browne-Wilkinson thought it 'uncontroversial'.[4] Yet in the law of trusts, as in equity more generally, it is often the most basic propositions that excite the most controversy. Indeed, in England, there has been little sign of judicial or academic enthusiasm for the development of Lord Browne-Wilkinson's second proposition.[5] The aim of this

* This chapter was prepared, in part, during a visit to the Melbourne Law School, University of Melbourne, and I am particularly grateful for the assistance of Andrew Robertson, Matthew Harding and Elise Bant. The views expressed here are my own and the usual disclaimers apply.

[1] *Westdeutsche Landesbank Girozentrale v Islington LBC* [1996] AC 669 (HL).

[2] Ibid 705.

[3] Ibid.

[4] Ibid.

[5] Approval of Lord Browne-Wilkinson's second proposition was given by Millett LJ in *Bristol and West Building Society v Mothew* [1998] Ch 1 (CA) 23–24. Lord Browne-Wilkinson's general approach was also approved by Judge Chambers QC in *Papamichael v National Westminster Bank plc (No 2)* [2003] EWHC 164, [2003] 1 Lloyd's Rep 341 (Comm) [222]–[226] and ('diffidently') by Mann J in *Re Farepak Food and Gifts Ltd* [2006] EWHC 3272 (Ch) [40]. Doubts were however cast by Rimer J in *Shalson v Russo* [2003] EWHC 3272 (Ch), [2005] Ch 281 [110]–[111]. For academic disapproval of Lord Browne-Wilkinson's approach see, eg W Swadling, 'Property and Conscience' (1998) 12 *Trust Law International* 228; R Meagher, D Heydon and M Leeming, *Meagher, Gummow & Lehane's Equity:*

chapter, however, is to suggest that the second proposition contains an important truth. In particular, with the assistance of other hints in Lord Browne-Wilkinson's speech in *Westdeutsche*, the second proposition can be developed into a positive formula: it will be argued that, if the conditions set out by each of the three parts of this formula are met, a non-express trust will arise. It is not claimed that, if those conditions are not satisfied, no non-express trust can arise; the positive formula provides only one of the various bases for such a trust. It will be argued that the positive formula can assist our understanding of three important recent decisions in disputes originating in New South Wales; and that those decisions may, in turn, play a role in the future development of English law. In fact, it may be that Lord Browne-Wilkinson's approach will share the experience of many English visitors to Australia: having found a more conducive environment abroad, it will return home with renewed vigour.

II. The Positive Formula

Before examining the three Australian decisions, it is necessary to analyse Lord Browne-Wilkinson's second proposition in a little more detail, and to show how it can be developed into a positive formula.

A. The Context

First, the second proposition needs to be seen in the context of the *Westdeutsche* decision itself. The Westdeutsche Landesbank (B) made a payment to the defendant local authority (A), mistakenly believing that it was under a contractual duty to do so. In performance of the apparent contract, A had also made some payments to B. The apparent contract was, in fact, void as beyond the powers of A. B claimed that A had a duty not only to repay the balance of B's initial payment, but also to pay compound interest on that sum. As the law then stood,[6] such a claim for compound interest was only possible if the local authority was found to have held the initial mistaken payment on trust. An authority in the bank's favour was *Chase Manhattan Bank v Israel-British Bank*.[7] In that case, the paying bank (B) owed money to the defendant bank (A), but mistakenly paid the sum twice. As A subsequently went into insolvency, B argued that the second payment had, from the moment of its receipt, been held on trust by A. Goulding J accepted this argument. His reasoning

Doctrine and Remedies, 4th edn (Chatswood, Butterworths LexisNexis, 2002) para [14–015]; B Häcker, 'Proprietary Restitution After Impaired Consent Transfers: A Generalised Power Model' (2009) 68 *CLJ* 324; R Chambers, 'Trust and Theft' in E Bant and M Harding (eds), *Exploring Private Law* (Cambridge, Cambridge University Press, 2010) 223, 242–43.

[6] See now *Sempra Metals Ltd v IRC* [2007] UKHL 34, [2008] 1 AC 561.

[7] *Chase Manhattan Bank v Israel-British Bank* [1981] Ch 105 (ChD).

depended on the view that a payor making such a mistake, whilst transferring legal title to the payment to the recipient, *retains* an equitable property right in the payment.[8]

In *Westdeutsche*, however, Lord Browne-Wilkinson pointed out some of the difficulties with this reasoning.[9] First, it rests on the view that a party who simply holds a right, free from any trust, has both a distinct legal interest in that right and a separate equitable interest. This view is untenable both historically and as a matter of principle. Historically, in a case where a party simply holds a right, there is no reason for a court of equity to intervene or to recognise any distinct equitable interest. As a matter of principle, equitable property rights, unlike legal property rights, necessarily depend on a relationship between specific individuals: any equitable property right of B is based on an initial duty owed to B by A.[10] The analysis of Goulding J is thus inconsistent with the first of Lord Browne-Wilkinson's four 'fundamental' propositions: that 'equity operates on the conscience of the owner of the legal interest'.[11] The point seems to be that, unless there is a specific reason for which A comes under a duty to B, there can be no trust. On Goulding J's analysis, A comes under a duty to B *because* B has a right under a trust; on Lord Browne-Wilkinson's analysis, it seems, it is A's duty to B which itself constitutes the trust.

This leads to the second difficulty with the analysis of Goulding J. The third of Lord Browne-Wilkinson's fundamental propositions is that '[i]n order to establish a trust there must be identifiable trust property.'[12] In other words, for a trust to exist, it must be the case that A is under a duty to B, and that A's duty relates to a specific right held by A. In a case where A receives a mistaken payment from B, but is unaware of B's mistake, it is difficult to say that A is under a duty to B *in relation to* the right he has acquired from B. This is not to deny that A comes under an immediate *prima facie* duty,[13] enforceable in an action for money had and received, to pay B the value of the mistaken payment. In each of *Chase Manhattan* and *Westdeutsche*, however, B wished to show that the mistaken payment was held by A on trust. In order to do so, B had to show that A's duty was not just a general duty to return the value of the payment, but was rather a duty that related *specifically* to the payment itself: to the right A acquired from B. If such a duty exists then A acts in breach of trust if, rather than holding the payment for B, he uses the payment for his own benefit. Yet if A is unaware of B's mistake in making the

[8] Ibid 119: 'a person who pays money to another under a factual mistake retains an equitable property in it and the conscience of that other is subjected to a fiduciary duty to respect his proprietary right'.

[9] *Westdeutsche* (n 1) 714–15.

[10] See, eg R Chambers, *An Introduction to Property Law in Australia*, 2nd edn (Sydney, Lawbook Co, 2008) para [13.90]; L Smith, 'Philosophical Foundations of Proprietary Remedies' in R Chambers, C Mitchell and J Penner (eds), *Philosophical Foundations of the Law of Unjust Enrichment* (Oxford, Oxford University Press, 2009); B McFarlane and R Stevens, 'The Nature of Equitable Property' (2010) *Journal of Equity* 1.

[11] *Westdeutsche* (n 1) 705.

[12] Ibid.

[13] *Prima facie* because it is subject to possible defences, such as the change of position defence.

payment, it is very difficult to see why A should be under such a duty not to use the right acquired from B for A's own benefit.[14] Moreover, if A were under such a duty, A would be precluded from using the change of position defence—even if A, relying in good faith on the payment from B, were to spend all or part of the sum received on expenditure which A would not otherwise have incurred, A would still be under a duty to account to B, as a trustee, for the whole sum received. This leads us back to Lord Browne-Wilkinson's second proposition, that A 'cannot be a trustee of the property if and so long as he is ignorant of the facts alleged to affect his conscience'.

In *Westdeutsche*, the bank's failure to satisfy Lord Browne-Wilkinson's second proposition ensured that no trust was recognised. The bank's payment had been made in June 1987, and it was only in November 1989 that it was first held that the type of contract under which the payment had been made was beyond the powers of a local authority.[15] In that two year period, it seems, the local authority had spent the money received by the bank, and retained no traceable substitute of the initial payment.[16] As a result, there was no point at which the local authority *both* held a specific right that could be identified as the product of the bank's payment *and* knew about the bank's error in making the payment. In other words, there was no point at which the local authority was under a duty to the bank in relation to a specific right held by the local authority—therefore, there was no trust.

B. Refining and Developing the Proposition

This chapter does not seek to defend the literal truth of Lord Browne-Wilkinson's second proposition. For example, the proposition assumes that, for a trust to exist, the conscience of 'the holder of the legal interest' must be affected. Such an assumption is understandable in the context of *Westdeutsche*, but it should not be applied generally as it is of course possible to have a trust of a purely equitable right. Indeed, the very common practice of intermediated securitisation depends on the existence of a chain of sub-trusts.[17] Similarly, the second proposition considers whether a party is a trustee 'of the property'. This term is perhaps best avoided, as trust assets can, of course, include a personal right, such as a bank account held by a trustee. A reformulated version of the proposition would therefore be:

> Since the equitable jurisdiction to enforce trusts depends upon the conscience of the holder of a right being affected, he cannot be a trustee of the right if and so long as he is ignorant of the facts alleged to affect his conscience.

[14] See, eg *Mothew* (n 5) 23 (Millett LJ); *Papamichael* (n 5) [226] (Judge Chambers QC).

[15] The decision of the Divisional Court in *Hazell v Hammersmith & Fulham LBC* [1992] 2 AC 1 (HL) was given on 1 November 1989.

[16] *Westdeutsche* (n 1) 700.

[17] See B McFarlane and R Stevens, 'Interests in Securities: Practical Problems and Conceptual Solutions' in L Gullifer and J Payne (eds), *Intermediated Securities: Legal Problems and Practical Solutions* (Oxford, Hart Publishing, 2009).

Lord Browne-Wilkinson's second proposition is entirely negative: it tells us only when a trust cannot arise. Nonetheless, with the assistance of a number of hints in Lord Browne-Wilkinson's speech, it may be possible to develop the proposition into a positive formula describing a set of circumstances in which a trust *will* arise. First, Lord Browne-Wilkinson suggested that, whilst Goulding J's reasoning is flawed, the decision in *Chase Manhattan* may be correct. Before going into insolvency, and whilst still holding the payment made to it by B, A became aware of B's mistake. Lord Browne-Wilkinson commented that: '[a]lthough the mere receipt of the moneys, in ignorance of the mistake, gives rise to no trust, the retention of the moneys after the recipient bank learned of the mistake may well have given rise to a constructive trust.'[18]

The second hint lies in Lord Browne-Wilkinson's discussion of the case of a thief who steals a bag of coins and then mixes its contents with other coins, or pays the stolen coins into a mixed bank account. Lord Browne-Wilkinson accepted that, in such a case, the thief can be 'required to disgorge the property which, in equity, represents the stolen coins'.[19] In *Westdeutsche*, the bank argued that this was due to the existence of a resulting trust, arising either at the time of the theft or on the mixing of the stolen money. Lord Browne-Wilkinson's view, however, was that:

> [T]he proprietary interest which equity is enforcing in such circumstances arises under a constructive, not a resulting trust. Although it is difficult to find clear authority for the proposition, when property is obtained by fraud equity imposes a constructive trust on the fraudulent recipient: the property is recoverable and traceable in equity.[20]

Using these hints in Lord Browne-Wilkinson's speech, it is possible to develop a positive formula, applying both in the case where A knowingly retains a mistaken payment, and in the case where A obtains a right by fraud. The positive formula states that a non-express trust will arise if three conditions are met. First, the same act or transaction must have involved both B's loss of a right (or acquisition of a duty) and A's acquisition of a right. Second, there must be a specific reason (such as B's mistake or A's fraud) for which there is no legal basis for A, as against B, to have the benefit of the right acquired by A. Third, A must know both that he has acquired the right, and of the facts constituting the reason why there is no legal basis for A, as against B, to have the benefit of the right. A must have that knowledge whilst holding either the right initially acquired, or a right that counts as a traceable product of that initial right.

It may be useful, at this point, to give three examples of the application of the positive formula. First, it is satisfied in a case, such as *Chase Manhattan*, in which A, having innocently acquired a right mistakenly transferred by B, becomes aware of

[18] *Westdeutsche* (n 1) 715.

[19] Ibid 716.

[20] Ibid. This statement was approved by Lawrence Collins J in *Commerzbank Aktiengesellschaft v IBM Morgan plc* [2004] EWHC 2771 (Ch), [2005] 2 All ER (Comm) 564 [36] but in *Shalson v Russo* (n 5), Rimer J at [111] doubted the proposition that property obtained by fraud is automatically held by the recipient on a constructive trust for the person defrauded.

B's mistake whilst still holding that right or right that counts as a traceable product of that initial right. The decision to be discussed in section IIIA, *Wambo Coal Pty Ltd v Ariff*,[21] demonstrates the application of the positive formula in such a case. Second, the formula may also be satisfied in a case where A holds a right on trust for B, and then transfers that right to C, who provides no consideration: if, and only if, C retains that right (or its traceable product) with knowledge of the trust in B's favour (or the facts giving rise to it), C will then hold that right on a non-express trust for B. It will be argued that the application of the positive formula to such a case is consistent with both the analysis of the High Court of Australia in *Farah Constructions Pty Ltd v Say-Dee Pty Ltd*,[22] to be discussed in section IIIB, and the broad approach of the Court of Appeal of New South Wales in *Heperu Pty Ltd v Belle*,[23] examined in section IIIC. Third, the decision of the High Court of Australia in *Black & Black v S Freedman & Co*[24] is consistent with this second example: a thief who pays stolen money into a bank account holds his right against the bank on trust for the victim of the theft; and if money is paid out of that account to an initially innocent volunteer who later gains knowledge of the theft, any traceable product of that payment retained by the volunteer will also be held on trust for the victim of the theft.

In *Black*, the reasoning of O'Connor J depended on the idea that a trust arises *as soon as* a theft occurs.[25] It is worth pointing out that such a trust cannot be justified by the positive formula. The first part of the formula is that the same act or transaction must involve both B's loss of a right (or acquisition of a duty) and A's acquisition of a right. This part is satisfied where B directly transfers a right to A by, for example, transferring his title to a $100 note to A. It is not satisfied where A simply steals B's $100 note; whilst A, by taking possession of the note, has gained a right (a purely possessory title), A's theft has not caused B to lose any right, as B of course retains title to the note.[26] If A then pays the $100 note into his bank account, however, then, assuming that A's account is in credit after the payment, the first part of the formula is met. For that payment involves both A's acquisition of a right against his bank, and B's loss of a right—the bank, as a bona fide purchaser for value without notice, gains good title to the note.[27] This means that, if the thief is to hold his possessory title on trust for the victim of the

[21] *Wambo Coal Pty Ltd v Ariff* [2007] NSWSC 589.

[22] *Farah Constructions Pty Ltd v Say-Dee Pty Ltd* [2007] HCA 22, (2007) 230 CLR 89, reversing [2005] NSWCA 309.

[23] *Heperu Pty Ltd v Belle* [2009] NSWCA 252, (2009) 76 NSWLR 230.

[24] *Black & Black v S Freedman & Co* (1910) 12 CLR 105 (HCA).

[25] Ibid 107: '[w]here money has been stolen, it is trust money in the hands of the thief, and he cannot divest it of that character.' This idea is doubted (with good reason) by Rimer J in *Shalson v Russo* (n 5) [110]. Rimer J assumes, however, that, in *Westdeutsche*, Lord Browne-Wilkinson also took the view that a trust arises as soon as a theft occurs; in fact, Lord Browne-Wilkinson's analysis (*Westdeutsche* (n 1) 715–716) does not depend on the finding of such a trust.

[26] As noted by Rimer J in *Shalson v Russo* (n 5) [110].

[27] See, eg *Miller v Race* (1758) 1 Burr 452, 97 ER 398.

theft, such a trust must arise on some other principle, distinct from the positive formula set out here.[28]

The first part of the positive formula is also met where B's mistaken payment to A consists of a bank transfer of $100. If each of B's account and A's account is in credit, B loses a right to claim $100 from B's bank, and A acquires a right to claim $100 from A's bank. If B's bank account is overdrawn, the test is still met, as B acquires a further duty: to pay his bank $100. If A's account, after receipt of the payment, is also overdrawn, however, the payment does not lead to A's acquisition of a right; it rather leads to A's loss of a pre-existing duty to pay his bank $100. Such a case is excluded from the positive formula as the formula seeks solely to describe one set of circumstances in which a *trust* will arise. As noted above, a trust exists only where A is under a duty to B in relation to a particular right and, where payment is made into an overdrawn account, there is no right of A that A may hold on trust for B. This does not mean that, in such a case, there is no *personal* right that B may have against A: as A has received a relevant benefit, B may still bring a claim for money had and received against A. Equally, if B's payment removes a duty owed by A to X, and that duty was secured by, for example, a charge held by X over some right of A, it may be the case that, under principles of 'reviving' subrogation, X's charge will revive in order to secure A's *prima facie* duty to pay B the value of the mistaken payment.[29] There are important and interesting links between the circumstances in which a non-express trust may arise, and those in which such reviving subrogation can give B an equitable security right; this chapter is, however, limited to an examination of a particular set of circumstances in which a trust may arise.

The second part of the positive formula is that there must be a specific reason (such as B's mistake or A's fraud) for which there is no legal basis for A, as against B, to have the benefit of the right acquired by A. It must be emphasised that, in the examples under discussion, there is a legal basis on which A has acquired the *right* in question: after all, only the operation of legal rules (be they common law, equitable, or statutory) can lead to A's acquisition of a right. If, for example, B transfers to A his title to a car, mistakenly believing that he is under a contractual duty to do so, then A does acquire B's title, as B did intend to transfer that very right to A. Similarly, if A steals money from B and pays it into a bank account, A does acquire a new right against A's bank. The fact that A has acquired a right, through the operation of one set of rules, does not prevent A's being under a personal duty to pay the value of that right to B;[30] nor does it prevent A's holding that right on trust for B. Indeed, A's acquisition of the right is a *pre-condition* of any such trust. The point is that, whilst there clearly is a basis on which A has acquired the right,

[28] For a full consideration of possible grounds for such a trust, see Chambers, 'Trust and Theft' (n 5).

[29] See, eg *Butler v Rice* [1910] 2 Ch 277 (Ch); *Banque Financière de la Cité SA v Parc (Battersea) Ltd* [1999] 1 AC 221 (HL).

[30] See, eg *Cressman v Coys of Kensington (Sales) Ltd* [2004] EWCA Civ 47, [2004] 1 WLR 2775 [24] (Mance LJ).

there is a specific reason (such as B's mistake or A's theft) for which A, as against B, should not have the benefit of that right.

The third part of the positive formula is that A must know both that he has acquired the right, and of the facts constituting the reason why there is no legal basis for A, as against B, to have the benefit of the right acquired by A. The influence of Lord Browne-Wilkinson's second proposition can be seen most clearly in the crucial role played by A's knowledge. Again, it should be emphasised that the positive formula is concerned only with the question of whether a trust arises. It is important to note that A may be under a *prima facie* duty to pay B the value of A's right even if A has no knowledge that he has that right, or of the facts meaning that there is no legal basis for A, as against B, to have the benefit of the right.[31] As noted above, for example, A was under such a duty, in each of *Chase Manhattan* and *Westdeutsche*, as soon as A received the mistaken payment from B. That immediate duty, however, did not relate to any specific right held by A: A could satisfy it by paying the relevant sum to B, whatever the source of that money. For a trust to arise, A must be under a duty in relation to a specific right and, on Lord Browne-Wilkinson's second proposition, such a duty can only arise where A has the relevant knowledge.

C. Clarifying the Positive Formula

The remainder of this chapter will be dedicated to testing the three-part positive formula by considering its application to three recent Australian decisions. It is first necessary, however, to make three points of clarification, each concerning the relationship of the positive formula to Lord Browne-Wilkinson's speech in *Westdeutsche*.

First, in his discussion of each of *Chase Manhattan* and the case of property acquired through fraud, Lord Browne-Wilkinson describes the trust, arising consistently with the positive formula, as a constructive, rather than a resulting, trust. As far as testing the positive formula is concerned, this distinction is irrelevant. It would be important if the right acquired by B under a constructive trust were different from that acquired by B under a resulting trust. If, for example, the constructive trust contemplated by Lord Browne-Wilkinson was one which arose only upon a court order creating it, the difference between a constructive and a resulting trust would be significant. It is true that, in his speech in *Westdeutsche* Lord Browne-Wilkinson does discuss remedial constructive trusts, in which 'the remedy can be tailored to the circumstances of the particular case'[32] so as, for example, to protect third parties who have acquired rights from A before any court order in B's favour. There is, however, nothing to suggest that Lord Browne-Wilkinson viewed trusts arising under the positive formula as remedial in this

[31] See, eg *Kelly v Solari* (1841) 11 LJ Ex 10.
[32] *Westdeutsche* (n 1) 716.

sense.[33] In particular, his Lordship considered that the possible introduction of remedial constructive trusts into English law was a question for a future case,[34] whereas he regarded the trusts recognised in each of *Chase Manhattan* and the case of property acquired through fraud as already established in English law.

It must be admitted that Lord Browne-Wilkinson's distinction between constructive and resulting trusts is also significant in so far as it might suggest that the positive formula set out in this chapter is *not* to be used to explain the two sets of circumstances in which, according to Lord Browne-Wilkinson, a resulting trust can arise. Those circumstances are, first, where B makes a voluntary payment to A, or pays wholly or in part for the acquisition of a right vested in either A alone or in the joint names of A and B; and, second, where B transfers a right to A on an express trust, 'but the trusts declared do not exhaust the whole beneficial interest'.[35] In *Westdeutsche*, Lord Browne-Wilkinson adopts what he calls the 'traditional' explanation of those resulting trusts: that they give effect to the common intentions of A and B, whereas a constructive trust, in contrast, is 'imposed by law against the intentions of the trustee'.[36] Of course, if that explanation is correct, then resulting trusts arise on a basis distinct from that of the positive formula set out in this chapter.

There are, however, a number of difficulties with the idea that the parties' common intention is the basis of the two types of trust identified by Lord Browne-Wilkinson as resulting trusts.[37] Further, if the positive formula set out here is accepted, it seems that it may well be broad enough to include each type of resulting trust.[38] That broader question cannot be pursued here, but it does lead us to the second point of clarification. In *Westdeutsche*, Lord Browne-Wilkinson expressly rejected the view, proposed by Birks, that resulting trusts are restitutionary responses to A's unjust enrichment at the expense of B.[39] Yet, the first two parts of the positive formula set out here may be viewed as identifying cases in which A is unjustly enriched at B's expense.[40] How then can the positive formula escape Lord Browne-Wilkinson's apparent objection to non-express restitutionary trusts? The answer is that the positive formula set out here differs from the analysis rejected by Lord Browne-Wilkinson.

[33] In *Papamichael* (n 5) Judge Chambers QC at [222] noted that, on Lord Browne-Wilkinson's view, the trust arising in *Chase Manhattan*, as a result of the recipient bank's knowledge of the paying bank's mistake, was 'an institutional resulting trust'.

[34] *Westdeutsche* (n 1) 716.

[35] Ibid 708.

[36] Ibid.

[37] It is, for example, difficult to argue that the resulting trust recognised in *Vandervell v IRC* [1967] 2 AC 291 (HL) was intended by Mr Vandervell: see, eg *re Vandervell's Trusts (No 2)* [1974] Ch 269, 294 (Megarry J).

[38] See B McFarlane, *The Structure of Property Law* (Oxford, Hart Publishing, 2008) 314–22.

[39] *Westdeutsche* (n 1) 708–09.

[40] See B McFarlane, 'Unjust Enrichment, Rights and Value' in D Nolan and A Robertson (eds), *Rights in Private Law* (Oxford, Hart Publishing, 2011).

First, the positive formula, if described in Birks' terminology, takes a much more restrictive view of the 'at the expense of B' requirement: it is limited to cases where the same event or transaction causes B to lose a right (or acquire a duty) and A to gain a right. In contrast, Birks, particularly in his later writing, took a wide view of the 'at the expense of' requirement, arguing that it could be met whenever there was a causal relationship between B's loss and A's gain.[41] For example, consider a case such as *Lipkin Gorman v Karpnale*.[42] A, a rogue partner, drew cheques on the bank account of a partnership (B), without authority. B's bank made payment to A and, consistently with the terms of its contract with B, debited those sums from B's account. It was clear that A thereby gained legal title to the money paid out by B's bank.[43] A then went to C's casino where he exchanged some of the money for chips with which he gambled. As gambling contracts were, at that time, void, C provided no consideration for the money it received from A. The House of Lords held that C was under a duty to pay to B the value of the overall gain it had made (roughly £150,000) from A's gambling with those chips. On Birks' view, it can be said that C was unjustly enriched at B's expense, as there was a clear causal link between the loss to B (the valid debiting of B's bank account) and the gain to C (the money it received from A's gambling). In contrast, the second part of the positive formula set out here is *not* satisfied—C has acquired a right, but that right was acquired from A, who, despite his lack of authority, had good legal title to the money paid out by B's bank. It cannot be said that C's acquisition of a right (caused by A's gambling in C's casino) was part of the same act or transaction as B's loss of a right (caused by B's bank paying out money to A). This distinction between the positive formula set out here and the view of Birks is important, as it meets Lord Browne-Wilkinson's first objection to Birks's argument: that 'the argument elides rights in property (which is the only proper subject matter of a trust) into rights in "the value transferred"'.[44] It is important to emphasise that the positive formula focuses on rights, rather than on value; and, as will be discussed in section IIIC below, this focus is in fact consistent with both the result of, and much of Lord Templeman's analysis in, *Lipkin Gorman* itself.

The second difference between the positive formula and Birks's analysis is that, under the third part of the positive formula, no trust can arise unless and until the supposed trustee acquires knowledge of both his acquisition of a right and of the facts meaning that there is no legal basis for A, as against B, to have the benefit of that right. This allows the positive formula to meet Lord Browne-Wilkinson's

[41] See, eg P Birks, *Unjust Enrichment*, 2nd edn (Oxford, Clarendon Press, 2005) 86–98; P Birks, '"At the Expense of the Claimant": Direct and Indirect Enrichment in English Law', in D Johnston & R Zimmerman (eds), *Unjustified Enrichment: Key Issues in Comparative Perspective* (Cambridge, Cambridge University Press, 2002).

[42] *Lipkin Gorman v Karpnale* [1991] 2 AC 548 (HL).

[43] *Commercial Banking Co of Sydney Ltd v Mann* [1961] AC 1 (PC).

[44] *Westdeutsche* (n 1) 709.

second, and principal, objection to Birks's analysis:[45] that it allowed for a trust to arise without A being aware of the facts alleged to affect A's conscience.

The third and final point of clarification relates to a warning note struck by Lord Browne-Wilkinson himself, when noting that his second proposition, even in its negative form 'may call for some expansion'.[46] The acknowledged complication comes from resulting trusts acknowledged in cases where a right has been put into A's name by B, without a gift being intended by B, and without A having any initial knowledge of B's action. In such a case, if a trust arises immediately, before A is even aware that he holds the right, this is inconsistent with any requirement that a trustee must have knowledge of the facts alleged to affect his conscience. Two points need to be made. First, even if a resulting trust arose immediately in such cases, this would not, in itself, be fatal to the positive formula: it would simply mean that such resulting trusts are not dependent on that formula, but instead arise under a different principle. Second, Lord Browne-Wilkinson's view was that in such cases, a resulting trust does *not* arise immediately, as there is

> so far as I am aware, no authority which decides that [A] was a trustee, and therefore accountable for his deeds, at any time before he was aware of the circumstances which gave rise to the resulting trust.[47]

On this view, in the period before A has knowledge, B can best be described as having what might be called a 'factual power': by providing A with the necessary knowledge, B can establish a trust. B's power is factual rather than legal as B's exercise of it is not a pre-condition of B's acquiring the right under the trust: B will acquire the right whenever A has the requisite knowledge, whether or not A gained that knowledge from B. In that way, *anyone* familiar with the facts of the case has the power, by informing A, to give B a right under a trust. In *Westdeutsche*, such a factual power existed during the period in which the local authority held the initial payment received from the bank, or a right counting as a traceable product of that right.[48] It is therefore important to distinguish B's factual power from a full blown right under a trust: on Lord Browne-Wilkinson's analysis, the existence of such a power does *not* mean that A holds any right on trust for B. Similarly, the positive formula set out here does not seek to describe when B may have a power to acquire a right; it is rather confined to cases where B acquires a right under a trust.

[45] Ibid.

[46] Ibid 705.

[47] Ibid 706. R Chambers, *Resulting Trusts* (Oxford, Clarendon Press, 1997) 201–12 takes a different view of the authorities.

[48] As noted by Judge Chambers QC in *Papamichael* (n 5) [226]: '[t]he later the acquisition of the knowledge the less chance that a trust will arise'.

III. The Australian Authorities

A. *Wambo Coal Pty v Ariff*[49]

In September, B, intending to make payment to X, mistakenly made a payment of $27,715 to A. That money was paid into an account which was $360 in credit. C was appointed as administrator and then liquidator of A. As liquidator of A, C ensured that $27,800 was paid from that account to C2, a company controlled by C, to meet C's expenses and fees as liquidator. That payment out was made at the start of October, before A or C was aware that B had made the first payment by mistake. At the end of October, B, again intending to make payment to X, made a second mistaken payment to A, into the same account, this time of $18,416. At the start of November, B realised its mistake in relation to each of the two payments, and informed A and C. In December, C ensured that a further payment of $17,600 was paid from the account to C2, again to meet C's expenses and fees as liquidator. The only credits made to A's account in the period between September and December were the two mistaken payments made by B. B had a simple restitutionary claim against A, but this claim was of no practical value, given A's financial position.[50] Could B instead look to C by claiming that C was under a duty to account to B for the sums paid out from A's account to C2?

Such were the essential facts of *Wambo*. The reasoning of White J in that case is perhaps the most direct judicial application of Lord Browne-Wilkinson's approach in *Westdeutsche*, and demonstrates some of the practical effects of its acceptance. As White J noted,[51] the only plausible basis for a claim against C was that: (i) A had held one or both of the mistaken payments on trust for B; and (ii) C was liable to account to B for some or all of the value of those payments, as a constructive trustee, under one of the two limbs of *Barnes v Addy*.[52]

The first point for decision, therefore, was whether A had, at any point, held the mistaken payments on trust for B. Counsel for Wambo (B) sought to rely on the judgment of Goulding J in *Chase Manhattan*, and argued that B had retained an equitable interest in the payments made to A. White J, closely following the reasoning of Lord Browne-Wilkinson in *Westdeutsche*, rejected this argument. He further noted that, on the facts, B clearly 'intended to part with the ownership of the money which it paid' and so 'did not intend to retain any equitable property in the money paid.'[53] Counsel for B also argued that, if there was no immediate trust, a trust could arise when A first became aware of the mistake. This argument depended on Lord Browne-Wilkinson's re-interpretation of *Chase Manhattan*.

49 *Wambo* (n 21).
50 As a result, White J described Wambo (B)'s direct restitutionary claim against Singleton (A) as giving rise only to 'a personal remedy of no value': ibid [67].
51 Ibid [31].
52 *Barnes v Addy* (1874) LR 9 Ch App 244.
53 *Wambo* (n 21) [36].

Counsel for Ariff (C) submitted that this re-interpretation was unconvincing and also submitted that, due to its dependence on the notion of a remedial constructive trust, it formed no part of English law.

It was argued above that Lord Browne-Wilkinson's analysis of *Chase Manhattan* did not, in fact, depend on the acceptance of a remedial constructive trust. White J took the same view, holding that the trust contemplated by Lord Browne-Wilkinson, whether resulting or constructive, 'is of an institutional rather than a remedial character.'[54] He also held that, whilst Lord Browne-Wilkinson's re-interpretation of *Chase Manhattan* is strictly obiter, it is 'consistent with principle'.[55] White J therefore held that, as the payments made by B had not only been made by mistake, but were also unaccompanied by consideration, '[i]t would be against conscience for [A] to use the moneys as its own once it knew of [B's] mistake'.[56] At that point, therefore, a trust arose. White J noted that Lord Browne-Wilkinson's analysis has been criticised by, for example, *Meagher, Gummow and Lehane*.[57] Nonetheless, he supported that analysis as consistent with cases in which a constructive trust is imposed in relation to property obtained by fraud and without consideration.[58]

Having found that a constructive trust would be recognised if A had knowledge of B's mistake, White J went on to consider the important question of what degree of knowledge is required for the trust to arise. He held that 'the appropriate question is whether the payee has such knowledge of the mistake as to affect his conscience because he is aware that he is not entitled to deal with the money as if he were the beneficial owner'.[59] A positive answer can be given not only in cases where the recipient has actual knowledge of the mistake, but also where he wilfully shuts his eyes to the obvious; or wilfully and recklessly fails to make such inquiries as an honest and reasonable person would make; or has knowledge of circumstances which would indicate the facts to an honest and reasonable person.[60] Applying this test it was found that C (whose mind was the mind of A) had sufficient knowledge of B's mistake before the second (but not the first) payment was made out of A's account and into C2's account.

B's claim then depended on showing that C was personally liable as a recipient of the second payment out of A's account. The payment had been made to C2 rather than to C himself. White J found, however, that C could be viewed as the true recipient: it was made at his direction and in respect of expenses due to him in his personal office as liquidator.[61] The question then was whether C's knowledge

54 Ibid [40]. See also *Papamichael* (n 5) [222] (Judge Chambers QC).
55 *Wambo* (n 21) [43].
56 Ibid.
57 Meagher, Heydon and Leeming (n 5) para [14–010].
58 *Wambo* (n 21) [43]. Reliance was placed, for example, on the decision of Bingham J in *Neste Oy v Lloyds Bank plc* [1983] 2 Lloyd's Rep 658 (Com Ct).
59 *Wambo* (n 21) [44].
60 Ibid.
61 Ibid [59].

sufficed to make him liable under the first limb of *Barnes v Addy*. The answer was yes: the fact C had (at least) wilfully shut his mind to the possibility that B's second payment had been mistakenly made was decisive.[62] As a result, C was liable to account to B as a knowing recipient of money held by A on constructive trust for B and paid to C2 in breach of that trust.

White J's analysis in *Wambo* matches almost exactly that which flows from the positive formula. The crucial question in deciding if a recipient of a mistaken payment holds that payment on trust was whether there was any point in time at which the recipient held that right, or its product, with knowledge of the fact that the payment had been mistakenly made. White J's analysis of how to test for such knowledge is also consonant with the positive formula. In particular, it is interesting to note that the test matches almost exactly that applied in English law to decide if a party is liable as a knowing recipient of trust assets under the *first* limb of *Barnes v Addy*.[63] The importance of this link will be discussed below, when *Farah*[64] is examined. First, however, a note of comparative caution must be struck. For, in interpreting the knowledge requirement, White J drew an analogy with the test applied under the *second* limb of *Barnes v Addy*.[65] In English law, that test requires dishonesty on the part of the defendant:[66] this sets a relatively high threshold for a claimant, and protects the defendant from the possibly severe joint and several liability for the trustee's breach of trust that is imposed where the second limb of *Barnes v Addy* is made out.[67] In *Wambo*, however, White J's preference for a test based on the second limb of *Barnes v Addy* led to no practical divergence from the approach preferred in this chapter. For White J's interpretation of the standard for liability under that second limb was not based on the higher 'dishonesty' test, as applied in English law, but rather on a wider test, including cases where the defendant has 'knowledge of circumstances which would indicate the facts to an honest and reasonable person'. It should therefore be emphasised that the practical effects of White J's analysis are identical to those of the approach preferred in this chapter.

B. *Farah Constructions Pty Ltd v Say-Dee Pty Ltd*[68]

It was suggested above that the knowledge requirement imposed by the third part of the positive formula should be exactly the same as that applied when deciding if a defendant is liable under the first limb of *Barnes v Addy* for the 'knowing receipt' of trust property. There is a practical advantage to such an approach: any difficul-

[62] Ibid [62].
[63] See, eg *BCCI v Akindele* [2000] EWCA Civ 502, [2001] Ch 437.
[64] *Farah* (n 22).
[65] *Wambo* (n 21) [44].
[66] See, eg *Barlow Clowes International v Eurotrust International* [2005] UKPC 37, [2006] 1 WLR 1476.
[67] See *Ultraframe (UK) Ltd v Fielding* [2005] EWHC 1638 (Ch) [1506] (Lewison J); S Elliott and C Mitchell, 'Remedies for Dishonest Assistance' (2004) 67 *MLR* 16.
[68] *Farah* (n 22).

ties in defining the knowledge requirement under the positive formula can be met by drawing on the test already applied in knowing receipt cases. More importantly, the approach is also justified in principle. For the very question asked in knowing receipt cases is the same as that to be asked in the mistaken payment case: has the defendant held a right on constructive trust for the claimant?[69]

This analysis of the nature of a knowing receipt claim can be developed by considering the decision of the High Court of Australia in *Farah*. The case has, of course, provoked much analysis, and its facts are well known. For present purposes, its importance consists in the view taken on one particular point: if A holds a right on trust for B, and transfers that right, without authority to C, what is the nature of any personal liability of C to B? For example, in *Wambo*, B contended that it had a direct restitutionary claim against C as C had been unjustly enriched by his receipt of assets held by A on trust for B. White J relied on the High Court's decision in *Farah* in stating that such a claim 'would appear to be unfounded.'[70] In *Farah*, the High Court did not in fact need to take a view on that question, as it found that Mrs Elias and her daughters (C) had not acquired any right to which a trust, or even a fiduciary duty, had previously attached.[71] For present purposes, however, the High Court's decision is significant for its discussion, and rejection, of a particular view adopted in the *Farah* litigation by the Court of Appeal of New South Wales. That view was that, where C receives a right as a result of a breach of trust or other fiduciary duty owed by A to B, then, even if C has no notice of A's breach, C may hold that right on constructive trust for B, such a trust arising to effect restitution for C's unjust enrichment at B's expense.[72] If correct, this analysis would subvert Lord Browne-Wilkinson's second proposition and would also render redundant the third part of the positive formula set out in this chapter.

In *Farah*, however, the High Court stated that it was a 'grave error' for the Court of Appeal of New South Wales to have adopted the view that, where C acquires a right as a result of a breach of trust or other fiduciary duty owed by A to B, C can hold that right on constructive trust for B even if C has no notice of A's breach.[73] That argument, based on unjust enrichment, had not been expressly put to the Court of Appeal, but it had been adopted by the court as 'it bears upon the true foundation of the first limb of *Barnes v Addy*', on which B had relied.[74] As the High Court pointed out, the Court of Appeal's view entailed not a reworking of that first limb but, rather, its abandonment.[75] For a crucial feature of liability under the first limb has always been that B must prove knowledge on C's part: C cannot be liable unless 'to his knowledge the money is being applied in a manner which

[69] See *re Montagu's Settlement Trusts* [1987] Ch 264 (ChD) 285 (Megarry V-C); McFarlane, *The Structure of Property Law* (n 38) 256–58.

[70] *Wambo* (n 21) [67].

[71] *Farah* (n 22) [115], [118].

[72] *Say-Dee Pty Ltd v Farah Constructions Pty Ltd* [2005] NSWCA 309 [216]–[217].

[73] *Farah* (n 22) [131].

[74] *Say-Dee* (n 72) [217].

[75] *Farah* (n 22) [153].

is inconsistent with the trust'.[76] English authorities have similarly emphasised the importance of knowledge;[77] indeed, 'knowing receipt' is the accepted short-hand name for the liability arising under the first limb of *Barnes v Addy*.

The key argument in favour of the unjust enrichment analysis preferred by the Court of Appeal of New South Wales was made both by Birks[78] and, writing extra-judicially, Lord Nicholls: it is the argument that 'equity should now follow the law'.[79] If, as recognised by the House of Lords in *Lipkin Gorman*, a strict liability unjust enrichment claim may protect a claimant's common law right, why should equitable rights receive less protection? The answer to this question lies not just in history, but also in principle. The first point is that the nature of a claim in knowing receipt is very different from a common law restitutionary claim, such as a claim for money had and received made against the recipient of a mistaken payment.[80] When seeking to rely on the first limb of *Barnes v Addy*, the claimant must show that the defendant is 'liable to account as a constructive trustee'. This is no empty formulation: as Mitchell and Watterson have recently shown,[81] a defendant liable for knowing receipt is under the same duties, and subject to the same remedies, as a trustee. For instance, to use an example given by Mitchell and Watterson,[82] consider a case where A holds title to a painting on trust for B and, without authority, transfers that title to C, who knows of the initial trust. C then sells the painting for \$5000. By the time that B discovers the unauthorised sale, the value of the painting has increased to \$50,000. C is liable for that larger sum, as he has the very same duty as A: to account to B for the title to the painting.[83] This leads to the second point:[84] it can be argued that C is not simply treated *as though* he were a trustee for B; rather, C's liability depends on the fact that he *did* hold a right on trust for B. It is at this point that a link can be drawn between liability in knowing receipt and Lord Browne-Wilkinson's analysis in *Westdeutsche*; and therefore between the approach of the High Court in *Farah* and of White J in *Wambo*. In order to make a claim in knowing receipt, B needs to show that C, at some point, held a right on trust for B. The facts giving rise to such trust—or, in Lord Browne Wilkinson's phrase, the facts causing C's conscience to be bound—are that C received, without

[76] *Re Blundell* (1888) 40 Ch D 370, 381 (Stirling J). See also *Consul Development Pty Ltd v DPC Estates Pty Ltd* (1975) 132 CLR 373 (HCA) 396 (Gibbs CJ) and 410 (Stephen J).

[77] See, eg *Montagu's ST* (n 69); *Akindele* (n 63).

[78] P Birks, 'Receipt' in P Birks and A Pretto (eds), *Breach of Trust* (Oxford, Hart Publishing, 2002).

[79] D Nicholls, 'Knowing Receipt: The Need for a New Landmark' in W Cornish, R Nolan, J O'Sullivan and G Virgo (eds), *Restitution: Past, Present and Future* (Oxford, Hart Publishing, 1998) 245.

[80] See, eg L Smith, 'Unjust Enrichment, Property and the Structure of Trusts' (2000) 116 *LQR* 412.

[81] C Mitchell and S Watterson, 'Remedies for Knowing Receipt' in C Mitchell (ed), *Constructive and Resulting Trusts* (Oxford, Hart Publishing, 2010).

[82] Ibid 138.

[83] See *re Rothko* 43 NY 2d 305; 372 NE 2d 291 (1977) (Court of Appeals of New York).

[84] It is not suggested that this second point necessarily flows from the analysis of Mitchell and Watterson (n 81), who rather seem to take the view that the knowing recipient is treated as though he were a trustee.

authority or any other defence,[85] a right that had been held on trust by A for B. On Lord Browne-Wilkinson's proposition, C can therefore only be liable to account, as a constructive trustee, if C had sufficient knowledge of those facts.

This link between the test for liability under the first limb of *Barnes v Addy* and the general question of when a constructive trust may be recognised can also be seen in two important English decisions: *re Montagu's Settlement Trusts*[86] and *BCCI v Akindele*.[87] In the former case, Megarry V-C, in a comment echoed by Lord Browne-Wilkinson's second proposition in *Westdeutsche*, stated that '[i]n determining whether a constructive trust has been created, the fundamental question is whether the conscience of the recipient is bound in such a way as to justify equity in imposing a trust on him.'[88] In the latter case, Nourse LJ held that, for liability in knowing receipt to arise, '[t]he recipient's state of knowledge must be such as to make it unconscionable for him to retain the benefit of the receipt.'[89] Of course, as noted by Nourse LJ, such a test, like any test based on knowledge, may be difficult to apply in practice; the important point for the present chapter, however, is that in developing and applying the knowledge-based test set out in a case such as *Wambo*, the courts should draw on decisions applying the first limb in *Barnes v Addy*. This is because the very same question arises in each set of cases: did the defendant, at the relevant time, hold a particular right with such knowledge of the facts alleged to affect his conscience that the defendant can be said to have held that right on trust for the claimant?

C. *Heperu Pty Ltd v Belle*[90]

In *Wambo*, White J drew an important analogy between the trust that arises in cases where the defendant retains a mistaken payment, knowing of the payor's mistake, and the trust that arises where the defendant holds a right that has been acquired through fraud and without consideration. This latter form of trust was considered in *Heperu*. As far as the positive formula set out in this chapter is concerned, the chief importance of the analysis of the Court of Appeal of New South Wales consists in its discussion of the trust that can arise where a fraud committed by A on B leads to the acquisition of a right by an innocent volunteer (C). The existence of such a trust can be seen to lie behind what the court in *Heperu* called the 'well-known principle',[91] recognised by *Black*, that:

> a person entirely innocent of a fraud who comes to know that he or she has received and still retains the proceeds of, or taken advantage of, a fraud to which he or she was not

[85] C will have a defence if, for example, C is a bona fide purchaser for value of the right formerly held on trust for B.

[86] *Montagu's* (n 69).

[87] *Akindele* (n 63).

[88] *Montagu's* (n 69) 277.

[89] *Akindele* (n 63) [69].

[90] *Heperu* (n 23).

[91] Ibid [92]. In *Black* itself, the formulation of the principle was attributed to Sir George Jessel MR: see *Black* (n 24) 106 (Griffith CJ).

a party, cannot knowingly seek to retain those proceeds or that advantage, without, in effect, becoming a party to that fraud and liable accordingly.[92]

This liability of the initially innocent volunteer may be explained as depending on the existence of a trust arising under the positive formula. This suggestion depends on a two-stage analysis, consisting first of the approach applied in *Wambo* and secondly of the approach advocated in *Farah*. Such a two-stage analysis can be used to explain the result in *Lipkin Gorman*, and thus tie up an end left loose in section IIC above. At the first stage of the facts in *Lipkin Gorman*, the same act (A's withdrawal of B's funds without B's authority) involved both A's acquisition of a right and B's loss of a right. Whilst A gained legal title to the money paid out by B's bank, the fact of B's lack of authority meant that there was a specific reason for which there was no legal basis for A, as against B, to have the benefit of that right. Further, A was of course aware of that fact. The three conditions of the positive formula were therefore met, and so A held the money received from B's account on trust for B. A then transferred some of the money held on trust to C, the casino. As gambling contracts were, at that time, void, C provided no consideration for the money received from A and was thus a volunteer. When C received the money, C was innocent, as C did not know, and had no reason to know of, the fraud practised by A on B. When, however, C later gained knowledge of that fraud, whilst still holding a right received from A, or any traceable proceeds of that right (that is, any right that could be identified as a product of the money initially received from A), C held that right on trust for B, and was so liable to account to B for its value. This liability can be seen as arising on the same basis as that arising under the first limb of *Barnes v Addy* and thus, as the High Court emphasised in *Farah*, as dependent on C's knowledge.

On this analysis, the casino's liability in *Lipkin Gorman* depended on its retention of traceable proceeds of the money paid to it by A with knowledge of the facts meaning that A held that money on trust for B. This view of *Lipkin Gorman*—which, of course, varies both from that explicitly adopted by the House of Lords, and from the analysis of Birks discussed in section IIC above—has already been set out and defended in detail.[93] It is admittedly unorthodox; but, significantly, in *Heperu*, the Court of Appeal of New South Wales seems to have adopted this reading of the case. Indeed, the Court of Appeal also analysed the decision in *Banque Belge pour l'Etranger v Hambrouck*[94] as resting on the same basis.[95] In that case, A fraudulently drew cheques on his employer's account with Banque Belge (B). As a result, B paid around £6000 to A's bank. A then wrote cheques, drawn on his account, in favour of his wife (C), who paid those cheques into her account

[92] *Heperu* (n 23) [92].

[93] See McFarlane (n 38) 293–98; L Smith, 'Simplifying Claims to Traceable Proceeds' (2009) 125 *LQR* 338; B McFarlane, 'Unjust Enrichment, Property Rights and Indirect Recipients' (2009) 17 *Restitution Law Review* 37.

[94] *Banque Belge pour l'Etranger v Hambrouck* [1921] 1 KB 321 (CA).

[95] *Heperu* (n 23) [137]–[144].

at a different bank. B, of course, was unable to debit the £6000 from the account held by A's employers. B therefore made claims against both C and C's bank. The cheques drawn on A's account were the only payments made into C's account, and C's bank paid the full value of that account into court. The Court of Appeal held that the money thus paid into court should be paid to B. That decision is consistent with the positive formula set out in this chapter, and with the two-stage analysis of *Lipkin Gorman* set out above.[96] It is significant that, in *Banque Belge*, Scrutton and Atkin LJJ each relied on the rules, set out in *re Hallett's Estate*,[97] that allow B to assert an *equitable* right in relation to traceable proceeds of a right initially held on trust for B. As the court noted in *Heperu*, *Banque Belge* can therefore be seen as an example of a common law court recognising and protecting a right under a trust, and permitting a beneficiary to enforce the trustee's duty to account by means of a common law claim for money had and received.[98] The non-express trust so enforced in *Banque Belge*, like the trust in *Lipkin Gorman*, can be seen as arising under the positive formula set out in this chapter. In this way, the decisions in *Banque Belge* and *Lipkin Gorman* can be used to support that positive formula and to cement the link, drawn by both Lord Browne-Wilkinson in *Westdeutsche* and White J in *Wambo*, between trusts arising in mistaken payment cases and trusts arising in cases of fraud.

As far as this chapter is concerned, therefore, the chief importance of *Heperu* lies in its analysis of *Banque Belge* and *Lipkin Gorman*. There are layers of irony here. First, whilst *Lipkin Gorman* has been lauded as the decision in which the House of Lords unequivocally recognised the role of unjust enrichment in explaining the action for money had and received, it may well be that the case itself did *not* in fact involve the defendant casino's being unjustly enriched at the claimant firm's expense. Secondly, and conversely, in *Heperu*, where this re-analysis of *Lipkin Gorman* was supported, it may well be that the case *did* in fact involve the defendant's being unjustly enriched at the claimant's expense, so that the two-stage trust analysis required in *Lipkin Gorman* was in fact unnecessary. On this view, the court in *Heperu* pointed out, correctly, that *Lipkin* was a two-stage trust case mistakenly analysed as a direct unjust enrichment case; but the court in *Heperu* also committed the converse mistake, by mistakenly analysing a direct unjust enrichment case as a two-stage trust case.

In *Heperu*, funds were provided by Landa and companies controlled by him (B) to Mr Cincotta (A), for investment by A on behalf of B. Over $2.7 million was provided, in six cheques, and it was intended by B that the funds would be paid into an account, to be managed for B's benefit, with Perpetual Trustees Ltd. In breach of his duties to B, A paid those cheques into an account held with Perpetual Trustees Ltd

96 For a full discussion of *Banque Belge*, see McFarlane, 'Unjust Enrichment' (n 93).

97 *re Hallett's Estate* (1880) LR 13 Ch D 696 (CA).

98 *Heperu* (n 23) [143]. The court referred to Smith, 'Simplifying Claims to Traceable Proceeds' (n 93) where it is demonstrated that a common law action for money had and received may be used to enforce a trustee's duty to account. See also *Roxborough v Rothmans of Pall Mall Australia Ltd* [2001] HCA 68, (2001) 208 CLR 516 [67] (Gummow J).

in the name of his then wife (C).[99] Funds were then withdrawn from that account and transferred into an account, also in C's name, at Westpac. The proceeds of that Westpac account were used by A for the benefit of himself and his family—some withdrawals were used to pay off credit card debts of C, as well as to meet principal and interest payments on mortgage debts secured on land co-owned by A and C. C had no knowledge of A's dealings with B; and whilst C had given A authority to operate the Westpac account, it was held that she had given him no such authority in relation to the Perpetual account.[100] C also had no knowledge of the payments made into her Perpetual account, or of the use which A made of that account. When the fraud was discovered, $1m was paid to B from the Westpac account. B sought to recover the remaining sum, of over $1.7 million, from C.[101]

It is true that, in *Heperu*—as in *Black*, *Banque Belge* and *Lipkin Gorman*—the defendant was an innocent volunteer who had not directly defrauded the claimant. There is a crucial difference, however, between *Heperu* and each of those cases: in the three earlier cases, the payment received by the defendant did not come directly from the claimant. In *Heperu*, in contrast, there was no point in time at which Mr Cincotta (A) acquired any right to the misappropriated funds—he simply paid B's cheques directly into C's account. As a result, the same act (acceptance of the cheques) caused both C's acquisition of a right and B's loss of a right: there was no intermediary standing between C's gain and B's loss. *Heperu* can thus be seen as a direct case, in which B can make the same strict liability restitutionary claim against C that can be made in a case such as *Wambo* against A, the direct recipient of B's mistaken payment. In *Wambo*, of course, owing to A's insolvency, B needed to rely on a trust in order to bring a claim against C, who was an indirect recipient of the mistaken payment. In *Heperu*, however, there were no such insolvency problems, and a simple claim for money had and received against C, as the direct recipient of B's payment, should have been *prima facie* available. On this view, there was no need for the court in *Heperu* to have embarked on an analysis of *Black*, *Banque Belge* or *Lipkin Gorman*.

The Court of Appeal of New South Wales held, however, that the simple money had and received claim was not available to B, as, where such a claim depends on C's acquisition of a right, it cannot arise before C knows that he has acquired that right.[102] Yet, whilst the question cannot be fully explored here, it is hard to see why such knowledge should be required[103]—the gist of B's claim is C's acquisition of a right, and if that right can be acquired without C's knowledge, there is no reason

[99] By the time of the litigation, Mrs Cincotta, having separated from her former husband, was known as Ms Belle.

[100] *Heperu* (n 23) [53]–[55].

[101] In a separate action, B also claimed that Perpetual Trustees Ltd was liable to B in conversion, and/or money had and received. The Court of Appeal of New South Wales dismissed those claims: *Perpetual Trustees Australia Ltd v Heperu Pty Ltd* [2009] NSWCA 84. An appeal was heard before the High Court of Australia but the case was settled before judgment was given.

[102] *Heperu* (n 23) [74].

[103] For a contrary view, in defence of the requirement, see J Edelman and E Bant, *Unjust Enrichment in Australia* (Oxford, Oxford University Press, 2006) 104.

why B's claim should depend on such knowledge. Certainly, if one sees B's claim as depending on C's unjust enrichment at B's expense, C's enrichment is established by his acquisition of a right, irrespective of his knowledge of that enrichment. The submission that C can be under a strict restitutionary duty as a result of acquiring a right of which he is unaware may seem unduly harsh on C; but it is of course tempered by the availability of defences. For example, in finding that a simple money had and received claim depends on C's knowledge of his acquisition of a right, the court in *Heperu* relied on *National Commercial Banking Corporation of Australia Ltd v Batty.*[104] In that case, A misappropriated cheques and paid them into a partnership account with B, the claimant bank. C, a fellow partner, was unaware of the payment in of the cheques. A withdrew the proceeds and applied them to his own use before C knew of the payment, or of A's wrongdoing. It was held that, even if it could be assumed that the sum credited to the partnership account represented the money of the bank, B had no claim against C: as C did not know of the payment into the partnership account, there was no point at which B could have brought a money had and received claim against C. Gibbs CJ stated that:

> Where, because of the action of a servant or agent acting outside the scope of his authority, or for that matter because of the action of a complete stranger, money has been paid into the account of the defendant, who has technically received it, although he is quite unaware of that fact, and the money is then misappropriated, still without the knowledge or intervention of the defendant, there seems to be no reason in justice or equity why the defendant should be answerable for the money simply because theoretically he had the means of knowing that the money was in the account. In principle, in those circumstances, the defendant ought not to be liable unless, before the money was misappropriated, he knew or ought to have known that he had possession or control of it.[105]

It is possible to support Gibbs CJ's statement, however, whilst still arguing that, when the payment into the account was made by A, C *did* come under a *prima facie* restitutionary duty to B: the same act (B's crediting of the account) had caused both B's loss of a right and C's acquisition of a right; and A's fraud meant that there was no basis for C, as against B, to have the benefit of the right acquired. A's subsequent disposal of the proceeds of the cheques, however, removed C's initial restitutionary duty: it gave C a defence by ensuring that C retained no benefit from his initial acquisition of the right. Of course, things would have been different if the elimination of C's benefit was due to C's own action *after* C had learned of his acquisition of the right, and A's fraud: C's knowledge is thus relevant not to the question of whether C is under an initial restituonary duty to B, but rather to the different question of whether that duty may be reduced, or eliminated, by a subsequent event reducing or eliminating the benefit gained by C.

On the view taken in this chapter, then, the facts of *Heperu* should be analysed in the following way. When A misappropriated B's cheques and paid them into C's account, C came under an immediate restitutionary duty to B. When A then spent

104 *National Commercial Banking Corporation of Australia Ltd v Batty* (1986) 160 CLR 251 (HCA).
105 Ibid [19].

the proceeds of those cheques, before C knew of the misappropriation, C's liability to B was reduced to the extent of any benefit retained by C at the point when C knew, or ought to have known, that she had acquired a right from B as a result of A's fraud. On the facts of *Heperu*, such benefit was limited to the $1m retained in the Westpac account (and later paid to B) and any necessary expenditure of C that was met by A's use of the proceeds of the cheques, such as the payment of C's credit card and mortgage debts. This analysis of *Heperu*, whilst differing from that of the court, is in fact consistent with the result in the case.[106] The court found that C's liability to B was limited to any benefits retained by C (as a result of the initial payment of the cheques into C's account) at 'the relevant time':[107] the time when C first knew, or ought to have known, of those payments, and the fact that they were fraudulently made: as a result, the court ordered that an inquiry be made into the extent of those benefits.

In *Heperu*, however, the court did not reach this conclusion through the relatively direct route advocated here. It seems that the court ordered the inquiry not with the purpose of identifying any *benefits* (ie value) attributable to the payment of the cheques into C's account and retained by C at the relevant time, but rather in order to locate any *property* (ie rights) attributable to that payment and retained by C at the relevant time. This was because, it seems, the court wished to identify rights held by C on trust for B. As we have seen, finding a trust of rights held by C was necessary in *Black*, *Banque Belge* and *Lipkin Gorman* as, in each of those cases, C was not a direct recipient from B, and so no simple money had and received claim was available. In *Heperu*, in contrast, C *was* a direct recipient from B, and so the question is not whether any *rights* retained by C can be identified as trust property; it is rather whether C's retention of any *value* prevents C from having a full defence to B's *prima facie* claim for money had and received. This mistaken focus on the retention of rights seems to have led to an odd concession by B's counsel in *Heperu* that C could not be liable for the value of any money taken from the Westpac account and used by A to pay C's credit card debts.[108] The payment of such debts did not lead to C's acquisition or retention of any right that could then be held by C on trust for B; but it did mean that C retained value, through the saving of a necessary expenditure, and so should have been relevant when determining C's liability to B.

This leads us to the final lesson to be taken from *Heperu*: in cases where C acquires a right as a result of a fraud practised by A on B, it is crucial to differentiate two claims B may have against C. The first claim is available only if C has acquired the right *directly* from B, and it is based on the same principle as that applying in a simple mistaken payment case. The same act has caused both B's loss of a right (or gain of a duty) and C's gain of a right; and there is a specific

[106] Once the concession made by B's counsel, discussed in the text below at n 108, is taken into account.

[107] *Heperu* (n 23) [42].

[108] Ibid [160].

reason (A's fraud) why C should not, as against B, have the benefit accruing from that gain of a right. As a result, C, as soon as he acquires his right, is under a restitutionary duty to pay the value of that right to B; that duty may arise even if C has no knowledge that he holds the right, nor of A's fraud. Defences are, however, available to C. In particular, if subsequent events reduce or eliminate the benefit retained by C as a result of the acquisition of the right then, if those events occur before C gains knowledge both of his holding of his right and of A's fraud, they will correspondingly reduce C's duty to B. It is suggested that the availability of such a claim is the simplest means to explain B's (limited) success in *Heperu*.

The first claim is not available if B's loss of a right (or gain of a duty) is only *indirectly* related to C's gain of a right. This will be the case if, as in *Black*, *Banque Belge*, or *Lipkin Gorman*, A's fraud leads first to A's acquisition of a right, and then to A's transfer of a right to C. In such case, B must rely on the second, different claim: that C held the right received from A (or a right counting as its traceable product) on a non-express trust for B, and so must account to B for that right. As the court usefully pointed out in *Heperu*, such a claim may be enforced by a common law action for money had and received.[109] It nonetheless depends on the establishment of a non-express trust; and the positive formula set out in this chapter provides one of the bases on which such a trust may arise. Under this positive formula, B's claim depends on showing that C held a right *with knowledge* of both his holding of the right and of A's fraud. It has been suggested here that the availability of this claim explains B's success in *Black*, *Banque Belge* and *Lipkin Gorman*.

One danger of confusing the two claims is that the first claim, like the second, will be seen as arising only if C has knowledge of A's fraud. This requirement could then be extended to mistaken payment cases, so that, for example, a claim in money had and received for the return of a mistaken payment would be said to depend on the recipient's knowledge of the payor's mistake. It would be unfortunate if such a development was to be furthered through drawing a mistaken analogy between two quite different claims. Certainly, Lord Browne-Wilkinson's second proposition, making the recognition of a trust depend on the trustee's knowledge, has no relevance to the separate question of whether knowledge is required for a claim for money had and received against the recipient of a mistaken payment.

IV. Conclusion

Building on Lord Browne-Wilkinson's analysis in *Westdeutsche*, this chapter has proposed a positive formula identifying one ground on which a non-express trust may arise. The formula states that a non-express trust will arise if three conditions are met. First, the same act or transaction must have involved both B's loss of a right (or acquisition of a duty) and A's acquisition of a right. Second, there

[109] Ibid [144], [153]

must be a specific reason (such as B's mistake, or A's fraud on B) for which there is no legal basis for A, as against B, to have the benefit of the right acquired by A. Third, A must know both that he has acquired the right, and of the facts constituting the reason why there is no legal basis for A, as against B, to have the benefit of the right. A must have that knowledge whilst holding either the right initially acquired, or a right that counts as a traceable product of that initial right.

It has been argued that, where the first two parts of the formula are satisfied, B will have a direct, restitutionary claim against A. If A is insolvent, however, or if B wishes to bring a claim against a third party (C), then B will need to show the right acquired by A was held by A on trust for B. One means for B to do this is to show that the third part of the formula has been satisfied. In *Wambo*, A acquired a right as a result of B's mistaken payment, and C then acquired a right that depended on the right so acquired by A. Initially, C knew nothing of B's mistake; but, when C gained knowledge of the mistake, he then held the right acquired from A, or any traceable product of it, on trust for B. C was then liable to account to B for the right so held. In *Farah*, the High Court rejected the view, adopted by the Court of Appeal of New South Wales, that, where A holds a right on trust for B, and transfers that right without authority to C, an innocent volunteer, C will immediately hold that right on trust for B. That analysis is consistent with the formula proposed here: if B wants to show that C is liable to account as a constructive trustee for the right acquired from A, B must show that C held that right or its traceable product with knowledge of the prior trust in B's favour. In *Heperu*, the Court of Appeal of New South Wales considered cases (such as *Black*, *Banque Belge* and *Lipkin Gorman*) where A acquired a right from B as a result of fraud, and then transferred that right or its traceable product to C, an innocent volunteer. The court's analysis of such cases is again consistent with the formula proposed here: C will be liable to account to B if B can show that C held the right received from A, or its traceable product, with knowledge of A's fraud.

It has thus been shown that the positive formula proposed here is consistent with, and supported by, the analysis of each of White J, sitting in the New South Wales Supreme Court in *Wambo*, of the High Court of Australia in *Farah*, and of the Court of Appeal of New South Wales in *Heperu*. If it is accepted that the formula can operate to determine the operation of such constructive trusts, a number of further questions arise. First, as noted in section IIC above, can the formula also be used to explain the operation of resulting trusts? Second, can the formula also apply in cases where the transaction involving B's loss of a right (or gain of a duty) and A's gain of a right also involves the passing of consideration from A to B? In particular, might the third part of the formula, with its focus on A's knowledge, assist in explaining the role of rescission in cases where the initial transaction between the parties involves a voidable contract? These broader questions are, no doubt, difficult ones; but it is equally certain that their resolution will benefit from a comparative analysis, drawing on developments not only in England and Australia, but across all equitable jurisdictions.

9

The Limits of Equity in Disputes over Family Assets

MATTHEW HARDING*

I. Introduction

In the common law world, couples who break up and seek a judicial allocation of property in their family assets will have their disputes determined either according to the statutory rules of family law or according to the judge-made doctrines of equity. In Australia, New Zealand and the Canadian provinces of Manitoba and Saskatchewan, comprehensive statutory regimes govern many such disputes, and it now seems fair to say that there is no longer a significant role for equity to play in the allocation of property in family assets in those jurisdictions.[1] By contrast, in other parts of Canada, and in England and Wales, statutory regimes govern only disputes between married couples, couples in civil partnerships (in England and Wales), and couples in registered relationships (in Nova Scotia).[2] In those parts of Canada and England and Wales equity continues to be applied, in determining the allocation of property in family assets, to a wide range of cases. Given that both statutory regimes and the doctrines of equity apply to family assets cases across the common law world, it is important to appreciate and understand any differences of approach to the question of allocation in the two bodies of law. Contributing to this understanding is my broad aim in this chapter.

* My thanks to Michael Bryan and Andrew Robertson for helpful discussions on the arguments in this chapter, and to Fiona Burns and Ben McFarlane for detailed comments.

[1] Australia: Family Law Act 1975 (Cth), ss 75, 78, 79 (extended to unmarried couples by the Family Law Amendment (De Facto Financial Matters and Other Measures) Act 2008 (Cth)) and Family Court Act 1997 (WA), ss 205ZD(3), 205ZG(4); New Zealand: Property (Relationships) Act 1976 (NZ), ss 8, 11, 13, 15, 18; Manitoba: Family Property Act CCSM c F25, ss 13, 14, 15; Saskatchewan: Family Property Act SS 1997 c F–6.3, ss 20, 21.

[2] Alberta: Matrimonial Property Act RSA 2000 c M–8, ss 7, 8, 19, 20; British Columbia: Family Relations Act RSBC 1996 c 128, ss 56, 59, 65; Nova Scotia: Matrimonial Property Act RSNS 1989 c 275, ss 12, 13 (extended to couples in registered relationships by the Vital Statistics Act RSNS 1989 c 494, Part II); Ontario: Family Law Act RSO 1990 c F3, ss 5, 19, 21, 23, 24; England and Wales: Matrimonial Causes Act 1973 c 18, ss 23, 24, 24A, 24B, 25 and Civil Partnership Act 2004 c 33, ss 65, 66. Note that same-sex couples can marry in Canada under the Civil Marriage Act SC 2005 c 33.

I focus on just one difference between statutory and equitable approaches to the allocation of property in family assets. Under statutory regimes, courts that must allocate property in family assets are typically empowered and sometimes required to take into account the likely future financial positions of the parties to the dispute when deciding on an allocation.[3] This means that, in at least some cases that are dealt with under these statutory regimes, some or all of an allocation of property in family assets will be made with an eye to how the parties are likely to be situated in the future, as opposed to how they have acted in the past. By contrast, courts applying equity to disputes over family assets do not usually take into account future needs when determining questions of allocation.[4] Notwithstanding the notoriously convoluted and multi-dimensional nature of equitable jurisprudence on property in family assets, the attention of courts applying equity is mostly fixed on past events rather than future needs when called upon to allocate.[5]

My specific aim is to consider how this difference in approach as between statute and equity might be justified. To that end, I examine a proposition that I take to be widely accepted: the proposition that, whatever the position under statute, in equity courts are constrained doctrinally not to have regard to future needs in the allocation of property in family assets. A person who was minded to assert this proposition would require an account of doctrinal constraints in equity explaining why regard to future needs is ruled out when the question of property allocation arises in a family assets case. I consider two such accounts: one that confines equity to norms of corrective justice; and one that confines equity to a limited set of applicable norms, including norms of corrective justice, none of which refer to future needs as grounds for allocation of property in family assets. I argue that there are large obstacles to accepting either the corrective justice account or the limited set account in respect of family assets cases in equity. It follows that there are reasons not to accept the proposition about doctrinal constraints in equity, at least to the extent that the proposition depends on either the corrective justice account or the limited set account. However, I conclude that, even if the proposition about doctrinal constraints in equity is rejected, there remain reasons to think that a court

[3] Family Law Act 1975 (Cth), ss 75, 79; Family Court Act 1997 (WA), ss 205ZD(3), 205ZG(4); Matrimonial Property Act RSA 2000 c M–8, ss 8, 20, Family Relations Act RSBC 1996 c 128, s 65; Family Law Act RSO 1990 c F3, s 24; Family Property Act CCSM c F25, s 14; Family Property Act SS 1997 c F–6.3, ss 20, 21; Matrimonial Causes Act 1973 c 18, s 25.

[4] In this paper, I will use the phrase 'future needs' as shorthand for 'likely future financial positions of the parties'.

[5] I say 'mostly' because equity does seem prepared take an interest in future needs in the setting of the doctrine of proprietary estoppel: see *Sledmore v Dalby* (1996) 72 P & CR 196 (CA). For the view that, because of doctrinal constraints in equity, future needs should not have been taken into account in *Sledmore v Dalby*, see: S Gardner, 'The Remedial Discretion in Proprietary Estoppel' (1999) 115 *LQR* 438, 460; S Bright and B McFarlane, 'Proprietary Estoppel and Property Rights' (2005) 64 *CLJ* 449; 476; B McFarlane, *The Structure of Property Law* (Oxford, Hart Publishing, 2008) 459–60; A Robertson, 'Unconscionability and Proprietary Estoppel Remedies' in E Bant and M Harding (eds), *Exploring Private Law* (Cambridge, Cambridge University Press, 2010) 402, 421–26. For a different view see E Cooke, *The Modern Law of Estoppel* (Oxford, Oxford University Press, 2000) 116–17.

applying equity should refrain from having regard to future needs in allocating property in family assets cases.

II. Doctrinal Constraints (1)—The Corrective Justice Account

Norms of corrective justice are norms that require the reversal of transactions pursuant to which benefits have passed from one party to another.[6] The reversal of a transaction that is demanded by a norm of corrective justice entails taking a benefit from a party who received that benefit under an impugned transaction, and giving it back to a party who lost it in the same transaction. Thus, as John Gardner has said, 'allocation back' is the distinctive form of norms of corrective justice.[7] Understood as norms that take the form of 'allocation back', norms of corrective justice are necessarily past-regarding: they operate only in circumstances where a transaction that has occurred in the past now requires reversal by an allocation back, and they specify, as grounds for that reversal by an allocation back, events that took place in the past in light of which the transaction may be impugned. In contrast to norms of corrective justice, norms of distributive justice require an allocation *tout court*, based on criteria other than the fact that a benefit has passed from one party to another under an impugned transaction.[8] Unlike norms of corrective justice, norms of distributive justice are not necessarily past-regarding and may specify, as grounds for allocation, future events or states of affairs. If equity is confined to norms of corrective justice in family assets cases, courts applying equity should not look to future needs when allocating property in family assets cases. If equity is not confined to norms of corrective justice, it may still be that equity should not look to future needs in family assets cases, but as norms of distributive justice can be future-regarding, further argument is needed to demonstrate this.

There are at least three obstacles to accepting the proposition that equity is confined to norms of corrective justice in family assets cases. One refers to the law as it is, and the other two are grounded in normative argument. The first obstacle is that the case law suggests that courts applying equity do not confine themselves to norms of corrective justice when allocating property in family assets. The second obstacle is that there is no reason to think that, just because there are two parties in a typical family assets case, only norms of corrective justice should apply. And the third obstacle is that, contrary to what is asserted by corrective justice theorists,

[6] This may include non-material benefits: see, eg E Weinrib, *The Idea of Private Law* (Cambridge MA, Harvard University Press, 1995) ch 5.

[7] J Gardner, 'What is Tort Law For? Part 1: The Place of Corrective Justice' (2011) 30 *Law and Philosophy* 1, 9–10. See also Weinrib, *The Idea of Private Law* (n 6) 62.

[8] On the distinction between the forms of corrective and distributive justice, see Gardner, 'What is Tort Law For?' (n 7) 11–13; Weinrib (n 6) 61–63.

a court may respond to Kantian right by applying both corrective and distributive norms in the resolution of private law disputes.

A. Courts Do Not Confine Themselves to Norms of Corrective Justice

It has been said that equity will intervene in disputes over family assets in circumstances where it would be unconscionable or inequitable for one party to assert or retain property in those assets, thereby denying that property to the other.[9] To say that equity intervenes in the family assets cases because one party denies property to the other is to imply that equity intervenes to effect a giving back of property that is withheld by one party from the other in circumstances where such a withholding is not justified, and this in turn suggests that the norms operative in such cases are norms of corrective justice. But talk of a defendant denying property to a claimant, while usefully deployed as a way of gesturing to the broad contours of equity's concerns in the family assets cases, tends to obscure an important distinction between types of norm that potentially operate in such cases. This is the distinction between norms that allocate property in family assets to the claimant on the one hand, and norms that require a defendant to act in light of such an allocation on the other hand: in shorthand, the distinction between property-allocating norms and action-requiring norms.[10] A reference to inequitable denial of property points to the demands of action-requiring norms, but tends to neglect property-allocating norms.

I leave open the question of how we should understand the action-requiring norms that are applied in equity in family assets cases. It may be that these action-requiring norms are invariably norms of corrective justice, requiring an allocation back to the claimant of what is unjustifiably withheld from her by the defendant. However, it may also be that the action-requiring norms applied in family assets cases are derivative norms, requiring the defendant to act so as to realise the demands of whatever property-allocating norms apply to the case, and if this is so, then the form of action-requiring norms might be corrective or distributive, depending on the form of the applicable property-allocating norms.[11] For present purposes, the important point to note is that property-

[9] See, eg *Gissing v Gissing* [1971] AC 886 (HL) 905 (Lord Diplock); *Muschinski v Dodds* (1986) 160 CLR 583 (HCA) 620 (Deane J).

[10] The distinction between property-allocating norms and action-requiring norms is reflected in the nature of the remedies that equity awards in family assets cases: there will typically be a declaration of trust, allocating property in an asset, followed by orders requiring the defendant to make a transfer of title or sell the asset and pay some or all of the proceeds to the claimant. Occasionally the court will declare the trust but refrain from making orders in the expectation that the defendant will act voluntarily in accordance with applicable action-requiring norms. For an example of a case where the court applied a property-allocating norm but refrained from applying an action-requiring norm: *Baumgartner v Baumgartner* (1987) 164 CLR 137 (HCA).

[11] See L Smith, 'Restitution: The Heart of Corrective Justice' (2001) 79 *Texas Law Review* 2115, especially 2126–28.

allocating norms and action-requiring norms are distinct, so that in determining whether equity operates only according to norms of corrective justice in family assets cases, attention must be paid not only to the action-requiring norms that underpin assertions about inequitable denial of the claimant's property, but also to the property-allocating norms that deliver property to the claimant in the first place. Those property-allocating norms are my focus in this chapter.

The case law reveals that, in family assets cases, courts applying equity have allocated property according to norms the form and content of which is largely unclear. That said, it does appear clear that the range of property-allocating norms applied in equity in family assets cases is not limited to norms of corrective justice. In Canada, courts have explicitly invoked the concept of unjust enrichment when making decisions about allocation.[12] Because a norm requiring the restitution of unjust enrichment always takes the form of 'allocation back' and is always accordingly a norm of corrective justice,[13] it might be thought that such cases reveal the application of corrective norms. However, it has been pointed out that in the Canadian cases, courts appear to have invoked the concept of unjust enrichment in order to give effect to distributive norms the content of which is uncertain.[14] To the extent that these criticisms of the Canadian cases are sound, it may not be said that in Canada equity operates solely according to corrective norms in family assets cases.

In England, courts have decided family assets cases in equity on the basis of the common intention of the parties. This suggests the application of distributive property-allocating norms. Recall that a norm of distributive justice demands an allocation based on a criterion other than the fact that a benefit has passed under an impugned transaction. In the common intention cases, the common intention of the parties, once established as a matter of fact directly, by inference or even by imputation, is treated as the criterion for allocation as between the parties concerned, both in the sense of supplying a ground for allocation and in the sense of quantifying proportions to be allocated to the parties.[15] There is no reference, in such cases, to an impugned transaction in light of which an allocation back to the claimant must be effected. Taken at face value, they are cases of distributive,

[12] *Pettkus v Becker* [1980] 2 SCR 834 (SCC); *Sorochan v Sorochan* [1986] 2 SCR 38 (SCC); *Rawluk v Rawluk* [1990] 1 SCR 70 (SCC); *Peter v Beblow* [1993] 1 SCR 980 (SCC).

[13] For Weinrib's account of the content of corrective justice in cases of unjust enrichment, see E Weinrib, 'The Normative Structure of Unjust Enrichment' in C Rickett and R Grantham (eds), *Structure and Justification in Private Law* (Oxford, Hart Publishing, 2008) 21; E Weinrib, 'Correctively Unjust Enrichment' in R Chambers, C Mitchell and J Penner (eds), *Philosophical Foundations of the Law of Unjust Enrichment* (Oxford, Oxford University Press, 2009) 31.

[14] See, eg the criticisms of the Canadian case law in J Mee, *The Property Rights of Cohabitees* (Oxford, Hart Publishing, 1999) ch 7, and note McLachlin J's discussion of public policy considerations in *Peter* (n 12) 992–95.

[15] *Pettitt v Pettitt* [1970] AC 777 (HL); *Gissing* (n 9); *Grant v Edwards* [1986] Ch 638 (CA); *Lloyd's Bank Plc v Rosset* [1991] 1 AC 107 (HL); *Midland Bank plc v Cooke* [1995] 2 All ER 562 (CA); *Stack v Dowden* [2007] UKHL 17, [2007] 2 AC 432.

not corrective, justice.[16] Moreover, English courts have been criticised for their propensity to impute a common intention to the parties in family assets cases, and this criticism suggests that those cases have really been decided by the application of unarticulated distributive norms specifying grounds for allocation other than common intention.[17]

In Australia and New Zealand, the character of property-allocating norms applied by courts in family assets cases is no clearer. In *Baumgartner v Baumgartner*, the High Court of Australia allocated property in a family home based on the fact that each of the parties to the dispute had contributed money to a pooled fund from which household expenses were met.[18] The reasoning of the majority of the court, Mason CJ, Wilson and Deane JJ, was obscure as to the nature of the property-allocating norm being applied;[19] some have described the case as one in which the restitution of unjust enrichment was effected,[20] suggesting the application of a corrective norm, but it is also possible to interpret the case as one in which a distributive norm was applied, the criterion for distribution most likely being some sort of indirect labour-based desert.[21] And in *Lankow v Rose*,[22] Tipping J

[16] English courts have traditionally given effect to the parties' common intention only in cases where it can be demonstrated on the evidence that the claimant has, in reliance on that intention, acted to her detriment: see *Gissing* (n 9) 905 (Lord Diplock); *Grant* (n 15) 646–48 (Nourse LJ); *Rosset* (n 15) 132–33 (Lord Bridge). It might be thought that detrimental reliance is a complicating factor in the common intention cases, making it difficult to assert that the criterion for allocation in such cases is either common intention or an unarticulated ground for distribution, rather than an impugned transaction of some sort that is evidenced by the detrimental reliance in question. However, detrimental reliance may be viewed as a fact that must be proven so that 'common intention' can qualify as a criterion for allocation, given the formality requirements that otherwise prevent a trust of land being created intentionally in the absence of writing. And recent common intention cases indicate that English courts may not in the future insist on proof of detrimental reliance: see S Gardner, 'Family Property Today' (2008) 124 *LQR* 422, 434–35, 443–44, referring to *Stack* (n 15) and *Abbott v Abbott* [2007] UKPC 53.

[17] On the imputation of common intention, see: J Mee, 'Joint Ownership, Subjective Intention and the Common Intention Constructive Trust' (2007) 71 *Conveyancer and Property Lawyer* 14; W Swadling, 'The Common Intention Constructive Trust in the House of Lords: An Opportunity Missed' (2007) 123 *LQR* 511; N Piska, 'Intention, Fairness and the Presumption of Resulting Trust after *Stack v Dowden*' (2008) 71 *MLR* 114; N Piska, 'Constructive Trusts and Constructing Intention' in M Dixon (ed), *Modern Studies in Property Law: Volume V* (Oxford, Hart Publishing, 2009) 203; S Gardner and KM Davidson, 'The Future of *Stack v Dowden*' (2011) 127 *LQR* 13.

[18] *Baumgartner* (n 10) 148–49 (Mason CJ, Wilson and Deane JJ).

[19] By contrast, in *Muschinski* (n 9), Deane J (whose judgment influenced the High Court in *Baumgartner v Baumgartner*) appears clearly to have applied a corrective norm. Bearing in mind that corrective norms effect 'allocation back' in view of an impugned transaction, how else is the following passage of Deane J's judgment (at 620) to be understood? '[T]he principle operates in a case where the substratum of a joint relationship or endeavour is removed without attributable blame and where the benefit of money or other property contributed by one party on the basis and for the purposes of the relationship or endeavour would otherwise be enjoyed by the other party in circumstances in which it was not specifically intended or specially provided that that other party should so enjoy it.'

[20] Toohey J stated in his separate judgment that the decision of the majority was 'consonant with an approach based on unconscionable conduct or one based on unjust enrichment': *Baumgartner* (n 10) 154. See also K Mason, J Carter and G Tolhurst, *Mason and Carter's Restitution Law in Australia*, 2nd edn (Sydney, LexisNexis, 2008) [135], [170].

[21] I discuss labour-based desert in another equitable setting in M Harding, 'Justifying Fiduciary Allowances' in A Robertson and H Tang (eds), *The Goals of Private Law* (Oxford, Hart Publishing, 2009) 341.

[22] *Lankow v Rose* [1995] 1 NZLR 277 (NZCA).

of the New Zealand Court of Appeal stated that, in order for an allocation of property to be made in the claimant's favour in a family assets case, it would be sufficient for the claimant to prove: (a) direct or indirect contributions to the assets; (b) that she had an expectation of property in the assets; (c) that her expectation was reasonable; and (d) that the defendant 'should reasonably expect to yield the claimant an interest'.[23] This approach to the question of allocation may imply a corrective norm, requiring the restitution of an enrichment yielded by the claimant's contributions. But it may also imply a distributive norm that operates even where there has been no transaction between the parties, specifying as the criterion for allocation the fact that, in the circumstances of the case, the claimant reasonably expected to gain property in the assets. It is not obvious from Tipping J's judgment which of these two norms is the weightier or how they operate together.[24]

I hope to have done enough to show that one obstacle to accepting the proposition that equity is confined to norms of corrective justice in family assets cases is that it is difficult to reconcile that proposition with the practice of courts. However, this obstacle is not insurmountable, because it is possible to insist that, whether or not the outcomes of family assets cases are defensible, equity should not apply distributive property-allocating norms in those cases and should instead confine itself to norms of corrective justice. To tackle the corrective justice proposition in this prescriptive sense, it is necessary to engage with the normative foundations of corrective justice itself.

B. Two Party Cases Are Not Always Cases of Corrective Justice

One obstacle to accepting the corrective justice proposition in a prescriptive sense is that there is no reason to assume that, simply because family assets cases raise private law disputes between two citizens about their rights and obligations inter se, those cases can be resolved rationally only by the application of norms of corrective justice. In his groundbreaking work on corrective justice in private law, Ernest Weinrib argues that 'private law is a justificatory enterprise that articulates normative connections between controversies and their resolutions'.[25] Given that private law entails bipolar disputes, between a particular claimant and a particular defendant, Weinrib argues that private law, if it is to realise its purpose as a justificatory enterprise, must specify as grounds for the determination of disputes norms that explain why *this* defendant is liable to *this* claimant. In other words,

[23] Ibid 294.

[24] This ambiguity in the New Zealand jurisprudence is even more pronounced in the leading judgment of Cooke P of the New Zealand Court of Appeal in an earlier case, *Gillies v Keogh*, where a notion of 'reasonable expectation' appears to have been invoked as a placeholder for a variety of corrective and distributive norms referring to unjust enrichment, 'contributions to assets', common intention, and elements of the doctrine of proprietary estoppel: *Gillies v Keogh* [1989] 2 NZLR 327 (NZCA) 330–35 (Cooke P).

[25] Weinrib (n 6) 12.

Weinrib argues that the reasons for the decisions of courts in private law cases must reflect the bipolarity of parties' relationships. For Weinrib, '[c]orrective justice is the pattern of justificatory coherence latent in the bipolar private law relationship of plaintiff to defendant';[26] this is because corrective justice presupposes just two parties, the party from whom a benefit has passed under an impugned transaction and the party to whom that benefit has passed under the same transaction. So Weinrib concludes that private law may operate as a justificatory enterprise, in light of the bipolarity of private law disputes, only to the extent that it is constituted by norms of corrective justice.

The statutory regimes of family law regulate disputes between two citizens about their rights and obligations inter se. If Weinrib is right, courts applying the rules of those statutory regimes to disputes over family assets are engaged in something other—or more—than the justificatory enterprise that is private law, notwithstanding the bipolar nature of the disputes, because the statutory rules operate according to both corrective and distributive norms. But can it really be said that a court allocating property in family assets under statute cannot articulate any normative connection between the parties' dispute and its resolution except by applying a norm of corrective justice specifying an impugned transaction as the ground for allocation? Surely applying a distributive property-allocating norm might articulate such a normative connection just as much as applying a corrective property-allocating norm does.[27]

The key is in apprehending that norms of distributive justice, while they often and perhaps typically apply in circumstances where more than two parties are in view, can apply to two party cases.[28] A property-allocating norm of distributive justice identifies potential candidates for allocation and specifies a criterion as the ground for allocation. In some circumstances, the criterion for allocation specified in a distributive norm may demand consideration of the positions of many persons. However, in other circumstances, the criterion for allocation specified in a distributive norm may demand consideration of the positions of only two persons. Take the family assets cases in equity in which courts allocate property based on a norm specifying common intention as the criterion for allocation.[29] In such cases, it is only parties whose common intention is proven who are considered as candidates for allocation, and the parties whose common intention is proven are the claimant and the defendant. The court is able to supply a reasoned justification for allocating a proportion to *this* claimant and another proportion to *this* defendant,

[26] Ibid 19.

[27] It is uncontroversial to assert that distributive property-allocating norms can supply a normative connection between human action and the acquisition of property. The question for present purposes is whether such a normative connection can be supplied that is consistent with the bipolar character of a private law dispute.

[28] See Gardner (n 7) 12–13.

[29] For the purposes of analysis, I am thinking here of cases where common intention is established directly or inferred, and not of cases where common intention is imputed to the parties.

in accordance with the criterion of their common intention. The bipolarity of the parties' relationship is thereby reflected, notwithstanding that a distributive norm is applied.[30]

Weinrib himself acknowledges that '[n]either corrective nor distributive justice lays exclusive claim to a certain slice of the empirical world',[31] and he accepts the possibility of a distributive norm applying in a two party case in private law.[32] His argument is that in a two party case in private law, distributive norms have only a 'contingent' relationship, whereas corrective norms have an 'essential' relationship, with the case.[33] It is unclear what Weinrib might mean by this distinction between contingent and essential norms: in a case where a distributive norm applies to only two parties, that norm would seem to have an essential relationship to the parties' dispute and its resolution, insofar as it is a bipolar dispute. Perhaps in drawing the distinction, Weinrib means to point to the requirements of Kantian right that underpin his theory of corrective justice, a matter that I take up in the next section of this chapter. Whatever Weinrib might mean, it is important to note that he does not seem to deny, nor could he deny, that courts can apply distributive norms in two party cases consistently with their purpose as institutions required to supply normative justifications in the adjudication of bipolar disputes. From the fact that a family assets case in equity is a two party case, it cannot be concluded that only norms of corrective justice should apply to the case.

C. Both Corrective and Distributive Norms Respond to Kantian Right

Another obstacle to accepting the corrective justice proposition in a prescriptive sense confronts those who would assert the proposition on the basis of a particular theory of the normative foundations of corrective justice: Weinrib's theory, according to which there is a special link between corrective justice and Kantian right. A good place to start exploring this aspect of Weinrib's theory is his claim that, in a private law case, a 'court has only one role: to give public expression to the meaning of [Kantian] right in a particular interaction'.[34] The meaning of Kantian right is specified by Kant's Universal Principle of Right, which, according to Arthur Ripstein, 'demands that each person exercise his or her choice in

[30] A property-allocating norm specifying common intention as the ground for allocation appears to fall within the notion of 'justice in transfer' that is referred to by Robert Nozick in his account of distributive justice: *Anarchy, State, and Utopia* (New York, Basic Books, 1974) ch 7. And as Gardner (n 7) 13 points out, Nozick's account of justice in transfer is an account of bipolar distributive norms.

[31] Weinrib (n 6) 70.

[32] Ibid 72, n 41.

[33] Ibid.

[34] Ibid 105.

ways that are consistent with the freedom of all others to exercise their choice'.[35] Kantian right points to the freedom of each individual person to be a self-directed chooser of her own ends, but only to the extent that this may be reconciled with the same freedom for everyone else. In Ripstein's neat phrase, it demands that 'no person be the master of another'.[36] So Weinrib's claim about the role of the court seems to be a demand that a court justify its decision in a private law case by specifying reasons for that decision that treat the parties as free according to what Ripstein describes as 'a system of freedom under universal law'.[37]

For Weinrib, the only way a court adjudicating a private law dispute may do this is by applying norms of corrective justice: '[c]orrective justice is *the* justificatory structure that pertains to the immediate interaction of one free being with another'.[38] I emphasise the word 'the' in that quotation because Weinrib's claim is not that applying a norm of corrective justice is just one among several ways in which a court might give meaning to Kantian right in deciding a case in private law; the claim is that a court cannot give meaning to Kantian right in a private law setting except by applying a norm of corrective justice. For present purposes, Weinrib's account of the way in which corrective justice gives meaning to Kantian right may be accepted.[39] I wish to concentrate instead on the possibility that, in addition to giving meaning to Kantian right by applying a norm of corrective justice, a court in a private law case might give meaning to Kantian right by applying a norm of distributive justice. If Kantian right underlies distributive norms that are available to courts in private law, then this presents an obstacle to accepting the corrective justice proposition, at least to the extent that one has a Kantian moral outlook.

Kantian right may underlie a distributive norm in any case where the ground for distribution specified by the norm points to the consent of the parties in question. As Ripstein argues, consent plays an important role in Kant's moral theory, being a way in which an individual may, consistently with the Universal Principle of Right, bring about the variation of her rights and obligations vis-à-vis another.[40] A person who consents to such a variation of her rights and obligations is not, to the extent that she has consented, an instrument of the purposes of another; rather, her moral position is changed in a way that is consistent with her freedom as a self-determining chooser of her own ends. As Ripstein puts it, '[b]y consenting, you can turn an act that would otherwise be another person's despotism over you into an exercise of your own freedom.'[41] And so, where a court deciding a private law case specifies the consent of two individuals as the ground

[35] A Ripstein, *Force and Freedom: Kant's Legal and Political Philosophy* (Cambridge MA, Harvard University Press, 2009) 35–36. I have relied heavily on Ripstein's book in preparing this section of the chapter.
[36] Ibid 36.
[37] Ibid 169.
[38] Weinrib (n 6) 19.
[39] For the account, see Weinrib (n 6) ch 5.
[40] Ripstein, *Force and Freedom* (n 35) 109–15.
[41] Ibid 47.

for a distribution between them, that court gives meaning to Kantian right notwithstanding that it applies a norm of distributive justice to the case. Arguably, the application of such a consent-based distributive norm characterises cases where courts allocate property in family assets based on the common intention of the parties: in such cases, the parties' common intention is the form of their mutual consent to a variation of their rights and obligations as against each other. On this view, the common intention cases supply a practical illustration of the theoretical possibility that distributive norms, as well as corrective norms, may respond to the requirements of Kantian right in private law.

III. Doctrinal Constraints (2)—The Limited Set Account

The obstacles to accepting the corrective justice account of doctrinal constraints in equity constitute reasons to reject that account. However, rejecting the proposition that courts applying equity are confined to norms of corrective justice does not necessarily entail abandoning the proposition that doctrinal constraints in equity rule out regard to future needs in family assets cases. This is because it is possible to accept that both corrective and distributive norms should apply in equity in family assets cases but at the same time insist that the set of applicable corrective and distributive norms is limited, and that none of the applicable norms permits consideration of future needs. The view that the set of applicable corrective and distributive norms in family assets cases is limited is not difficult to discern in the case law. For example, in the foundational case of *Pettitt v Pettitt*, Lord Morris of Borth-y-Gest expressed a view that may be attributed fairly to all of the Law Lords who heard the appeal in that case.

> In the absence of some new legislative provisions giving some discretionary powers to a court to adjust ... legal or equitable interests in property the duty of a court, if disputes arise, must be to reach conclusions as to where those interests belong.[42]

This statement is entirely consistent with the view that allocations of property in family assets might occur in accordance with distributive, as opposed to corrective, norms, as the endorsement of a distributive common intention-based norm in *Pettitt v Pettitt* itself confirms. Nonetheless, the statement assumes a distinction between distributions of property in accordance with a limited set of relevant norms, which it is the duty of a court applying equity to achieve, and *re*distributions of property in accordance with an open-ended set of irrelevant norms, which it is the duty of a court applying equity to avoid.

[42] *Pettitt* (n 15) 803; see also 793 (Lord Reid), 807–08 (Lord Hodson), 812–13 (Lord Upjohn), 820–21 (Lord Diplock).

How might a person who holds the limited set view of doctrinal constraints in equity argue against a court taking future needs into account when allocating property in family assets? One possibility might be to argue that future needs can never figure in the criterion for distribution of a sound norm of distributive justice, and that the set of applicable property-allocating norms in equity is composed only of sound corrective and distributive norms. An argument to the effect that future needs never figure in sound norms of distributive justice is certainly possible,[43] and in order to rule it out altogether sustained normative argument is required.[44] However, I wish to leave that line of argument to one side here. If sound norms of distributive justice were circumscribed so as always to rule out regard to future needs, the statutory regimes of family law could not, to the extent that they demand that future needs be taken into account in family assets cases, operate in accordance with the requirements of justice. Again, this conclusion is not impossible—such regimes might give expression to norms of charity, for example[45]—but in my view it is counterintuitive enough to warrant continuing on the assumption that sound norms of distributive justice can at least sometimes refer to future needs.

Two further arguments against admitting a distributive norm referring to future needs into the limited set of applicable property-allocating norms in family assets cases now come into view. First, there is the argument that equity should allocate property only in accordance with norms specifying as grounds for allocation events that took place before the parties brought their case to court, and never in accordance with norms specifying as grounds for allocation future events or states of affairs. Put simply, the argument is that the set of applicable norms that apply to family assets cases should be limited to past-regarding, as opposed to future-regarding, norms. This argument makes an appeal to the value of certainty in law; parties, including third parties, should be able to rely on the assurance that property disputes will be determined based on what has been said and done in the past, and not what will be said and done in the future.[46]

Secondly, there is the argument that a court that allocates property in accordance with future needs in a family assets case in equity fails to provide a sufficient

[43] For an argument that needs never figure in sound norms of distributive justice, see Nozick, *Anarchy, State, and Utopia* (n 30) ch 7.

[44] For an effective attack on Nozick's theory of distributive justice, see G Cohen, *Self-Ownership, Freedom and Equality* (Cambridge, Cambridge University Press 1995) chs 1–3.

[45] On the distinction between justice and charity, see J Gardner, 'The Virtue of Justice and the Character of Law' (2000) 53 *Current Legal Problems* 149; J Gardner, 'The Virtue of Charity and Its Foils' in C Mitchell and S Moody (eds), *Foundations of Charity* (Oxford, Hart Publishing, 2000) 1.

[46] In this regard, the argument resembles the argument against discretionary remedialism in equity: see P Birks, 'Proprietary Rights as Remedies' in P Birks (ed), *Frontiers of Liability: Volume 2* (Oxford, Oxford University Press, 1994) 214; P Birks, 'Three Kinds of Objection to Discretionary Remedialism' (2000) 29 *University of Western Australia Law Review* 1; P Birks, 'Rights, Wrongs and Remedies' (2000) 20 *OJLS* 1. However, the two arguments are different: one could hold the view that discretionary remedialism in equity is impermissible and yet approve of the application of a determinate rule demanding that future needs be taken into account in any case raising the question of property allocation in family assets.

justification of its decision, given the bipolar nature of the dispute between the parties before it. Earlier, I discussed the claim that only by applying a norm of corrective justice may a court sufficiently justify its decision to the two parties before it in a private law dispute. I rejected that claim because of the possibility of norms of distributive justice applying to two party cases. Nonetheless, it remains the case that a court that applies a norm of distributive justice to a two party case only provides a sufficient justification of its decision where it applies a norm that is specific to those two parties. This is because in a two party case, an allocation in favour of one party necessarily diminishes the allocation to the other. The court must be able to explain to the party whose allocation will be diminished why *her* allocation must be diminished so as to augment the allocation of the other party, as opposed to that other party's position being improved in some other way, perhaps by recourse to a state-sponsored social welfare system. Therefore, the argument goes, a court in a private law case that allocates property to one party because of her future needs insufficiently justifies to the other party why *her* allocation must be correspondingly diminished.

These two arguments about doctrinal constraints in equity, appealing respectively to the value of certainty and to the justificatory enterprise that is private law, are strong arguments, and I wish to accept them for present purposes. Accepting the arguments entails accepting that there are limits to how courts applying equity might take future needs into account when allocating property in family assets cases. For one thing, if equity should confine itself to past-regarding norms in family assets cases, a court applying equity should never allocate property based solely on the fact that one party to the case is likely in the future to be worse off than the other party to the case.[47] And if equity should operate only according to norms that reflect the bipolarity of the parties' relationship, a court should never allocate property to a party to the case before it so as to reduce a burden that would otherwise have to be borne by the state through the provision of social welfare to that party.[48]

That said, accepting arguments about doctrinal constraints in equity that confine it to past-regarding and bipolar norms does not necessarily entail accepting the proposition that doctrinal constraints in equity rule out regard to future needs in family assets cases. This is because, in some family assets cases in equity, property-allocating norms of distributive justice may be at large that: (a) are past-regarding in the sense of specifying past events as grounds for allocation; (b) are bipolar in the sense of applying only to the claimant and the defendant; but (c) require a consideration of the future needs of the parties.

[47] Ben McFarlane's assertion that 'the court cannot take advantage of A and B's presence before it to adjust their rights according to some … question of their respective needs' may therefore be accepted: McFarlane, *The Structure of Property Law* (n 5) 460.

[48] In contrast, alleviating the state's burden of social welfare may be a goal of statutory family law regimes: see *Attorney-General of Nova Scotia v Walsh* [2002] SCC 83, [2002] 4 SCR 325 [114]–[117] (L'Heureux-Dubé J).

The argument to establish the possibility of such norms begins with the observation that among the events that have occurred before two parties take a dispute over family assets to court is the formation and maintenance of the family relationship itself. How this event is to be understood depends in large part on deeper philosophical questions about the moral contours of family life. Answers to these questions might be arranged on a spectrum. At one end of the spectrum is the view that in certain circumstances, by coming together as a couple, two individuals cease in some respects to continue to be individuals and instead form a single moral subject—a community—with a unity of purpose.[49] Close to this end of the spectrum is another view, according to which a couple may come to share purposes but not to form a single moral subject: this is the view of marriage that Ripstein attributes to Kant.[50] Further along the spectrum, and moving away from these communitarian views, is the view that the moral world of individual persons who enter into a relationship as a couple may be constituted in part by norms of trust and trustworthiness, norms that attach to the form of life that the couple have chosen.[51] And further again from the communitarian end of the spectrum is the view that, by choosing to live as a couple, two individuals might voluntarily undertake to be bound by specific obligations, either explicitly or because such obligations are conventionally understood to arise in a relationship such as that which the couple has formed.[52] Finally, at the non-communitarian end of the spectrum is the view that living as a couple does not change the moral world of individuals: on this view, the moral position of a person vis-à-vis her partner is no different than her position vis-à-vis a stranger.[53]

On any but the last of these views, the formation and maintenance of a family relationship may generate norms that would not otherwise apply to the parties whose relationship it is. In what follows, I wish to concentrate on the possibility of one relationship-specific norm in particular: a norm, arising from a couple relationship, taking the form of an obligation to provide material support to one's partner. The possibility of such a norm is consistent both with a communitarian view that a couple's identity might be fused or their purposes united by virtue

[49] See M Sandel, *Liberalism and the Limits of Justice* 2nd ed (Cambridge, Cambridge University Press, 1998) 149–50, describing the 'constitutive conception' of community.

[50] Ripstein (n 35) 75, n 22.

[51] See S Gardner, 'Rethinking Family Property' (1993) 109 *LQR* 263, 286–89; C Rotherham, *Proprietary Remedies in Context* (Oxford, Hart Publishing, 2002) 198–99, 212–13, 221–30. Unlike Gardner and Rotherham, I do not think that in family assets cases a legally enforceable distributive norm could be grounded in the demands of trust and trustworthiness, because I do not think that those demands typically take the form of obligations: see M Harding, 'Manifesting Trust' (2009) 29 *OJLS* 245; M Harding, 'Responding to Trust' (2011) 24 *Ratio Juris* 75.

[52] See S Munzer, 'Property as Social Relations' in S Munzer (ed), *New Essays in the Legal and Political Theory of Property* (Oxford, Oxford University Press, 2001) 36, 70.

[53] See S Okin, *Justice, Gender, and the Family* (New York, Basic Books, 1989) 108–09, arguing that Rawlsian norms of distributive justice apply both to the family and to other social institutions. For Rawls' reply to Okin, reflecting the view that family relationships can generate otherwise inapplicable distributive norms, see J Rawls, *Justice as Fairness: A Restatement* (Cambridge MA, Belknap Press, 2001) 162–68.

of their relationship, and with a more individualistic view that individuals may voluntarily undertake specific obligations upon entering into, or during, a couple relationship. I wish to argue that such a norm is both past-regarding and bipolar, but that in certain circumstances it demands consideration of future needs. I therefore wish to argue that, to the extent that such a norm has arisen in the relationship of parties who seek an allocation of property in their family assets in equity, it may be accepted by those who would insist that equity is confined to a limited set of past-regarding and bipolar norms. And this means that taking the limited set view of doctrinal constraints in equity does not entail rejecting the possibility of future needs being taken into account in family assets cases in equity.

But before making that argument, I must consider whether a norm demanding the provision of material support ever arises in relationships the breakdown of which triggers disputes over family assets in equity. It is uncontroversial to assert that a norm demanding the provision of material support may arise in a marriage. In the recent family law case of *Miller v Miller; McFarlane v McFarlane*, Lord Nicholls, referring to marriage, stated that '[m]utual dependence begets mutual obligations of support'.[54] And it is also possible that the equitable presumption of advancement in the law of resulting trusts has sometimes been viewed by courts as resting on an obligation of support that a husband owes to his wife.[55] However, given that the allocation of property in family assets on the dissolution of a marriage is dealt with under statutory family law regimes, to demonstrate that a norm demanding the provision of material support may arise in a marriage is to say nothing about the position of parties whose cases must be determined in equity. The question, then, is whether such a norm can ever arise in the relationships of couples who are not married.

This question admits of no easy answer. As scholars who study family relationships have pointed out, the variety of family forms means that it is difficult to make general claims with any degree of certainty about the normative worlds of unmarried couples.[56] The Canadian case of *Attorney-General of Nova Scotia v Walsh* illustrates the difficulty.[57] There, the Supreme Court of Canada was asked to decide whether or not the failure to extend a statutory family law regime to unmarried couples constituted impermissible discrimination under the Canadian Charter of Rights and Freedoms. In finding that there was no discrimination, a majority of

[54] *Miller v Miller; McFarlane v McFarlane* [2006] UKHL 24, [2006] 2 AC 618 [11].

[55] See the discussion in R Chambers, *Resulting Trusts* (Oxford, Oxford University Press, 1997) 30–31. By contrast, it would seem that courts have thought that a wider obligation of advancement underlies the presumption of advancement in parent/child relationships: see J Glister, 'The Presumption of Advancement' in C Mitchell (ed), *Constructive and Resulting Trusts* (Oxford, Hart Publishing, 2010) 289.

[56] See, eg R Probert, 'Equality in the Family Home?' (2007) 15 *Feminist Legal Studies* 341; G Douglas, J Pearce and H Woodward, 'Cohabitants, Property and the Law: A Study of Injustice' (2009) 72 *MLR* 24; M Maclean and J Eekelaar, 'The Perils of Reforming Family Law and the Increasing Need for Empirical Research, 1980–2008' in J Miles and R Probert (eds), *Sharing Lives: Dividing Assets* (Oxford, Hart Publishing, 2009) 25.

[57] *Walsh* (n 48).

the Court drew a sharp distinction between the norms that operate in a marriage and the norms that operate in the relationships of unmarried couples.[58] However, L'Heureux-Dubé J dissented, arguing that, in view of the realities of contemporary family life, in at least some cases the relationships of unmarried couples are likely to be characterised by the same norms as the relationships of couples who are married.[59]

In my view, there are reasons to doubt that the sharp distinction drawn by the majority in *Attorney-General of Nova Scotia v Walsh* is sound. For one thing, even in jurisdictions where statutory family law regimes have not been extended in full to unmarried couples, there exist legislative provisions that enforce norms arising from the relationships of such couples in matters like the maintenance of children and provision for a surviving partner and children upon the death of the other partner to the relationship.[60] Moreover, in some cases decided in equity, courts have appeared willing to accept that the relationships of unmarried couples might generate otherwise inapplicable norms.[61] But more importantly it seems quite implausible to suggest that in no case may the relationship of an unmarried couple assume the same normative dimensions as the relationship of a married couple. In circumstances where two individuals maintain a longstanding relationship as a couple, it is difficult to see why they could never come to owe each other obligations of material support simply because they have not voluntary undertaken such obligations in a public ceremony of marriage. Obligations may be voluntarily undertaken in other ways and, in any event, from some philosophical perspectives obligations might arise even though they have not been voluntarily undertaken, say because those obligations have been generated by the alignment of a couple's purposes.[62] My argument therefore rests on the claim that a norm demanding the provision of material support may arise from the relationship of an unmarried couple and therefore may be relevant in at least some family assets cases in equity. I now return to that argument, to demonstrate that a norm demanding the provision of material support is both past-regarding and bipolar in nature.

A norm demanding the provision of material support is past-regarding in the straightforward sense that it arises either upon the formation of a couple relationship or upon the maintenance of a couple relationship, by virtue of a voluntary undertaking or the fusion or alignment of the purposes of the two parties to that relationship. Taken as a property-allocating norm of distributive justice in the setting of a family assets case in equity, then, such a norm specifies as the ground

[58] Ibid [31]–[64] (Bastarache J, McLachlin CJ, Iacobucci, Major, Binnie, Arbour and LeBel JJ concurring. Gonthier J agreed in a separate judgment).

[59] Ibid [76]–[173].

[60] In England and Wales see, eg Inheritance (Provision for Family and Dependants) Act 1975 (provision on death); Children Act 1989 sch 1 (capital provision for children); Family Law Act 1996, pt IV (occupation orders) and sch 7 (transfers of tenancies).

[61] I have discussed this point elsewhere: see M Harding, 'Defending *Stack v Dowden*' (2009) 73 *Conv* 309.

[62] See text to nn 65–67 below.

for an allocation of property in family assets an event that has occurred before the parties have taken their case to court.

The bipolarity of a norm demanding the provision of material support may be a more complex matter, depending on how the event giving rise to the norm is viewed philosophically. Because a couple relationship gives rise to such a norm, its range of application can be no greater than the parties to that relationship, so if the norm implicates more than one person, it must be a bipolar norm. However, on a Kantian view of morality, a norm demanding the provision of material support might not implicate more than one person. In his discussion of Charles Fried's account of contract as promise, Weinrib argues that the morality of promising cannot explain contract law on Kantian grounds, because from a Kantian perspective the morality of promising is a matter of the virtue of the promisor.[63] On this view, although the promisor has voluntarily undertaken an obligation by making a promise, the promisee may not enforce the obligation as owed to her. For Weinrib, then, promising is a matter of Kantian ethics rather than Kantian right, and a voluntarily undertaken obligation, taken on its own, is unenforceable in private law because private law is confined to giving meaning to Kantian right.[64]

One way of responding to this argument is to insist that the morality of promising is a matter of Kantian right and that therefore voluntarily undertaken obligations, taken on their own, are enforceable in law.[65] However, it may not be necessary to do this work to convince a Kantian that a norm arising from a couple relationship and demanding the provision of material support can be legally enforceable. According to Ripstein, Kant argues that certain relationships—relationships of status—are characterised by norms that, although they have not been consented to, establish claims of right.[66] For Kant, one such relationship is marriage, a relationship in which 'each spouse's purposes become the other's'.[67] So on a Kantian view, the status of marriage gives rise to norms requiring each spouse to pursue the ends of the other, and these norms establish reciprocal claims of right, enforceable in law. A norm demanding that each spouse provide material support to the other may be viewed in this light: providing materially for one's spouse seems clearly to be entailed in pursuing the ends of that spouse. If all that is accepted, then a norm demanding the provision of material support may be bipolar, and therefore legally enforceable, in the sense demanded by Kantians, precisely because it expresses a relation of right. Of course, it is possible to accept this argument but insist that the argument applies only to the status relationship of marriage, in which case the argument has no

[63] Weinrib (n 6) 50–53, discussing C Fried, *Contract as Promise: A Theory of Contractual Obligation* (Cambridge MA, Harvard University Press, 1981).

[64] See Weinrib (n 6) 113, arguing that Fried 'lock[s] into the wrong section of the Kantian moral universe'.

[65] For an argument consistent with the proposition that the morality of promising is a matter of Kantian right, see D Kimel, *From Promise to Contract: Towards a Liberal Theory of Contract* (Oxford, Hart Publishing, 2003) 22–27.

[66] Ripstein (n 35) 70–77.

[67] Ibid 75, n 22.

traction in the setting of equity. However, Kant's view appears to be that it is the unity of purpose in a marriage that generates unconsented-to norms specific to that status relationship, and as I have argued already there is no reason to assume that such a unity of purpose can never occur outside of marriage. Thus, from a Kantian perspective, relationships of marriage and other relationships characterised by a unity of purpose can give rise to a bipolar norm demanding the provision of material support that is, all else being equal, enforceable in private law.

Finally, I come to future needs. How might a past-regarding and bipolar norm demanding the provision of material support lead to a court taking future needs into account when allocating property in family assets? The answer to this question is in two parts. First, a norm arising from a couple relationship and demanding the provision of material support may survive the breakdown of the relationship. This is not to say that such a norm necessarily requires a person to provide materially for her former partner on an ongoing basis after the breakdown of their relationship, as occurs in family law when spousal maintenance orders are made. The breakdown of a couple relationship typically indicates that at least one of the parties to that relationship is choosing to cease to be bound by norms arising from the relationship. Respect for this choice entails legal recognition that relationship-specific norms no longer apply to the parties, and this imperative must be balanced against the demands of those relationship-specific norms themselves. However, to the extent that a norm demanding the provision of material support has arisen in a couple relationship, there appears to be no reason why the choice of one of the parties to exit that relationship should operate so as to cancel the demands of that norm altogether.[68] Arguably, an appropriate balance between the competing demands of, on the one hand, a relationship-specific norm requiring the provision of material support and, on the other hand, respect for the choice of one of the parties to cease to be bound by that norm may be found in a once-and-for-all allocation of property in family assets. Such an allocation responds to the requirements of the relationship-specific norm but, because it is a once-and-for-all response to that norm, it leaves the parties to face each other in the future unburdened by the norms that previously regulated their interactions as a couple.[69]

Secondly, a court that applies, in this once-and-for-all way, a relationship-specific norm demanding the provision of material support must make an assessment of what constitutes material support in the circumstances of a family relationship breakdown. It is here that consideration of future needs comes into play. The court may have regard to future needs in order to quantify an allocation of property that will, once and for all, accord with the requirements of the norm demanding the

[68] The extent to which the choice of *both* parties to cancel the demands of a relationship-specific norm should be respected is a more difficult matter: see *Radmacher (formerly Granatino) v Granatino* [2010] UKSC 42, [2010] 3 WLR 1367.

[69] For a discussion of some of the difficulties in balancing relationship-specific norms and respect for the choice to exit a couple relationship: C Frantz and H Dagan, 'Properties of Marriage' (2004) 104 *Columbia Law Review* 75; H Dagan, 'The Limited Autonomy of Private Law' (2008) 56 *American Journal of Comparative Law* 809, 819–24.

provision of material support. Thus, future needs themselves do not constitute the ground for allocation. The ground for allocation is the obligation to provide material support, an obligation arising from a past-regarding and bipolar norm. Future needs are taken into account in working out what, in the circumstances of the case, might best achieve the discharge of the obligation, having regard to other imperatives in play such as the demand that the choice to exit the family relationship be respected. An analogue may be found in the activities of courts asked to assess damages to be paid to a claimant who is successful in an action in the tort of negligence. In such cases, the ground for an allocation to the claimant is the defendant's breach of a duty of care owed to the claimant, and the allocative norm applied by the court is therefore both past-regarding and bipolar.[70] However, the court may have regard to future possibilities when quantifying the allocation that will come closest to satisfying the requirements of the applicable allocative norm.

IV. Conclusion: Beyond Doctrinal Constraints

To summarise, then, there are large obstacles to accepting the proposition that doctrinal constraints in equity rule out regard to future needs in family assets cases. If the proposition is understood as resting on an argument that equity is confined to norms of corrective justice, it is at odds with the practice of courts, and it fails to take into account the possibility that distributive norms may apply, consistently with the requirements of Kantian right, in two party cases. If the proposition is understood as resting on an argument that equity is confined to a set of corrective and distributive norms that are past-regarding and bipolar, it faces a hurdle in the possibility of a past-regarding and bipolar norm of distributive justice requiring that future needs be taken into account in giving effect to an obligation, arising from a couple relationship, to provide material support to one's partner. A proponent of the limited set view may avoid this hurdle only by making the implausible argument that the relationship of an unmarried couple can never give rise to an obligation to provide material support, or by asserting that such an obligation may be cancelled by the choice of one party to exit the relationship in question.

However, it is important to remember that rejecting the proposition that doctrinal constraints in equity rule out regard to future needs in family assets cases does not, by itself, clear the path for courts applying equity to develop the law in this direction. There may be obstacles to doing so that have nothing to do with doctrinal constraints. In concluding, I wish to point to four such obstacles. Before courts applying equity may take future needs into account when allocating property in family assets cases, these four obstacles must be overcome.

[70] Of course, on Weinrib's view, allocative norms in negligence law are always norms of corrective justice: Weinrib (n 6) ch 6.

First, even if it is accepted—and I think that it should be accepted—that a norm demanding the provision of material support can arise from the relationship of an unmarried couple, courts still face a difficulty in ascertaining a range of relationships, apart from marriage, in which this norm arises. And precisely what the norm demands in the setting of a particular relationship, especially in view of the requirement to respect the choice of at least one party to exit the relationship, is an equally difficult question. Earlier, I alluded to the work of scholars who have studied family relationships, and the conclusions that such scholars have reached based on empirical studies suggest that it is not possible to generalise about the normative worlds of unmarried couples. Given this empirical deficit, courts may not be in a position, when deciding family assets cases in equity, to draw inferences from the facts of the cases before them that can provide a sound platform for the application of a principle requiring that future needs be taken into account when allocating property. Of course, legislatures contemplating the design of statutory family law regimes face the same problem, but legislatures may respond to a wider range of norms than courts when developing law to deal with family assets cases, and this wider range of norms may enable rational decisions about property allocation to be reached notwithstanding the empirical deficit. For example, legislatures may respond to a norm demanding that the state's burden of social welfare be alleviated if possible in circumstances where a party will exit a couple relationship in need,[71] or a norm taking into account the disproportionate burden of poverty that is borne by separated women.[72] These are norms that courts applying equity may not respond to because of doctrinal constraints.

Secondly, courts must be able to justify why a norm demanding the provision of material support should lead to an allocation of property, rather than an allocation in the form of a personal remedy. From the fact that an obligation to provide material support is recognised, it cannot be concluded that property will, or should be, allocated to the partner entitled to support.[73] And more broadly, the question whether or not an allocation in a family assets case should take the form of property, with the consequences for third parties that this entails, has received different answers in the case law to date. In Canada, courts are willing to award either a proprietary or a personal remedy in response to a successful claim in a family assets case.[74] In England, the doctrine of proprietary estoppel may deliver either a proprietary or a personal remedy, but the common intention constructive trust always has proprietary consequences.[75] In Australia and New Zealand, proprietary relief has been the norm, but its availability and scope has been a

[71] See above n 48.

[72] For a discussion of this issue, see Frantz and Dagan, 'Properties of Marriage' (n 69) 119–24.

[73] See *National Provincial Bank v Ainsworth* [1965] AC 1175 (HL).

[74] *Peter* (n 12) 995–1000 (McLachlin J).

[75] For discussion of the remedial consequences of proprietary estoppel see: *Crabb v Arun District Council* [1976] Ch 179 (CA) 198 (Scarman LJ), *Gillett v Holt* [2001] 1 Ch 210 (CA) 235 (Robert Walker LJ), *Jennings v Rice* [2002] EWCA Civ 159, [2003] 1 P & CR 100 [22]–[36] (Aldous LJ).

matter of debate.[76] The various arguments for and against the award of proprietary remedies must be resolved before it can be said with confidence that a property allocation is the appropriate response to a norm demanding the provision of material support. Relevant considerations are likely to include the nature of the assets in question,[77] the connection—if any—between the needs of the parties upon the breakdown of the relationship and the contributions that the parties have made to the assets during the life of the relationship, the accommodation needs of the parties now that their relationship has ended, and the positions of third parties.

Thirdly, a court that allocates property in a family assets case in equity based on future needs will almost certainly make new law.[78] In circumstances where the legislature has decided not to extend the operation of a statutory family law regime to unmarried couples, thus indicating its desire that future needs not be taken into account when courts allocate property between unmarried couples upon the breakdown of their relationships, it is arguable that courts should refrain from developing the law in this direction. Of course, mere legislative silence on the question of future needs in the setting of disputes between unmarried couples should not carry much weight. If legislative silence on legal problems arising from relationship breakdowns always constituted a conclusive reason for courts not to make new law in response to those problems, none of the developments in equitable doctrine in family assets cases over the past forty years could be justified. But in circumstances where the legislature has recently and explicitly considered whether or not future needs should be taken into account in disputes over family assets between unmarried couples, and has deliberately decided against taking this step, courts may be constrained institutionally to apply equity in a way that is consistent with that decision.[79] The jurisdiction where this institutional constraint may be most evident today is England: in recent years the Law Commission of England and Wales has considered in detail how the law should respond to disputes over family assets between unmarried couples, and in light of (or despite) that work the legislature has refrained from changing the current law.[80] It may be that, in this climate, English courts should for the time being decline to develop equity so as to respond to future needs in family assets cases.[81]

[76] See, eg *Muschinski* (n 9) 614–15, 623 (Deane J); *Lankow* (n 22) 282 (Hardie Boys J), 289 (Gault J); *Giumelli v Giumelli* [1999] HCA 10, (1999) 196 CLR 101, 113; *John Alexander's Clubs Pty Ltd v White City Tennis Club Ltd* [2010] HCA 19, (2010) 241 CLR 1 [126]–[130].

[77] For example, have the assets been acquired or held for family purposes, or for investment or other purposes? For a discussion of this question, see *Miller* (n 54) [20]–[22] (Lord Nicholls), [149]–[153] (Baroness Hale).

[78] Although, as I alluded to above (n 5), there is arguably some precedential support for such a move in the case law on the doctrine of proprietary estoppel.

[79] For a discussion of the problems that can emerge when courts strike out on their own in such circumstances, see Harding (n 61) 317–22.

[80] Law Commission, *Cohabitation: The Financial Consequences of Relationship Breakdown* (July 2007, Law Com No 307), especially Part 4. For the government response, dated 6 March 2008, postponing reform '[f]or the time being', see http://www.justice.gov.uk/news/announcement060308a.htm, accessed 7 July 2011.

[81] For a different view, see Gardner and Davidson, 'The Future of *Stack v Dowden*' (n 17) 18–19.

Finally, there is a risk that a court that develops equity so as to take future needs into account in family assets cases may thereby distort equitable doctrines with a range of application wider than family assets cases. This risk would appear to be especially great in the setting of the doctrine of proprietary estoppel. Courts applying the doctrine of proprietary estoppel have shown themselves willing to respond to future needs when quantifying the relief to be awarded to a successful claimant.[82] As I hope to have demonstrated in this paper, there are no doctrinal impediments to developing proprietary estoppel in this way, insofar as the doctrine applies to family assets cases against the backdrop of a couple relationship in which a norm demanding the provision of material support has arisen. However, as Simon Gardner has pointed out, proprietary estoppel is not limited to such cases: it applies in both family and commercial settings. As Gardner indicates, by developing proprietary estoppel to respond to a norm that is specific to couple relationships, courts risk delivering a doctrine that cannot be justified in all of the cases to which it might be applied.[83] In recent times, judges have demonstrated an awareness of the possibility that equitable doctrines might operate differently depending on whether they are applied in a family or a commercial setting.[84] However, despite this awareness, the risk of doctrinal distortion is unlikely to be eliminated altogether while doctrines like proprietary estoppel apply to both family and commercial cases.

These four considerations show that there are reasons for doubting that courts applying equity should have regard to future needs in family assets cases. However, as I hope to have shown in this chapter, there are large obstacles to accepting the proposition that the different treatment of future needs as between the statutory regimes of family law and equity may be justified by pointing to doctrinal constraints in equity. Rather, equity has available to it doctrinal resources that permit future needs to be taken into account in family assets cases, even once relevant doctrinal constraints have been applied. The assumption that, in family assets cases, courts allocating property under statute may have recourse to a wide range of corrective and distributive norms via the exercise of judicial discretion, while courts applying equity may not, may well be sound. However, questions about the limits of equity in disputes over family assets, and in particular questions about whether regard to future needs is beyond those limits, are unlikely to receive satisfactory answers by focusing solely on doctrinal constraints. Those answers must also be sought elsewhere.

[82] *Sledmore* (n 5), discussed above n 5.
[83] Gardner (n 5) 460.
[84] *Stack* (n 15) 439 (Lord Hope), 449 (Baroness Hale).

10

Constructive Trusts: Understanding Remedialism

MICHAEL BRYAN*

I. Introduction

This chapter examines that over-analysed concept, the remedial constructive trust, in the light of two developments. The first development is the promulgation of the *Restatement (Third) of the Law of Restitution and Unjust Enrichment (Third Restatement)* prepared by Andrew Kull.[1] The publication of the Restatement is a considerable scholarly achievement. Like the *Restatement (First) of Restitution (First Restatement)*, prepared by Warren Seavey and Austin Scott and published in 1937, it encompasses both restitution for unjust enrichment and restitution for wrongs. It will undoubtedly shape the direction of the American law of restitution for many years to come, and its provisions and commentary will influence academic debate about unjust enrichment and restitution outside the USA. This paper is concerned only with the provisions of the Restatement dealing with the award of a constructive trust. Paragraph 55 provides:

1. If a recipient is unjustly enriched by the acquisition of legal title to specifically identifiable property at the expense of the claimant or in violation of the claimant's rights, the recipient may be declared a constructive trustee, for the benefit of the claimant, of the property in question and its traceable product.
2. The obligation of a constructive trustee is to surrender the constructive-trust property to the claimant, on such conditions as the court may direct.
3. Constructive trust is authorized as a means to rectify or avoid unjust enrichment of the recipient at the expense of the claimant. Where constructive trust would yield a

* Many of the arguments in this paper evolved from discussions with my colleague, Elise Bant, but responsibility for errors is solely mine.

[1] American Law Institute, *Restatement (Third) of Restitution and Unjust Enrichment Tentative Draft* (approved May 2010) ('*Third Restatement*'). This paper is based on *Tentative Draft No 6* (March 12, 2008).

> recovery greater than the claimant's loss, the remedy is subject to limitation to protect innocent recipients and certain third parties. See §§ 50, 56(4) and 61(1).[2]

Paragraph 160 of the *First Restatement of Restitution* had more succinctly provided:

> Where a person holding title to property is subject to an equitable duty to convey it to another on the ground that he would be unjustly enriched if he were permitted to retain it, a constructive trust arises.

Paragraph 160 of the *First Restatement* was widely thought to epitomise the view that American law, in contrast to English law, espouses the remedial constructive trust.[3] It was a view promoted by Austin Scott, the author of the paragraph.[4] Whether one agrees depends on the meaning to be assigned to 'remedial'. The *Third Restatement* avoids the terminology of institutional and remedial constructive trusts while nonetheless locating § 55 within the Remedies part of the Restatement. In spite of the basic definitional problems, however, the genie has escaped from the American bottle and spread its message across the globe. The remedial constructive trust is recognised in Canada,[5] Australia[6] and New Zealand.[7] In England the 'remedial' constructive trust is recognised by denial; it is said to be the type of constructive trust not awarded under English law.[8]

The second recent development discussed in this chapter is the High Court of Australia's decision in *John Alexander's Clubs Pty Ltd v White City Tennis Club Ltd*.[9] The High Court held that a contract between two parties which (on one view of the facts) empowered one of them to exercise an option to buy land for purposes agreed between both parties, gave rise to neither a fiduciary relationship nor an entitlement to a constructive trust on *Pallant v Morgan*[10] principles. In so doing the High Court set aside the constructive trust imposed by the New South Wales Court of Appeal over the land. The High Court recognised the concept of a

[2] The qualifications are important and are discussed below. Under *Third Restatement* §50(4) a claimant cannot claim a constructive trust over consequential gains made by an innocent defendant which would not have been recoverable in a personal claim for unjust enrichment. §56(4) goes on to provide that, against an innocent recipient, proprietary restitution, if otherwise justified, will be by way of an equitable lien instead of a constructive trust. §61 provides that a claimant will not be permitted to obtain a profitable recovery in restitution at the expense of adequate provision for creditors and dependants of the recipient.

[3] R Maudsley, 'Proprietary Remedies for the Recovery of Money' (1959) 75 *LQR* 234, 237. See also C Rotherham, *Proprietary Remedies in Context* (Oxford, Hart Publishing, 2002) 12–16.

[4] A Scott, 'Constructive Trusts' (1955) 71 *LQR* 39, 41.

[5] *Pettkus v Becker* [1980] 2 SCR 834 (SCC); *Soulos v Korkontzilas* [1997] 2 SCR 217 (SCC).

[6] *Muschinski v Dodds* (1985) 160 CLR 583 (HCA); *Bathurst City Council v PWC Properties Pty Ltd* [1998] HCA 59, (1998) 195 CLR 566; *John Alexander's Clubs Pty Ltd v White City Tennis Club Ltd* [2010] HCA 19, (2010) 241 CLR 1.

[7] *Gillies v Keogh* [1989] 2 NZLR 327 (NZCA); *Lankow v Rose* [1995] 1 NZLR 277 (NZCA); *Fortex Group Ltd (in rec & liq) v MacIntosh* [1998] 3 NZLR 171 (NZCA) 175–77 (Tipping J).

[8] For a recent example of denial, see *De Bruyne v De Bruyne* [2010] EWCA Civ 51 [48] (Patten LJ).

[9] *John Alexander's Clubs* (n 6). See K Mason, 'Deconstructing Constructive Trusts in Australia' (2010) 4 *Journal of Equity* 98.

[10] *Pallant v Morgan* [1953] Ch 43 (ChD).

remedial constructive trust even if the facts of the *John Alexander's Clubs* case did not justify its award. This recognition informs the discussion of the timing of the imposition of the constructive trust,[11] as well as of the availability of alternative personal relief.[12] A strong impression conveyed by the High Court judgment is that the issue now is not *whether* Australian law recognises the remedial constructive trust, but *how*, as a matter of process, the trust can be accommodated within the existing structure of personal and proprietary relief, so that third parties can be identified and have their interests protected under a remedial scheme which is otherwise directed to achieving 'inter partes' justice.

This chapter has two main arguments. The first concerns current judicial usage of the adjective 'remedial' in the term 'remedial constructive trust'. One of the reasons why the remedial constructive trust is suspect is that the terminology employed to explain the concept is unstable. The conclusion reached is that all proprietary constructive trusts are remedial in the limited sense that a court can always award personal relief as an alternative to the making of a proprietary order.[13] The precise relationship between proprietary and personal relief depends, however, on the category of constructive trusteeship in question. The second argument is that the debate about the merits of proprietary remedies has placed excessive emphasis on the insolvency implications of the award of proprietary relief, even in contexts where insolvency has no part to play.[14] One of the signal merits of the *Third Restatement* is that it draws attention to a number of compelling reasons for ordering proprietary relief which have nothing to do with the insolvency implications of constructive trusteeship. These reasons are germane not only to the award of a constructive trust in cases of unjust enrichment or as the response to a commission of a wrong, these being the concerns of the *Restatement*, but to many other constructive trusts as well. The extent to which weight *ought* to be given to non-insolvency considerations is, however, a separate question, and I argue that the distinction adopted by the *Restatement* between 'two party' constructive trust cases and 'three party' constructive trust cases for the purpose of taking into account creditor interests is unsound.

A premise of both arguments made in this chapter is that, in spite of surface differences in terminology and in the rhetoric of constructive trusteeship, common law jurisdictions have adopted broadly similar criteria governing the imposition of a constructive trust as a proprietary remedy. Statements that English law does not recognise the remedial constructive trust whereas the concept is recognised

[11] *John Alexander's Clubs* (n 6) [118].

[12] Ibid [126]–[129].

[13] The converse does not of course follow. Constructive trusteeship imposed solely as a vehicle for personal relief does not have a proprietary order option. See, eg the constructive trust awarded in cases of knowingly, or dishonestly, assisting in a breach of fiduciary obligation: *Royal Brunei Airlines Sdn Bhd v Tan* [1995] 2 AC 378 (PC); *Farah Constructions Pty Ltd v Say-Dee Pty Ltd* [2007] HCA 22, (2007) 230 CLR 89.

[14] An exception to this generalisation is W Swadling, 'Policy Arguments for Proprietary Restitution' (2008) 28 *Legal Studies* 506 which examines some of the non-insolvency reasons for imposing constructive trusts.

in (say) the USA or Australia overlook features of the constructive trust which are common to all jurisdictions which enforce such trusts.[15] It would be surprising if the position were otherwise since the personal and commercial reasons for making a claim to specific property are much the same in all these jurisdictions. Moreover, there is nothing in the cases to suggest that core values such as commercial certainty and the primacy of property rights are evaluated differently in constructive trust litigation in the various common law jurisdictions.

II. Institutional and Remedial Constructive Trusts

The distinction between institutional and remedial constructive trusts has been a persistent feature of constructive trust discourse since it was first articulated by Roscoe Pound in 1920.[16] The intellectual history of the distinction provides an example of how a modest insight into the application of legal doctrine can be inflated into high theory. Pound did not *contrast* institutional and remedial constructive trusts. In his view all constructive trusts were remedial, although the nature of the relief awarded varied. In some cases the constructive trust provided a remedy 'better suited to the circumstances of a particular case, where the suit was founded on another theory, as in cases of reformation, specific performance, of fraudulent conveyance, and of what the civilian would call the exclusion of unworthy heirs',[17] while in others the trust effected specific restitution of a received benefit on the ground of unjust enrichment. In neither class of case was any 'institutional' resemblance to the express trust perceived. While noting that some decisions treated the trust as 'something substantive'[18] Pound left the reader in little doubt that he considered such thinking to be erroneous. In short, the distinction between institutional and remedial constructive trusts was drawn solely for the purpose of rejecting it.

A preliminary definitional problem is to determine the precise meaning of the words 'institutional' (or 'substantive') and 'remedial' in this context.[19] Judicial usage is not uniform and the characterisation of a constructive trust as institutional or

[15] Recent examples of national distinctiveness include *De Bruyne* (n 8) [48] (Patten LJ): no remedial constructive trusts in English law; *Wambo Coal Pty Ltd v Ariff* [2007] NSWSC 589 [40] (White J): 'The remedial constructive trust is part of the law of Australia'.

[16] R Pound, 'The Progress of the Law 1918–1919' (1920) 33 *Harvard Law Review* 420, 420–21. That Pound did not consider his formulation to be significant is indicated by the opening words of the article: 'Little that is new is involved in the decisions upon equity during the past year.' Pound distinguished between remedial and *substantive* constructive trusts. The current conceptualisation of remedial and *institutional* constructive trusts is most likely attributable to Maudsley, 'Proprietary Remedies' (n 3) 237. See Rotherham, *Proprietary Remedies in Context* (n 3) 12–13.

[17] Pound, 'The Progress of the Law' (n 16) 421 (citations omitted).

[18] Ibid 422.

[19] P O'Connor, 'Happy Partners or Strange Bedfellows: The Blending of Remedial and Institutional Features in the Evolving Constructive Trust' (1996) 20 *Melbourne University Law Review* 735; Rotherham (n 3) 26–32.

remedial depends on the type of constructive trust under consideration. Two kinds of distinction are drawn in the decisions and the academic literature.

A. Classification According to Whether the Constructive Trust is 'Practically Certain' or Not

Constructive trusts which do not belong to a recognised category of constructive trust are remedial.[20] *Ford and Lee's Principles of the Law of Trusts* distinguishes between situations where it is 'practically certain' that if a court were invited to declare a constructive trust, it would, subject to the application of equitable bars, so declare, and other situations where it is uncertain whether a constructive trust will be granted.[21] The authors instance the constructive trust imposed by Australian law over stolen money[22] and the trust imposed over land or other valuable property under a specifically enforceable contract as examples of the institutional constructive trust. On the other hand, the *Baumgartner* constructive trust[23] and constructive trusts imposed in estoppel cases are classified as remedial.

The point of classifying the 'practically certain' constructive trust as institutional is, as *Ford and Lee* remind us, that these trusts are not simply remedies. A great deal of planning of commercial transactions assumes that a constructive trust will vest equitable title in well-recognised and recurring situations. Reliance on the 'practically certain' constructive trust enables the application of Statute of Frauds writing requirements to be deliberately avoided in some cases.[24] However, conceding the commercial value of the distinction, constructive trusts are not easily divisible between the 'practically certain' and all the rest. What the proposed distinction perhaps means is that a proprietary constructive trust is almost certainly to be imposed upon proof of relevant criteria for some types of constructive trust, such as those listed by *Ford and Lee*, whereas in other cases the choice between proprietary and personal relief will be more evenly balanced. How choices between proprietary and personal remedies are made will be examined later in this chapter. For the moment it is enough to note that the category of 'practically certain' constructive trusts is not as secure as *Ford and Lee*'s list suggests. For example, in view of the controversy surrounding the decision in *Chase Manhattan Bank NA v Israel-British Bank (London) Ltd*,[25] it would take a brave lawyer to conclude that it is 'practically

[20] *De Bruyne* (n 8) [48] (Patten LJ).

[21] *Ford and Lee's Principles of the Law of Trusts* para [22.660] (revised 2010).

[22] *Black v S Freedman & Co* (1910) 12 CLR 105 (HCA).

[23] *Baumgartner v Baumgartner* (1987) 164 CLR 137 (HCA).

[24] Cf the role of the constructive trust or, alternatively, the application of the principle that equity will not allow a statute to be used as an instrument of fraud, in *Halloran v Minister Administering National Parks & Wildlife Act 1974* [2006] HCA 3, (2006) 229 CLR 545.

[25] *Chase Manhattan Bank NA v Israel-British Bank (London) Ltd* [1981] Ch 105 (ChD). See R Calnan, *Proprietary Rights and Insolvency* (Oxford, Oxford University Press, 2010) paras [4.142]–[4.167] for the argument that no proprietary remedy should have been awarded, inter alia, because where money is paid by mistake the payee has not obtained the payer's property. Compare the position taken

certain' that a constructive trust will be imposed over a mistaken payment. The point is underlined, as far as American law is concerned, by the *Third Restatement* which would impose a constructive trust over a mistaken payment where the payee is solvent, while describing the trust in that situation as a 'superfluous or even meaningless remedy', but would withhold the constructive trust where the payee is insolvent.[26] In constructive trust jurisprudence very little is 'practically certain'.

B. Classification According to Date and Manner of Imposition

An institutional constructive trust arises by operation of law from the date of the circumstances giving rise to the constructive trust, the role of the court being simply to declare its existence. A remedial constructive trust, on the other hand, is created by court order after consideration of all the circumstances of the case. This distinction between institutional and remedial constructive trusts was drawn by Lord Browne-Wilkinson in *Westdeutsche Landesbank Girozentrale v Islington London Borough Council*: 'an institutional constructive trust ... arises by operation of law as from the date of the circumstances which give rise to it: the function of the court is merely to declare that such trust has arisen in the past.'[27] In contrast, a remedial constructive trust is a judicial remedy giving rise to an enforceable equitable obligation: the extent to which it operates retrospectively to the prejudice of third parties lies in the discretion of the court.'[28] Both key terms in this version of the institution/remedy dichotomy require scrutiny.

Lord Browne-Wilkinson's analysis of 'institutional' adopts in substance Scott's analysis of the constructive trust as being a trust 'construed' from the circumstances of the case, rather than 'constructed' by court order.[29] Confusingly, however, and illustrative of the unstable terminology in this area, what for Lord Browne-Wilkinson is an institutional constructive trust was for Scott a remedial constructive trust.[30]

The 'institutional' constructive trust, on this definition, is critical to the determination of priority disputes where the declaration of a pre-existing trust will result in the claimant enjoying priority over interests created after the date of the occurrence of the events which give rise to its recognition. A possible objection to defining 'institutional' in this way is that the court's function is not wholly declaratory. The

in the *Third Restatement* that the question whether the recipient has been enriched is 'unknowable': §55, Comment g.

26 *Third Restatement* §55, Illustration 1.

27 *Westdeutsche Landesbank Girozentrale v Islington London Borough Council* [1996] AC 669 (HL) 714 (Lord Browne-Wilkinson). See also *Parsons v McBain* [2001] FCA 376 [10]–[18].

28 *Westdeutsche* (n 27) 714–15.

29 A Scott and W Fratcher, *The Law of Trusts,* 4th edn (Boston, Little Brown, 1987) §462.4. Compare G and C Bogert, *The Law of Trusts and Trustees,* 2nd edn (St Pauls, West Publishing Co, 1977) § 461–472. Scott's analysis was approved in *Muschinski* (n 6) 614 (Deane J). See also *Parsons* (n 27) [10].

30 Scott's insistence that a backdated constructive trust was remedial has been criticised by other American writers: See, eg S Palmer, *The Law of Restitution*, vol 1 (Boston, Little Brown, 1978) 1, 6.

definition ignores the significance of judicial intervention in fashioning the terms of relief. Constructive trust relief, like other equitable relief, can be conditioned on the imposition of terms, the best known example being the constructive trust imposed over property legal title to which has passed under a rescinded voidable contract. Although the constructive trust arises at the date of election the court's role in imposing terms designed to restore the parties to their pre-contractual position will mean that the precise rights and obligations of the parties will only be determined at the date of judgment. Failure to comply with the conditions of relief will preclude avoidance of the contract and will confirm the beneficial title of the recipient of the property.

Lord Browne-Wilkinson assumed that English law did not recognise remedial constructive trusts: 'whether English law should follow the United States and Canada by adopting the remedial constructive trust will have to be decided in some future case when the point is directly in issue.'[31] But on his analysis it is hard to see why constructive trusts imposed in estoppel cases are not remedial in view of their prospective effect and the role of the court in fashioning relief.[32] Moreover, the readiness of the House of Lords in *Stack v Dowden*[33] to adopt a multi-factored approach in determining whether the criteria for a 'common intention' constructive trust have been met, ranging beyond the express and inferred intentions of the parties at the time of purchase, is more suggestive of the flexibility of remedialism than the predictability of the institutional constructive trust.

Lord Browne-Wilkinson's remedial constructive trust, in the sense of a constructive trust imposed by court order which can[34] operate prospectively from the date of judgment is the most controversial version of the remedial constructive trust. In Australia, where it applies, the only reason why it has caused few problems in practice is because courts have imposed it as an (often superfluous) vindicatory remedy in cases where no third party interests are in issue. As a proprietary remedy it has usually been awarded in precisely those cases in which its proprietary characteristics are irrelevant.

An example of a superfluous award of a prospective remedial constructive trust is the High Court of Australia's decision in *Muschinski v Dodds*.[35] The plaintiff and defendant, a de facto couple, purchased land as legal tenants in common with a view to developing a cottage on the land as an arts and crafts centre while living in a prefabricated home on the property. The plaintiff had paid ten-elevenths of the costs of the project by the time it was abandoned. Abandonment was due to

[31] *Westdeutsche* (n 27) 716.

[32] B McFarlane, *The Structure of Property Law* (Oxford, Hart Publishing, 2008) 466–71.

[33] *Stack v Dowden* [2007] UKHL 17, [2007] 2 AC 432 [69] (Baroness Hale). See now *Jones v Kernott* [2011] UKSC 53.

[34] Contrast: Bogert (n 29) §461–472 for whom the prospective operation of the remedial constructive trust was mandatory. See also the minority judgment in *Rawluk v Rawluk* [1990] 1 SCR 70 (SCC). D Waters, 'The Constructive Trust in Evolution: Substantive *and* Remedial' (1991) 10 *Estates and Trusts Journal* 334.

[35] *Muschinski* (n 6).

refusal of planning permission by the council and to the termination of the parties' relationship. A majority of the High Court, Brennan and Dawson JJ dissenting, held that the plaintiff was entitled to equitable relief in addition to the half-share in the property to which she was entitled under the tenancy in common. Mason and Deane JJ imposed a constructive trust for the benefit of both parties 'to repay to each her or his respective contribution and as to the residue for them both in equal shares.'[36] The constructive trust was to take effect prospectively, from the date of the publication of the High Court's reasons '[l]est the legitimate claims of third parties be adversely affected.'[37] The third judge who found in favour of the plaintiff, Gibbs CJ, saw no need to invoke the law of constructive trusts. He held that the plaintiff was entitled to equitable contribution for the amount in excess of half of the purchase moneys she had paid, secured by an equitable charge over the defendant's half-share.[38]

Deane J's judgment in *Muschinski* provides an instructive example of how traditional equitable doctrine can respond to contemporary problems which legislation has failed to address. But did the prospective remedial constructive trust in *Muschinski* achieve any purpose which could not have been accomplished by the award of some other recognised equitable relief? There was no evidence of third parties whose interests might have been prejudiced by the imposition of the trust. Even if creditors had claims on the property, the accounting order, secured by an equitable charge over the defendant's share of the property, proposed by Gibbs CJ, would have achieved a fair balance between the interests involved. As we will see, this is exactly the solution advocated by the *Third Restatement*. Moreover, the constructive trust imposed by Deane J was unusual. It did not entitle the plaintiff to an enhanced proportionate share in the co-owned property; it simply secured repayment of her contributions to the failed joint venture. Unlike the beneficiaries of most constructive trusts the plaintiff did not gain any increased share in the disputed property by reason of the trust's imposition.

If the facts of *Muschinski* were to recur today, in a situation to which family law property reallocation legislation did not apply, it is unlikely that a constructive trust would be imposed. Recent High Court authority has disapproved of the award of constructive trust relief which 'goes beyond the necessities of the case.'[39] It would be hard to justify the necessity of a constructive trust in a case of a failed joint venture where the accounting is not complex and orders can be effectively secured by the imposition of a charge or lien.

The *Third Restatement*, true to Scott's vision of the constructive trust, has rejected the 'date of judgment' trust. A restitutionary constructive trust imposed under §55 'exists' from the moment of the transaction out of which the trust

[36] Ibid 623–24 (Deane J).

[37] Ibid 623.

[38] Ibid 598. Gibbs CJ ultimately concurred with Mason and Deane JJ for the purpose of establishing a majority decision for the relief awarded.

[39] *John Alexander's Clubs* (n 6) [129]. See also *Bathurst City Council v PWC Properties Pty Ltd* [1998] HCA 59, (1998) 195 CLR 566, 584–85; *Giumelli v Giumelli* [1999] HCA 10, (1999) 196 CLR 101.

arises; alternatively, the trust arises on the date of judgment but 'relates back' to the transaction between the parties.[40] The commentary to the paragraph insists that the dating of the trust from the circumstances which give rise to its recognition does not amount to a rejection of the remedial character of the trust. Private law remedies generally operate in this backdated fashion. The amount of damages payable in tort or for a breach of contract may be determined by the court in a contested case, but the obligation to pay damages arises when damage occurs, assuming that proof of damage constitutes part of the cause of action. A damages award is therefore a response to a pre-existing state of affairs determined by the court.

Potential prejudice to third parties where a constructive trust is claimed under the *Third Restatement* is prevented not by a 'date of judgment' rule but by limiting the impact of the constructive trust in some 'third party' cases. For example, §50(4) provides that a claimant cannot recover more than her loss against an innocent recipient, and §61 provides that a claimant will not be permitted to invoke the constructive trust as a profit-disgorgement remedy at the expense of adequate provision for creditors and dependants of the innocent recipient.

The version of the remedial constructive trust promulgated by the *Third Restatement* is therefore not a 'discretionary date of imposition' trust of a kind rejected by English law. The date of imposition is the date of the circumstances giving rise to the trust. Specific provisions protect third party claimants while preserving a limited priority in insolvency for the constructive trust beneficiary, in some cases relegating her to the status of an equitable lien claimant. It is a straightforward matter to apply this model of the remedial constructive trust to cases of unjust enrichment and restitution for wrongs, where the date of receipt of benefit or of commission of wrong can usually be ascertained relatively easily. It would be a more complex matter to extend the model to other applications of the constructive trust, such as the 'common intention' constructive trust where there is often no clearly established date on which the claimant acted to her detriment in reliance on an intention or understanding that she would obtain an interest in the defendant's property.[41] But common law jurisdictions can learn at least two lessons from the *Restatement* model. First, a constructive trust is capable of being remedial without the date of imposition being, as Lord Browne-Wilkinson assumed, a matter for the exercise of judicial discretion. Secondly, a successful claimant need not necessarily enjoy all the incidents of a constructive trust. The *Restatement* limits the impact of the trust, for example on creditors, by denying to the claimant the profit-disgorgement incidents of constructive trusteeship. The same outcomes might be reached in jurisdictions outside the USA by devices such as imposing terms and conditions on the imposition of the trust or by requiring claimants to elect

[40] *Third Restatement* §55, Comment e.
[41] *Stack v Dowden* (n 33).

the award of the remedy so that its proprietary force derives from the date of election.[42]

III. Personal Relief as an Alternative to a Proprietary Order

Neither of the two senses of the word 'remedial' discussed above is wholly adequate, or sufficiently established by authority, to provide a settled meaning of the term 'remedial constructive trust'. But there is another sense in which all proprietary constructive trusts are remedial. If the criteria for the award of a constructive trust either have been met, or would have been met but for the absence of traceably identifiable property over which the trust can be imposed, personal relief is available, subject to the recognised bars to equitable relief, as an alternative remedy. On this analysis constructive trusts are not divisible between the institutional and the remedial. All proprietary constructive trusts[43] entitle the claimant to the award of a personal remedy provided that the criteria for the award of the constructive trust are satisfied.

Choosing the appropriate remedy is not, however, usually straightforward. Remedialism in the law of constructive trusts is not simply a matter of selecting the appropriate remedy on the given facts of the case. This is because the principles governing constructive trust relief depend on the nature of the claim in which relief is sought. Moreover, the relative ease or difficulty with which a proprietary remedy can be obtained is still explicable only in terms of the history of the cause of action in which proprietary relief is claimed. In some cases, such as constructive trusts imposed in cases of breach of fiduciary obligation, the proprietary remedy evolved out of equity's accounting procedures. In other cases, such as estoppel, proprietary and personal relief were from a relatively early stage recognised as remedial alternatives, while in yet other cases, such as restitution for unjust enrichment, remedial alternatives developed from parallel common law and equitable causes of action which, outside the USA at least, have still not been fully integrated. These different histories continue to obscure our understanding of the proprietary and personal alternatives of constructive trusteeship.

A. Breach of Trust and Other Fiduciary Obligations

The trustee's liability to make over property acquired in breach of fiduciary obligation to the trust, or to a beneficiary absolutely entitled to the property, arises out

[42] E Bant, 'Trusts, powers and liens: An exercise in ground-clearing' (2009) 3 *Journal of Equity* 286.

[43] This does not mean that constructive trusteeship awarded solely as a formula for personal relief, for example for knowingly or dishonestly assisting the commission of a breach of fiduciary obligation, generates a proprietary remedy. See n 13 above.

of the trustee's duty to account for the management of trust assets. The accounting process may reveal that trust property has been misappropriated by the trustee, or that the trustee has acquired assets from third parties in breach of his duty of loyalty.[44] The primary duty of the trustee is to account to the beneficiary for gains improperly acquired, but an order directing the trustee to transfer specific property to the trust will often be more convenient and economical than requiring the property to be valued for the purpose of ordering the trustee to pay the account assessed.

Considerations of convenience and ease of assessment are often overlooked in enumerating the advantages of the constructive trust. Few would consider that the claimant's convenience on its own justifies priority over the claims of creditors to the trustee's property. But in what the *Third Restatement* terms the 'two-party context', where the defendant is solvent, the constructive trust is a realistic remedy where the value of property is hard to establish or where the recovery of specific property is less costly than proof and recovery of its value. The constructive trust is employed in many fiduciary cases as a vindicatory remedy, being 'a flexible means of achieving specific restitution, justified by remedial economy and convenience to the claimant.'[45] For example, where a partner to a mining joint venture improperly uses information obtained in a fiduciary capacity to purchase for himself land under which valuable minerals have been discovered, a constructive trust over the land will often be a simpler remedy to enforce than a series of accounting orders which assess the present and future profits accruing to the fiduciary as a result of his breach of duty.[46]

Reasons of convenience also explain the constructive trust controversially ordered in *Boardman v Phipps*.[47] Critics of the decision have argued that the plaintiff beneficiary's relief should have been limited to an account of profits, either because Boardman was that rare bird, an honest fiduciary acting in breach of obligation, or because the constructive trust entitled the plaintiffs to shares which they had not previously owned and which could not have been purchased by the trust.[48] But while taking the accounts of the capital distributions and dividends already declared posed no problems, valuing the shareholdings in a recently reorganised private company would have been more complicated. Since it was assumed that there were no creditor or other third party interests to be prejudiced it was surely simpler to order a transfer of Boardman's and Tom Phipps's shares to

[44] R Chambers, 'Liability' in P Birks and A Pretto (eds) *Breach of Trust* (Oxford, Hart Publishing, 2002) 26–30. The beneficiaries can adopt or reject the traceable proceeds of misappropriated property: *Foskett v McKeown* [2000] UKHL 29, [2001] 1 AC 102, 130 (Lord Millett).

[45] *Third Restatement* (n 1) §55, Comment c.

[46] *LAC Minerals Ltd v International Corona Resources Ltd* (1989) 61 DLR (4th) 14 (SCC) 49 (La Forest J); *Third Restatement* (n 1) §55, Illustration 4. Assessing the capitalised value of a wasting asset such as a mine has presented courts with particular difficulties in assessing profit. Contrast *Chameleon Mining NL v Murchison Metals Ltd* [2010] FCA 1129 [1037] (Jacobson J) where the account ordered was described as 'difficult' and 'complex' but was nonetheless preferred to a constructive trust.

[47] *Boardman v Phipps* [1967] 2 AC 46 (HL).

[48] G Jones, 'Unjust Enrichment and the Fiduciary's Duty of Loyalty' (1968) 84 *LQR* 472, 481–86.

the plaintiff than to undertake a potentially complex valuation exercise. Moreover, the order made by Wilberforce J in *Boardman v Phipps* established an equitable framework for bargaining between the parties. The plaintiff could take the shares, thereby assuming a greater share of the commercial risk of the company which had been reorganised by Boardman's efforts, or take cash from the defendants for the shares, leaving Boardman and his co-defendant in control of the company. Not the least of the advantages of the constructive trust is that, like the injunction, the court order leaves open the possibility of negotiating a release from its application.[49]

Are there other applications of constructive trusteeship which are premised on the notion of the defendant accounting to the beneficiary as if he were an express trustee? Liability to account for having knowingly received property in breach of fiduciary obligation has come under intense judicial and academic scrutiny in recent years. On one view, equitable liability is always personal since the restitution of equitable property received or its traceable proceeds can be accomplished by an equitable proprietary claim without imposing the burden of establishing the defendant's knowledge on the plaintiff.[50] The plaintiff is entitled to recover trust property unless the defendant can show that he is a good faith purchaser for value without notice. But another view is that 'knowing receipt' liability can be either personal or proprietary, a proposition supported by some of the cases.[51] In a recent essay Charles Mitchell and Stephen Watterson have argued that a knowing recipient is liable to account in the same way that an express trustee must account for property received on the terms of the trust.[52] A consequence of their analysis of the constructive trustee as an 'as if express trustee' is that the constructive trustee will be subject to at least some of the core obligations of an express trustee, such as getting in, preserving and restoring trust property. The model is canvassed as the alternative to recognising recipient liability as a species of strict liability for unjust enrichment. A consequence of applying the 'as if express trustee' analysis to recipients is that the relief available against the recipient is not limited to restoring the value of the enrichment but includes gain-based remedies where the recipient has made a successful investment.

[49] Cf G Calabresi & A Melamed, 'Property Rules, Liability and Inalienability: One View of the Cathedral' (1972) 85 *Harvard Law Review* 1089.

[50] M Bryan, 'Recipient Liability under the Torrens System: Some Category Errors' in C Rickett and R Grantham (eds) *Structure and Justification in Private Law* (Oxford, Hart Publishing, 2008) 339. On this view, the onus rests on the recipient to show that he is a good faith purchaser for value without notice.

[51] Cf the order made by the New South Wales Court of Appeal in *Say-Dee Pty Ltd v Farah Constructions Pty Ltd* [2005] NSWCA 309 reversed sub nom *Farah Constructions* (n 13). The application of 'knowing receipt' principles to indefeasible title under the Torrens system still raises problems: *Super 1000 v Pacific General Securities* [2008] NSWSC 1222, (2008) 221 FLR 427 [215]–[234] (White J).

[52] C Mitchell and S Watterson, 'Remedies for Knowing Receipt' in C Mitchell (ed) *Constructive and Resulting Trusts* (Oxford, Hart Publishing, 2010) 115. For a criticism of this analysis see W Swadling, 'The Fiction of the Constructive Trust', 64 (2011) *Current Legal Problems* 399.

Where the constructive trust can be analysed in terms of the constructive trustee being an 'as if express trustee', so that the express trustee's liability to account becomes applicable it is easy to establish the terms on which proprietary and personal relief will be available. The law of express trusts provides an established remedial framework which can be adapted fairly easily to constructive trusts, having regard to the obvious differences that the constructive trustee has not been selected by a settlor and is not expected to perform the ongoing management obligations of an express trustee. Similar principles apply to the liability of a trustee de son tort, which lies on the borderline of the law of express and constructive trusts, being an express trust in all but the circumstance that the defendant was not appointed an express trustee.[53]

B. Estoppel

The constructive trust imposed in proprietary estoppel cases does not arise out of an obligation to account, and perhaps in consequence the law of estoppel is more explicitly remedial than other areas of equity to which the constructive trust applies. In early decisions on proprietary estoppel the defendant was ordered to transfer specific property to the plaintiff,[54] or, as in *Dillwyn v Llewelyn*,[55] a declaration that the plaintiff was entitled to the fee simple in land on which he had expended money was referred to a judge in chambers to settle a conveyance which complied with the terms of the order. The constructive trust was not premised on the defendant's liability to account, and the defendant was not a constructive trustee, as in the fiduciary cases, on the basis of being an 'as if express trustee'. It is relatively rare nowadays for a plaintiff in an estoppel claim to be awarded the fee simple in the defendant's land, but in these cases the constructive trust serves only as the contemporary substitute for the chancellor's jurisdiction to order directly a conveyance of land to be executed.

The academic literature on the aims of proprietary estoppel is substantial, and it is unnecessary for present purposes to explore the contested rationales of expectation enforcement, compensation for reliance loss or, more generally, the prevention of unconscionable conduct as grundnorms for equitable relief.[56] The practice

[53] D Heydon and M Leeming, *Jacobs' Law of Trusts in Australia,* 7th edn (Chatswood, LexisNexis Butterworths, 2006) para [1303]; *Mara v Browne* [1896] 1 Ch 199 (CA).

[54] *Hunt v Carew* (1649) Nelson 47, 21 ER 786; *Lester v Foxcroft* (1700) Colles 108, 1 ER 205. E Cooke, *The Modern Law of Estoppel* (Oxford, Oxford University Press, 2000) 42–43.

[55] *Dillwyn v Llewelyn* (1862) De GF&J 517, 45 ER 1285.

[56] S Bright and B McFarlane, 'Personal Liability in Proprietary Estoppel' [2005] *Conv* 14; S Gardner, 'The Remedial Discretion in Proprietary Estoppel: Again' (2006) 122 *LQR* 492; N Hopkins, 'Conscience, Discretion and the Creation of Property Rights' (2006) 26 *Legal Studies* 475; A Robertson,' The Reliance Basis of Proprietary Estoppel Remedies' [2008] *Conv* 295; A Robertson, 'Unconscionability and Proprietary Estoppel Remedies' in E Bant and M Harding (eds), *Exploring Private Law* (Melbourne, Cambridge University Press, 2010) 402.

of awarding personal relief in estoppel cases is well established.[57] Provided that a tender of compensation is not used as a means of forcing an inequitable solution on a claimant,[58] there is a convincing case for awarding personal relief more often than now occurs.[59] Assuming that estoppel enforces, at least in some cases, the plaintiff's reasonable expectations, there is no more reason why expectation enforcement in property law should result in an award of proprietary relief than the enforcement of expectations in contract law should routinely attract an award of specific performance.[60] But, regardless of doctrinal aim, courts apply what a leading writer has termed a 'remedial equation' in estoppel cases.[61] Where proprietary rights and personal licences to occupy land have been granted in 'two party' estoppel cases[62] the award will often reflect the claimant's subjective attachment to the land, no doubt as a result of expenditure incurred on it.[63] In such cases the award of proprietary relief is similar to the application of specific performance in awarding the plaintiff the subjective value of what was promised under the broken contract.[64] The significance of the claimant's subjective preference for specific property in the award of constructive trusts is discussed in more detail below.

C. Unjust Enrichment

Where constructive trusts are imposed in cases of breach of fiduciary obligation and estoppel the proprietary and personal remedial alternatives arise either directly from proof of the elements of the cause of action, in the case of estoppel, or as relief giving effect to the outcome of the accounting process applied to trustees and other

[57] *Unity Joint Stock Bank Mutual Banking Association v King* (1858) Beav 72, 53 ER 563; *Dodsworth v Dodsworth* (1973) 228 EG 1115 (CA); *Morris v Morris* [1982] 1 NSWLR 61 (NSWSC); *Giumelli v Giumelli* [1999] HCA 10, (1999) 196 CLR 101; *Jennings v Rice* [2002] EWCA Civ 159.

[58] *Milton v Proctor* (1989) NSW ConvR ¶55,450, ¶58,254 (Mahoney JA).

[59] See Bright and Macfarlane, 'Personal Liability in Proprietary Estoppel' (n 56).

[60] This is also true if relief in estoppel is, or should be, confined to protection of the plaintiff's reliance interest. See S Bright and B McFarlane, 'Proprietary Estoppel and Property Rights' (2005) 64 *CLJ* 449; Robertson, 'The Reliance Basis' (n 56); J Mee, 'The Role of Expectation in the Determination of Proprietary Estoppel Remedies' in M Dixon (ed), *Modern Studies in Property Law*, vol 5 (Oxford, Hart Publishing, 2009) 389.

[61] Robertson, 'Unconscionability and Proprietary Estoppel Remedies' (n 56) 403.

[62] Personal relief is usually appropriate where the interests of identified third parties are taken into account: *Giumelli* (n 57).

[63] *Dillwyn* (n 55); *Pascoe v Turner* [1979] 1 WLR 431 (CA); *Sullivan v Sullivan* [2006] NSWCA 312; *Thorner v Major* [2009] UKHL 18, [2009] 1 WLR 776 (where the varying extent of the improved farm property was held to be irrelevant). Against: *Sledmore v Dalby* (1996) 72 P&CR 196 (CA) where the fact that the representee was making only minimal use of the improved property suggested that the subjective attachment to the property was low. In the event it was held that the representee's equity had expired.

[64] D Friedmann, 'Economic Aspects of Damages and Specific Performance Compared' in D Saidov and R Cunnington (eds), *Contract Damages: Domestic and International Perspectives* (Oxford, Hart Publishing, 2008) 65, 68–69.

fiduciaries. In both cases the alternatives are derived, directly or indirectly, from proof of the elements of the cause of action.

The law of unjust enrichment differs from both these models.[65] In the USA the law of unjust enrichment is remedial, in that the basic elements of an unjust enrichment claim are common to the award of personal and proprietary relief, and the only additional requirements for the award of proprietary relief relate to proof of traceably identifiable property and to the court being satisfied that legitimate third party interests will be securely protected.[66] But the imposition of restitutionary constructive trusts for unjust enrichment does not work so simply in Australia. It is not the case in Australia that a limited number of recognised 'unjust factors' result in the award of personal or proprietary restitution, the precise nature of the relief awarded depending on proof of identifiable property and the balancing of the interests of third parties. Instead, proprietary restitution for unjust enrichment is disguised by labels which conceal the reality of a reversal of unjust enrichment. So some proprietary restitution which could most transparently be analysed in terms of failure of basis is concealed by judicial invocation of the principle of preventing unconscientious conduct.[67]

In other cases an unjust factor is recognised but a proprietary remedy is awarded only upon the application of criteria which bear no relation to the proprietary characteristics of the relief being ordered. For example, personal restitution for mistake can be obtained upon proof that the mistake caused the payment to be made[68] but recent authority suggests that proprietary relief will only be available where the mistake is known to the payee.[69] The criteria for the award of a proprietary remedy having, as its primary characteristic, the power to bind third parties should not depend on the state of knowledge of the second party recipient, who may in practice be quite unaffected by its award.[70]

Finally, and more controversially, the role of the resulting trust in reversing unjust enrichment has not been recognised by Australian courts.[71]

[65] But note the attempt to bring the claim to proprietary restitution for mistake within the fiduciary paradigm in *Chase Manhattan* (n 25).

[66] See *Third Restatement* §55, Comment a.

[67] *Muschinski* (n) 6.

[68] *Barclays Bank Ltd v WJ Simms, Son & Cooke (Southern) Ltd* [1980] 1 QB 677 (Comm); *Kleinwort Benson Ltd v Lincoln County Council* [1999] 2 AC 349 (HL); *David Securities Pty Ltd v Commonwealth Bank of Australia* (1992) 175 CLR 353 (HCA).

[69] *Westdeutsche* (n 27) 715 (Lord Browne-Wilkinson); *Wambo Coal* (n 15).

[70] The knowledge of the third party will be relevant under the doctrine of notice. For a fully worked out scheme of proprietary recovery based on second and third party knowledge, see McFarlane, *The Structure of Property Law* (n 32) Chapter 4.

[71] R Chambers, *Resulting Trusts* (Oxford, Clarendon Press, 1997); R Chambers, 'Is There a Presumption of Resulting Trust?' in Mitchell, *Constructive and Resulting Trusts* (n 52) 267. Contrast: W Swadling, 'Explaining Resulting Trusts' (2008) 124 *LQR* 72.

It would be possible, as an exercise in the reviled 'top down reasoning',[72] to hypothesise a law of unjust enrichment operating on the principle:

> return that property to me: you have been unjustly enriched at my expense, unless you can establish a defence such as change of position. If you cannot return my property because you no longer have it, and you cannot establish a defence, pay me the value of the property you received.

Such a principle ought to be attractive to any legal system which places a premium on the protection of private property rights. It would prioritise proprietary remedies, leaving the personal claim as residual relief to be awarded where the property had been disposed of in circumstances which do not entitle the recipient to the benefit of change of position or other relevant defence.

In practice the law of unjust enrichment does not work like this. Proprietary restitution in common law jurisdictions is the exception, not the rule, and even as an exception its availability has been criticised.[73] The reasons for its marginalisation are partly historical and partly policy-based. Historically, the fragmented treatment of equitable relief, including proprietary relief, by nineteenth century writers meant 'any common underpinnings linking together the situations in which a remedy was granted remained hidden.'[74] At the policy level several concerns have inhibited the development of proprietary restitution. One is the impact of proprietary restitution on the legitimate claims of unsecured creditors. Another concern, less often discussed in the literature, is that there is no social utility in imposing constructive trusts over property for which market substitutes can easily be obtained.[75] These concerns are legitimate, but it is unclear why they should be more significant in the law of unjust enrichment than in estoppel where the award of proprietary relief is fairly common.

Assuming the existence of a law of restitution for unjust enrichment based on proof of legally recognised 'unjust factors', three techniques could be applied to prevent proprietary relief from being imposed where it might prejudice the legitimate interests of third parties. One is to impose limitations on the award of a proprietary interest where the interests of a third party, such as a creditor or dependant, are in issue, for example by remitting the plaintiff's claim to that of an equitable lien. This is the approach adopted by the *Third Restatement*.[76] A second is to restrict the potential application of such orders by requiring plaintiffs to elect to rescind the transaction under which the recipient obtained title, thereby protecting the security of title of parties who obtained an interest in the property

[72] K Mason, 'Do Top-Down and Bottom-Up Reasoning Ever Meet?' in Bant and Harding, *Exploring Private Law* (n 56) 19.

[73] Swadling, 'Policy Arguments for Proprietary Restitution' (n 14).

[74] D Ibbetson, *A Historical Introduction to the Law of Obligations* (Oxford, Oxford University Press, 1999) 283.

[75] The analogy with specific performance is obviously relevant in this context: *Aristoc Industries Pty Ltd v RA Wenham (Builders) Pty Ltd* [1965] NSWR 581 (NSWSC).

[76] *Third Restatement* §61(1).

prior to election.[77] These two techniques have the merit of being explicitly directed to the consequences of imposing a proprietary remedy, in terms of potential third party prejudice and entitlement to the benefits of asset appreciation. The third technique, that of superimposing additional requirements on the 'unjust factor' such as the defendant's knowledge of the claimant's mistake, is less appropriate than the other two because the additional requirements are not directed to the consequences of imposing a proprietary, as opposed to a personal, order.

IV. Motivations and Policies

The comments to §55 of the *Third Restatement* distinguish between constructive trusts imposed in two-party cases and constructive trusts imposed in three-party cases. The distinction is a reminder that although the potential impact of the remedy on third party interests is a critical consideration in constructive trust cases it is not the only consideration. Indeed, there are many cases in which third party claims are not relevant at all.

Some of the reasons why, in a two-party case against a solvent defendant, a constructive trust is preferred to alternative equitable relief have already been mentioned. One consideration is the comparative simplicity of the remedy. In cases where it is available the account of profits is a complex remedy to administer. Equitable accounting procedures, although simpler than the action of account at common law, can be procedurally complex and time-consuming.[78] Where accounts are taken upon failure of a joint venture, assessment may have to be remitted to an independent accountant and the determination of the state of the accounts is likely to be a lengthy process.[79] Complexity of calculation is not a reason for refusing relief, but where the constructive trust is an alternative it will generally be simpler than an accounting remedy to administer and enforce.

As the *Third Restatement* observes, '[c]onstructive trust in a two-party case is a flexible means of achieving specific restitution, justified by remedial economy and convenience to the claimant'.[80] The remedy is superfluous where money is claimed from a solvent defendant since, assuming that the plaintiff's money can be identified, a proprietary order is no more advantageous to a claimant than a personal remedy. But it is useful where restitution is sought of a chattel 'when the property has special value for the claimant; when it has appreciated in value; when its value might be difficult to establish; or when recovery of a specific thing is merely less costly than proof and recovery of its value'.[81] In other words, the constructive trust

[77] Bant, 'Trusts, Powers and Liens' (n 42).

[78] R Meagher, D Heydon and M Leeming, *Meagher, Gummow & Lehane's Equity: Doctrine and Remedies*, 4th edn (Chatswood, Butterworths LexisNexis, 2002) para [25–005].

[79] *Chameleon Mining* (n 46) [1037] (Jacobson J).

[80] *Third Restatement* §55, Comment c.

[81] Ibid.

in a two-party case is a simple vindicatory remedy. Just as specific performance enforces the plaintiff's subjective wish to secure the precise performance of the agreed contract even if alternative performance might economically be no less valuable,[82] so the constructive trust enforces the plaintiff's subjective preference to obtain an interest in identified property, whether that preference is for restitution, enforcement of a reasonable expectation, or for obtaining the fruits of the defendant's wrongdoing. This is most obviously the case where a constructive trust is imposed over property transmissible under a specifically enforceable contract, since the constructive trust reinforces the plaintiff's claim to property which has special value, or at least no readily available market substitute.[83]

Subjective preference is also enforced in those proprietary estoppel cases where the intensive nature of the work undertaken on the defendant's land creates a strong subjective attachment to the land which cannot be satisfied by a monetary payment.[84] It may also explain some instances of the award of a constructive (or resulting) trust for unjust enrichment, defining subjective preference for this purpose to include a desire to exploit the value of the property, as well as a desire to derive personal enjoyment from its use.[85] Finally, the aim of most common intention, Australian-style unconscionability and Canadian-style unjust enrichment constructive trusts imposed in family home cases is not usually to satisfy any desire or expectation on the part of the plaintiff to live in the property claimed, but a desire to unlock and realise the appreciated capital value of the home, usually by means of its sale soon after the beneficial interests have been judicially defined. Unless specific creditors have been identified,[86] and subject to existing mortgages taken over the home, the family home cases are analysed as 'two-party' contests; a combination of the likelihood of sale occurring soon after the judicial definition of beneficial title and conveyancing practice designed to alert purchasers to the realities of the sharing of beneficial title in the home[87] minimise the risks of third parties being adversely affected by enforcement of the trust. A positive feature of the *Third Restatement*'s treatment of constructive trusts is that it highlights the vindicatory functions of the trust, particularly in fulfilling a claimant's simple wish to claim or recover specific property, that are sometimes overlooked in debates about the role of proprietary relief.

The position changes when a constructive trust is imposed in what the *Third Restatement* terms a 'three-party' contest, so that the claimant's aim is to achieve priority over unsecured creditors, as well as later secured creditors who are not good

[82] Friedmann, 'Economic Aspects of Damages and Specific Performance Compared' (n 64) 68. Expectation damages for breach of contract also give effect, in monetary form, to the plaintiff's subjective preference, subject to restrictions where the preference is unreasonable: *Tabcorp Holdings Pty Ltd v Bowen Investments Pty Ltd* [2009] HCA 8, (2009) 236 CLR 272.

[83] K Barnett, 'Substitutability and Disgorgement Damages in Contract' in Bant and Harding, *Exploring Private Law* (n 56) 377.

[84] *Dillwyn* (n 55).

[85] *Black* (n 22); *Nelson v Nelson* (1995) 184 CLR 538 (HCA); *Brown v Brown* (1993) 31 NSWLR 582 (NSWCA).

[86] As in *Parsons* (n 27).

[87] *Stack v Dowden* (n 33) [50]–[52] (Baroness Hale) on the role of Land Registry practice in identifying third party interests (and on how that practice might be taken further).

faith purchasers or who cannot assert an indefeasible title to the disputed property. The *Third Restatement* adopts the conventional, but not uncontroversial, view that where D has been unjustly enriched at the expense of P, D's creditors cannot stand in a better position than D.[88] The creditors, it is argued, would be unjustly enriched at P's expense if their claim could be satisfied out of P's property.[89] The argument rests on the assumption that the creditors are voluntary risk takers whereas the unjust enrichment claimant is the victim of a defective, and therefore involuntary, transaction which justifies the award of a proprietary remedy.[90]

The assumption that creditors, including tort victims, are voluntary and presumably rational assessors of commercial risk is disputable. It is not the aim of this paper to evaluate the competing arguments.[91] More relevant for present purposes is the *Third Restatement*'s strategy for resolving 'three-party' disputes. Although the principle that a constructive trust claim will defeat unsecured creditor claims is confirmed by §55 the application of the principle is modified in practice by countervailing rules which limit the scope of the trust. One is the application of tracing rules which are 'rough but not altogether arbitrary in their application because they serve to protect the creditor's position'.[92] Another, already mentioned, prohibits the constructive trust claimant from claiming more than her loss where an innocent defendant has realised consequential gains which could not have been captured by the plaintiff in a personal claim for unjust enrichment.[93] Moreover, a constructive trust claimant will not be entitled to obtain a profitable remedy in restitution at the expense of adequate provision for creditors and dependants of the recipient.[94] The practical effect of these restrictions is to make the equitable lien, and not the constructive trust, the effective proprietary remedy in 'three-party' cases.

V. Identifying 'Two-Party' and 'Three-Party' Proprietary Restitution

The most problematic feature of the *Third Restatement*'s scheme of proprietary restitution is the distinction it draws between 'two-party' and 'three-party' restitution contests. In the abstract there is a great deal to be said for a scheme of propri-

[88] Cf *Attorney-General for Hong Kong v Reid* [1994] 1 AC 324 (PC) 331 (Lord Templeman). See A Hicks, 'The Remedial Principle of *Keech v Sandford* reconsidered' [2010] *CLJ* 287, 316–18.

[89] *Third Restatement* §55, Comment d.

[90] Exponents of risk analysis include D Paciocco, 'The Remedial Constructive Trust: a Principled Basis for Priorities' (1989) *Canadian Bar Review* 311; E Sherwin, 'Constructive Trusts and Bankruptcy' (1989) *University of Illinois Law Review* 297; A Burrows, 'Proprietary Restitution: Unmasking Unjust Enrichment' (2001) 117 *LQR* 412.

[91] Swadling, 'Policy Arguments for Proprietary Restitution' (n 14). S Worthington, 'Property, Obligations and Insolvency Policy' (2005) 4 *Journal of International Banking and Finance Law* 100; Calnan, *Proprietary Rights and Insolvency*, (n 25) paras [1.146]–[1.156].

[92] *Third Restatement* §55, Comment g.

[93] *Third Restatement* §50(4); §56(4).

[94] *Third Restatement* §61(1).

etary remedies which differentiates between disputes where third party interests will be affected and others where they will be absent. But the major objection to such a scheme is that every 'two-party' claim is potentially a 'three-party' claim; a constructive trust which provides appropriate relief 'inter partes' may be rendered inequitable by the fact that creditors have claims to the property in dispute which have not been identified in the course of the constructive trust litigation.

Viewed solely from the perspective of promoting 'fair process' in litigating constructive trust claims, *Chase Manhattan*[95] is an 'easy' case for the law of proprietary restitution, in spite of the extensive academic literature debating the merits of the decision. The interests of creditors in the insolvent Israel-British Bank were well known, and it would have been a relatively straightforward if time-consuming exercise for the court to have taken account of them, had it been required to do so.[96] The more difficult question is to determine how, if at all, such interests should be evaluated in competition with the proprietary unjust enrichment claim. Should they be completely ignored, a solution suggested by the outcome of the *Chase Manhattan* litigation? Should the constructive trust claimant be remitted to a personal remedy provable in insolvency? Should some creditors, such as those ignorant of the mistake, be favoured over others? Or should an equitable lien be preferred to a constructive trust, along lines indicated by the *Third Restatement*? There are no easy, and no certainly no automatic, answers to these questions, but at least any exercise in evaluating the competing interests would have been informed by a full understanding of what these interests were. *Chase Manhattan* is unambiguously a 'three-party' case.

In contrast, other cases are ambiguously 'three party' cases because the existence or the precise extent of third party claims are unknown. The claim in *Boardman v Phipps*[97] was analysed as a 'two-party' claim in view of the undoubted solvency of the principal defendant. The parties to the dispute had no incentive to explore the appropriateness of the constructive trust on the assumption that creditors might have claims on Boardman's property. The convenience of the remedy, though not the criteria for its award, was accepted by courts and litigants alike. In a constructive trust dispute neither party may have an interest in identifying third party claims which might complicate questions of proof and qualify any beneficial interest awarded. In the *John Alexander's Clubs* case, for example, entitlement to an unregistered equitable mortgage over the property to which the constructive trust was claimed was only directly brought to the attention of the New South Wales Court of Appeal after it had declared the existence of a constructive trust which would have prejudiced the mortgagee's security.[98] The High Court held that there was evidence of the mortgage of which account should have been taken by the Court of Appeal in

[95] *Chase Manhattan* (n 25).
[96] In *Chase Manhattan* Goulding J was only invited to decide whether the plaintiff was entitled to a constructive trust. No question of tracing and claiming the mistaken payment arose: ibid 116.
[97] *Boardman* (n 47).
[98] *White City Tennis Club Ltd v John Alexander's Clubs Pty Ltd* [2009] NSWCA 19.

determining equitable relief[99] but the decision nonetheless illustrates the difficulties courts can experience in determining whether a constructive trust is being claimed in the context of a 'two party' or a 'three party' case.

The issue is an important one for Australian law which awards remedial constructive trusts in 'two-party' cases but which attempts to circumscribe proprietary relief in 'three-party' cases where the legitimate personal or proprietary interests of third parties would be prejudiced. The High Court's decision in *John Alexander's Clubs* attempts to identify the boundary between the two types of case by imposing procedural requirements on constructive trust claimants designed to flush out the existence of third party interests. For example, any person who will be affected by the making of a proprietary order is a 'necessary party' who must be joined to the litigation.[100] Further, where for any reason the third party has not been joined, that party has standing to have the constructive trust order set aside.[101] The decision recognises that a doctrine of remedial constructive trusts which permits a constructive trust to be imposed in 'two-party' cases in order to give effect to the claimant's subjective preference to own or to recover property, or to exploit its economic value, will only be workable if it is supplemented by adjectival provisions directed to identifying whether the dispute is in fact a 'three-party' contest. Without the existence of such provisions any scheme for awarding constructive trusts such as that proposed by the *Third Restatement* carries the risk of 'proprietary overkill' by failing to identify all the interests at stake when a proprietary claim is made.

VI. Conclusion

The remedial constructive trust has its detractors but the author of this chapter is not among their number. Debates about the merits of the trust have been bedevilled by the failure on the part of supporters and critics alike to define their terms. In the limited sense of the term identified in this chapter the remedial constructive trust has long existed. Whenever the constructive trust is employed as a proprietary remedy the alternative of ordering personal relief must always be considered, and choice exercised according to flexible but structured criteria. This is as true of trusts which take effect from the circumstances giving rise to their award as it is to trusts taking effect from the date of judicial decree. Paragraph 55 of the *Third Restatement* offers a blueprint for a model of remedial constructive trusteeship. Its techniques, such as remitting plaintiffs to equitable lien protection and conditioning relief on the making of provision for creditors, repay close study. By distinguishing between 'two-party' constructive trust cases and 'three-party' cases the *Restatement* highlights the role of subjective preference in two-party claims to constructive trusts.

[99] *John Alexander's Clubs* (n 6) [127].
[100] Ibid [131].
[101] Ibid [137].

The *Restatement* also reminds us that priority on insolvency is not the only policy consideration which determines the availability of proprietary relief. Every 'two-party' claim, however, is in danger of being converted into a 'three-party' claim by reason of unascertained creditor claims. The spectre of potential creditor claims is more worrying, from the court's perspective, than the reality of creditors contesting the constructive trust claim since the latter can be resolved by a variety of techniques, including the application of priority rules. Assuming that courts continue to impose constructive trusts to fulfil a variety of 'two party' and 'three party' aims, only carefully crafted adjectival provisions which identify relevant third party personal and proprietary interests and join them to the constructive trust litigation can make remedialism in constructive trust law workable.

11

Thoughts on Equity in New Zealand and New South Wales

ANDREW BUTLER AND TIM MILLER*

I. Introduction

We mean no disservice when we say that the law of equity and trusts in New South Wales is notoriously conservative. By conservative we mean an insistence by many within the New South Wales legal community—be it bench, bar, or academy—that equity and trusts law maintains a particular historical, intellectual and, ultimately, doctrinal position which is said to be purer and closer to the true traditions of equity and trusts.[1] For this group, New South Wales is seen as the last outpost of the true equity.[2] Certain developments elsewhere, such as Canada and New Zealand, are regarded with suspicion, if not treated with outright scorn. This view is probably no more apparent than in the preface to the fourth edition of *Meagher, Gummow and Lehane's Equity: Doctrines and Remedies*, where its authors suggest that:

> In New Zealand, the prospect of any development of equitable principle seems remote short of a revolution on the Court of Appeal. The blame is largely attributable to Lord Cooke's misguided endeavours. That one man could, in a few years, cause such destruction exposes the fragility of contemporary legal systems and the need for vigilant exposure and rooting out of error.[3]

A not dissimilar sentiment has been expressed more recently by Young JA in his short review of the fourth edition of Samantha Hepburn's *Principles of Equity and Trusts*.[4] Though generally positive about Hepburn's book, his Honour did note

* We thank Matt Dodd and Rupert Rouch for their research assistance.

[1] But see M Kirby, 'Equity's Australian Isolationism' (2008) 8 *Queensland University of Technology Law & Justice Journal* 444.

[2] The only hope for equity in New Zealand, on this view, would have been if New Zealand had never separated from New South Wales! For an overview of New Zealand's short existence as a part of New South Wales see P Joseph, *Constitutional and Administrative Law in New Zealand*, 2nd edn (Wellington, Brookers, 2001) para [2.3].

[3] R Meagher, D Heydon and M Leeming, *Meagher, Gummow & Lehane's Equity: Doctrine and Remedies*, 4th edn (Chatswood, Butterworths LexisNexis, 2002) xi.

[4] P Young, 'Book Review: Principles of Equity and Trusts' (2010) 84 *Australian Law Journal* 657, reviewing S Hepburn, *Principles of Equity and Trusts*, 4th edn (Annandale, Federation Press, 2009).

rather disapprovingly that 'a New South Wales equity lawyer does notice that the book strays from the narrow way in that there is some reliance on New Zealand thinking which has been abrogated in New South Wales courts'.[5]

Adherence to the so-called 'narrow way' is no doubt a badge of honour for many. This proudly atavistic approach to the law of equity reflects the view expressed by Viscount Simonds over 50 years ago in *Chapman v Chapman* that in equity

> the range of authority can only be determined by seeing what jurisdiction the great equity judges of the past assumed and how they justified that assumption … It may well be that the result is not logical, and it may be asked why, if the jurisdiction of the court extended to this thing, it did not extend to that also. But, my Lords that question is as vain in the sphere of jurisdiction as it is in the sphere of substantive law. We are as little justified in saying that a court has a certain jurisdiction, merely because we think it ought to have it, as we should be in declaring that the substantive law is something different from what it has always been declared to be, merely *because we think it ought to be so*. It is even possible that we are not wiser than our ancestors. It is for the legislature, which does not rest under that disability, to determine whether there should be a change in the law and what that change should be.[6]

However, as Kirby J has observed, this approach is not necessarily the result of uncritical acceptance of the wisdom of old, but rather:

> The strong passions that are engendered in Australia over the development and reformulations of equitable doctrine represent a tribute brought to the table by highly knowledgeable lawyers who cherish the important, ameliorating role that equity doctrine and its remedies have played over the centuries. Because equity is often concerned with the incidents of property rights, there is a natural and proper anxiety on the part of knowledgeable lawyers about any unthinking tinkering with long settled rules that give the shape of certainty to the important investment decisions of citizens and promise predictability to the expression and affirmation of their legal expectations.[7]

It is clear, therefore, that New South Welsh equity has much to offer. At times it makes the New Zealand approach to equity, and in particular, the simplification project initiated by Lord Cooke, appear as if it always elects the Gordian knot solution, rather than taking the time, as many New South Welsh judges and academics would purport to do, to tease out the distinct threads of equitable doctrines and maxims, so that the metaphorical equitable rope is not unnecessarily severed (or perhaps, more accurately, so it is not unnecessarily frayed).

By the same token, we are of the view that 'New Zealand thinking' has a thing or two to teach New South Welsh and, more broadly, Australian equity. The purpose of this chapter, therefore, is to stimulate a discussion on the areas where we think New Zealand has something worthwhile to offer Australian equity. The broad theme of this chapter is that it is acceptable for the law (be it common law or statute) and equity to both interact and mingle, where appropriate. In general,

[5] Ibid.
[6] *Chapman v Chapman* [1954] AC 429 (HL) 444.
[7] Kirby, 'Isolationism' (n 1) 44.

it will be appropriate where the purpose and function of the two can properly be regarded as the same. We begin with a general defence of this view and then move on to discuss its application by reference to the topics of exemplary damages, causation of loss for breach of non-custodial fiduciary duties, and equitable estoppel. We should stress, however, that because the coverage of this chapter is wide, the focus is more on broad themes than doctrinal niceties or in-depth case studies. Further, as the title suggests, the principal focus is on New Zealand and New South Wales, but with some consideration of other jurisdictions where appropriate.

II. The Influence of 'Other Law'

Any discussion of the differences between equity in New Zealand and New South Wales must start with that most loaded of terms, 'fusion'. Of course, there is nothing controversial in the fact that there has been a fusion of jurisdictions, in the sense that the courts in New Zealand and Australia exercise both common law and equitable jurisdiction. Rather, the controversy lies in what results from that fact.

The orthodox view in New South Wales appears to be that nothing substantive results from this fusion. That is, 'the Judicature procedure was not designed of itself to be a source of change of substantive rules, whether legal or equitable'.[8] To state otherwise is to buy into what *Meagher, Gummow and Lehane* describes as the 'fusion fallacy':

> The fusion fallacy involves the administration of a remedy, for example, common law damages for breach of fiduciary duty not previously available either at law or in equity, or the modification of principles in one branch of the jurisdiction by concepts which are imported from the other and are thus foreign, for example by holding that the existence of a duty of care in tort may be tested by asking whether the parties concerned are in fiduciary relations.[9]

In this section we begin by picking up on the second example given in this passage: that of borrowing. In doing so, we challenge the idea that it is impermissible for equity to borrow from the common law. To be clear we are not saying that there is a case for arguing that such 'borrowing' was intended by, or is a necessary or automatic consequence of, the administrative fusion of common law and equitable jurisdictions (so-called 'automatic fusion').[10] As Mason P noted in his judgment in *Harris v Digital Pulse*, 'that would be a fusion fallacy of a different sort, because there is much authority supporting the proposition that the fusion effected by the statute was of an administrative and procedural character'.[11] What we want to examine

[8] Meagher, Heydon and Leeming, *Equity* (n 3) para [2–105].
[9] Ibid.
[10] J Edelman, 'A "Fusion Fallacy" Fallacy?' (2003) 119 *LQR* 375, 377.
[11] *Harris v Digital Pulse Pty Ltd* [2003] NSWCA 10, (2003) 56 NSWLR 298 [139].

and challenge from a normative perspective is the proposition that courts in developing the law of equity should not borrow from the common law.

We have suggested in the introduction to this chapter that there appears to be a real concern in New South Wales that equity maintains its historical and doctrinal purity. Although this concern could be criticised as a form of uncritical 'ancestor worship',[12] there is a certain attraction to the view that such purity is a worthwhile end in itself. However, as we have already foreshadowed, there is clearly more to this view than that. A principal concern, among others, is that equity continues to fulfil its proper role vis-à-vis the law. As noted in an article by Meagher and Maroya:

> It is one thing to say, as Lord Redesdale is said to have, that yesterday's equity is tomorrow's law: 'A great part of what is now strict law was formerly considered as equity, and the equitable decisions of this age will unavoidably be ranked under the strict law of the next.' That is a pellucid observation of equity's 'supplementary' function, but it is otherwise a fact that hardly needs acclaiming or bewailing. It is quite another thing to declare that today's law will be tomorrow's equity. And that, it will be noted, Lord Redesdale did not say. That is an entirely different proposition, and one that sits quite uncomfortably with equity's corrective and supplemental function. In order for equity to perform its function, there must remain alive some meaningful distinction between equitable and legal doctrine, between equitable and legal remedies.[13]

There is force in these comments. They should sit at the forefront of one's mind when considering whether the common law might provide some guidance on how the law of equity ought to develop. However, what they say to us is that courts should be cautious about, but not completely dismissive of, the possibility that the common law might, at times, provide a guide to equity's development.

We are encouraged in this view by three considerations. First, it is simply ahistorical to suggest that equity has never developed by analogy with the common law. As Mason P notes in *Harris v Digital Pulse*, equity has, at times, developed in this way, even before the reforms of the Judicature Acts. Examples of this phenomenon are, 'collected under the rubrics of the maxim "equity follows the law" or equity's "concurrent jurisdiction"'.[14] Further, the Judicature Acts placed no restriction on equity continuing to develop in this way.[15] Of course, this does not mean that equity *ought* always to develop by analogy with the common law—that is a question that must be addressed in the particular instance in which it arises. Mason

[12] See M Kirby, 'Constitutional Interpretation and Original Intent: A Form of Ancestor Worship' (2000) 24 *Melbourne University Law Review* 1, 1 where Kirby J, writing extra-judicially, borrows the phrase from Binnie J in describing the 'original meaning/intent' approach to constitutional interpretation.

[13] R Meagher and A Maroya, 'Crypto-Fiduciary Duties' (2003) 26 *University of New South Wales Law Journal* 348, 349 citing *Spect v Spect* (1891) 26 P 203, 205 (Harrison J) and *Roxborough v Rothmans of Pall Mall Australia Ltd* [2001] HCA 68, (2001) 208 CLR 516, 554 (Gummow J). See also P Keane, 'The 2009 WA Lee Lecture in Equity: The conscience of equity' (2010) 84 *Australian Law Journal* 92.

[14] *Harris* (n 11) [143]. For instance, limitation by analogy: see Tipping J's comments in *Murray v Morel & Co Ltd* [2007] NZSC 27, [2007] 3 NZLR 721.

[15] On this point, see the remarks of Professor Tilbury cited by Mason P in *Harris* (n 11) [154].

P's point does show, however, that the evolution of equity by analogy with the common law is not as doctrinally suspect as some would have it.

Secondly, Meagher and Maroya's view is premised on there always being harsh common law rules, which in turn require equity to step in to correct and supplement. While it is true that equity has in the past, and sometimes still does, fulfill this role vis-à-vis the common law there is a certain absurdity in their implication that the historical harshness of the common law be maintained so that equity can come to the rescue. It is fair to say that the common law has evolved significantly from the inflexible writs of old (or at least has attempted to) in order to bring a more modern, flexible, fact-sensitive approach to the resolution of legal disputes. On occasion, equity has gone the opposite way. As a result, it may be that, in some circumstances, the common law can correct or at least provide some guidance to the law of equity.

The final consideration we want to address concerns the normative point. Butler has suggested elsewhere, when commenting on *Day v Mead*[16] in an article dedicated to the late Lord Cooke, that

> it has to be accepted that equity does not operate in a time warp. What counts is not why, historically, certain positions were adopted in equity, but rather whether those positions ought to be maintained in light of modern conditions. Among those modern conditions is the test of legal rationality, which asks whether there is a principled reason for the position to be maintained. One of the considerations relevant to that is whether a particular component of the legal system is operating in a manner cognisant of the rules and principles operating in other areas.[17]

We should stress that this approach is not necessarily synonymous with Professor Burrows' view that 'where, on close examination, like cases are not being treated alike … fusion of common law and equity is required in order to eradicate that inconsistency'.[18] This is because there may be very good reasons to treat what at first blush appear to be like cases differently in order to preserve or give effect to the different purposes and functions of law and equity. We discuss this point further below in relation to comments made by Elias CJ in *Premium Real Estate v Stevens*.[19] This is not to say, however, that law and equity cannot borrow from one another in deciding how to carry out their distinct functions or provide the same response where their particular function is truly the same. We appreciate also that the required level of similarity and therefore the permitted level of borrowing is something about which reasonable minds may differ.

The test of legal rationality outlined above suggests also that equity can, and should where appropriate, take cues in its development from developments in

[16] *Day v Mead* [1987] 2 NZLR 443 (NZCA).

[17] A Butler, 'Simplicity and Innovation in the Law of Equity and Trusts: The Cooke Era' (2008) 39 *Victoria University of Wellington Law Review* 167, 173.

[18] A Burrows *Fusing Common Law and Equity: Remedies, Restitution and Reform* (Hong Kong, Sweet & Maxwell, 2002) 3, cited in Edelman, 'Fusion Fallacy' (n 10) 377–78.

[19] *Premium Real Estate v Stevens* [2009] NZSC 15, [2009] 2 NZLR 384 (the neutral citation has the parties as *Stevens v Premium Real Estate*).

statute law. It is to this topic that we briefly now turn. In New Zealand, the seeds of this approach were sown by Cooke P in his judgment in *Day v Mead*. In this case, the President, as he then was, reasoned that Parliament's recognition of the concept of contributory negligence in the Contributory Negligence Act 1947 provided support for recognising a similar concept in equity (the particular case being concerned with a proven breach of fiduciary law).[20] In his view:

> Whether or not there are reported cases in which compensation for breach of a fiduciary obligation has been assessed on the footing that the plaintiff should accept some share of the responsibility, there appears to be no solid reason for denying jurisdiction to follow that obviously just course, especially now that law and equity have mingled or are interacting. Moreover, assuming that the Contributory Negligence Act does not itself apply, it is nevertheless helpful as an analogy, on the principle to which we in New Zealand are increasingly giving weight that *the evolution of Judge-made law may be influenced by the ideas of the legislature as reflected in contemporary statutes and by other current trends.*[21]

One would imagine that for many in the New South Welsh legal community (and elsewhere) Cooke P's view that equity may be influenced by contemporary statutes and other current trends is a dangerous one. In the first place, this is because the assertion that law and equity are now mingled in a substantive sense lacks foundation (although it is obviously correct—in fact trite—to say that they 'are interacting'). Secondly, at a more general level, it is because it shows a preparedness to question and override long-established principles of equity in the name of whatever is currently in vogue. This could legitimately be seen as problematic because it does not account for the reality that policy, as expressed in statutes, is often as changeable as the fortunes of those who govern. Any attempt to tailor an equitable doctrine to the particular policy of the government of the day risks undermining years of carefully crafted judge-made law and with it the independence of the judicial enterprise.[22] The final objection is likely to be that if developments in statute law are to influence the development of equity, this should only be through direct legislative intervention.[23] On this view, it is not for the courts to divine some sort of notional parliamentary intention by looking to what Parliament has done in other areas of the law.

As to the first objection, we reiterate the point made above about the test of legal rationality. Those observations apply equally to the second objection. That objection also has less force in situations where policy choices are contained in enduring statutes (that is, statutes that successive governments have chosen not to alter in any material way) or where there is bipartisan support for a particular legislative measure. At the time judgment was given in *Day v Mead*, for instance, the Contributory

[20] For Australian criticisms of this approach see Meagher, Heydon and Leeming (n 3) 838; K Handley, 'Reduction of Damages Awards', in P Finn (ed), *Essays on Damages* (Sydney, Lawbook Co, 1992) 127. But see Butler, 'The Cooke Era' (n 17).

[21] *Day v Mead* (n 16) 15–16 (emphasis added).

[22] For other potential criticisms see Butler (n 17) 173.

[23] See the comments of Viscount Simonds in *Chapman* cited above (n 6).

Negligence Act 1947 was 40 years old. It was hardly, at that time, a trend susceptible to the winds of political change. Indeed, it remains in force some 25 years or so after the Court of Appeal gave judgment in *Day v Mead.*

As to the objection that changes in equity should only come through express legislative action, the simple answer—in the New Zealand context anyway—is that legislative attention to reform of the law of equity and trusts is notoriously lacking. A prime example is the successive but ultimately fruitless attempts to reform trusts law in New Zealand.[24] This phenomenon can be explained, in part, by the fact that for many law reformers equity and trusts are not particularly 'sexy' subjects. It may be attributable also to what many who try to familiarise themselves with equity perceive as its extreme opaqueness. We are reminded here of a passage from an article by Professor Worthington. Speaking about the lack of knowledge among law graduates in the areas of property law and equity, she observed:

> One suspects that student experience of Equity and Land Law courses has much to answer for. At their worst, the 'fog' of some equity teaching and the unrelenting doctrinaire nature of some Land Law courses mean that students commonly approach all 'property' issues with a mixture of dread and resignation.[25]

The important point, therefore, is that the judiciary has, for the most part, been left to attend on its own to the development of equity and trusts. That being the case, it appears less unobjectionable for the judiciary to consider what Parliament has done elsewhere when considering whether and what direction (if any) the law of equity ought to take.

III. Exemplary Damages

We now discuss an example where we think Australian equity should adopt a remedy from the common law; that is, exemplary damages. We do so for two reasons: first, the fusion debate is most often played out in the area of remedies, thus making this example a logical starting point; secondly, the availability of this remedy was rejected by the New South Wales Court of Appeal in *Harris*, but it is yet to be considered by the High Court of Australia.

In New Zealand it is now well-established that 'common law' remedies, including exemplary damages, can be awarded for breaches of equitable obligations. This has been the case since at least the time of the Court of Appeal's decision in *Day v Mead*. Any doubt about that was removed in *Aquaculture Corporation v New*

[24] Although the Law Commission does appear to be finally turning its mind to possible reforms in the law of trusts: see New Zealand Law Commission, *Review of Trusts Law in New Zealand* (NZLC IP19, 2010).

[25] S Worthington, 'Rehabilitating Personal Property Law as a Serious Topic for Research and Teaching' (2002) 36 *Canadian Business Law Journal* 238, 238. The passage was cited extra-judicially by Gummow J in W Gummow, 'Equity: Too Successful?' (2003) 77 *Australian Law Journal* 30, 30.

Zealand Green Mussel Co Ltd where, in holding that exemplary damages were available in an action for breach of confidence, Cooke P said:

> For all purposes now material, equity and common law are mingled and merged. The practicality of the matter is that in the circumstances of the dealings between the parties the law imposes a duty of confidence. For its breach a full range of remedies should now be available as appropriate, no matter whether they originated in common law, equity, or statute.[26]

Cooke P's comments were subsequently endorsed by the Supreme Court of Canada in cases such as *Norberg v Wynrib*.[27] There, exemplary damages are now an accepted part of equity's remedial landscape.

In England the position remains unsettled. It is fair to say that while there has been some extra-judicial support for the availability of exemplary damages in equity, the case law on this issue there appears to be virtually non-existent.[28] Perhaps the nearest that the issue has come to judicial consideration is in the High Court's relatively recent decision of *Max Mosley v News Group Newspapers Limited*.[29] In this case Mosley sought compensatory as well as exemplary damages in an action for breach of confidence or, more accurately, the extended version of that action based on rights of privacy as protected by Article 8 of the European Convention on Human Rights. Eady J, while recognising the 'arguments both ways',[30] held that in England exemplary damages should not be made available for breach of confidence (at least in the context where the Article 8 right to privacy was in play). In reaching this view, one of the judge's principal concerns appeared to be that an award of exemplary damages in this context—something that he described as amounting to a fine—may not be a justified limitation on the countervailing right to freedom of expression protected by Article 10 of the Convention.

Of course, caution needs to be taken in treating this as an equity case. As Eady J recognised, while breach of confidence has roots in equity, its status in England is not altogether clear.[31] That this is so is illustrated by the fact that the case was heard in the Queen's Bench, not Chancery, division.

We pause to note here that the impact of the availability of exemplary damages for breach of confidence on the right to freedom of expression has not been considered in New Zealand case law. Its relevance would not have been readily apparent

[26] *Aquaculture Corporation v New Zealand Green Mussel Co Ltd* [1990] 3 NZLR 299 (NZCA) 301, cited with approval by Elias CJ in *Premium Real Estate* (n 19) [33].

[27] *Norberg v Wynrib* [1992] 2 SCR 226 (SCC).

[28] See England and Wales Law Commission, *Aggravated, Exemplary and Restitutionary Damages* (Law Com No 247, 1997).

[29] *Max Mosley v News Group Newspapers Limited* [2008] EWHC 1777 (QB).

[30] Ibid [84], citing the comments of Cooke P in *Aquaculture* (n 26) 301.

[31] For a useful discussion on the origins of breach of confidence, see G Hammond, 'The Origins of the Equitable Duty of Confidence' (1979) 8 *Anglo-American Law Review* 71.

in *Aquaculture*, with the New Zealand Bill of Rights Act 1990 passed a few months after the Court of Appeal's decision in that case.[32]

In our view, to the extent that Eady J suggested that an award of exemplary damages could never be a justified limit on the right to freedom of expression, he may have gone too far. We would argue that in jurisdictions in which there are rights instruments that protect the right to freedom of expression, such as New Zealand and England, the effect of an award of exemplary damages on that freedom should be considered on a case by case basis. In essence, it is but another ingredient to throw into the discretionary mix.

In Australia, and more particularly in New South Wales, exemplary damages in equity have received a rather mixed reception. In *Harris*, the Court of Appeal by a majority overturned the decision of Palmer J to award exemplary damages for breach of fiduciary duty.[33] Spigelman CJ preferred a narrow view, finding that exemplary damages are not available for a breach of fiduciary duty where the breach of duty is also a breach of contract. Heydon JA was more emphatic, finding that exemplary damages are never available in equity. Mason P, on the other hand, took the view that an award of exemplary damages ought to be available in equity.

As Anthony Duggan has suggested, there were two key questions at issue in *Harris*. First, whether New South Wales currently permits an award of exemplary damages in equity; secondly, and if not, should the court change the law?[34] As to the first question, it was clear that prior to Palmer J's judgment at first instance, an award of exemplary damages in equity had not been made in New South Wales or anywhere else in Australia.[35] The question, therefore, was really the broader one of whether the courts' equitable jurisdiction was capable of providing a punitive remedy performing the same function as exemplary damages do at common law. Palmer J took the view that equity could provide such a remedy. In reaching this view, his Honour placed some reliance on the criminal jurisdiction that the Chancery courts exercised in the sixteenth and seventeenth centuries, suggesting that this showed that 'the concept of punishment was by no means foreign to the Chancery courts'.[36] Palmer J also went on to suggest that there are elements of punishment and deterrence in equity's approach to remedies in modern times: for example, the varying liberality of the allowances for care and skill that may be awarded when a defaulting fiduciary is made to account for profits, or the strict rule that even an honest fiduciary must not make a profit without his principal's consent.[37]

[32] The Court of Appeal's judgment in *Aquaculture* was given on 11 June 1990, with the New Zealand Bill of Rights Act 1990 not coming into force until 19 September 1990.

[33] *Digital Pulse Pty Ltd v Harris* [2002] NSWSC 33, reversed in *Harris* (n 11).

[34] A Duggan, 'Exemplary damages in equity: a law and economics perspective' (2006) 26 *OJLS* 303, 303.

[35] Though in *Bailey v Namol* (1994) 53 FCR 102 (FCA) 112–13, the Full Federal Court cast doubt on their availability, citing with approval Somers J's statement in *Aquaculture* (n 26) that 'equity and penalty are strangers'.

[36] *Harris* (SC) (n 33) [164].

[37] Ibid [165], [167].

On appeal, none of the judges thought that Chancery's historical criminal jurisdiction provided a sound basis for finding a pre-existing jurisdiction to award exemplary damages in equity. (For our own part, we would tend to agree.) However, there was disagreement in the Court of Appeal as to whether modern equitable remedies included punitive elements. Spigelman CJ and Heydon JA both thought that those remedies cited by Palmer J, and others cited by the respondents on appeal such as higher awards of interest in the case of gross breaches of trust, could not be properly categorised as punitive.[38]

It is beyond the scope of this chapter to address their Honours' reasons for taking this view, particularly those set out in Heydon JA's lengthy and tightly reasoned judgment. We do, however, make two points. First, as Mason P noted in his judgment, although equity does not set out to punish it nonetheless 'reveals itself readier to select a more stringent remedy if the fiduciary's default is deserving of punishment, for example because it was deliberate and/or motivated by greed'.[39] So while punishment may not be de jure in equitable remedies, it is, certainly at times, de facto.

Secondly, there is clearly an element of deterrence in some of equity's remedial responses. As Edelman J has observed, after noting that exemplary damages at common law sometimes perform a solely deterrent function,[40] 'the central purpose of an account of profits is also to provide such deterrence, [meaning that] in many cases the jurisdiction of equity is already co-existent with one central rationale for exemplary damages'.[41] Other examples abound. For instance, in the New Zealand Supreme Court's recent decision in *Premium* (discussed further below), Blanchard J suggested, in the context of a disloyal real estate agent, that, 'the double sanction of damages and forfeiture of moneys received or receivable by way of remuneration is equity's method of *deterring* disloyal behaviour by fiduciaries'.[42]

We now wish to turn to the second question considered in *Harris*: whether equity in New South Wales *ought* to award exemplary damages.[43] We have already suggested that the test of legal rationality requires a court to ask itself whether there is a principled reason for a position to be maintained in light of developments in other areas of the law. There is, perhaps, some support for the view that all the judges in *Harris* were prepared to ask this question, with all at least notionally willing to consider whether there was a suitable analogy with other areas of the law.

Spigelman CJ was not convinced there was suitable analogy at common law for equity to draw upon, saying that:

[38] See also Keane, 'The conscience of equity' (n 13) 107–08.

[39] *Harris* (n 11) [165]–[166].

[40] Where, for instance, damages are to be paid by an insurer.

[41] Edelman (n 10) 377.

[42] *Premium* (n 19) [89] (emphasis added).

[43] Of course that is not to say that the functions of remedies currently available in equity are not relevant to normative question, but rather that they are not a complete answer either way.

> In his judgment, Mason P poses the question of whether the development of equity jurisprudence should proceed by way of analogy with tort or by way of analogy with contract. It is not apparent to me that analogical reasoning at this level of generality is appropriate. Each is a distinct body of law with its own integrity.[44]

The Chief Justice did go on to suggest, however, that if there is a suitable analogy with fiduciary law, it is with the law of contract. In his view, contract is a better analogy because, among other things, even though fiduciary duties are imposed by operation of law, 'the highest of authority has described the imposition of fiduciary obligations in terms of "undertaking" and "agreement"'.[45] He then reasoned that as exemplary damages are not available for breach of contract in Australia, by analogy they should not be available for breach of fiduciary duty.

Heydon JA took a different route. While not explicitly recognising it, 'he proceeded on the basis that development of equity by analogy with the common law was clearly possible'.[46] In his Honour's view, however, exemplary damages were best regarded as a form of criminal sanction and, accordingly, were inappropriate in equity.

Mason P, perhaps unsurprisingly, regarded the appropriate analogy as that of tort, where exemplary damages are available in Australia. He regarded the contract analogy as a weak one, suggesting, among other things, that:

> There are some similarities between fiduciary duties and contractual relationships, but the differences predominate. Most notably, fiduciary obligations are imposed by law (like torts) and they arise out of a relationship and/or conduct, as distinct from merely giving effect to the negotiated private arrangement that is contract. And there is no principle of efficient breach underpinning remedies for breach of fiduciary relationship: indeed the different function of remedies like account of profits shows that equity repudiates the type of efficiency encompassed in the contractual notion of efficient breach.[47]

If pressed to choose, we would agree that the more appropriate analogy is tort (however, only if the analogy is drawn at a very general level). We think rather that, at the normative level, the better question is whether awarding exemplary damages is consistent with the function and purpose of fiduciary law. In this regard, the following comment of Palmer J at first instance is apposite: '[c]onsistency in the law requires that the availability of exemplary damages should be co-extensive with its rationale'.[48] As Mason P points out '[t]hat rationale is the composite goal of punishing, deterring and vindicating a person who is the victim of wrongdoing clearly proscribed'.[49] We see those rationales as being entirely consistent with the duty of loyalty demanded of fiduciaries, and fiduciary law's

[44] *Harris* (n 11) [29].
[45] Ibid [36].
[46] Edelman (n 10) 378.
[47] *Harris* (n 11) [184].
[48] *Harris* (SC) (n 33) [170].
[49] *Harris* (n 11) [195].

attendant prophylactic purpose. And bearing in mind that exemplary damages are awarded where a defendant 'has acted in a highhanded or contumacious way',[50] it surely cannot be said that there will never be an occasion for exemplary damages to play a role in equity where the wrongdoer's conduct is of such a nature.

The New Zealand experience also suggests that the recognition of exemplary damages has not undermined the role of equitable remedies. The discretionary nature of equitable remedies is preserved; however, there is one more tool available to equity in support of its flexible and contextual remedial approach. Where there is conduct justifying an award, a judge may choose to provide that remedial response in addition to the others available. In New Zealand there has been no opening of the floodgates, with awards remaining extremely rare and the amounts of exemplary damages relatively modest, typically in a range of $15,000 to $30,000.[51]

Finally, we note that David Morgan has suggested that a move to a single category of civil wrongs in Australia, along the lines envisaged by Professor Burrows[52] and Edelman J,[53] would be one way for exemplary damages to attach to what we would currently regard as a breach of an equitable wrong.[54] In our view he rightly concludes that this is unlikely to happen in Australia in the near future, but Morgan suggests that such an approach may already be emerging in New Zealand and Canada. We would certainly agree that in terms of remedies this appears to be the case in New Zealand, where there appears to be a gradual movement towards a single category of monetary award for all 'civil wrongs' regardless of whether the wrong has its origins in equity or the common law (though the development of a single category of substantive civil wrong seems unlikely). Dr Walker has suggested that the 'high watermark'[55] of this approach is Tipping J's judgment in *Premium*, where drawing on the academic work of James Edelman (non Justice Edelman of the Supreme Court of Western Australia), his Honour said:

> I close by saying that I have throughout these reasons used the single unqualified word 'damages' without reference to the historical source of the cause of action upon which they are based. I do not regard it as necessary or appropriate to speak any more of common law damages, equitable damages or, indeed, equitable compensation. An understanding of the historical source of the cause of action will often be helpful for substantive purposes but, when monetary relief is being referred to, the single word 'damages' can be used, with the descriptor confined to the nature of the damages rather than their historical origin.[56]

[50] Butler (n 17) 174.

[51] Ibid 176.

[52] A Burrows, *Fusing Common Law and Equity* (n 18).

[53] J Edelman, *Gain-Based Damages: Contract, Tort, Equity and Intellectual Property* (Oxford, Hart Publishing, 2002).

[54] D Morgan, '*Harris v Digital Pulse*: The availability of exemplary damages in equity' (2003) 29 *Monash Law Review* 377, 395–96.

[55] C Walker, 'What is Damage(s)?' (2010) *New Zealand Law Society Intensive: Current Issues in Remedies* 1, 2. Also see the comments at 23.

[56] *Premium* (n 19) [111], citing Edelman, *Gain-Based Damages* (n 53).

Like Walker, we are generally comfortable with New Zealand's law of remedies heading this way. However, this is subject to a very important proviso. That is, the award of a particular remedy in a particular instance must be both cognisant of, and consistent with, the purpose and function of both the cause of action giving rise to the (successful) claim and the remedy itself informed, properly, by their history. We pick up on this theme in the next section.

IV. Causation of Loss by Breach of Fiduciary Duty

A key theme throughout this chapter is that New South Welsh equity stands apart from equity in other parts of the world because of its conservatism—particularly when contrasted with the New Zealand approach. It is interesting to note, therefore, that Jamie Glister suggests in his chapter in this book, and elsewhere,[57] that the New Zealand position on causation and equitable compensation for breach of a non-custodial fiduciary duty is stricter than the position taken in the rest of the Anglo-Commonwealth.

As Glister notes, it is commonly understood that the strict *Brickenden* rule no longer represents the law in New Zealand, as appears to be the case elsewhere. Instead, there is a 'small causal get-out'[58] where, in simple terms, it can be proved that the principal would have suffered the relevant loss even if there had been no breach of fiduciary duty. Tipping J explained this 'get-out' in the following terms in *Bank of New Zealand v New Zealand Guardian Trust Co Ltd*:

> Questions of foreseeability and remoteness do not arise in this kind of case either. Policy dictates that fiduciaries be allowed only a narrow escape route from liability based on proof that the loss or damage would have occurred even if there had been no breach.[59]

Relying on the application of this test by the majority of the Supreme Court in *Premium*, Glister argues that in New Zealand the standard of proof for getting through this narrow escape route is something higher than the balance of probabilities. He says for that reason there is a stricter standard in New Zealand than in the rest of the Anglo-Commonwealth. We are not convinced. As we will seek to explain, the issue in *Premium,* when analysed closely, was not causation, but quantum. Further, we argue that while *Premium* might represent a fairly strict line about quantum, we consider the Court's remedial response appropriate in the circumstances. This is an area where we do not think that the remedial response in equity should necessarily be the same as that provided for, in this case, a statutory wrong. In particular, we do not agree with the Chief Justice's apparent view in *Premium* that the remedial response to a fiduciary's breach of its disclosure obligations

[57] J Glister, 'Breach of fiduciary duty: *Brickenden* lives on (*Premium Real Estate v Stevens*)' (2011) 5 *Journal of Equity* 59.

[58] Ibid 9.

[59] *Bank of New Zealand v New Zealand Guardian Trust Co Ltd* [1999] 1 NZLR 664 (NZCA) 687, cited with approval in *Amaltal Corporation Ltd v Maruha Corporation* [2007] 3 NZLR 192 (NZSC) [30].

should, for all intents and purposes, be the same as the courts' remedial response to a breach of a statutory prohibition on misleading conduct in trade. But first, the facts in *Premium*.

Premium concerned a valuable property located on Auckland's North Shore. The Stevens were the owners of that property, and had hoped to sell it for \$3m. This was not to be, and in the end they agreed to sell the property to Larsen for \$2.575m. When the Stevens accepted this offer, their property had been on the market for over one month. And the Stevens had previously rejected one offer from another buyer, in the sum of \$2.2m. In that instance they had counter-offered, unsuccessfully, with \$2.8m. This became important later.

Subsequent to selling their property to Larsen, the Stevens learnt that Larsen, who had bought the property through the Mahoenui Valley Trust, had purchased it not for domestic use but rather for speculation. The Stevens were displeased enough to litigate, and commenced proceedings in which they argued that if they had known that there was speculative value in the property they would have held out for a higher market price. They formulated and advanced this case theory in the knowledge that Larsen had obtained a valuation report for the purposes of obtaining finance, and that this had valued the (then) Stevens' property at \$3.57m.

The Stevens litigation had as its principal target Riley, the agent they had engaged to help them sell their property. After the sale by the Stevens to Larsen, Riley had accepted a contract from Larsen to on-sell the property for him. Riley succeeded in doing so, ultimately selling it five months later, after 'an international marketing campaign', for \$3.555m to buyers in Hong Kong.

In the High Court, Courtney J awarded compensation to the Stevens for either breach of section 9 of the Fair Trading Act 1986,[60] or breach of fiduciary duty, as essentially the difference between the true market value in April 2004 (which she estimated to be approximately \$3.25m) and the amount the Stevens received from Larsen (\$2.575m). On appeal the Court of Appeal chose not to start from an objective market price. Instead, it considered the price at which the Stevens might have been prepared to sell the property had Larsen's speculative intentions been disclosed to them. So rather than calculating the losses starting from \$3.25m, the Court of Appeal preferred to base its calculations of equitable compensation on the sum of \$2.8m—the amount the Stevens would have been prepared to accept, based on the amount of the counter-offer they had made to another party before Larsen had showed an interest in buying the Stevens' property.

The majority in the Supreme Court agreed for the most part with Courtney J's assessment,[61] with Elias CJ instead preferring the Court of Appeal's approach.

[60] The Australian equivalent is section 52 of the Trade Practices Act 1974.

[61] The majority's substantive reasons were given in a judgment by Blanchard J (on behalf of himself and McGrath and Gault JJ), with Tipping J concurring but giving a separate judgment on the issue of

Glister concludes that the majority's approach represents a strict approach to causation, saying of the causation issue:

> The majority held that the defendant had not adequately shown that the plaintiffs would have sold at $2.8m: 'to say as the Court of Appeal did that the Stevens were likely to have sold it at $2.8m, too easily permits the errant fiduciary to find the "narrow escape route".' This result is important because it arguably shows that, more than a simple disagreement over whether a fact had been proved on the balance of probabilities, the majority thought that the defendant had a higher standard of proof to satisfy.[62]

As noted above, we are of the view that the disagreement between Elias CJ and the majority was not so much about *causation*, but rather the appropriate *quantum* of loss. Let us explain.

In simple terms, in order to get through the narrow escape route, Premium needed to show on the balance of probabilities that the relevant loss would have occurred even if there had been no breach. In this case, the breach was a failure by Riley (imputed to Premium) to disclose to the Stevens what she knew about Mr Larsen (ie, that he was a property speculator). All the judges agreed that Premium was not able to show on the balance of probabilities that the relevant loss would have occurred even if the breach had not been committed. Further, they did not accept the view of Courtney J that if the relevant disclosure were made the Stevens would have retained the property and, therefore, an asset worth $3.25 million. Instead, they all agreed that, had there been the required disclosure, the Stevens would have in all likelihood sold the house at a higher price.[63] The disagreement was about how the higher price and, therefore, the relevant loss, were to be established.

As a result of the disagreement just outlined, the issue was not really one of causation of loss, but rather of how the quantum of the loss caused was to be assessed. This is apparent from Blanchard J's judgment where, after citing the narrow escape route test from *Guardian*, he said:

> The same general approach should be taken when the matter in issue is restricted to the quantum of loss. The same policy goals apply to both. That policy is designed to deter fiduciary breaches by limiting the circumstances in which fiduciaries in breach can escape or reduce their liability for the consequences of the breach. It would be artificial, and inconsistent with that policy to distinguish between causation and quantum issues. Where there is a normal or prima facie measure of loss, the fiduciary must positively show that it is not the appropriate measure. The normal and natural measure of loss, when a fiduciary breach has affected the price at which the property is sold, is the difference between the sale price and market value. Policy dictates that the fiduciary is to demonstrate that the plaintiff's loss was actually less (or non-existent). If there is any doubt about that, the doubt should be resolved against the fiduciary.[64]

why the Court was able to order Premium to refund its commission and also compensate the Stevens for their loss.

[62] Glister's chapter in this volume, text to ns 87–88 (footnotes omitted).
[63] *Premium* (n 19) [10], [40] (Elias CJ), [86] (Blanchard J).
[64] *Premium* (n 19) [85].

In essence, therefore, the majority thought that a narrow escape route type rule should also be applied to quantum, with the burden resting on the defendant to adduce evidence proving on the balance of probabilities that the normal or prima facie measure of loss is not appropriate. In *Premium* itself, the majority were not convinced that Premium had discharged this burden. In their view, the evidence did not establish that the Stevens would have still sold the house for $2.8 million had the breach not occurred. As Blanchard J pointed

> The evidence relied on for [the Court of Appeal's] conclusion all was directed to the time before the failure by Premium to make the disclosure the Stevens should have received. The Court appears to have overlooked in its assessment that the Stevens still believed that their property was worth $3m (the figure which appeared in the condition in the Parnell agreement) and were not especially concerned to acquire the Parnell property. In our opinion Courtney J was right to think that the Stevens, who were, as she found not in a rush to sell, would have reappraised the situation if told that Mr Larsen was a speculator. The possibility that they may have sought other valuation advice cannot be disregarded. It is also likely, indeed probable, that they would have extended the sale period, and if they did so, it was quite possible that they would have achieved a sale at what the Judge has determined to have been the current market value of $3.25m. An orthodox measure of loss was therefore to use this figure. To depart from it, and to say as the Court of Appeal did that the Stevens were likely to have sold it at $2.8m, too easily permits the errant fiduciary to find the 'narrow escape route'.[65]

The use of the narrow escape route language is, therefore, apt to mislead in this context, implying as it does that a causation enquiry is being undertaken. In our view, once it is accepted that Blanchard J's remarks were made in the context of a quantum analysis it is apparent that there is no issue of a higher evidential threshold (either in terms of causation or quantum). If Premium could have shown, for instance, that, on the balances of probabilities, $2.8m was all that the Stevens could ever have hoped to have received, even if the relevant disclosure had been made, that figure may very well have represented the appropriate quantum. In the absence of such evidence, however, Premium had not discharged what the majority considered was its burden of showing on the balance of probabilities that the 'normal measure' ought not to be applied.

In endorsing the majority's view, we recognise that Elias CJ was alive to, and rejected, this line of argument. She did not accept the majority's view that it was correct to start with the 'normal measure', for which the defendant then had the burden of proving did not apply, saying:

> The approach in *Brickenden* in addressing difficulties of proof of hypothetical facts should not be extended to be generally applicable to quantification of loss attributable to breach of fiduciary duty. Proof of loss is a necessary element in the claim for compensation which must be established by the claimant on the evidence to the satisfaction of the court. I do not accept in this assessment there is room for presumptive measures of loss for which it is for the defendant fiduciary to disprove. Application of such presumptions

[65] Ibid [86].

> seems to me to amount to 'equitable by-pass of the need to establish causation'. It is the case, as McLachlin J suggests [in *Canson Enterprises Ltd v Boughton & Co* [1991] 3 SCR 534], that causation of loss must be assessed on a 'common sense' basis. But that does not obviate the need for the court to come to a conscientious determination on all the evidence.[66]

In this instance, the Chief Justice was of the view that the relevant loss was a loss of chance to sell their house at a higher price. After weighing the available evidence, she considered the best evidence of what the Stevens could have hoped to have received was the $2.8 million they were previously prepared to accept (ie, their counter-offer in negotiations with a potential buyer before Mr Larsen came into the picture). Accordingly, the relevant loss of chance was one to sell their property at this figure.

In our view, the Chief Justice's approach is not to be favoured. It fails to take account of the wrong committed and the consequences that flowed from that wrong. Premium owed the Stevens a fiduciary duty of loyalty. As a part of this duty, it had a positive obligation to inform the Stevens that Mr Larsen was a speculator. For there truly to be a remedy for the wrong committed, the measure of loss had to take account of the consequences of Premium's breach of duty. As the majority point out, if the relevant duty was performed the Stevens would have certainly reassessed their position.[67] Commenting on this point, Professor Geoff McLay has observed that '[s]urely being informed that one's property is being bought by a speculator, whose business method is to buy properties at a low price to resell at a high one, might predispose one to hold onto the property to seek a similar higher value for oneself'.[68] It makes little sense, therefore, to assess their loss by reference to what they were prepared to accept for the house before Premium's disclosure obligation arose or, indeed, when Premium unbeknownst to the Stevens was in breach of that duty. It makes much more sense to assess loss by reference to the market value of the house, as established on the facts. In our view, the majority's approach is consistent with the need to give a remedy that both enforces the duty to keep the Stevens informed and that, consistent with fiduciary law's prophylactic function,[69] deters other fiduciaries from committing the same breach. In that sense, therefore, we do not see the Supreme Court's approach as standing apart from the rest of the Anglo-Commonwealth.

The final issue that we discuss in this section is Elias CJ's apparent view that the approach to assessing the compensation payable in *Premium* should be the same, regardless of whether the wrong committed is framed as a breach of a fiduciary obligation or a breach of some other common law or statutory duty. As outlined above, to the extent that is the Chief Justice's view, we respectfully disagree.

[66] Ibid [41].
[67] Ibid [82].
[68] G McLay, 'Equitable Damages' in A Butler (ed), *Equity and Trusts in New Zealand*, 2nd edn (Wellington, Thomson Reuters, 2009) 942–43.
[69] A Butler, 'Fiduciary Law' in Butler (ed), *Equity and Trusts in New Zealand* (n 68) 478.

The Chief Justice's view on this issue is illustrated at two points in her judgment, among others. The first is in her discussion of causation, where she does not appear to think that there should be any meaningful difference in approach between equity and the common law. Commenting on the contrary view, she observed that:

> Causation of loss attributable to breaches of duties of care and skill on this approach is assessed on common law principles, but loss attributable to breach of duties of loyalty is assessed on the basis of a more 'stringent' approach to causation. Such refinement seems to retreat from the position reached in *Aquaculture*.[70]

The second point is in her discussion of the trial judge's views on the different amounts owing by Premium depending on whether the conduct was analysed as a breach of fiduciary duty or a breach of the statutory prohibition on misleading conduct in trade (contained in section 9 of the Fair Trading Act 1986). It will be remembered that Courtney J found that the Stevens would have retained their house had there been the required disclosure. And quantum was assessed by calculating the difference between the price at which the Stevens sold to Mr Larsen ($2.575m) and the value of the asset they lost (of $3.25m), which came to $675,000. Courtney J, while applying this same measure under the Fair Trading Act claim, discounted the compensation payable by 50 per cent 'to reflect the actual causative effect of the conduct'. Her Honour took the view that the Stevens had sold their property at an undervalue partly because of their own mistaken belief about it was worth. Commenting on this difference in approach, Elias CJ said that '[i]t seems wrong in principle for such different results [to occur] when both claims are concerned to make good loss caused by the same wrongful conduct'.[71] In other words, the remedial response should be the same regardless of cause of action.

We make the following observations. First, as to causation, we do not accept the Chief Justice's apparent view that there should be no meaningful difference between the approach in equity and common law. The stricter approach to causation for breaches of *fiduciary duties* is necessary in order to enforce and vindicate the *nature* and *content* of the duty of loyalty expected of fiduciaries. Fiduciary duties are accorded particular weight because of the circumstances in which they arise; that is, the particular vulnerability of the principal to the actions of its fiduciary, in its role as fiduciary. That said, we would accept that the approach to causation ought to be the same where the nature and content of the duty are the same in equity and the common law. We have in mind here concurrent duties of care in equity and at common law. But it is a step too far to suggest that breaches of fiduciary duties, which have no analogue at common law, should be subject to common law causation rules.[72]

[70] *Premium* (n 19) [37].
[71] Ibid [50].
[72] See McLay, 'Equitable Damages' (n 68) 927.

Secondly, building on the first point, we do not agree that measure of quantum should necessarily have been the same in *Premium* whether assessed as breach of a fiduciary duty of disclosure or a breach of a statutory prohibition on misleading conduct in trade (or indeed a tortious duty not to make negligent misstatements). Our concern here is essentially the same as that in relation to causation. To assume that the measure of loss is the same assumes the nature and content of the duties are the same. This is clearly not the case. A statutory prohibition on misleading statements in trade is a broad-brush prohibition covering both misleading acts and omissions. It applies, therefore, to a much larger class of relationships than a fiduciary duty of disclosure. The policy rationale and approach to negligent misstatements is different again. While it is true that a fiduciary's failure to perform its duty of disclosure may also amount to misleading conduct in trade, or a negligent misstatement (by omission), the role of fiduciary law is to prevent that happening in the context of the fiduciary-principal dynamic. It is this dynamic that, rightly in our view, the law of equity has marked out as deserving of particular protection. It seems to us that if one says that the remedial response always should be the same however the wrong is classified, that is tantamount to saying there is no need for a fiduciary duty of disclosure or, indeed, a tortious duty not to make negligent misstatements. All that would be needed is a singular civil wrong of misleading conduct. That may be where the law ultimately heads. But in our view, such a step, if were to occur, would need to happen in a clear and coherent way, and not through a remedial back door.

In terms of *Premium* itself, this may have meant that it was appropriate for Courtney J to discount the award under the Fair Trading Act, to make allowance for the effect of the Stevens' mistaken belief, but not to impose the same discount in equity. In saying this, we recognise that in *Day v Mead* it was established that similar discounts can be made in equity. It is beyond the scope of this chapter to go into the merits of *Day v Mead*. We do, however, make two observations.[73] The first relates to the importance of context. It will be remembered that in *Day v Mead*, Mr Day, an 'experienced and mature man of business',[74] had, at the behest of his solicitor, Mr Mead, twice invested in a company that ultimately failed. It was in relation to the second investment that the trial judge and the Court of Appeal thought it appropriate to reduce Mr Day's compensation by 50 per cent. By the time of this second investment he 'had considerable knowledge of the operations of the company'.[75] On that basis, the Court's reluctance to let all the blame rest with Mr Mead is perhaps understandable. We do not see the situation in *Premium* as being in any way analogous.

The second point is that in *Day v Mead*, Cooke P stressed that such allowances would be very rare, saying:

[73] For further discussion see ibid 955.
[74] *Day v Mead* (n 16) 449.
[75] Ibid 448.

> Of course, before reducing an award on the ground that the claimant has been partly the author of his or her own loss, the Court will have to give much weight to the well-established principle that, largely for exemplary purposes, high standards are expected of fiduciaries.[76]

We close this section by recognising an important, pragmatic point. That is, as Glister points out, a large part of the disagreement between the majority and Chief Justice (and indeed the courts below) was about facts. As he points out:

> *Premium Real Estate v Stevens* might be a simple example of judges differing on whether or not a particular fact has been proved. It might be that the majority of the Supreme Court thought that Premium has not demonstrated on the balance of probabilities that the Stevens family would have sold at $2.8m, whereas the Court of Appeal and Elias CJ thought that this fact had indeed been established.[77]

While we do not necessarily agree with Glister's view as to the effect of *Premium*, we certainly take his point. It suggests that the outcome in *Premium*, like in most other cases, may have ultimately been a matter of facts and not of law.

V. Estoppel

We want to move at this point to the topic of equitable estoppel, which in New Zealand is now treated as a unified doctrine. In this section we argue that this has not given rise to 'loose thinking', and is instead a sensible simplification of a series of needlessly separate doctrines. Dr Every-Palmer has observed that, historically,

> at least 16 different doctrines of estoppel, each with distinct triggering requirements and remedial possibilities, have received judicial recognition. Some of these doctrines have been unique to equity, others unique to the common law, and there has been at least one common to both. The inconsistent use of terminology together with the evolution of these various doctrines over time has left behind a jumble of principles, rules, and maxims.[78]

New Zealand courts have attempted to sift through this apparent jumble and 'now recognise a unified doctrine of equitable estoppel based on the unconscionability principle'.[79]

Before discussing this unified doctrine, we note that there is some evidence that this unified doctrine even encapsulates common law estoppel. For instance, in *Gold Star Insurance Co Ltd v Gaunt*, Holland J said that there 'may now be

[76] Ibid 452.

[77] Glister, 'Breach of fiduciary duty (n 57) 70.

[78] J Every-Palmer, 'Equitable Estoppel' in Butler (ed) (n 68) 605 (footnotes omitted).

[79] Ibid 603, citing, inter alia, *Gold Star Insurance Co Ltd v Gaunt* [1998] 3 NZLR 80 (NZCA) 86 (Holland J); *National Westminster Finance NZ Ltd v National Bank of NZ Ltd* [1996] 1 NZLR 548 (NZCA) 549 (Tipping J); *Juzwa v Hill* [2007] NZCA 222 [15] (Robertson J).

no distinction in result between what we once called common law estoppel and equitable estoppel'.[80] Further, in giving judgment for the court in *National Westminster Finance NZ Ltd v National Bank of New Zealand*, Tipping J expressed the view that '[t]here is a single doctrine of estoppel with a variety of manifestations'.[81] In our view, this tends to make sense in light of the fact that there is often a significant overlap in the substantive coverage of each doctrine, and 'the restricted remedial possibilities under common law estoppel (it acts only as an evidentiary principle) goes against the trend of the modern authorities to make the widest possible range of remedies available'.[82] As to the unified doctrine, the key elements that a plaintiff must prove are:

(a) a belief or expectation has been created or encouraged through some action, representation, or omission to act by the party against whom the estoppel is alleged;
(b) the belief or expectation has been reasonably relied on by the party alleging the estoppel;
(c) detriment will be suffered if the belief or expectation is departed from; and
(d) it would be unconscionable for the party against whom the estoppel is alleged to depart from the belief or expectation.[83]

Two important qualifications to this test should be noted. First, Holland J has suggested that, where the circumstances require it, it is possible to depart from strict criteria and to direct attention to overall unconscionable behaviour.[84] Secondly, even where an estoppel is made out, the courts have a broad discretion as to the quantum and form of the remedy.[85] We return to these themes shortly.

Outside of New Zealand the position is less settled. In the English context, Lord Neuberger of Abbotsbury MR has suggested extra-judicially that estoppel in England ought to adopt a unified doctrine; although not one including common law estoppels, 'which will inevitably be subject to different principles'.[86] He has suggested, for instance:

> [M]ay not estoppel now be seen as a generic term for a claim by a plaintiff who has changed his position in the reasonable and foreseeable belief that a defendant's act, statement, silence or inaction has a particular consequence, so that it would now be

[80] *Gold Star* (n 79) 86.
[81] *National Westminster NZ* (n 79) 549.
[82] Every-Palmer (n 78) 611–12 citing *Aquaculture* (n 26) 301–02 (Cooke P).
[83] Ibid 613, citing *Hawke v B R Metcalfe Construction Ltd* (HC Hamilton, AP131/90, 5 June 1992) (Fisher J) 4–5; *Gold Star* (n 79) 86 (Holland J); *Gillies v Keogh* [1989] 2 NZLR 327 (NZCA) 346 (Richardson J).
[84] *Gold Star* (n 79) 86.
[85] *Hawke* (n 83) 4.
[86] D Neuberger, 'Thoughts on the law of equitable estoppel' (2010) 84 *Australian Law Journal* 225, 237.

> unconscionable for the defendant to repudiate that consequence (wholly or to an extent), at least without giving the plaintiff some compensation.[87]

As Lord Neuberger recognises, however, such a doctrine has yet to be recognised by the House of Lords or the Supreme Court.[88]

In the Australian context, some commentators have suggested that the High Court of Australia has recognised a unified doctrine of equitable estoppel,[89] citing in particular comments to that effect by Mason CJ and Wilson J in *Waltons Stores (Interstate) Ltd v Maher*.[90] For our own part, however, we are sceptical, as is Lord Neuberger, about whether this really is the case, given that other members of the High Court are yet to express a similar view.[91]

One gets the feeling that there is limited fondness for such a unified doctrine in New South Wales. While the authors of *Meagher, Gummow and Lehane* appear to be uncharacteristically non-committal on the unification issue, they do seem to prefer instead to analyse each type of estoppel individually.[92] Further, Handley J—who has written extensively on equitable estoppel[93] and given a number of the New South Wales Court of Appeal's judgments in the area[94]—is of the firm view that there should be no overarching doctrine of estoppel in equity (let alone one that also includes common law estoppel). In a recent article, he said of Lord Neuberger's tentative suggestion that there ought to be such a unified doctrine that:

> Proprietary estoppel and promissory estoppel are purely equitable and they operate directly to change the rights of the parties. The purely equitable estoppels are based on equitable causes of action which were enforceable by a suit in Chancery before the Judicature Acts. It will be seen therefore that the different forms of estoppel have different elements, they operate differently and they have different results. We no more need a single overarching doctrine of estoppel than we need a single overarching doctrine of torts.[95]

[87] Ibid.

[88] Since the time of writing the English Court of Appeal has released its judgment in *ING Bank NZ v Ros Roca SA* [2011] EWCA Civ 353. In *ING*, all three judges (Rix, Carnwath, and Stanley Burnton LJJ) appeared to think that the facts could be analysed in terms of *either* estoppel by convention or promissory estoppel. Stanley Burnton LJ thought, for instance, the distinction was 'largely one of terminology' at [76]. However, none of the judges thought it was necessary for the Court to decide whether there ought to be a single overarching principle of estoppel. If appealed to the Supreme Court, this case could provide a good opportunity for the recognition of a single, overarching doctrine in England.

[89] See, eg Every-Palmer (n 78) 610; P Parkinson (ed), *The Principles of Equity*, 2nd edn (LawBook Co, Sydney, 2003) para [712] (cited in Neuberger, 'Thoughts on the law' (n 86) 237).

[90] *Waltons Stores (Interstate) Ltd v Maher* (1988) 164 CLR 387 (HCA) 404.

[91] See the comments in Neuberger (n 86) 237.

[92] See Meagher, Heydon and Leeming (n 3) paras [17–005]–[17–025].

[93] See, eg K Handley, *Estoppel by Conduct and Election* (London, Sweet & Maxwell, 2006).

[94] For a recent example, see the judgment in *Delaforce v Simpson-Cook* [2010] NSWCA 84.

[95] K Handley, 'Further thoughts on proprietary estoppel' (2010) 84 *Australian Law Journal* 239, 234.

Lord Neuberger was alive to, but not ultimately convinced by, these concerns. He observed of the unified doctrine that:

> There are problems with this idea; thus, it would probably involve weakening proprietary estoppel or strengthening other estoppels, as 'proprietary estoppel is an extremely muscular doctrine' (according to Wilken and Villiers, *The Law of Waiver, Variation and Estoppel* (2 ed) p 100). Further, the different estoppels can be said to involve different features, *but it may be said with some force that the differences are more hypothetical than practical, and, insofar as they have any effect that they should not exist.*[96]

We tend to agree with Lord Neuberger's conclusion that the problems are probably more hypothetical than real. Having said that, the points Handley makes have merit. Bearing them in mind, we think that there are two areas that a sensible articulation of the unified doctrine should adequately address. First, what is meant by unconscionability? And secondly, would some forms of estoppel be unduly strengthened by the supposed availability of all equitable remedies?[97]

Justice Handley regards the idea that unconscionability is the organising principle in equitable estoppel—let alone Holland J's suggestion in *Gold Star* that a finding of unconscionability could, of itself, found an estoppel—as unpalatable. Justice Handley has said of certain English judgments that have used the language of unconscionability, that they 'created a public nuisance by encouraging the notion that unconscionability was a freestanding principle capable of generating legal rights outside established principles'.[98] The particular fear is that unconscionability will become shorthand for whatever a particular judge thinks fair in the circumstances. Keane CJ, in explaining what is wrong with this,[99] cites the following explanation by Pomeroy of the role of 'conscience' in equity:

> '[C]onscience' which is an element of the equitable jurisdiction came to be regarded, and has so been regarded, and has so continued to the present day, as a metaphorical term, designating the common standard of civil right and expediency combined, based on general principles and limited by established doctrines, to which the court appeals and by which it tests the conduct and rights of suitors—a judicial not a personal conscience.[100]

The High Court of Australia expressed a similar view in *Tanwar Enterprises Pty Ltd v Cauchi*, observing that:

> The terms 'unconscientious' and 'unconscionable' … describe in their various applications the formation and instruction of conscience by reference to well developed principles. … It is to those principles that the court has first regard rather than entering

[96] Neuberger (n 86) 237 (emphasis added).

[97] Putting to the side the added complication of the inclusion of common law estoppels.

[98] Handley, 'Further thoughts' (n 95) 239.

[99] Keane (n 13) 98.

[100] J Pomeroy and S Symons, *A Treatise on Equity Jurisprudence*, 5th edn (San Francisco, Bancroft-Whitney, 1941) vol 1, 94.

> into the case at that higher level of abstraction involved in notions of unconscientious conduct in some loose sense where all the principles are at large.[101]

The key concern really, then, is that often unconscionability is not so much a legal test but rather a conclusion reached through the application of 'well developed principles'. To the extent that the New Zealand position is that there can be an estoppel in circumstances where the elements of an estoppel are *not* made out, but the conduct is regarded by the particular judge as sufficiently unconscionable, we would agree that that is somewhat problematic. This is a point on which New Zealand equity should certainly take heed of Australian concerns, and on which some clarification from the Supreme Court would be welcome.

That said, we would also agree with Lord Neuberger's suggestion that the 'correct question in every case, whether commercial or domestic (or hybrid) should simply be whether it was reasonable for the plaintiff to have relied on the defendant's encouragement'.[102] As Lord Neuberger and, indeed, Every-Palmer suggest, the reasonableness of the plaintiff's reliance will fall to be assessed in light of equity's treatment of like cases in the past. In that way equity's 'well developed principles' will continue to be applied. There appears to be a limited risk, therefore, that some ill-defined notion of unconscionability will be applied to found an estoppel in a way that unduly interferes in, for instance, commercial dealings. New Zealand courts are as reluctant as any 'to render equitable assistance to well-resourced, well-advised commercial parties with similar bargaining power dealing at arm's length'.[103] We would have thought it likely, therefore, that a case such as *Yeoman's Row Management Ltd v Cobbe*,[104] where the House of Lords found that there was no estoppel in circumstances where experienced commercial parties had chosen to enter into an agreement binding in honour only, would receive similar treatment in New Zealand. In that context, Mr Cobbe's reliance simply was not reasonable.

Moving now to the risk that other equitable estoppels could be unduly strengthened if they are lumped in with proprietary estoppel, this too is more apparent than real. The concern seems to be that if all forms of estoppel are simply lumped together, this might lead to proprietary remedies being awarded in circumstances in which they would not normally be expected. Michael Kirby touches on this anxiety in his observation, cited in the introduction to this chapter, that '[b]ecause equity is often concerned with the incidents of property rights, there is a natural and proper anxiety on the part of knowledgeable lawyers about any unthinking tinkering with long settled rules'.[105]

101 *Tanwar Enterprises Pty Ltd v Cauchi and Ors* [2003] HCA 57, (2003) 217 CLR 315 [20].

102 Neuberger (n 86) 233. On the increased emphasis on reasonableness in proprietary estoppels, see N Piška, 'Hopes, Expectations and Revocable Promises in Proprietary Estoppel' (2009) 72 *MLR* 998.

103 Every-Palmer (n 78) 620.

104 *Yeoman's Row Management Ltd v Cobbe* [2008] UKHL 55, [2008] 1 WLR 1752.

105 Kirby (n 1) 44, cited above, text to n 7.

In our view this anxiety is ill-placed. This is because there is little risk that a proprietary remedy will be awarded in a situation not properly regarded as giving rise to a proprietary estoppel. While New Zealand courts generally reserve a wide remedial discretion, this does not mean that they do not have regard to the historical basis on which a particular remedy is awarded. This means it will continue to be the case that outside the proprietary estoppel context, any award is typically assessed using a reliance measure.[106] Further, even where an expectation measure is applied, it is not clear to us how that could ever translate into a proprietary remedy in circumstances where there was never any expectation created by the defendant that the plaintiff was to receive some form of proprietary interest.

VI. Conclusion

In this chapter, we have attempted to show, by reference to several selected examples, the sorts of considerations and tensions at play in the interaction of law and equity. The purpose of this exercise has been to show, among other things, that substantive fusion of law and equity is justifiable *in some circumstances*. We recognise that one could fairly say that we have set up a New South Welsh straw man which we have then knocked down with selected pot shots. And conversely, we have been all too sympathetic to the New Zealand way. This was not our intention. We think the occasional pedantry and the consistent intellectual rigour that is evident in the New South Welsh approach is to be welcomed. Further, for the most part, developments in the law of equity should be case-by-case and considered, and not go further than is strictly necessary. What should not be accepted, however, is that pedantry and conservatism are worthwhile ends in themselves. Rather, what is needed is a continual reassessment of the rationale for the maintenance of a certain position in light of modern conditions and novel factual scenarios. Where the rationale for a position does not stack up, courts should be prepared to make changes. And in making changes courts can legitimately draw on developments in other areas of law.

We close with the rhetorical question, 'Where would the law be now, if not for Lord Atkin's preparedness to strike out in a new direction in *Donoghue v Stevenson*?' While people might legitimately disagree about various doctrinal aspects of the negligence cause of action, few would do away with it altogether. Like the common law, equity must not be allowed to atrophy.

[106] Every-Palmer (n 78) 637–39.

INDEX

www.ingramcontent.com/pod-product-compliance
Ingram Content Group UK Ltd.
Pitfield, Milton Keynes, MK11 3LW, UK
UKHW020832290926
15470UKWH00009B/1853/J

9 781849 462198